The Dewey School

The Dewey School

The Laboratory School of the University of Chicago 1896-1903

WITH AN INTRODUCTION BY JOHN DEWEY

Katherine Camp Mayhew
and
Anna Camp Edwards

AldineTransaction
A Division of Transaction Publishers
New Brunswick (U.S.A.) and London (U.K.)

First paperback printing 2007
Copyright © 1965 by Atheron Press.

All rights reserved under International and Pan-American Copyright Conventions. No part of this book may be reproduced or transmitted in any form or by any means, electronic or mechanical, including photocopy, recording, or any information storage and retrieval system, without prior permission in writing from the publisher. All inquiries should be addressed to AldineTransaction, A Division of Transaction Publishers, Rutgers—The State University, 35 Berrue Circle, Piscataway, New Jersey 08854-8042. www.transactionpub.com

This book is printed on acid-free paper that meets the American National Standard for Permanence of Paper for Printed Library Materials.

Library of Congress Catalog Number: 2006045517
ISBN: 978-0-202-30874-6
Printed in the United States of America

Library of Congress Cataloging-in-Publication Data

Mayhew, Katherine Camp.
    The Dewey school : the laboratory school of the University of Chicago, 1896-1903
        p. cm.
    Includes index.
    ISBN 978-0-202-30874-6 (alk. paper)
    1. University of Chicago. University Elementary School. 2. Education—Experimental methods. 3. Dewey, John, 1859-1952. I. Edwards, Anna Camp, 1876-1956. II. Title.

LD7501.C4C625   2007
372.07109773'11—dc22   2006045517

Editor's Foreword

In 1894 John Dewey moved his position as Chairman of the Philosophy Department at the University of Michigan to assume the position as Chairman of the Department of Philosophy, Psychology, and Pedagogy at the University of Chicago. He would remain there until 1904, his departure prompted in great part by his dissatisfaction regarding his wife's treatment by the administration in her role of principal of the Laboratory School. If Dewey's relation to that school was a reason for his leaving Chicago, it was no less an important factor in his decision to go to Chicago originally. At this time Dewey was anxious to translate his more abstract ideas into practical form and he saw the position at Chicago affording him a rare opportunity to do this. For in any given term he might be found ranging across the continuum of theory and practice, teaching "The Logic of Ethics" and "Philosophy of Education" and administering the practical affairs of the Laboratory School.

The school itself was conceived by Dewey as having an organic functional relation to the theoretical curriculum. Just as Dewey was anxious to merge philosophy and psychology and to relate both of these disciplines to the theoretical study of education, similarly he saw the school as a laboratory for these studies analogous to the laboratory used in science courses. This effort to merge theory and practice is perhaps the major characteristic of Dewey's entire professional career. In the opening sentence of Dewey's remarks in his essay in this volume, "The Theory of the Chicago Experiment," we see the extent to which this problem preoccupied him: "The gap between educational theory and its execution in practice is always so wide that there naturally arises a doubt as to the value of any separate presentation of purely theoretical principles."

We have ample opportunity to analyze and evaluate Dewey's educational theory *per se*. He wrote at least five major treatises on the subject, and in a very real sense most of his abstract philosophy was indirectly concerned with a theory of education. What this volume provides is a firsthand account of Dewey's educational policies as they were actually put into practice during the eight-year period from 1896 to 1904. This presents us with the unusual opportunity of examining educational practice in order to see and understand its underlying theory. It is difficult indeed to see how that theory could continue to be so grossly misinterpreted if critics would read the careful descriptions of policy, curriculum, and method that we find here. It can easily be seen that the clichés characterizing the typical criticisms of Dewey's educational thought are grossly inaccurate. The school is seen to be far from "permissive," for the role of the teacher as a responsible agent is clearly defined. The school is not "child-centered," but rather "society-centered," constantly focusing as it does on social life and social occupations. The school is not "directionless." One of the most valuable aspects of this book is its description of the ways in which the notion of growth as an educational end is manifested in school practice. The reader is constantly struck by the postulation of flexible but definite aims and these aims are stated in terms of clearly discernible skills and attitudes. This attention to concrete detail is characteristic of the entire volume and as a result we have a thorough description of the role of the teacher, the principles of scientific method translated into concrete pedagogical principles, and the revolutionary Deweyan concept of discipline.

And the account is authentic. Dewey not only included the aforementioned essay and an introduction as well but also made it known, in an authorized biographical essay written by his daughter, that: "Mayhew and Edwards, who were teachers in the school, give a full and authoritative account [in *The Dewey School*] of its work, which makes it unnecessary to discuss it here."*

This volume is the result of a labor of love. It is an accurate and thorough account of one of the most important educational experiments yet undertaken in America, and as a result it has considerable historical significance. Yet its greatest value perhaps lies in the insight it provides into the richness and complexity of John Dewey's abstract philosophy of experimentalism.

Reginald D. Archambault
Brown University

* Jane M. Dewey, ed., "Biography of John Dewey," in P. A. Schilpp, ed., *The Philosophy of John Dewey* (New York, 1951) p. 28.

PREFACE

The increasing number of progressive schools throughout the world shows the wide and fast growing interest on the part of parents and educators in an educational experience for their children which they do not find in schools of the more traditional types. This interest renders an account of an early organized experiment in progressive education suitable and timely.

This school was a coöperative venture of parents, teachers, and educators, and was carried on at the University of Chicago during the years from 1896 to 1903. Under the direction of John Dewey, then head of the University's unified departments of Philosophy, Psychology, and Pedagogy, the undertaking grew out of a genuine desire to work out with children an educational experience more creative than that provided by even the best of the current systems.

The school was a laboratory for the departments of Psychology and Pedagogy where Mr. Dewey's educational theories and their sociological implications were worked out in accord with the then new psychological principles and in association with colleagues and students, the teachers in the school, and the parents of the children. It was never a "practice" school.

The book has been called *The Dewey School* not because Mr. Dewey as its head ever exercised any of the dominance too often evident in a "One man's school." Rather was the title chosen out of gratitude to the great person who made the school possible by his objective and impersonal attitude of faith in the growing ability of every individual, whether child or teacher. Mr. Dewey was never dominating. His respect for the opinions of even the youngest and least experienced of his staff bore fruit in the creative character of the work done. Only a person who has worked in such an atmosphere can understand what inspiration to creative work such freedom gives. After all, teaching is a creative social art. Mr. Dewey's philosophy expressed through his personality stimulated others and released their powers so that all who understood his point of view worked freely and coöperatively under his guidance.

The subtitle of the book, *The Laboratory School of the University of Chicago,* indicates its relation to the University, always a source of direct and indirect help and backing. Without this direction from experts, the teachers, functioning creatively in their daily experience, would have traveled many more blind alleys than they did. Had this experiment been allowed to come to fruition, it would have presented the first example of a unified enterprise in education at all age levels.

The slowly evolving curriculum of the Dewey School in both subject-matter and method was the result of the combined experimental efforts of trained specialists. These chapters should reveal that it was scientifically developed. Great emphasis was given to the use of directed experimental method in all areas of study. The main hypothesis was that life itself, especially those occupations and associations which serve man's chief needs, should furnish the ground experience for the education of children. The classrooms in this laboratory school were the proving grounds where teachers—specialists in their subjects— would discover, by trying, the particular experiences that would enrich the child's present life, making it a growing process and an ever more real and satisfactory preparation for the future. The hypothesis was that freedom to express in action is a necessary condition of growth, but that guidance of such expression is an equally necessary condition, especially of childhood's freedom. Learning, a main issue to the teacher, was seen as a side issue to the child, a by-product of his activity. The test of learning was the increasing ability of the child to meet new situations through habits of considered action which were even more social in character. It was found that satisfaction and emotional stability accompany such growth. The development of the curriculum was in relation to the immediate interests of growing children and thereby revealed the chief interests of the different psychological levels of this span in their life development. A type of education in which there is steady maintenance of coöperative processes and constant use of the scientific principle of objective testing of ideas through action and evaluating the results of such action for future planning, has significant implications for the world ferment of the day.

The authors were both teachers in the school. Katherine Camp Mayhew, as vice-principal, was in charge of the developing curriculum; she was also head of the science department. Anna Camp Edwards was a teacher of history in the early experimental period and later as a special tutor followed through the work of all other departments at older age levels, an experience which has aided her in interpreting the value of Mr. Dewey's philosophy of education in the present crisis.

The scope of this study was decided upon and its plan worked out by the authors in close consultation with Mr. Dewey, who has guided the entire development of the book. Throughout these consultations Mrs. Edwards acted as secretary and custodian of the records from which the selections used were made. In order that the manuscript should have literary unity, it became apparent that the composition and writing must be done by one of the authors. Mrs. Edwards has served in this capacity for all the chapters except the seventeenth. She is responsible for the amalgamation and editing of all the records and contributions from the various accredited sources. Mrs. Mayhew taught science and mathematics in the school for seven years. This and her wide later experience are the backgrounds of the seventeenth chapter and for her many invaluable contributions to all the other chapters of the book, especially her account of how the school developed the approach to history as the story of man's progress through invention, exploration, and discovery.

The original manuscript of this book was too large for publication. All the chapters were reduced in size, and two chapters omitted from the body of the book. These two chapters, however, have been included in the form of an appendix. The first, *The Evolution of Mr. Dewey's Principles of Education*, was written by Mrs. Anna Camp Edwards; the second, *The Theory of the Chicago Experiment*, by Mr. Dewey himself.

From 1896 to 1899 extensive accounts of the experimental school were published in the *University Record*. During 1900 the reports of the school appeared in a series of nine monographs entitled the *Elementary School Record*. These were later bound in one volume which soon was out of print. The records of 1901 and 1902 consisted of typed reports and summaries carefully collected and edited by Laura L. Runyon. These were never printed. The sources upon which the writers have drawn include the publications and documents mentioned above, the current and later writings of Mr. and Mrs. Dewey, and those of alumni and friends of the school. The school was deeply indebted to Mrs. Alice C. Dewey for her exceptional insight in solving many of its problems. She also collected and preserved a large part of the source materials. Mrs. Dewey's death in 1927 made impossible her plan to write the history of the school in collaboration with Mrs. Mayhew. Following her death, the authors undertook the work at Mr. Dewey's request and gratefully acknowledge their debt to Mrs. Dewey.

In the following pages much material has been taken from hitherto unpublished accounts of the school. The writers have also used extracts from published articles by the following: Georgia F. Bacon, Althea Harmer Bardeen, Lillian Cushman Brown, Hattie Hover Harding, Charles F. Harding, Katherine Andrews Healy, Nellie Johnson O'Conner, May Root Kern, Laura L. Runyon, and Katherine C. Mayhew. Special mention should be made of the never failing support of Mr. and Mrs. George H. Mead and their constant faith in the educational worth of the school. The first account of the undertaking, *The School and Society,* a series of three lectures on the school by Mr. Dewey, was edited by Mr. and Mrs. Mead, assisted by Katherine Camp Mayhew and Althea Harmer Bardeen.

Appreciation is expressed to Miss Bacon, Mrs. Brown, Miss Runyon, Sara French Miller, D. P. MacMillan, and Mary Tough for counsel in the early planning of the manuscript; to Elsie Clapp for her suggestions in relation to the needs of teachers; to Harry O. Gillette for access to letters and information collected by a graduate student for an unfinished thesis and to the few records of the last year of the school, preserved in the present School of Education of the University of Chicago; to George W. Locke, Anna Bryan, Grace Fulmer, E. C. Moore, Frank H.

Manny, W. A. Baldwin, and Helen Thompson Wooley; also to many pupils of the school, parents, former teachers, graduate students, and visitors at the school for their loyal support. Appreciation is also expressed to Marion Le Brun Pigman for her aid in the first revisions of the manuscript; to Elizabeth F. Camp, John L. Childs, Richard H. Edwards, Galen M. Fisher, Price H. Gwynn, Jr., Mr. and Mrs. Paul R. Hanna, Mrs. Harriet Hover Harding, Mrs. Katherine Andrews Healy, and Mrs. William Kent for valuable suggestions on the manuscript. The authors are indebted to several friends and alumni of the school for making it possible to include a number of the illustrations, thus giving much added interest and value to the story of the experiment.

Gratitude is due above all to Mr. Dewey for his written contributions, his permission to quote his writings freely, and for the generous donation of his time and thought, and to Evelyn Dewey (Mrs. Granville Smith, Jr.) for the final editing of the manuscript.

INTRODUCTION

The account of the Laboratory School contained in the pages that follow is so adequate as to render it unnecessary for me to add anything to what is said about its origin, aims, and methods. It is, however, a grateful task to express my appreciation of the intelligent care with which the theory and practice of the school have been reported. Because of their long connection with the school, the authors have a first-hand knowledge, while their responsible share in the work of the school has enabled them to make an authoritative statement of its underlying ideas, its development, and the details of its operation. The entire history of the school was marked by an unusual degree of coöperation among parents, teachers, and pupils. It is particularly gratifying to have this living evidence that the coöperative spirit still continues.

My gratification is far from being merely personal. The volume has historic interest and value, since it is a record of one of the earlier efforts in this country in the direction of experimental and progressive schools. But this historic interest is not all. This educational movement is still going on and is far from having reached its goal; its unsolved problems are still many. The book has, I think, a good deal to contribute now and here. It is timely as well as historical in interest. There is one point in particular which may be singled out for its present bearing. The problem of the relation between individual freedom and collective well-being is today urgent and acute, perhaps more so than at any time in the past. The problem of achieving both of these values without the sacrifice of either one is likely to be the dominant problem of civilization for many years to come. The schools have their part to play in working out the solution, and their own chief task is to create a form of community life and organization in which both of these values are conserved. The school whose work is reported in this volume was animated by a desire to discover in administration, selection of subject-matter, methods of learning, teaching, and discipline, how a school could become a coöperative community while developing in individuals their own capacities and satisfying their own needs. I am sure the present value of the volume is not exhausted in its account of this phase of the school's life. But the present importance of the issue emboldens me to believe that it is especially timely at the present juncture.

JOHN DEWEY

CONTENTS

PART III

EDUCATIONAL USE OF SCIENTIFIC METHOD

PART IV

PERSONNEL—ORGANIZATION—EVALUATION

APPENDICES

PART I

HISTORICAL DEVELOPMENT AND ORGANIZATION

CHAPTER I

GENERAL HISTORY

THE following pages tell the story of one of the earliest experiments in what later came to be known as *progressive education*. This experiment was an integral part of the University of Chicago during the years 1896 to 1904, and was an undertaking which aimed to work out, through the University, a school system which should be an organic whole from the kindergarten to the university. Conducted under the management and supervision of the University's Department of Philosophy, Psychology, and Education, it bore the same relation to the work of that department that a laboratory bears to biology, physics, or chemistry. Like any such laboratory it had two main purposes: (1) to exhibit, test, verify, and criticize theoretical statements and principles; and (2) to add to the sum of facts and principles in its special line. In consequence, it was often called the *Laboratory School*. The name is significant. John Dewey, when called to be the head of the department in 1894, had arrived at certain philosophical and psychological ideas which he desired to test in practical application. This desire was not merely personal, but flowed from the very nature of the ideas themselves. For it was part of the philosophical and psychological theory he entertained that ideas, even as ideas, are incomplete and tentative until they are employed in application to objects in action and are thus developed, corrected, and tested. The need of a laboratory was indicated. Moreover, the inclusive scope of the ideas in question demanded something more than a laboratory of experimentation in its restricted technical sense. The materials with which they dealt were the continuing development of human beings in knowledge, understanding, and character. A school was the answer to the need.

During the years at Chicago, Mr. Dewey's thought along these lines was greatly stimulated and enriched. One of the important influences affecting the distinct advance in the psychological formulations of this period was the coöperative thinking and pooled results of a close-knit group of colleagues, all concentrating under one leadership. James R. Angell was then working out his ideas of functional psychology. George H. Mead, who earlier had been a colleague of Mr. Dewey's at the University of Michigan, was developing the psychology of the act on the basis of wide biological knowledge, and James H. Tufts collaborated with Mr. Dewey in a course for the parents of the school. These men and others in related departments of the University made up a united and enthusiastic group of investigators and teachers.

Mr. Dewey's thinking was further supplemented by the work of the various study clubs of which he was a member and the groups of graduate and undergraduate students under his direction. He early joined the Illinois Society for Child Study, which included among its members many able educators. In the transactions of this society, which were being watched and commented upon by leaders in psychological thinking, Mr. Dewey took an active part. A number of his earliest statements were published by this organization and by the newly organized National Herbart Society.

As a result of all this original and coöperative effort, there were gradually built up the psychological and sociological principles, which, together with their many implications, form the basis of Mr. Dewey's theory of education. Statements of these appeared from time to time in various periodicals and in other forms.[1]

---

[1] This selected list of statements published at the time contains the essential elements in Mr. Dewey's philosophy of education: (1) "The Results of Child-Study Applied to Education," *Transactions of the Illinois Society for Child Study*, January, 1895; (2) "Interest as Related to Will," in National Herbart Society, *Second Supplement to the Herbart Yearbook for 1895*; (3) "The Reflex-Arc Concept in Psychology," *Psychological Review*, July, 1896; (4) "Pedagogy as a University Discipline," *University (of Chicago) Record*, September, 1896; (5) "Ethical Principles Underlying Education," in National Herbart Society, *Third Yearbook* (Chicago, 1897);

Many of the interested group and their friends were parents, and the idea of a school which should test in practice these newly stated principles of education grew out of their desire that their own children should experience this kind of schooling. The ideas of the group were formulated by Mr. Dewey in a privately printed brochure, "Plan of Organization of the University Primary School." This plan as summarized by Mr. Dewey follows.[2]

"Because of the idea that human intelligence developed in connection with the needs and opportunities of action, the core of school activity was to be found in occupations, rather than in what are conventionally termed studies. Study in the sense of inquiry and its outcome in gathering and retention of information was to be an outgrowth of the pursuit of certain continuing or consecutive occupational activities. Since the development of the intelligence and knowledge of mankind has been a coöperative matter, and culture, in its broadest sense, a collective creation, occupations were to be selected which related those engaged in them to the basic needs of developing life, and demanded coöperation, division of work, and constant intellectual exchange by means of mutual communication and record. Since the integration of the individual and the social is impossible except when the individual lives in close association with others in the constant free give and take of experiences, it seemed that education could prepare the young for the future social life only when the school was itself a coöperative society on a small scale. Therefore, the first factor in bringing about the desired coördination of these occupations was the establishment of the school itself as a form of community life.

"The primary skills, in reading, writing, and numbers, were to grow out of the needs and the results of activities. Moreover, since basic occupations involve relations to the materials and forces of nature, just as the processes of living together

(6) "Principles of Mental Development as Illustrated in Early Infancy," *Transactions of the Illinois Society for Child Study*, October, 1899; (7) *The School and Society* (Chicago, The University of Chicago Press, 1899).
    [2] John Dewey. Written for the Authors.

involve social invention, organization, and establishment of human bonds, making the development of individuals secure and progressive, knowledge was to grow out of the active contact with things and energies inherent in consecutive activities. History, for instance, was to be a deepening and an extension of the process of human invention and integration. The development of character and the management of what is ordinarily called *discipline,* were to be, as far as possible, the outgrowth of a shared community life in which teachers were guides and leaders. The substratum of the educative process was thus to develop from the idea that the young have native needs and native tendencies of curiosity, love of active occupation, and desire for association and mutual exchange which provide the intrinsic leverage for educative growth in knowledge, understanding, and conduct.

"The significance of these principles for the educational experiment that was undertaken can best be gathered from the account of the actual life of the school. The controlling aim of the school was not the aim of present *progressive education.* It was to discover and apply the principles that govern all human development that is truly educative, to utilize the methods by which mankind has collectively and progressively advanced in skill, understanding, and associated life.

"The basic principle necessarily demanded a very considerable break with the aims, methods, and materials familiar in the traditional school. It involved departure from the conception that, in the main, the proper materials and methods of education are already well-known and need only to be furthered, refined, and extended. It implied continual experimentation to discover the conditions under which educative growth actually occurs. It implied also much more attention to present conditions in the life of individuals, children, and contemporary society than was current in schools based chiefly upon the attainments of the past. It involved the substitution of an active attitude of work and play and of inquiry for the processes of imposition and passive absorption of ready-made knowledge and preformed skills that largely dominated the traditional school. It implied a much larger degree of opportunity for initiative, discovery, and independent communication of intellectual freedom than was characteristic of the traditional school.

"Thus the name *Laboratory School* (originally suggested by Ella Flagg Young) gives a key to the work of the school. A laboratory is, as the word implies, a place for activity, for work, for the consecutive carrying on of an occupation and in the case of education the occupation must be inclusive of all fundamental human values. A laboratory also implies directive ideas, leading hypotheses that, as they are applied, lead to new understandings. It demands also workers, who without being enslaved to the past, are acquainted with achievements of the past in science and art, and who are possessed of the best skills that have been worked out by the coöperative efforts of human beings. Like every human enterprise the Laboratory School came far short of achieving its ideal and putting its controlling ideas into successful operation. But some knowledge as to what the ideals and ideas were is necessary to give unity and coherence to an account of its detailed work."

The practical difficulties of creating a new school as compared with the formulation of theoretical principles were recognized from the start. The idea of education as growth was new. Since growth is the characteristic of all life, education is all one with growing; it has no end beyond itself; it goes on during the whole life span of the individual; it is the result of the constant adjustment of the individual to his physical and social environment which is thus both used and modified to supply his needs and those of his social groups. All these new theoretical statements presented practical difficulties. There were no precedents for this type of schooling to follow, and there was need to study the growing child in relation to his environment and to experiment with subject-matter and method to find what ministered best to his growth.

With faith in the soundness of the experimental approach to education that should test in practice the value of the theory, the school opened in January, 1896, in a private dwelling with sixteen pupils and two persons in charge. The first six months was a "trial-and-error" period and was chiefly indicative of what not to do. The school reopened on a new basis in October, 1896, at 5718 Kimbark Avenue with thirty-two children ranging in age from six to eleven and a staff of three regular teachers, one in charge of science and the domestic arts, one of literature and history, and one of manual training. A part-time instructor in music was also on the staff, and three graduate students gave all or part of their time to the school. The school continued at these headquarters until January, 1897, when, owing to inadequate space, it removed to the old South Park Club House, at the corner of Rosalie Court and 57th Street. The number of teachers was increased and new pupils were received, making the enrolment forty-five.

By December, 1897, the staff of teachers had grown to sixteen, the children numbered sixty, and the school again faced the need of larger quarters. In October, 1898, the school opened in an old residence at 5412 Ellis Avenue. At this time the school took on its subsequent departmental form, thus harmonizing with the University. A sub-primary department was added to include children of four and five. Eighty-two children were enrolled. New quarters included a gymnasium and manual training rooms in a barn connected with the house by a covered way. Art and textile rooms occupied the large attic rooms. The science department had two laboratories, one for combined physics and chemistry, and one for biology. The history department shared three special rooms with the English department. Domestic science now had a kitchen large enough for two groups to work together and two dining rooms properly equipped for serving.

In these quarters the school entered upon another stage of its history. The experience of two years and a half of success and failure afforded a basis out of which there grew an ever developing curriculum. Through the years 1900, 1901, and 1902 the school continued to increase in numbers until it reached a maximum of one hundred and forty children. The teaching staff increased to twenty-three teachers and instructors with about ten assistants (graduate students of the University). With its increase in size the organization of the teaching staff had become more formal in character. Mr. Dewey continued as Director, and Ella Flagg Young of the Department of Education was Supervisor of Instruction. Mrs. Dewey's previous informal connection now became official as principal of the school. She was also director of the Department of English and literature, and had general oversight of the language expression of the school. The relationship with the University continued as before, insuring stability and continuity to the work, as well as providing the advantages of expert advice, planning, and supervision of instruction.

The administration of the school was, particularly in its formative years, so much a matter of the coöperation of those directing and teaching that it is difficult to say where executive or administrative responsibilities ended and those of teaching began. As head of the Department of Pedagogy, Mr. Dewey was at all times head of the Laboratory School; but for the first three years of its existence the various administrative duties fell in great part to members of the teaching staff, were informally determined in conference with the director, and shifted constantly to meet temporary exigencies and changing needs. The teaching staff in these years, therefore, was the administrative, with the exception of certain administrative functions, chiefly financial, which were carried out by the University Department of Pedagogy. In later years when the greatly increased staff necessitated a more formal organization, the school was departmentalized, and while the administrative staff was still composed of teachers, a division of responsibility was made. One, as principal, took charge of all contacts with parents, graduate student-teachers, and visitors, and one, as vice-principal, continued to assume responsibility for the curriculum. At this time also, a supervisor from the Department of Pedagogy of the University was added to the staff. She also conducted classes with the pedagogical students working in the school and doing laboratory work as assistants,[3] where the prin-

---

[3] Principal and director of history, Georgia Bacon, 1900–1901; principal and director of the language instruction, Alice Chipman Dewey, 1901–1903; vice-principal and director of science, Katherine Camp; supervisor, Ella Flagg Young.

ciples and practices of the school were discussed and related. The early meetings, of the experimental years, however, being smaller, had included, in addition to the teachers, all of the Fellows, and most of the students and instructors in the University's Department of Pedagogy.

In retrospect, the coöperation of the many departments of the University, particularly in all forms of science is acknowledged with gratitude. Heads of these departments, as well as individual staff members, were generous with their time and facilities. In addition to this whole-hearted aid in material ways, intellectual resources were freely put at the disposal of the teachers. Of immeasurable, stabilizing value was the relationship to the University. As the laboratory of the Department of Pedagogy, the school shared with the other laboratories of the University the benefits of such intimate relationship. This gave an easy accessibility for teachers desiring it to many scientists who were, or since have become, leaders of thought and accomplishment in their various fields. Many of these men had, in addition to special attainments, unusual pedagogical interests which led to their giving constant intellectual and material help to the teachers of the school.[4]

As time went on, it became clear that this experiment in education required also experimental administrative methods. A school that was a social institution modeled after the organization of an ideal home required a special arrangement and organization of its directing factors. Instead of a group of

---

[4] Perhaps the University of Chicago possessed in the beginning many more scientists later to achieve international distinction than had been gathered together in any other new university. At that time Thomas C. Chamberlain was elaborating his planetesimal theory of the origin of the solar system and came to talk about it to the children. John M. Coulter planned and guided the experiments on plant relations. Others who coöperated were Charles O. Whitman in zoölogy, Jacques Loeb in physiology, W. I. Thomas and George Vincent in sociology, Frederick Starr in anthropology, Rollin D. Salisbury in geography, Albert A Michelson in physics, Alexander Smith in chemistry, and Henry C. Cowles in ecology. The school was indebted to numerous persons in other departments of the University especially to Mr. and Mrs. William D. MacClintock, to G. E. Hale, Wallace Atwood, and to the members of Mr. Dewey's departments for continuous coöperation particularly to George H. Mead, James H. Tufts, and James R. Angell.

persons who planned on paper a program which they then required a staff of teachers to teach to the pupils, these experimenters were confronted with a different problem. The aid of the teachers (as well as of the pupils) was a fundamental and primary requisite to even the theoretical formulation of an educative program. Plainly, therefore, all three factors, administrators, teachers, pupils, must share in the functions of managing and executing the teacher-learning process. Indeed, such an experiment in education as this could not go on except through a group of persons all of whom were intellectually and socially coöperating in a constantly developing educational plan. In such an endeavor the parents of the children were also factors, whose help was essential in countless ways for the successful accomplishment of the experiment. The focus of all this coöperative endeavor was the child—his physical and mental growth in a well-balanced and, therefore, happy fashion. Along many lines of approach help and suggestion flowed in and were integrated and correlated by the child's activities. At the request of the authors, Mr. Dewey has recently made the following comment on the relation of the theory to the practice in the actual working out of the school.

"In dealing with principles underlying school activities, it is easy, especially after a lapse of years, to read into a statement of them what one has learned in subsequent experience. Another danger more serious and more difficult to avoid lies in the gap between any formal statement of principles and ideals and the way things work out in actual practice; in the temptation to idealize the latter by assuming a greater conformity with theoretical principles than is attained. The concrete circumstances of school life introduce many factors that are not foreseen and taken account of in theory. This is as formal and static as the life of teachers and children in school is moving and vital.

"The principles stated were not intended to serve as definite rules for what was done in the school. They furnished a point of view and indicated the direction in which it was to move. Not merely the concrete material, the subject matter of the pupils' studies, but the methods of teaching were developed in the course of the school's own operations. This development signifies, of course, that the experience of one year taught something about what was to be done the next year and how it was to be better done. But it also meant something more than this,—material and methods which worked with one group of children would not give the same results with another group of supposedly about the same attainments and capacities, and quite radical changes would have to be introduced in the actual process of teaching."

The school always faced a serious financial situation. In five years it had outgrown three buildings, none of which had been adequately equipped. Because tuition fees had been kept low [5] for the sake of the parents who might otherwise have coveted in vain such an education for their children, there had been a yearly deficit. Each year, however, this deficit had been met by the parents and friends, staunch supporters of the school who had caught a vision of its worth and meaning for their own and other children. At the beginning the University assured Mr. Dewey only the sum of $1,000 to cover the initial expense. This sum, moreover, was not in cash but in tuitions of graduate students who were to teach in the school. At the end of the first six months the generous gift of $1,200 by Mrs. Charles R. Linn enabled the school to begin anew in the fall of 1896 with a staff of three teachers. In the years following funds to cover the deficit were forthcoming from the loyal group of parents and friends.

In 1902, the Chicago Institute (formerly the Cook County Normal School of Chicago) heavily endowed by Mrs. Emmons Blaine, and the University of Chicago consummated a plan whereby the former became incorporated with the University. Two other schools had been included in the merger, the Chicago Manual Training School and the South Side Academy. The Chicago Institute was primarily a school for training teachers and was under the leadership of Colonel Francis W.

---

[5] Tuition paid in 1901-2 was as follows: for children from four to six years, $75.00 per year; for older children attending the forenoon session only, $90.00 per year; for children attending the afternoon session also, $105.00 per year.

Parker. The faculty of the Institute numbered thirty-five persons. There were about one hundred students in the pedagogical and one hundred and twenty in the academic departments, one of which was an elementary school and kindergarten. The University accordingly found itself possessing two elementary schools. One, a practice school for the training of teachers under the leadership of Colonel Parker, was heavily endowed. The other, the Laboratory School of the University's Department of Pedagogy directed by Mr. Dewey, had no endowment, but had been, even then, characterized as one of the "greatest experiments in education ever carried on." Both schools were progressive; both had made outstanding contributions to the principles and practice of education. But while similar in these larger aspects of general purpose, the two schools differed rather widely in theory, method, and practice.

For the solution of the problem thus presented, various plans had been discussed by the President and Trustees of the University. Of these, two plans only seemed feasible. The first was to continue both schools as separate organizations; one, the Dewey School, to be a laboratory of the Department of Pedagogy of the University, the other to be a practice school for the training of elementary teachers. The difficulty, which seemed to make this plan impracticable, was the lack of endowment for the Dewey School. The only solution, apparently, was the second plan—merging the two schools. It had also been proposed that if the two elementary schools were merged, a new secondary school should be formed by combining the South Side Academy and the Chicago Manual Training School. Mr. Dewey was to be head of this secondary school, and it was to be regarded as part of the University's Department of Pedagogy so long as Mr. Dewey remained in charge of that Department. At the same time this secondary school was to be carried on in connection with the transplanted Chicago Institute.

The President and his Committee of Administrators, not having followed closely the development of the Laboratory School, made a serious error of judgment in supposing that the plan of merging the two elementary schools, so different in theory and method, would seem advisable or welcome to the parents, teachers, or administrators of the Dewey School. All parents, teachers, and administrators were in accord in their opinions that both schools would suffer from such procedure, and that the Dewey School, being the smaller, and bereft of its leader, would be swallowed up and lost in the larger school. Therefore, after much discussion and planning, they secured the permission of the University authorities to continue the school separately, under the official name of the *Laboratory School of the University of Chicago,* provided they could raise and guarantee to the University for the space of three years the sum of $5,000 annually. A committee of parents, fired with zeal to save the school, raised this amount in a comparatively short time with pledges for the years to come, and for one year longer the school continued at the same place and under the same administration as before.

During this year (1903), however, Colonel Parker died, and negotiations for the amalgamation of the two schools were again resumed and finally consummated. Mr. Dewey accepted the directorship of the School of Education with his understanding that the regular teaching and administrative staff of the Laboratory School was to be taken over by the School of Education and was to continue in office indefinitely. The Laboratory School accordingly moved into the newly completed School of Education building in the fall of 1903, and the School of Education then became the united faculties, students, and administration of four schools, The Chicago Institute, The Chicago Manual Training School, The University of Chicago Laboratory School, and the South Side Academy.

It seems fitting at this point to quote briefly an address by Mr. Dewey on the occasion of the first combined meeting of the parents of the four schools which had joined forces to become the School of Education. Upon the background of the history of these four schools, he states the ideal of the School of Education as he conceived it: [6]

---

[6] John Dewey, "Significance of the School of Education," *The Elementary School Teacher,* March, 1904.

"The significance of the School of Education, put in terms of its origin, lies in the bringing together of all factors of the educational problem. . . . It now incarnates in itself all the elements which constitute the theoretical educational problem of the present. In other words, we have right here in concrete, actual institutional form all the factors which any writer on education of the present day would lay down as involved in the problem of education. We have the so-called practical and utilitarian element. This comes not merely from the Chicago Manual Training School, but from the stress laid from the first in the Cook County Normal School (Chicago Institute) upon manual training, and the important place given in the Laboratory School to social occupations. Thus the motor, the executive side of the individual is appealed to. The School of Education recognizes that an "all-around education" is a mere name if it leaves out of account direct interest in seeing things and in doing things. The so-called practical and utilitarian factor is thus here not an isolated and independent thing, but the utilization of an otherwise wasted (and hence perverted) source of energy. But the School also stands for the most thorough-going recognition of the importance of scientific and cultural elements in education. Moreover, the School stands for these things, not merely within its own structure, but through the training of teachers and the promulgation of sound educational theory for educational progress and reform far beyond itself. . . . To have initiated these distinct and independent portions of an educational system represented here, was a great achievement. To stop here, not to recognize the growth that may come from their fusing into a vital whole, would be a calamity all the greater because of what has been achieved in the past. . . .

"Such growth can only come as a result of the coöperative effort of teachers, parents, and children. There is one kind of coeducation to which no one takes objections—one which is absolutely indispensable if the future of the school is to be as significant as its own past exacts of it. This coeducation of teachers, children, and parents by one another. I say *by* one another rather than *with* one another, for I think that coeducation is not the passive reception of the same instruction side by side, but the active participation in the education of one by others. If the School is to move along steadily and as a whole within itself, it must be because it moves along with a body of parents who have intrusted their children to it, and because in turn the parents move along sympathetically with the endeavors, experiments, and changes of the school itself. . . .

"In spite of all the advances that have been made throughout the country, there is still one unsolved problem in elementary and secondary education. That is the question of duly adapting to each other the practical and utilitarian, the executive and the abstract, the tool and the book, the head and the hand. This is a problem of such vast scope that any systematic attempt to deal with it must have great influence upon the whole course of education everywhere. The School of Education, both in its elementary and secondary departments, is trying to make its contribution to this vexed question. Utility and culture, absorption and expression, theory and practice, are indispensable elements in any educational scheme. But, as a rule, they are pursued apart. As already indicated, the different schools which have entered into combination here make it necessary for the School of Education to fuse hitherto separated factors. In this attempt we shall need your sympathetic intelligence. . . .

"In the second place, I wish to enlist your sympathy with the social ideals and spirit which must prevail in the School of Education, if it is to be true to its own past. We trust, and shall continue to trust, to the social spirit as the ultimate and controlling motive in discipline. We believe, and our past experience warrants us in the belief, that a higher, more effective, more truly severe type of personal discipline and government may be secured through appeal to the social motives and interests of children and youth than to their antisocial ones. . . . It must be possible on some other basis to secure and maintain a wholesome social and moral spirit in the school. It cannot be too definitely stated that it is only to this class that the

School of Education wants to appeal for members of its student body. . . . The moral and social influence which the members of the student body exert upon each other is far more potent for good in the long run than any device that teachers can set up and keep going; and the presence or absence of this influence must go back largely to home influences and surroundings.

"The School of Education wishes particularly, then, the cooperation of parents in creating a healthy moral tone which will render quite unnecessary resort to lower and more unworthy motives for regulating conduct, in the cultivation of a democratic tone, an *esprit-de-corps,* which attaches itself to the social life of the school as a whole, and not to some clique or set in it, . . . May we remind you that a school has a corporate life of its own; that, whether for good or bad, it is itself a genuine social institution—a community. The influences which center in and radiate from this corporate social life are infinitely more important with respect to the moral development of your children than is simply class-room instruction in the abstract. May I close with an exhortation to bear in mind the fundamental importance to yourselves and to your children, as well as to the School, of the maintenance of the right sort of social aims and spirit throughout the school as a whole."

These words seemed to promise a new era of fulfilment and expansion for the ideals of the Laboratory School. Those who had piloted this ship on its seven-year voyage of discovery thought at last they had found fair sailing. It proved, however, only a brief season of good passage, for Mr. Dewey's resignation followed in the spring of 1904. This action was quite as unpremeditated on his part as it was unexpected to his associates. Early in the spring he was told that at the time of the merging of the four schools assurances had been given to the Trustees of the Chicago Institute that certain members of the administrative staff of the elementary school would be eliminated at the close of the first year after the merger. Mr. Dewey had been entirely ignorant of these assurances, found himself unable to accept them and resigned, first as Director of the School of Education and shortly after as Head of the Departments of Philosophy, Psychology, and Pedagogy.

Only the passing of time has made it possible to state the reasons for this unhappy ending to so many relationships and undertakings. With the resignation of Mr. Dewey and the subsequent dispersal of all save three or four of the faculty of the Laboratory School, this experiment in education ended. The brief year of union with the School of Education at Chicago marked the close of the career of the Laboratory School, as the present School of Education can in no sense be regarded as the heir of either its purposes or its methods. There are many progressive schools which have extended the work of the Dewey School along certain lines, but nowhere has its closely knit social organization of children, parents, teachers in a university laboratory been achieved. Owing perhaps to the mechanized character of American life, there has been a distinct failure on the part of modern progressive schools to appreciate what the fundamental occupations of living—cooking, sewing, carpentry, and all principal manual-training activities—may do when clarified and organized as a means, *par excellence,* of preserving the investigative attitude and the creative ability of the growing child in socially directed expression. Day by day he gains both in his skill to control situations and to direct his own activity to further and more desired ends; he also becomes gradually conscious of his gain. This results in an integrated child, able to work more and more on his own initiative and under his own guidance—a child who is maturing, who is both educating and being educated, and whose education continues throughout life.

When the four schools united, there were, from the Laboratory School, a number of children who had received in that school practically all of their education. Although their curriculum had always been different from that of the children of the other schools, it was said of them a few months later, "Either these are exceptional children, or they have been exceptionally trained." They were, however, like other children of varying degrees of ability and types of temperament. They were exceptional only as they represented a group of parents who had caught a vision of a sort of education which they desired to have their children experience.

The sense of frustration with which these parents viewed the apparent shipwreck of their high hopes was to some degree lessened by the conviction that what they had desired had been for a brief time fulfilled. As the years passed they grew more and more comforted by the fact that what had seemed to die, continued to live, and was extending its influence throughout America, and even to foreign lands, such as China, and Mexico; to the early schools of Soviet Russia and to those of many European countries.

CHAPTER II

EXPERIMENTAL BASIS OF CURRICULUM

THE Laboratory School was both a department of the University and a place where parents sent children to be educated. As such it required conditions which would insure freedom for investigation on the one hand, and normal development for child life on the other. This meant the planning of a curriculum which was not static in character, but one which ministered constantly to the changing needs and interests of the growing child's experience. It involved careful arrangement of the physical and social set-up of the school and a discriminating search for subject-matter which would fulfil and further the growth of the whole child. It meant study and observation in order that the materials and agencies used to present this subject-matter should be in agreement with the child's changing attitudes and abilities, and would link what was valuable in his past experience to his present and his future. It required experimentation as to classroom methods in the use of this material so that it entered vitally into growth in such a way that control gained by the child in one situation might be carried on to the next, thus insuring continuity of experience, a habit of initiative, and an increasing skill in the use of the experimental method. As a child's social growth is largely a matter of adaptation to group relations, it was of primary importance that the subject-matter selected should be social in character and thus give free play to the child's group behavior and guide the expression of his individual interests toward social ends. It was important that the guidance should be of such a character that the child never felt imposed upon by adult standards, but developed his own standards out of habitual social behavior, that is, behavior free from conscious competition or biased criticism of others' products.

The task that lay before those who worked out the educational implications of these newly formed theories was a difficult one. It was difficult because it necessitated the discarding of many established methods of teaching and learning. It meant the careful study of the story of education, especially of those periods and types of civilization when there was no rift between experience and knowledge, when information about things and ways of doing grew out of social situations and represented answers to social needs, when the education of the immature member of society proceeded almost wholly through participation in the social or community life of which he was a member, and each individual, no matter how young, did certain things in the way of work and play *along* with others, and learned, thereby, to adjust himself to his surroundings, to adapt himself to social relationships, and to get control of his own special powers.

"He must learn by experience" is an old adage too little heeded by modern methods of schooling. Too often these methods take for granted that there is a short cut to learning, and that knowledge apart from its use has meaning for the developing mind. The memorizing of such knowledge has come to be a large part of present-day education, with the result that great masses of young lives have been denied the thrill of experimental living, of finding the way for themselves, of discovery, of invention, of creation. The fine aspiring tendril of childhood's native curiosity, like the waving tip of a growing vine, seeks the how and why of doing—its intellectual food. It is early stunted in many children. The strong urge to investigate, present in every individual, is often crushed by the memorizing of great masses of information useless to him, or the learning of skills that he is told may be useful to him in the far-away future, the sometime, and the somewhere. Only those in whom the urge to know will not be denied break away into new trails by virtue of individual and experimental effort, and when directed in the use of the scientific method, climb to the highest peaks of living; the majority travel a wide made-easy way of schooling into a dead level of mediocrity.

It was necessary, therefore, for these experimenters in a new practice to ignore and forget certain practices and precepts of the old psychology. They must hold steadily before their mental eyes the newer psychological principles and chart a course of pedagogical thinking and practice. This new psychology recognized that the normal functioning mind of the child cannot operate or develop alone in a physical world. It requires, in addition to the continual stimulus of first-hand experience, that of contact with other minds and social agencies, and of recourse to the accumulated knowledge and past experience of the race. In other words, educative schooling must furnish a social and intellectual as well as a physical environment, in which the child may become increasingly familiar with all kinds of relationships and be trained to consider them so far as is necessary in his individual and experimental activities. In general, the problem and purpose of this new type of schooling was, first of all, to aid the child to develop his own individuality by expression of his ideas in deed as well as in word, and thus become a freely maturing person. Always, however, it was an important duty of those guiding this process to help the child gradually to shape his expressions to social ends, and thus make them, through his growing control, more and more effective in the corporate life of the group.

Such free use of his powers by every child presupposes that he be studied and understood. Those planning the activities must see each child as an ever changing person, both because of what he undertakes and undergoes in his social group, and because of the changing needs of the succeeding stages of his development. They must carefully select and grade the materials used, altering such selection, as is necessary in all experimentation, in accord with the available materials, whether at hand or remote.

The plan for the life of the school, in this experiment of education, was a simplified and ordered continuation of the life of the home. In this environment, both new and familiar, the child, conscious of no break in his experience, could learn to become a useful member of a larger social group. Guided and stimulated to social action, he would naturally judge the value of his action by the responses of others. He gets the feel and the thrill of using his individual powers for social ends and becomes more and more expert in making his contribution socially effective. Coöperative effort involves interest in and consideration of others; he more and more naturally becomes alert to their needs and generous to share with them his opportunities. An increasing fund of personally tested knowledge accumulates from these experiments in human relationships and becomes the foundation upon which he builds his future social ideals. Increasing confidence in himself as the guiding agent of his activities makes him a recognized and responsible member of the group with the result that he is an increasingly integrated and happy child, because he is satisfied, adjusted to, and helpful in the control and modification of his physical and social environments.

In the ideal back of the plan two cardinal principles were held in mind. First, in all educative relationships the starting point is the impulse of the child to action, his desire responding to the surrounding stimuli and seeking its expression in concrete form. Second, the educational process is to supply the materials and the positive and negative conditions—the let and hindrance—so that his expression, intellectually controlled, may take a normal direction that is social in both form and feeling. These principles determined the entire school's operation and organization, as a whole and in detail. Study and performance of the basic and simplified occupations of life taught teachers and children *how* to do. In finding how to do, sense became alert to note and select materials to do *with*. Interest made minds receptive to facts and the best ways of doing. Knowledge became the child of experience, and the way of learning an alluring one. It was, however, often a difficult one to find. There were many false leads followed, but in the end a faint trail was made to which the hope still clings that it may prove the pathway to the promised land.

Starting with the activities familiar and natural to little children (fundamental and familiar activities of the home), the school conceived itself as an institution intermediate between the home and the larger school organization of the community, growing naturally out of the one and into the other. All activity having to do with such basic and continuing needs of life as shelter, clothing, and food became the central focus of a developing curriculum. With this unifying factor, all life, whether of the home, school, or larger community, was seen as one and the same continuous, changing social life. Similarly the infant, the school child, and the grown man were recognized as one and the same, though changing, individual. In consequence, the story of the corporate life of this school is a biography, for it was as truly a living, growing organism as was any of its smaller or larger members.

In the informal address to the parents and teachers toward the close of the third year of the school, Mr. Dewey gave a somewhat detailed account of the practices of the school in relation to its theoretical principles. Extracts from the stenographic notes of the address serve to give a bird's-eye view of the way in which the studies and activities of its curriculum were related or grew out of the daily experience of the children. These extracts are supplemented by portions of a circular published during the school's first year.[1]

"When the school was started, there were certain points which it seemed worth while to test—four questions, or problems in mind. First, what can be done, and how can it be done, to bring the school, now a place where the child comes, learns certain lessons, and then goes home, into closer relation with the home and neighborhood life; how bridge the gap, and break down the traditional barriers, which unfortunately now separate the school from the rest of the child's everyday life? This does not mean, as sometimes interpreted, that the child should study in school things he already has learned at home, but that, so far as possible, he should take the same attitude and point of view at school as at home; that he should feel the same interest in going to school because he finds there things worth doing for their own sake and just as interesting as

---

[1] John Dewey, "The University Elementary School, Studies and Methods," *University Record*, May 21, 1897.

the plays and occupations of his home and neighborhood. Again, the same motives which keep the child at work and growing should be used in the school as in the home, so that he shall not feel that he has one set of reasons which belongs to the school and another which is used in the home.

"Second, how can history and science and art be introduced so that they will be of positive value and have real significance in the child's own present experience? How can they be made to represent, even to the youngest child, something worthy of attainment in skill or knowledge; something just as worthy to him because it is, at his level, as truly satisfying intellectually and emotionally as anything a high school or college student might be able to get at his period of education? It is true, many modifications have been made in the traditional primary curriculum of most schools. Statistics recently collected, however, show that seventy-five to eighty per cent of the first years of a child in school is spent upon the form, not the substance of learning; is given to the mastering of the symbols of reading, writing, and arithmetic. There is not much positive nutriment in this. Its purpose is important, but it does not represent the same kind of addition or increase in a child's whole intellectual and moral experience that is represented by the positive subject-matter, now postponed to the later years of the child's education. One purpose, then, of the experiment is to see how much can be given to the child of the experiences of the world about him that is really worth his while to get; how far first-hand experience with the forces in that world and knowledge of its historical and social growth will enable him to develop the capacity to express himself in a variety of artistic forms. From the strictly educational side this has been the chief problem of the school. It is along this line that we hope to make our chief contribution to education in general. To this end, those subjects which have a positive content and intrinsic value of their own, and which call forth the inquiring and constructive attitude on the part of the pupil are made the core of the school work.

"In the third place, how can instruction in the formal, symbolic branches of learning—the mastering of the ability

to read, write, and use figures intelligently—be gained out of
other studies and occupations as their background? How can
the child be made to regard symbols as instruments and methods needful in his study of those subjects which appeal to him
on their own account? It is clear that need, when felt by the
child, would supply the motive for getting technical capacity,
and the question of the adjustment of these two sides of the
work would be solved. It is not the purpose, as has been stated,
of this school that the child learn to bake and sew at school,
and to read, write, and figure at home. It is true, however, that
these subjects of reading, writing, etc., are not presented during the early years in large doses. Instead, the child is led by
other means to feel the motives for acquiring skill in the use
of these symbols, motives which persist when competition,
often the only motive in the early years of many schools, ceases.
In this school, as well as in all schools, if a child realizes the
motive for acquiring skill, he is helped in large measure to
secure the skill. Books and the ability to read are, therefore,
regarded strictly as tools. The child must learn to use these,
just as he would any other tools. This implies that he shall
have arrived at some conception of what they are for and have
some end in view or motive for using them, and that the actual
learning to read shall *grow* out of this motive. Accordingly, no
special effort is made to teach children to read in the sixth
year, or even in the seventh, unless the indications are that
the child is awakening to his needs in that direction. The premature teaching of reading, in the present school system, involves undue strain on the eyes and the nervous system, takes
time away from subjects which have a positive content, and
devotes it to a purely formal study, which the child can master
with much less strain and more quickly when he is ready for
it. The aim is thus to familiarize the child with the use of
language as a means of discovering something otherwise unknown and of sharing with others what he himself has found
out. Hence reading is taught in close connection with other
subjects, science and history, not as a subject by itself. As soon
as the child has an idea what reading is for and has a certain
amount of technical facility, printed material is supplied him,

not as a text-book, but as an additional tool in his equipment. The prevalent use of text-books has two evils. First, the child forms a habit of depending upon them and comes almost instinctively to assume that the book is the chief, if not the only way, of getting information. Then, the use of books, as texts, throws the mind into a passive and absorbing attitude. The child is learning instead of inquiring.

"In the fourth place, individual attention is secured by small groupings of children and a large number of teachers, who attempt to supervise systematically the intellectual and physical work of the child. This insures attention, so far as those in charge are capable of giving it, to the general well-being and development of each child. It also enables them to carry on in connection with school work a certain amount of investigation of the psychological and physiological needs and powers of individual children. . . .

"The use of the hand, and other motor organs in connection with the eye, is the great instrument through which the children most easily and naturally gain experience and come in contact with the familiar materials and processes of ordinary life. It affords unrivalled means for securing and holding attention. It is full of opportunities for cultivating the social spirit through the opportunities it affords for division of labor and mutual coöperation, and supplies the child with motives for working in ways positively useful to the community of which he is a member. The use of the hand is again the best possible instrument for cultivating habits of industry and continuity in work, and of securing personal deftness and dexterity at the plastic period. When conducted in a free instead of mechanical spirit, it develops more than any other one instrumentality, ingenuity in planning and power in execution. The constant testimony is that nothing compares with it as a means of arousing the child to a positive sense of his own power, and of encouraging him in expression and construction. Furthermore, such training affords constantly recurring opportunities for related work in other directions. Cooking, for example, is a natural avenue of approach to simple but fundamental chemical facts and principles and to a study of the plants as articles of food. Similarly, a study of the materials and processes involved is carried on in connection with sewing, and includes a study of the history of invention, of geography (localities of production and manufacturing, with lines of distribution), and of the growth and cultivation of plants, like cotton and flax which furnish the raw material. Recourse to measurement is had in these subjects. The carpentry work, in particular, constantly calls for calculation and gives the child a command of numerical processes in a related way, and a genuine number sense is thus cultivated. Three main lines of manual training are pursued regularly, shop-work with wood and tools, the cooking, and the work with the textile fabrics. There is also much other hand-work incident to the experimental sciences. Indeed experience verifies the statement that hand-work, in variety and amount, is the most easy and natural of all ways to keep an attitude of combined effort and interest on the part of the child. The purpose, therefore, of those teaching and directing is to direct these activities, to systematize and organize them so that they shall not be as haphazard and wandering as they customarily are in child's play and home life. One of the most difficult problems is to enable the children to work continuously and definitely, and to help them pass from one phase of an activity to another.

"Carpentry, cooking, sewing, and weaving—all require different sorts of skill and represent, as well, some of the most important industries of the everyday outside world. The questions of living under shelter, of living in a home, of daily food and clothing, of protection through the home, and the support of life through food are basic things for all higher civilization. A child's interests are so direct and immediate that these things appeal to him. He gets through such activities, also, a training of the sense organs, of touch, of eye, and the ability to coordinate hand and eye. They furnish, as well, a healthy sort of exercise. They are more natural to child life than to keep continually quiet, to work at a book, or to engage in more formal modes of action. In addition, there is a continual appeal to memory, to judgment in adapting ends to means. Training in habits of order, of industry, and of neatness in the care of tools, or utensils are also by-products, for the child gets at things in a systematic instead of a haphazard way.

"All the children (boys and girls being treated alike) have cooking, sewing, and carpentry, besides incidental work with paper and pasteboard. From one to two hours a week are given to sewing, cooking, and carpentry respectively. Each group of children prepares its own luncheon once a week, being responsible for the setting of the table, reception of guests, and the serving of the meal. This is found to afford a positive motive for the cooking, as well as to give it a social value. In the carpentry shop no rigid series of exercises is followed. The aim is to adapt the tools and materials to the muscular and mental power of the child. The things made are, in the first place, the articles needed in the school work. For example, wands, dumb-bell racks, and wand-racks have been made for the gymnasium, and simple balances, with lead weights, test-tube racks, and simple experimental apparatus, for the laboratory. All of this active individual experience makes a background, especially in the earlier groups, for the later studies. Children get a good deal of chemistry in connection with cooking, of number-work and geometrical principles in connection with their theoretical work in carpentry, and quite an amount of geography very easily and naturally in connection with sewing. History enters in as the story of industrial development and growth of various inventions.

"Upon the whole, greater attention has been given to the relation of the positive subject-matter to the activity program, than to any other one aspect. History is introduced at a very early period and is conducted on the principle that it is a means of affording the child insight into social life. It is treated, therefore, not as a record of something which is past and gone, but as a way of realizing what enters into the make-up of society and of how society has grown to be what it is. Treated thus, as a mode of insight into social life, great emphasis is laid upon the typical relations of humanity to nature, as summed up in the development of food, shelter, habitation, clothing, and industrial occupations. This affords insight into the fundamental processes and instruments which have controlled the development of civilization and also affords natural and frequent opportunities for adjusting the work in history to that in manual training on the one side, and to science on the other.

"The younger children begin with the home and the occupations of the home. In the sixth year (of the child) these lead to a study of the occupations outside the home, the larger social industries—farming, mining, lumbering—that they may see the complex and various occupations on which life depends. They experiment with raw materials, with the various metals and observe materials new to them, noting what they are like and their uses. This makes a beginning of scientific study.

"The following year takes up the historical development of industry and invention. Starting with man as a savage, the typical phases of his progress upward are followed, until the iron age is reached when man has begun to enter upon a civilized career. The object of this study of the primitive period is not to keep the child in the primitive period, but rather to show him the steps of progress and development, especially along the line of invention, by which man was led into civilization. There is a certain nearness, after all in the child, to primitive forms of life. It is much more simple, and by throwing emphasis on the progress of man and the way advances took place, it is hoped to avoid the objections that are made, and validly so, of paying too much attention to savage life.

"It is at this point that the study of history, as such, really begins, as the story of primitive life cannot properly be called history. In the school about this time a year was given to the world wide explorations and discoveries, which developed an idea of the world as a whole and served as an introduction to the history of the settlements in America. Study of the early fur traders of North America, who established the trade routes, led naturally to the settlement of Chicago. This with some local history prefaced the general American history of the next two or three years. Greek and Roman history were then introduced, and finally, the regular chronological order of the development of civilization is adopted.

"As regards the study of literature, perhaps the most striking departure from methods pursued in other progressive schools is that literature is regarded as a social expression. It is approached, therefore, through the medium of history, instead of studying history through the medium of literature. This method puts the latter subject in its proper perspective, and avoids the danger of distracting and over-stimulating the child with stories which to him (however they may be to the adult) are simply stories. In developing the work upon Greek life, for example, it was found that practically all the books for children are composed from the strictly literary side. Many of them in addition make the myth fundamental, instead of an incident to the intellectual and social development of the Greek people.

"Both nature study (that is the study through observation of obvious natural phenomena) and experimental work are introduced from the beginning. The science is very much more difficult to arrange and systematize. There is so little to follow, so little that has been already done. It is impossible to exaggerate this statement. The slight amount of work in science that has been developed in any systematic way for the use of children, which purposes to cultivate their powers of noting the habits of plants and animals and of observing things with reference to their uses, is almost negligible. The earth is, perhaps, the focus for the science study as practically all of the work relates to it sooner or later, and in one way or another.

"Children of six as well as those of ten work in the laboratory, and with equal profit, both as regards the development of their intelligence and the acquisition of skill and dexterity in manipulation. The attempt is not to give them analytic knowledge of objects or minute formulations of scientific principles, either of which are incomprehensible to a child of this age. The object is to arouse his spirit of curiosity and investigation and awaken him to a consciousness of the world in which he lives, to train the powers of observation, to instil a practical sense of methods of inquiry, and gradually to form in the mind images of the typical moving forces and processes involved in all natural change. The results thus far show an eager and definite response to this mode of approach.

"Another aspect of the science studied is the application of natural forces to the service of man through machines. Last year a good deal of work was done in electricity, based on the telegraph and the telephone. Things that could easily be grasped were taken up. In mechanics, they have studied locks and clocks with reference to the adaptation of the various parts of the machinery to accomplish their work. Cooking also gives opportunity for unconscious absorption of a great many mechanical ideas of heat and water. In general, the scientific work in this school differs from that of other schools in having the experimental part of both physics and chemistry emphasized. It does not confine the science work to nature study, the study of plants and animals. This does not imply that the latter is less valuable, but does maintain that physical science should be brought into the program from the first, by introducing larger generalizations in a story form.

"As regards the spirit of the school, the chief object is to secure a free and informal community life in which each child will feel that he has a share and his own work to do. This is made the chief motive towards what are ordinarily termed order and discipline. It is believed that the only *genuine* order and discipline are those which proceed from the child's own respect for the work which he has to do and his consciousness of the rights of others who are, with himself, taking part in this work. As already suggested, the emphasis in the school upon various forms of practical and constructive activity gives ample opportunity for appealing to the child's social sense and to his regard for thorough and honest work.

"Genuine, as distinct from artificial, moral growth is measured by the extent to which children practically recognize in the school the same moral motives and relations that obtain outside. This can be secured only when the school contains the social conditions and presents the flexible, informal relations that prevail in everyday life. When school duties and responsibilities are of a sort found only in the school, comparatively little aid is secured for the all-round healthy development of character. When school conditions are so rigid and formal as not to parallel anything outside the school, external order and decorum may be secured, but there is no guarantee of right growth in directions demanded by the ordinary walks of life. When what is expected of children is based on the requirements of school lessons and school order, as laid down by textbook or teacher, not by work of positive value to those doing it, external habits of attention and restraint may be formed, but not power of initiative and direction, nor moral self-control. Hence the emphasis in the school laid upon social occupations, which continue and reinforce those of life outside the school, and the comparative freedom and informality accorded the children. These are means, not an end. Moral responsibility is secured only by corresponding freedom. Hence the school work on the moral side is to be judged, not by passing external occurrences or external evidences or attitudes, but by its efficiency in promoting healthy growth of character in the child and a general modification of disposition and motive, both of which are slow processes and not sudden transformations.

"For genuine intellectual development it is impossible to separate the attainment of knowledge from its application. The divorce between learning and its use is the most serious defect of our existing education. Without the consciousness of application, learning has no motive to the child. Material thus learned is separated from the actual conditions of the child's life, and a fatal split is introduced between school learning and vital experience—a split which reflects itself in the child's whole mental and moral attitude. The emphasis in the school upon constructive and so-called manual work is due largely to the fact that such occupations connect themselves easily and naturally with the child's everyday environment. They create natural motives for the acquiring of information and the mastery of related methods through the problems which they introduce.

"As to methods, the aim is to keep alive and direct the active inquiring attitude of the child, and to subordinate the amassing of facts and principles to the development of intellectual self-control and of power to conceive and solve problems. Immense damage is done whenever the getting of a certain quantity of information or the covering a certain amount of ground is made the end, at the expense of mastery by each child, of a method of inquiry and of reflection. If children can retain their natural investigating tendencies unimpaired, gradually organizing them into definite methods of work, when they reach the proper age, they can master the required amount of facts and generalizations easily and effectively. Whereas, when the latter are forced upon them at so early a period as to crush the natural interest in searching out new truths, acquiring tends to replace inquiring.

"The social spirit of the school thus furnishes the controlling moral motive of the child. His own alert inquiring attitude is his intellectual spur. Along with this goes the possibility of attention to individuals as such. For purposes of convenience the children are divided into small groups of eight to twelve according to the kind of work and the age of the children. It is expected that the teacher will give attention to the specific powers and deficiencies of each child, so that the individual capacities will be brought out, and individual limitations made good. This attention extends to the physical as well as the intellectual side. Each child receives a personal physical examination in the gymnasium, and all defects are reported to the parent in order that the child may have the special exercises needed to build him up. He also is examined in the psychological laboratory of the University, with reference to his sense organs and motor powers. Almost twenty per cent of the children in the school have been thus far reported to their parents as needing either special exercises or the attention of a competent medical specialist to the eyes, ears, or throat.

"The School is often called an experimental school. In one sense this is the proper name, for it is an experiment school—with reference to education and educational problems in which an attempt is being made to find by experience whether and how these problems may be worked out. A characteristic of experiment is change or modification of the original method or plan. There are two points upon which the ideas and policy of the school have been modified, where the point of view has changed in process. When the school was small, it was intended to mix up the children,—the older and the younger—to the end that the younger might learn unconsciously from the older. There seemed moral advantages to both, in having the older assume certain responsibilities in the care of the younger. As the school grew, it became necessary to abandon this policy and to group the children with reference to their common capabilities or store of knowledge. These groups are based not on ability to read, write, etc., but on the basis of community of interest, general intellectual capacity and mental alertness, and the ability to do certain kinds of work. In other ways, however, children of different groups are still mingling, as they move about and come in contact with different teachers. Thus the gap between groups is bridged and the step-ladder system of the public school avoided. . . .

"The children also meet in general assemblies for singing and for the report of the school work as read by different members of the groups. All hear the report of what each group is doing. This mixture of the ages is also secured by giving to the older children for a half hour a week, responsibility for the work of some of the younger groups. This enables them, especially in hand-work, to enter into the activity of the younger children by coöperating with them.

"As a result of experience, the other chief modification has been with regard to specialization on the part of teachers. It was assumed, at first, that an all-round teacher would be the best, and perhaps it would be advisable to have one teacher teach the children in several branches. This theory, however, has been abandoned, and it has been thought well to secure teachers who are specialists by taste and training—experts along different lines. One of the reasons for this modification of the original plan was the difficulty of getting scientific facts presented that were facts and truths. It has been assumed that any phenomenon that interested a child was good enough, and that if he were aroused and made alert, that was all that could be expected. It is, however, just as necessary that what he gets should be truth and should not be subordinated to anything else. The training of observation by having the child see wrong is not so desirable as sometimes it has been thought to be. The difficulty of getting scientific work presented except by those who were specialists has led to the change in regard to other subjects as well.

"On the other hand, however, it has been recognized that, in the effort to avoid the serious evils of the first situation, there is a tendency to swing from one extreme to the other. That when specialists are employed the result is often that each does his work independently of the other, and the unity of the child's life is thus sacrificed to the tastes and acquisitions of a number of specialists. It seemed, however, not a question of the specialist but of the expert. When manual training, art, science, and literature are to be taught, it is a physical and mental impossibility that one person should be competent in all these lines of work. Superficial work is bound to be done in some one of them, and the child, through not having a model of expert workmanship to follow, acquires careless and imperfect methods of work. The school, accordingly, is endeavoring to put the various lines of work in charge of experts who maintain agreement and harmony through continued consultation and coöperation. When the different studies and occupations are controlled by reference to the same general principles, unity of aim and method are secured. The results obtained justify the belief that the undue separation, which often follows teaching by specialists, is a result of lack of supervision, coöperation, and control by a unified plan."

This principle of guidance by experts referred to by Mr. Dewey was continued throughout the school's existence and was fundamental to the plan. Experience showed that the social spirit of the school successfully avoided the dangers of too narrow and therefore isolated specialization in subject-matter and method.

PART II

THE CURRICULUM—SOCIAL OCCUPATIONS

CHAPTER III

EXPERIMENTAL PRACTICES
DEVELOPING THE CURRICULUM

IN studying the developing curriculum of the Laboratory School, two periods may be recognized. The practices of the first period (1896 to 1898) were largely experimental and guided by the theoretical premises of its hypothesis, native insight as to the nature of children, practical acquaintance with certain fields of subject-matter, and first-hand experience in the use of scientific method. Those of the second period (1898 to 1903) grew out of or were revised on the basis of the courses and methods that had proved successful in the first.

In planning a school program that was to be an experiment in coöperative living, the child was the person of first concern. There were certain theoretical premises in its underlying hypothesis—certain general principles—which were to be aids in understanding its purposes and in guiding its practices.

[1] "The primary business of school is to train children in coöperative and mutually helpful living, to foster in them the consciousness of interdependence, and to help them practically in making the adjustments that will carry this spirit into overt deeds. The primary root of all educative activity is in the instinctive, impulsive attitudes and activities of the child. . . . Accordingly, the numberless spontaneous activities of children, plays, games, mimic efforts, even the apparently meaningless motions of infants are capable of educational use, are *the foundation-stones* of educational method.

"These individual tendencies and activities are only organized and exercised through their use in an actual process of co-

[1] John Dewey, "Froebel's Educational Principles," *Elementary School Record*, No. 1, February, 1900.

operative living; the best results follow when such a process reproduces on the child's plane the typical doings and occupations of the larger, maturer society into which he is finally to go forth; and it is only through such productive and creative use that valuable knowledge is secured and clinched."

FOUR NATIVE IMPULSES

The problem therefore became one of how to utilize the child's individual tendencies, his original impulses to express himself with such growing power and skill as to help him contribute with increasing effectiveness to the life of his group. For purposes of convenience, these native impulses are roughly classified and described by Mr. Dewey under four heads: the social, the constructive, the investigative, and the expressive.

The social impulse of a little child is shown in his desire to share with his family and others the experiences of his limited world. This self-centered interest in his own immediate environment is capable of a continuing expansion; it is the taproot of his intellectual life. His desire to tell about things, to share his ideas with others, takes advantage of all possible ways of expression and communication and influences his growth profoundly. The language instinct, the simplest form of the social expression of a child, is, therefore, a great, perhaps the greatest, of all educational resources.[2]

The child's impulse to do, to make—*the constructive impulse* —finds expression first in play, in rhythmic movement, in gesture, and make-believe; then becomes more definite and seeks outlet in shaping raw materials into tangible form and permanent embodiment. As these self-initiated social and constructive efforts of the child, aided by skilful direction from without, are shaped to his own definitely imaged and desired ends,

---

[2] All the expressive arts, modeling, painting, drawing, etc., might be included either under this heading or that of the constructive impulse. Mr. Dewey suggests that the impulse to this kind of expression probably originates in both the social and constructive impulses of the child, that they are in reality refinements of them. For purposes of convenience, however, these expressions are grouped under a separate heading of artistic activities.

they result in helpful contributions to the common work and play. The very sense of having helped out turns back into and enhances the child's estimate of his own power. He finds for himself a consummate value in such a realization and is stimulated to further and better efforts. Little by little, a constructive way of acting becomes habitual and results in a developing experience for the child and for the group, an experience which is continually refined and enriched as it enlarges day by day.

The impulse to investigate and experiment is often a combination of the constructive and the conversational impulses. Hence, in the school, there was no distinction made between the experimental science for the little children and the work done in the carpentry shop. They liked best of all to do things just to see what would happen. The teacher's part was to contrive that one result should lead through one meaning to another, to ever more meaningful results.

The expressive impulse, like the investigative, seems to follow the communicating and constructive impulses; it is their refinement and full manifestation. All the utensils and materials necessary to express ideas were, therefore, at hand when the desire to do so sprang out of the children's activities.

EXPERIMENTAL USE OF NATIVE IMPULSES (FIRST TWO YEARS)

These fourfold desires—to communicate, to construct, to inquire, and to express in finer form—are the child's natural springs for action. His growth depends upon their use and exercise. The story of the developing curriculum is seen, therefore, to be the story of the attempts to meet and utilize these deep-lying urges to expression and creative effort.

At the start, there was no previous school experience which had attempted to meet the psychological conditions of learning implied in the concept of the organic circuit. Only a few theoretical principles had been formulated by Mr. Dewey which were privately printed during the fall of 1895. Nor were there any precedents as to a plan for school organization. The experience of the first six months, therefore, was largely revealing of what not to do. Aims, plans, and methods were, accordingly, reconsidered, at its close, and on the basis of its successes and particularly of its failures, many revisions were made in the school's curriculum, its organization, and administration. The school's original purpose still held, namely, to give each child the opportunity and method for doing those things he really wanted to do and such guidance in the process that his concept of their social meaning continually developed.

TYPE OF TEACHER

With the growing realization that the developing program of the school was a program of related activities, the conception of the requirements of the teacher in charge of these activities, her abilities, natural aptitudes, and training, likewise took on a different aspect. The need of specialists whose backgrounds and training had fitted them for teaching certain subjects became apparent. Accordingly, from the beginning, in the building of such a staff, a specialist in science was included as a member of the teaching force.

ORGANIZATION OF CURRICULUM THROUGH ACTIVITIES

The addition of elementary nature study or science, of literature and history, to the three R's of the old curriculum, together with the multiplication of the means of expression (the so-called special studies, music, drawing, coloring, modeling) has disturbed the unity and balance of traditional primary education in many school systems. The result has been a confused and distracted child. To any one in intimate contact with young children, the glaring lack of continuity in most school programs, even in many of the better progressive types, seems quite beyond belief. The continuity that the word *growth* implies seems something apart from many teachers' conception of the nature of school activity. In many advanced private as well as public schools the young child's day is still compartmented into tiny cubicles of time without sufficient care for either social or intellectual relations. The pressing problem then, even as now, became how to utilize all these subjects and means of expression in an educative way, how to organize them about a common center, give them a thread of continuity, and make each reinforce the others.

A common center was found for the Laboratory School in the idea of the school-house as a home in which the activities of social or community life were carried on. The ideal was so to use and guide the child's interest in his home, his natural environment, and in himself that he should gain social and scientifically sound notions of the functions of persons in the home; of plant and animal, including human life, and their interdependence; of the sun as the source of all energy; of heat as a special form of energy used in the home (as in cooking); and of food as stored energy. The materials about him and the things that were being done to and with them furnished the ideas for the initial start and choice of the activities which occupied the children in the shop, laboratory, kitchen, and studios. These ideas were chosen for study not alone because of their direct, clear, and explicit relationship to the child's own present environment and experience, but also because of their indirect, veiled, and implied relationship to the past out of which present conditions have developed and to the future which is dependent upon the present. They started the child in his present, interested him to relive the past, and in due time carried him on to future possibilities and achievements in an ever developing experience. In brief, they furnished a thread of continuity because they were concerned with the fundamental requisites of living.

From the teacher's standpoint, the development of these ideas afforded occasions and opportunities for the enrichment and extension of the child's experience in connection with his activities. The reconstructed story of the building of the homes of the primitive peoples, as the youngest group imagined and reënacted it, took on a character as real in historical quality as the authentic accounts of the homes of the ancient Greeks—the history learned by older groups. New words and short sentences, both read and written, added themselves easily to the vocabularies of the youngest children, while *literature* embodying beauty of the written word was given to them in myth and story that had to do with the activities they were carrying on. From the teacher's point of view, the child was learning art as he drew, daubed, or modeled the idea that urged him to expression. He, however, unconscious that he was learning anything, expressed in line or color, clay, wood, or softer fabric, the thing that in him lay and in so doing, no matter how crude the result, tasted of those deep satisfactions that attend all creative effort. Little did the experimenting child realize that he was studying physics as he boiled down his cane or maple syrup, watched the crystallization process, the effects of heat on water, and of both on the various grains used for food. He reinvented Ab's trap for the sabre-toothed tiger, quite oblivious that he was rediscovering the use of a certain kind of lever. The teacher knew, although he did not, that he was studying the chemistry of combustion as he figured out why fire burned, or weighed, burned, and weighed again the ashes from the different woods or coal and compared results. The coal in the bins in the cellar was traced to the mines and the fossil plants. The coal beds were located as were all the products used in the activities. From the teacher's standpoint, this was geology and geography, or biology as the children examined the seeds, their distribution, and use as food, or the life of the birds and animals in the open fields. From the child's standpoint, however, these ideas were interesting facts or skills that he learned as he went about his various occupations; they were reflected, as it were, in the series of activities through which he passed in becoming conscious of the basis of social life.

In their constructive work the younger groups made their own jute-board pencil boxes, their book covers, and other articles needed in the school life. They selected the material for, measured, cut, and basted the dish towels for their laboratory kitchen. As they relived imaginatively the life and occupations of primitive man and reconstructed his environment and needs, they built into sand or clay or stone their ideas of the types of shelter used at this stage of life. They rediscovered the best kind of stone for making the weapons that he needed for protection from the wild animals or the best kind of clay for many uses in the way of utensils. As a by-product, they learned many geological facts, the source of the clay from the silt of rivers, the different kinds of stone, and the reasons for their differences.

In the laboratory, the child experimenter boiled water, collected steam, tried to "keep it in," and discovered its power as well as its heat. Under the same careful guidance, he planted corn in cotton and in soil; he kept it in the dark or in the light, in air and in a vacuum, weighing or measuring before and after, and learning what changes, if any, had been brought about by the growing plants. In the kitchen, also a laboratory, he husked, shelled, pounded, ground (for this he had made a mill in the shop), parched, soaked, and cooked corn which he had obtained from an interested farmer, when on a visit to his farm. The weighing and measuring were on scales, in measures, or with thermometers made by the children themselves. For the simple reason that they could not weigh or measure and thus carry on something which claimed both their interest and effort without knowledge of and skill in the use of the symbols of weight and measurement, they learned the value of numbers, quite unaware that they were studying mathematics. Pints and pounds, halves, quarters, thirds became familiar devices to attain desired ends. The study of social life furnished the thread of continuity, linking all these modes of experience—whether constructive or experimental. It had a direct aspect as revealed in the physical and social environment of the present or an indirect as in history and literature.

The following is a necessarily brief sketch of the school's first two years of rapid growth and experimentation. There were many trials of different types of subject-matter with different groups of children which were discarded as not suitable either because of the character and training of the teacher, and the background of the children, or because the materials and equipment necessary were not available. With the younger groups, the meaning of the home was developed in detail. When very young, the child was led to consciousness that it was the center and source of all things necessary to his well-being. In it he found food, shelter, and comfort, all of which came through the agency of various persons—his mother, his father, the milkman, the grocery boy, and others.

He learned that he and his home were dependent upon life without, particularly the life of the farm. A model farm was built in a large sand pan, and the study extended itself to what constitutes a typical farm locality—the kind of land for pasture, for meadow, or for the grain fields. The process was, of necessity, one of constant sharing by all. The practical methods of communication, the use of language, of reading, of writing, of measuring, took on importance in the eyes of the children and were thus naturally included in their daily program. The seasonal changes as exhibited in the relation of sun and earth, the vegetables and animal life, and the occupations of human life were, of course, constantly emphasized.[3]

The plan of the year's work was to make the study of social life the center of attention and to follow its development, in part at least, from its earliest beginnings through the barbaric stage to the opening of authentic history. Starting with the most primitive ways of living, it took up the beginnings and growth of industry through discovery and invention and their effect on social life.

The finding of metals was developed differently each year. Each group discovered the various ores, worked out in their own way their smelting process and the way in which such discoveries reacted upon the lives of those concerned. Usually the discovery of iron was taken up in great detail. Much discussion disclosed the many uses for this metal and the fact of its frequent occurrence in many localities. The construction of miniature smelting places introduced the problems of air supply and fuel in small bulk and the difficulty of right application of heat. Other incidental problems were met and solved. The kindling point of different materials, which the children burned in small smelting places, was discovered. The latter were of necessity tiny kilns rather than the large pit smelting places of the early metal industry. As they worked, the chil-

---

[3] "School Record, Notes, and Plan XXI. The University of Chicago School," *University Record*, April 21, 1897.

dren thought out the effect this new industry would have upon the social life of people, as requiring a division of labor, and attempted to carry out such an organization in their own efforts to work together on a single smelting place, under the leadership of one person. Great emphasis was laid upon the development of the metal industry. It was a dramatic picture of the effect upon civilization of invention and discovery which resulted in control of the material which is basic to all other industries. The organization on the social side necessary for its production gave the children a picture of the beginnings of our industrial society.[4] The subject of the governmental development, which had entered incidentally into previous discussions, was now taken up as a subject by itself. The methods of transportation, necessitated by the beginning of commerce, and the barter of the new iron weapons, carried on by the more advanced tribes, were also discussed.[5]

In their study of social life, the older children of Groups V and VI (eight to ten years old) passed through the phases of primitive living more quickly than the younger groups and soon came to the period when man had settled into permanent homes. The life of the early Greek peoples was chosen as forming the easiest transition from the imagined records of primitive lives to the records of authentic history. Again there were no precedents to follow, and the question arose as to how to present history subject-matter to young children. What would be a good starting point? Again the guiding principle answered—it must be something closely related to their own life and therefore of interest to them. Experiment only could tell whether this interest lay in the manner of living, the social and political institutions, commerce, art, literature, religion, or thought. It was a serious problem to select from

---

[4] Little time was given to the Bronze Age, as but a limited portion of mankind passed through this stage. This was found to be a mistake. The greater fusibility of copper and tin, together with the fact that they are found in a native state (thus making the processes simpler) would have made a more natural approach to the greater step of the discovery and use of iron.

[5] "Report of the University Elementary School," *University Record*, February 11, 1898.

all the wealth of collected knowledge that which should prove of most value for the child.

A beginning was made with social life of the early Greeks. Their social groupings were studied and questions asked. How did these come to be, and what were the relations of these social groups to each other? An attempt was made to trace the activities of the Greeks and to study their methods of warfare, commerce, and political and domestic life. This led to a study of their fortifications, their weapons, and war chariots, their ships and methods of navigation, their forms of government, and governing officers, the making and execution of their laws, their homes, schools, farms, and cities. This study of institutions proved very interesting, but not entirely satisfactory. Full interest was lacking. The difficulty seemed to be that all these things persisted in remaining objective and far away from the children in spite of the fact that they had once had to do with the reality of living. The work was too abstract and detailed for this age of development, too formal and too remote from present personal interest. The dynamic quality was lacking, that which made life moving and vital. It did not furnish images enough. What was to be done?

Again, the recent past experience seems to have been scrutinized for a suggestion of the next best step. These children were already thoroughly familiar with the myths of Greece so these did not seem to demand further attention. The line of approach lay somewhere between the myth-tale and such a study of Greek life as already had been attempted. This was finally found in what might be called a study of Greek characters. The myth and the organization of a Greek home were left almost wholly out of account, and a study was made of the great men of Greece, for in their deeds, shared by the whole nation, the common life of Greece found its best and most complete expression.

Interest in individuals is strong in children of this age. It is the period when they revel most in their own newly discovered individuality. Early peoples have the same experience. Their history is the history of heroes, and it is not less history because it takes the form of biography in which the emotional life of a whole people is expressed, so clearly and concisely that it is readily grasped by the child.

The children gleaned much of the material for this study themselves, did almost all of their own reading, and reproduced on paper many of the tales of the Iliad, the Odyssey, Herodotus, and Plutarch. The events and persons involved were never to them mere historical happenings of a long time ago or characters who were dead and gone. They were living men and women anxious to do certain things to and with other men and women. As the study progressed, there was a gradual passage from the concern of a single hero to those of a people who desire a common end and, therefore, act cooperatively. The gradual growth of people led by inspired individuals to the common aims and united efforts of a corporate group is richly illustrated by Greek development and formed a basis of transition to the story of the organization and administration of the corporate life of the Roman people.

A study of the social life of the Romans had already been attempted with a younger Group (ten years), but here again experience proved the children were too immature to appreciate enough of the definite contribution made by this civilization to make the study worth their while. On the background, however, of their study of the development of the Greek community life, it was hoped that these older children might become familiar with the trend of historical events and gain pictures of the social life of the times and the political evolution of a state. On the whole, however, this second experiment also was not wholly a success and did not warrant another trial with children of this age. The study of the Roman state was finally developed more satisfactorily in the later years with older children.[6]

For all groups during these two years the science work was a study of the plant as something which does work.[7] Attention was first directed accordingly to the active functions, such as

---

[6] Group IX (thirteen to fourteen years), Teacher, E. C. Moore, *University Record*, December 16, 1898.

[7] Course outlined by John M. Coulter, and under direction of Katherine Andrews.

breathing and circulation, and the analysis of structure was made simply to locate the parts which do the work. The younger children, as compared with the older, showed a much keener interest in this observational work and preferred it to the experimental. Their drawings and records evidenced more freedom and less formality in their habits of noticing and recording. The older children studied the adaptation of plants to their environment. This included the different species found in different soils, and at different elevations, and brought out the relation of moisture to plant growth. A vacant lot was selected; the character of the soil in the high and in the low places was studied; and the different plants native to each environment and their groupings were noted.

With children of nine and ten years, the science included also a study of electricity as they saw it in everyday use.[8] The electric battery or cell was used as a starting point, and the climax of their first investigations in this field was the installation of an electric bell in the school-room. Simple experiments led as steps up to the understanding of the electric bell and later of the telegraph and telephone.

The work in cooking with the older groups was also largely experimental in character. The making of jelly from cranberries and apples gave occasion for emphasizing or introducing many physical processes, such as the effect of boiling water in disintegrating solid matter and in hastening the process of evaporation. These were demonstrated by experiment. The change of water into steam and back again into water, through the condensation process, was noted and voluntarily related to observation of the same process elsewhere. The effect of heat and cold upon the density of the material was brought out when the class saw that the hot liquid strained much more easily than the cold, and that the juice grew solid much faster when placed out of doors. A number of children began at this time to relate processes noted in cooking to similar proc-

---

[8] The time spent was three to four hours weekly for ten weeks. The children worked individually, the discussion and a few of the more complicated experiments being conducted by the group as a whole. Course was first given by Katherine Camp.

esses in nature. The resemblance of thick boiling liquids to geysers and volcanoes was noticed, and generalizations were made about the expansive tendency of heat and the fact that steam demands more space than the water from which it was formed.

The custom of a weekly luncheon worked well for the older groups also in expressing and developing a social spirit. The work of getting lunch was variously distributed among the different children. Some calculated and measured the amount of cocoa needed, others measured and weighed hominy and water. Others set the table, while two wrote stories to read for the entertainment of the others. On a special occasion the ten-year-old group prepared a luncheon for twenty-two people. The meal consisted of bean soup and cocoa, and the children themselves bought the milk, bread, and butter needed. In the meantime, some of Group IV (nine years) set the tables and some wrote stories to be read at table for the entertainment of Group V (ten years). Among these stories were *Robin Hood, Sun and the North Wind, Puss in Boots, Apollo and the Python,* and others on original themes.

Opportunity was constantly given for expression in various mediums. By means of crayon, pencil, color, and scissors, as well as through the spoken and written word, the children were encouraged to record the memories of a walk, the apples they had gathered, the story they had heard, or the process they had imagined or carried through. One of these younger groups attempted graphically to represent the evolution of the house, from the earth lodge and cave to the Greek temple. The time given to the constructive work in shop, to the development of design and the decorative arts in laboratory or studio, to the writing of records, the related number work, or the reading and language drill in both English and French was so interwoven and incidental to the activities carried on in the study of social life, scientific observations, and experiments as to make it impossible to differentiate or calculate at all the amount given to each of these subjects.

The physical health of the children was constantly considered. Until the spring of 1897, the work of this department was carried on at the University. Later, a large hall in the school was equipped and used for plays and games of the younger children, the rhythmic drills with wands and dumbbells, and the apparatus work or basket ball of the older groups. There was constant supervision of individual children and their special needs.

In addition to its relation to the grace and rhythm of bodily movement music was also always included as a course of study for all groups. This study was in accord with the methods of Calvin B. Cady. Its purpose was to develop the musical intelligence of the pupils by aiding them to form and express complete mental images of music. Music is idea expressed in tone, and a simple melodic phrase is intellectually and musically a complete idea which must be grasped and gradually unfolded by the child into its essential elements of melody, rhythm and harmony.

This curriculum pertains to the School from 1896 to 1898 and represents what has been referred to as the "early period of the developing curriculum." In this experimental school, the concern was to discover not alone what subject-matter suited each stage of developing child life, but also to see what could be done with materials and activities never before used in classes of small children. The use of these spontaneous activities in the classroom necessitated great freedom for change, for omission, or for repetition later found necessary. As a result, the school program was always more or less tentative in character, and shifts in it were frequently made. Certain subjects were found excellent for use at this or that age or with this or that group or teacher. Others proved unsuitable. There was a continual change and revision of both subject-matter and method on the basis of experience and in accord with the tastes and training of the teacher and the resources of the environment and equipment.

STAGES IN CHILD GROWTH

The practical experience of the School so far had demonstrated that there were certain stages in child growth. These were never sharply defined, but merged into and overlapped one another. Certain needs and abilities characteristic of these stages were recognized, and a beginning had been made in selecting activities and skills appropriate to those needs and abilities. Experiment had proven that those studies which had been of fundamental value to the child's expression had also enlarged his mental horizons and carried him on into deeper living. As the result of such a critical interpretation of the practices of the School from the point of view of both the teacher and the learner, a clearly defined principle of mental growth emerged which was of primary importance in understanding the needs of the growing child and in planning a program which should answer to those needs.

The statement made by Mr. Dewey of this principle of the psychological order of development is the basis of the subsequent organization and administration of the School, both as to the more permanent groupings of the children and the choice of its subject-matter and method.[9]

In the organization of the Elementary School, three stages or periods are recognized. These, however, pass into one another so gradually that the children are not made conscious of the changes. The first extends from the age of four to eight or eight and a half years. In this period the connection of the school life with that of the home and neighborhood is, of course, especially intimate. The children are largely occupied with direct social and outgoing modes of action, with doing and telling. There is relatively little attempt made at intellectual formulation, conscious reflection, or command of technical methods. As, however, there is continual growth in the complexity of work and in the responsibilities which the children are capable of assuming, distinct problems gradually emerge in such a way that the mastery of special methods is necessary.

Hence in the second period (from eight to ten), emphasis is put upon securing ability to read, write, handle, number, etc., not in themselves, but as necessary helps and adjuncts in relation to the more direct modes of experience. Also in the various forms of handwork and of science, more and more conscious attention is paid to the proper ways of doing things, methods of reaching results, as distinct from the simple doing itself. This is the special period for securing knowledge of the rules and technique of work.

---

[9] "The University Elementary School, General Outline of Scheme of Work," *University Record*, December 30, 1898.

In the third period, lasting until the thirteenth year, the skill thus acquired is utilized in application to definite problems of investigation and reflection, leading on to recognition of the significance and necessity of generalizations. When this latter point is reached, the period of distinctly secondary education may be said to have begun. This third period is also that of the distinctive differentiation of the various lines of work, history and science, the various forms of science, etc. from one another. So far as the methods and tools employed in each have been mastered, so far is the child able to take up the pursuit each by itself, making it, in some sense, really a study. If the first period has given the child a common and varied background, if the second has introduced him to control of reading, writing, numbering, manipulating materials, etc., as instruments of inquiry, he is now ready in the third for a certain amount of specialization without danger of isolation or artificiality.

The picture of the first two years of this experiment in education is somewhat blurred, for it was a period of quest, a trying out first of this trail, then of that. Many of these trails were blind; failure was as frequent as success; but out of the seeming confusion grew a skeleton pattern for the courses and method of the later years. Out of it also came a clearer understanding of the child mind, its functioning, its changing powers and interests. Out of it grew a clearer picture of education as beginning, continuing and ending with life—a unified and rhythmic experience out of which is born and nourished day by day the individual life of the spirit which is the child, the person.

Subsequent experience revised the early statement of the psychological order of development after the eleventh year. The School's experience with the third stage of growth and the beginnings of the secondary period was not long enough to warrant much positive information after the thirteenth year.[10] The growth stages are covered by the chapters in this volume as follows:

---

[10] The age of the children in any group may be found by adding three to the number of the group, for example: Group I—age 4 years; Group II—age 5 years, etc.

THE FIRST STAGE OF GROWTH

Chapter IV.—Groups I and II (4–5 years)
Chapter V.—Group III (6 years)

TRANSITION STAGE

Chapter VI.—Group IV (7 years)
Chapter VII.—Group V (8 years)

SECOND STAGE OF GROWTH

Chapter VIII.—Group VI (9 years)
Chapter IX.—Group VII (10 years)

TRANSITION STAGE

Chapter X.—Group VIII (11 years)
Chapter XI.—Group IX (12 years)

THIRD STAGE OF GROWTH AND BEGINNING OF SECONDARY PERIOD

Chapter XII.—Group X (13 years)
Chapter XIII.—Group XI (14–15 years)

CHAPTER IV

HOUSEHOLD OCCUPATIONS

GROUPS I AND II (AGES FOUR AND FIVE)

THE setting for the youngest children of the school was not ideal from the point of view of convenience, modern equipment, or exposure. It was, however, sufficiently like the children's own homes to give a sense of familiarity to their first away-from-home experience. The home of the school, a large dwelling-house on Ellis Avenue, faced east. It had a wide angled, covered porch, but the large living-room, most suitable for a kindergarten room in other respects, lay on the northern side of the house. This very fact was turned to an advantage for it made the teacher more alert to the need of many outdoor excursions for play on the porch or in the yard, trips to the park and its great gardens, to the Museum, or just on walks that were filled with talk of the children's own observations. The room had great eastern windows and a fireplace. Owing to lack of funds, it was rather sparsely furnished aside from the tables and chairs necessary for work and the daily luncheon. The very bareness of the room, however, seemed to please the children, for it gave them the freedom for their plays and games often lacking in their home environment. At its rear was the old library of the house. Some of the shelves in this large room were kept for the school reference books; others were adapted for extra locker space for the little children. By happy chance, therefore, the dressing and undressing, the taking off and putting on of overshoes, and all the daily activities incident to the coming in and going out of little children, so important to their gradual development of control and independence, were carried on in their own quarters.

56

Such were the quarters of the sub-primary department that opened for the first time in the fall of 1898 with eight children. In January of the next year, the number grew to twenty. The children were divided into two groups, the four-year-olds, Group I, and the five-year-olds, Group II. The number of boys and of girls was about equal. Daily attendance in each group averaged about nine. Later the enrolment of the sub-primary department was increased to twenty-four in order to bring the average attendance to ten or eleven. These children were not exceptional save as they represented to an unusual degree parents of various professions whose confidence in the plan and its sponsors had aroused a hope and a desire for this different and more social type of training for their children. The daily program was as follows:

> 9:00– 9:30....Hand-work.
> 9:00–10:00....Songs and stories.
> 10:00–10:30....Marching and games such as "Follow the Leader" while the room was being aired and personal wants cared for.
> 10:40–11:15....Luncheon.
> 11:15–11:45....Dramatic play and rhythms.

This order was not a fixed one. It varied with the work the children were doing. Sometimes an outdoor excursion to places near-by was taken. The aim was to have a period of relaxation follow a period of fixed interest, so as not to keep them at one kind of work too long. The periods of hand-work included constructive work, play with blocks, drawing, painting, modeling in clay, work in the sand, or any suitable medium of expression.

Mid-morning luncheon was served every day. The children took entire charge of setting the table, serving, waiting upon each other, and of washing and putting away the dishes. The menu consisted of one tablespoon apiece of a prepared cereal, served with cream and sugar, a cracker and a small glass of milk, or cocoa on cold days. This menu served twenty-four children and three teachers for $5.00 a month. Fruit was served to children whose parents found the above menu objectionable.

TEACHERS' PROBLEMS AND PRINCIPLES

The first year the teacher in charge,[1] who had previously taught the primary department of a public school, also directed the reading and writing of some of the older groups. A year later she married, and a graduate of the Free Kindergarten Association of Armour Institute took over the direction of the groups with the help of two assistants.[2] These teachers in charge of this new sub-primary department had their own problems. In the light of a new but partial understanding of the little child as a growing person, both courage and faith were needed. They had need of courage to discard whatever they had learned of old methods and materials that could not be adapted to the sort of teaching disclosed by a new understanding of mind in the making. They had need of faith to trust for guidance to the child's own selective power in and instinctive control of the activities induced by his surroundings. The watchword was "continuity," in order to avoid breaks in the child's experience which would retard, hamper, or frustrate the spontaneous expression of his intellectual life— his thought in action.

The small child of four, who with others, faced the teacher of these youngest groups, feels himself a person, like other children of his age. He has long since passed out of the short period when instinct and simple emotion have control. The tentative beginnings of his intellectual life are well established. He has ridden rough shod over the indulgence and correction of his home guardian, has chosen what he liked, and rejected what he disliked; he has seen the way he would go and the thing he would do, and has both gone that way and done that thing. The consequent pleasurable experience of these first choices, these breaks away from his mother's plan and of following his own will-o'-the-wisp desires, have given him a new sense of freedom and of the power for independent action.

---

[1] Florence La Victoire.

[2] Georgia Scates, Grace Dolling, Jessie Taylor, pupils of Anna Bryan, head of Free Kindergarten Association of Armour Institute, who took an active interest in developing the sub-primary curriculum.

He has tasted the apple of life and found it to his liking. He has, to some extent, achieved his own intellectual ends, such as they are, and has formed his own habit of judging for himself.[3] "He has a method of thinking, as inevitably his own as was that of his mother or that of any other caretaker who made him see his own way by compelling him to react against her way." The teacher's problem was to simplify and clarify this passing out from the small center of the narrow and intense life of the family, where instinct and emotions have been the guides to action, into the larger and more diffused activities, which demand intellectual control. How could she make their present living a continuation of the old, so that it would continually lead on to a new and larger experience?

As play is the child's natural avenue for expression, a teacher must consider his knowledge of the physical and social world about him with its materials and relationships. Play is neither purely psychical, nor purely physical, but involves the expression of imagery through movement, with a social end in view. It is not to be identified with anything which he externally does. It rather designates his mental attitude as a whole. His sensations of color, sound, taste, or touch all function in order to carry on, assist, or reinforce this play, and his mind naturally selects material with reference to its maintenance and continuation.[4] "Play is the free movement, the interplay, of all the child's powers, thoughts, and physical movements, embodying in a satisfying form his own images and interests. At this age, he is still so unskilled in action that he practically lives in a world of imaginative play which comes through the cluster of suggestions, reminiscences, and anticipations that gather about the things he uses. The more natural and straightforward these are, the more definite basis there is for calling up and holding together all the allied suggestions which his imaginative play really represents. The simple cooking, dishwashing, dusting, etc., which the children do are no more

---

[3] Alice C. Dewey, "The Place of the Kindergarten," *The Elementary School Teacher*, January, 1902.

[4] John Dewey, "Froebel's Educational Principles," *The Elementary School Record*, June, 1900.

prosaic or utilitarian to them than would be, say, the game of the Five Knights. To children, these occupations of every-day life are surcharged with a sense of the mysterious values that attach to whatever their elders are concerned with. The materials, then, must be real, as direct and straightforward, as opportunity permits. The house life in its setting of house, furniture, and utensils, together with the occupations there carried on, offers material which is in a direct and real rela-tionship to the child, and which he naturally tends to repro-duce in imaginative form."

The program was relatively unambitious compared with that of many kindergartens, but it may be questioned whether there are not certain positive advantages to be seen in this limitation to activities that are so fundamental to human liv-ing that they continually lead out into new fields and open up new paths for exploration. Each activity, because of its in-timate relation to the needs of life, calls for expansion and enlargement, creates a demand for further activity, reveals a further need, and suggests something to satisfy that need, brings in new controls, new materials, and more refined modes of activity. The little child's liking for novelty and variety, his need of renewed stimulus, are satisfied and supplied with no sacrifice of the unity of his experience.

The life of the school touched civic and industrial life at many points. Many concerns were brought in, when desirable, without going beyond the unity of the main topic which helped to develop and foster in the child a sense of continuity and security, a feeling of at oneness with life which is at the basis of attention and fundamental to all intellectual growth. From the child's standpoint, this unity lay in the subject-matter—in the fact that he was always dealing with one thing—namely, home life. Emphasis was continually passing from one phase of this life to another; one occupation after another, one piece of furniture after another, one relation after another received attention. They all, however, contributed to one and the same mode of living, although bringing now this feature, now that into prominence.

Upon the whole, constructive or "build-up" work (with of

course the proper alternation of story, song, and game connected so far as desirable with the ideas involved in the construction) seemed better fitted than anything else to secure two factors—*initiation in the child's own impulse,* and *termination upon a higher plane.* It brought the child into contact with a great variety of material such as wood, tin, leather, or yarn. It supplied a motive for using these materials in real ways, instead of going through exercises having no meaning save a remote symbolic one. It called into play alertness of the senses and acuteness of observation. It demanded clear-cut imagery of the ends to be accomplished and ingenuity and invention in planning. In addition, it made necessary concentrated attention and personal responsibility in execution, while the results were in such tangible form that the child was led to judge his own work and improve his standards.[5]

It was taken for granted that the little child is highly imitative and open to suggestions, that his crude powers and immature consciousness need to be continually enriched and directed through right channels. It was understood that the psychological function of both suggestion and imitation is to reinforce and to help out, not to initiate. Both must serve as added stimuli to bring forth more adequately what the child is already blindly striving to do. It was accordingly adopted as a general principle that *no activity should be originated by imitation. The start must come from the child through suggestion; help may then be supplied in order to assist him to realize more definitely what it is he wants.* This help was not given in the form of a model to copy in action, but through the medium of suggestions to improve and express what he was doing. The same principles applied even more strongly to

[5] It is a pleasure again to acknowledge our great indebtedness to Miss Anna Bryan and her able staff of the Free Kindergarten Association, for numberless suggestions regarding both materials and objects for constructive work. Our obligations are also due to Miss La Victoire who inaugurated the sub-primary program in this school, and who, coming to the kindergarten the previous year from successful primary work, was highly effective in affiliating the kindergarten to the spirit of the best modern primary work. In later years Miss Georgia Scates, Miss Dolling, and Miss Elsie Port as well as others trained by Miss Bryan, all aided in developing the sub-primary program of the school.

what is called dictation work. Nothing, however, seemed more absurd than to suppose that there was no middle term between leaving a child to his own unguided fancies and likes and controlling his activities by a formal succession of dictated directions. Neither was it thought that the teacher should not suggest anything to the child until he has consciously expressed a want in that direction. On the contrary, it was believed that a sympathetic teacher is quite likely to know more clearly than the child himself what his own instincts are and mean. Such a teacher can discriminate between use of imitation and suggestion so external and unreal to the child as to be thoroughly non-psychological, and use so justified through organic relation to the child's own activities as to fit in naturally and inevitably as instruments to help a child carry out his own wishes and ideals. In organic relations, images, in process of expression, are compelled to extend and relate themselves to other images, in order to secure proper expression. This expansion or growth of imagery is the medium of realization and is secured when the materials of expression are provided and the end to which these are the means, is recognized by the child.[6] Mr. Dewey points out in this connection that the process of learning, under such conditions, conforms to psychological conditions, in so far as it is *indirect*. Attention is not upon the *idea of learning*, but upon the accomplishing of a real and intrinsic purpose—the expression of an idea.

DAILY PROCEDURE

The first days in school were spent in getting acquainted.[7] Each child finds out through talk and play with other children that they too have homes where many of the same familiar

---

[6] A teacher could supply the requisite stimuli and needed materials for expression. A suggestion of a playhouse that came from seeing objects that had already been made to furnish one or from seeing other children at work, was often quite sufficient definitely to direct the activities of a normal child of five.

[7] Statements in regard to the children of four and five cover a period of five years, from 1898 to June 1903. All other statements that cover an experience with children of nine and ten, embrace a space of seven years.

things are done with this difference or that. The teacher finds that the children under her care will learn much from each other and sees in it both a help and a problem. Every one soon began to have a feeling that here was a place belonging to him, where simple ways were without haste and pressure. In his own home, adults, always engaged in their own pursuits, had hurried him in his play. Here, he found he could play as he wished and take his own time, as long as he did not block others' play. Here, also, he could express freely the natural social interest in other children normal to his age. In one group for example, the children grew acquainted with each other and their surroundings by telling of their summer experiences. One little boy made an old-fashioned well like one on the farm he had visited, and another child made a basket with eggs like the one he had used. They soon were grouped or grouped themselves according to their favorite plays or games or way of expressing themselves, and these groups closely coincided with the actual ages of the children. The four-year-old children were satisfied with mere activity, regardless of means and ends. At first, this age preferred to play alone, but with skillful management the climbing, jumping, running, and rolling were guided into group games where the children learned to accommodate themselves to others and to express themselves in the presence of others.

SELECTION AND DEVELOPMENT OF ACTIVITIES

During the early weeks, both groups took many walks in the parks where their attention was directed to the homes of the birds, the insects, and the animals. They noticed the empty birds nests, brought some home, and talked of where the birds were going at this time of year and why. The gathered autumn leaves and drew them with paints or colored crayons. These expressions gave many clues to individual interests and talents. The repeated emphasis on home experiences loosened tongues, and the outside world came creeping in. Each child's own home life was used as a basis to build talks about the other children's homes and families, and the various persons helping in the occupations of the household. The family's dependence upon the daily visit of the milkman, grocer, iceman, postman, and the occasional visits of the coalman and others was also discussed.

At this age, children are forthright into action, and an idea straightway becomes drama. At first little or nothing suffices for the setting of the stage. Any folded piece of paper is adequate for the postman's letter. The child's fertile imagination at first requires none of the props and aids of stage setting, properties, or costume. Very soon, however, his idea enlarges and is translated through action into the postman's cap, his bag, the mail box, or the two-wheeled mail cart of those days drawn by a paper horse. Again the horizon shifts as new ideas rise over the border line of consciousness. The child wants to go further with the mail man than the corner post-box. The mail man takes letters from the box. "Where does he take them? To the post-office! Let's go." From the many avenues along which a little child can journey out into a larger world the teacher must help to choose those trails that are not blind but lead into main thoroughfares of thought and action.

In the autumn, when the activities of the world of both nature and man are inspired and influenced by the need of preparing for the cold days of winter, the thoughts of little children are easily directed to the seasonal changes and the necessary occupations which they cause. It was easy for the children in these groups to see the connection between the squirrel in the park, busy storing nuts in the hollow tree, and their mothers preserving fruit in their own kitchens.

But the child's many kinds of food, articles of clothing, and large and complicated house required many questions. Many of the answers to the latter seemed to open paths into one main avenue which led back to the farm. They made a trip to a farm and saw the orchards, the harvesting of the fruit, and the fields with their shocks of corn. This visit was the beginning of many activities, which varied, of course, with teacher, children, and circumstances. Part of the group played grocery store and sold fruit and sugar for the jelly-making of the others.

Some were clerks, some delivery boys, others mothers, and some made the grocery wagons. The clerks were given measuring cups with which to measure the sugar and cranberries and paper to wrap the packages to take home. This led under guidance into a discussion of the large storehouse. It was considered as a roomy place where a great deal of fruit could be kept. From time to time it supplied the grocery store which held only enough for a few days. A wholesale house was constructed out of a big box. Elevators would be necessary, a child volunteered, for storehouses have so many floors; and these were made from long narrow corset boxes, a familiar wrapping in every household of that day.

Early cold days made it easy and natural for another group to decide that one of the necessary things for the mother to do was to get the warm clothing ready for the family. Out of this talk developed a play of the dry-goods store, in which three classes joined together. The children planned to play and decided the parts which grew in scope from day to day. Several children were the mothers coming to the dry-goods store to shop. Others were the clerks who arranged and decorated the windows with various materials. The mothers chose those they thought most suitable for warm clothing. All selected warm colors and judged of material largely by feeling it. A table was taken for a counter and on it were put scissors, thread, thimbles, and needles—all that would be needed for the making of clothing. After buying the material at the store, the mothers tried to match it in thread, in tape, and different kinds of silk. These attempts were interesting to watch. A third group of children made street cars out of chairs on which the mothers could ride to the store. One child was the conductor and punched the tickets, and a triangle was used for a car bell. Or again, two of the children became horse and wagon and delivered the goods, while another child was the bundle wrapper. They enjoyed the game so much that it was played all over again the next day.

Still another group approached the occupations of the household from a different angle. In the discussion (and aided by suggestion) the children decided that mother has so much to do that she must have some one to assist in the general work of the house. They then organized and dramatized the work of washing and ironing, constructing the necessary utensils as they went along. The work for the two groups varied little save that the older children did more of their own construction. In making their scrub boards, for example, these children themselves measured the required lengths with rulers, and were also able to do their own sawing. Most of these children could count to fourteen and could understand the figures on the rulers.

It was found that the preparation for, the eating and clearing away of the mid-morning luncheon gave a continuous set of activities affording many opportunities for self-management and initiative in which the youngest child gradually came to competent control of the whole procedure. Each child must help in preparing for a group action. The counting of the chairs was a coveted task. Each chair was named for each child many times until the idea dawned that one can count the children and then count the chairs. This new method gradually extended to the counting of the spoons and other necessary articles, and a familiarity with the use of numbers in counting was gained. It was useful also to know that if you give one-half an apple to each child, four apples are enough for eight children, or if one cupful of flaked wheat is enough for two children, four cups must be used for eight.

Many operations difficult for small persons to surmount grew out of table setting. There were many materials to handle—chairs, cups, plates, spoons, napkins and food. They must learn with more and more success to carry properly, to place, to pour, to serve, and to wash and wipe the dishes. In all these processes, the thinking done and the decisions made involved coöperation in a project with a social end. The giving and receiving of directions required definiteness of speech and courtesy of manner in social relationships. To play host and hostess involved consideration of others, for equals in age and experience as well as adults. Interest was always evident, and growth in development was shown by an increased sense of responsibility.[8] On great occasions, such as Thanksgiving or Christmas, the menu for the luncheon was elaborated and extended to include the actual cooking of one food, such as cranberries or pop corn. When popping corn the children's apparent interest was not in why the corn popped, but in the kind of dish to use, how to hold it over the fire, and most of all in the popped corn, the ticklish process of its sharing and the delightful one of its consumption.

Toward the end of the second year, when getting the lunch, certain children, generally the older ones, began to ask why they couldn't always cook the cereal and to show an interest in the material of different dry cereals which they served. This interest in material and competency to plan and carry through alone the operations necessary for the mid-morning luncheon were some of the indications that a child was ready to undertake the more intricate processes of cooking, which, in this school, was a definitely developed subject-matter. Its scientific implications were easily emphasized with all ages, because of the natural social end of the luncheon. Five years of experience resulted in the decision to postpone systematic use of cooking with heat to the six-year groups, when interest in experimentation as consciously planned and directed experiment begins to develop. With younger children, it was another case of skimming the cream from an activity which might be used to great advantage at a later period when desire to experiment with an end in view had awakened.[9]

The program for these groups was always flexible. It was adapted to the seasons and to special events such as Thanksgiving and Christmas. Birthdays were celebrated when one group entertained the other or an older group. At some sea-

---

[8] The luncheon was generally prepared and cleared away in twenty minutes and in consequence, entailed on the part of the teacher just the kind of setting that would prevail in any well-ordered home where utensils and material were chosen and arranged for a young child's use.

[9] "Overestimation of the child's ability is drawing on the future. It puts in the child's way material for which he is not ripe and is sure to bring on that attitude of indifference which is characteristic of that unfortunate being known as the *blasé* kindergarten child." Alice C. Dewey, "The Place of the Kindergarten in Education," *Elementary School Teacher*, January, 1902.

son of the year, usually the second quarter, the work included the building of a play house. This was a group enterprise. Cottages with one or two rooms, the smallest known to the children, were made of blocks. Day by day details were added. Streets were made with sidewalks to connect with other streets. Lamp-posts were added and the stepping stones across the streets. These ideas were the children's own and developed without direct suggestion. When interest flagged, they were aided (by prearrangement of material and situation) to carry on into a new phase of the idea. The streets and sidewalks of their toy town finished to their satisfaction, a hint was sufficient to direct attention and effort to the interior arrangements of their cottages. They outlined the rooms with six-inch blocks and with smaller ones placed in them the necessary furniture. Another group of children cut their houses from brown paper and drew the sidewalks.

As they worked there was talk of the wood that was used in the construction of real cottages. Speculation was rife as to where it came from and its many uses. Answers came easily—tables and chairs and the woodwork in the houses were suggested. Finally, one child volunteered that trees were made of wood also. Some one else then suggested that trees could be chopped down to get the wood. These details taken from the records serve to show how the self-originated ideas of the children were allowed to develop into self-expression and to extend and enlarge into larger and more complicated execution. Only enough aid was given to avoid "blocks" in expression and the consequent dulling of interest and waste of effort in a "slowed up" process.

An expedition to a hardware store to see what tools a carpenter might use to build a house made one child want to build his own house to take home. Large boxes were used. The older children measured and cut all the paper for the walls. The little children tacked down the matting on the floors, made a table for the dining-room by fastening legs on a block. For chairs, they nailed a back to a cube and tacked on a leather seat. The older children made tables and chairs from uncut wood, which they measured and sawed by themselves. When finished, these were shellacked and the seats upholstered with leatherette and cotton. Some of the children painted the outside of the house so that its walls should "be protected from the weather." Inside it was papered "for ornament," and the necessary furniture for each room decided upon, made from cardboard, wood, or tin, and put into place. One of the results of this phase of the project was a gain in each child's ability to carry out his own ideas. He was put to it to execute and to show individual results. He thus secured the feel of accomplishment according to the measure of his success.

All the hand-work of these groups involved the use of large muscles. That of Group II was a little more advanced than that of Group I. The latter, for example, were given two pieces of wood to make a chair—one, 4 x 1 inches, the other a 1 x 1 inch cube. Their problem was to find a way of putting them together. Group II, however, was given a cube and a long strip of wood which they measured and sawed to length, before constructing the chair. A leather cushion for the chair was given to the younger children, cut the right size to fit the chair; while the older children were given a large piece from which to cut the cushion to their own measurements. This work was given slowly, a few steps at a time, not too closely connected, but in such a way that each step appealed to the child as a fairly complete whole in itself. Recognition also was given to the desire all children have—time to play with what they have made.

REPORT OF GROUP TEACHERS

At the end of each quarter, each group teacher reported on the work of the group. These reports were for the information of her colleagues and those directing the experiment; they enabled the writer to evaluate her series of activities and in the light of its success or failure, to plan her succeeding program. Extracts from such an evaluation of a quarter's activities, in terms of the gain in development made by the children who engaged in them, may help to point out how necessary such reports were to the success of the entire experiment. These classroom findings became the basis of informal and seminar discussion out of which came the revision that made for whatever progress in education this experiment may have achieved.

[10] Our chief aim has been to help each child in Group I to gain control of himself and the few simple materials at hand. In reality, this is the beginning of his mastery of the whole material world. The environment is new to each, likewise the social relations. It took some time to become accustomed to both in order to adjust to both. As a group, they have begun to recognize to some extent each other's rights and to feel a certain amount of responsibility for keeping the whole kindergarten in good condition. They have gained some control over their own bodies, especially their hands. This is proved by their ability to arrange materials, build with blocks, and to construct a few, simple objects of paper, tea-lead, or clay. In this work and play, they have used water-colors to express their ideas. The drawing so far can scarcely be called drawing; it is mostly an occasional test of the impressions the child has received and of the skill he is acquiring in the way of giving expression along these lines. The modeling in clay is beginning to assume a somewhat more definite shape, and the results are sometimes in accord with the names they bear. For the most part, there is still more pleasure in the mere handling of the material, and the name is discovered after the object is finished.

The work with Group II has been somewhat more definite so far as progress is concerned. The children have all gained considerable skill in building with blocks and have a pretty good idea of the right position and relation of these blocks to produce the desired effect. Free play has been given and then directed when they have shown signs of finding their own limitations in the use of material. Sometimes, each child does his separate piece of work in his own way; sometimes, each does his own as all of the rest do theirs; and sometimes, all work together, each doing a part on some one thing. This latter plan is not altogether successful at the beginning, but the children later get much pleasure out of such coöperative work and play. The only models used for work in clay and color so far have been fruits and vegetables. These have been fairly well reproduced. The drawing has been interesting in its different stages, but progress is not marked. Much has been from imagination, with an occasional reproduction of experience such as their visit to the baker or the blacksmith shop. The games have grown from those which give pleasure through the mere exercising of the body to those which deal a little more with the imagination and the dramatization of actual experience. This has enlarged their ideas of social relations.

Each child begins to feel in a small way the pleasure that comes

---

[10] Group Teachers, Bertha Dolling, Elsie Port.

with sharing, as he relates his experience in the morning circle or brings from home something in which all are interested. Sometimes this is a story or a song, a book or a pet toy; whatever it is, they are all learning in a sweet, unconscious way to give and have pleasure in giving. The more timid children are beginning to offer a remark or two, and this is encouraged as aften as possible. The spirit of helpfulness is often shown in the arranging of the chairs or dusting before kindergarten, in putting on their own wraps as far as possible, and in helping others who need it.

Some number work has been done with all of the children, more in the second group than in the first. In Group I, each child can count beads, children, blocks, or other objects up to six. With one or two when six is reached, there is uncertainty and indefiniteness. The finger will touch two or three beads while counting one, or will count four or five while touching two. With the larger number of children, however, sixteen and seventeen seem to be the limit. Two is about as large a number as they try to handle in combinations. They will make number lessons for themselves, studying two beads of one color, two of another, or perhaps two of one form and one of another. In Group II perhaps one or two of the children can count to fifty or one hundred, but the actual comprehension of number with the majority of the group stops with twenty or twenty-one.[11] The group works with twos, threes and fours, and can make simple combinations of these numbers.

SUMMARY

A spirit of freedom and mutual respect on the part of both teachers and children was as apparent in these groups as in the older. Each child came to see that orderly self-direction in his activity was essential to group effort: he learned to stop pounding because it interfered with the group's story-telling, even though he didn't choose to join the activity of the group. The "good" way of doing things developed in each situation, and the best order of proceeding with the activity was formulated by teachers and children as a result of group thought. Therefore, "discipline," so-called, was not from above, but was evolved as a result of the participation by both teacher and children in a group activity, and a school spirit developed which fostered social sensitivity and conscience. The teacher's

---

[11] This limit was probably due to the fact that the class numbered twenty-one.

part in the developing play of these years is to see that the child really carries out his self-initiated game in such a way that, without unnecessary aid from her, the play proceeds in orderly development to its finish. This aid takes the form of an intelligent shared interest which when necessary removes "blocks" in the child's action so that it is free and unhampered to follow the gleam of his own impulses.[12] The purpose was that the flow of dynamic energy from these native desires to do and to make should be used to attain that measure of skill in action which would enable him to accomplish his end without undue and discouraging effort. The satisfaction of this accomplishment would then carry over and give rise to the new gleam of a larger purpose. In order that this flow of power and purpose might be uninterrupted, it was necessary that the activities be continuous. Those of one day or week or period of development must grow out of the preceding and into the succeeding one, in order that the native powers and acquired skills of every child may be continuously stimulated and built into habits of acting which can cope with the changing conditions of his activity. This was an ideal in the school. Needless to say, there were often breaks in this desired continuity; subject-matter that did not carry the idea on nor the child's original impulse over into the next period of growth. Discussion as to reasons for this failure led to elimination or revision.

In the process of getting what he wanted, the child learned many things as to the ways and means of getting it. Little by little in this school of experiencing, he was taught control. His impulse to act grew less immediate. He schooled himself to wait, to think, and plan a bit before acting. Success and failure in dealing with means in regard to ends exercised his judgment of the quality and value of means as appropriate to purpose. When the conditions were right, and the let and hindrance were in the right proportion for the continuous development of his action, he gradually built up a background

---

12 These "blocks" occur often for reasons hidden in the child's past, sometimes because of interference of unsocially developed children who get "a kick" out of interruption *per se.*

of both satisfactory and unsatisfactory experience, which gave him a basis for wider choice and more definite preference.

Ideally, then, he was well started in his growing process.

As a member of a group, he had learned the rudiments of co-operation, and something of the pleasure of sharing. He had experienced the satisfaction of doing and of making the concrete image of his idea. The latter (ideally) self-originated, was accomplished largely through imitation and guided by suggestion. Little by little, however, he had been thrown on his own to choose his play or the material with which to develop his thought, and he was already beginning to investigate and experiment, to use "the test and prove" method. In the process he had learned, by succeeding and failing, the subsequent pleasurable or disagreeable sensations, the satisfactory or unsatisfactory feelings. Thus, he built up a background of experience that had depth as well as range and quality as well as efficiency. His were the rewards of a construction that truly expressed his purpose, the pleasurable sensations of the sand swiftly dropping through the fingers, the softness of the easily molded clay, the bright color of the paints vividly reproducing the mental image, the melody of the songs, or the rhythm of the dances. All blended into a living and expressing that was truly artistic in its quality, however crude its product.

CHAPTER V

SOCIAL OCCUPATIONS SERVING THE HOUSEHOLD

GROUP III (AGE SIX)

GROUP III averaged about seventeen in number. Their headquarters were in one of the best rooms in the house, which also served as the biological laboratory. This room had an eastern and southern exposure, with a big bay-window, closet, and alcove. Here stood the vivarium and aquarium that provided homes for the many living things—plant and animal—collected by the children.

In this room the children of Group III spent an average of one and a half to two hours a day. This time was used for social exchange of their ideas and plans and the dramatization of the occupations they were undertaking. A blackboard and a sand-table were available and free floor space for games. The group was divided for the work necessitating individual attention, but went as a whole to assembly and chorus singing. The entire group joined twice a week with the seven-year-olds in plays and games, outdoors and in the gymnasium. Two or three times a week, they returned to the sub-primary rooms for a half hour of play and music with the younger children.

Group III was in charge of a teacher trained in science. She was responsible for the physical condition of the children, and the parents came to her for consultation. She had an assistant.[1] The school period for these children was from nine to twelve, a half-hour longer than that of the sub-primary groups. There was no mid-morning luncheon as their going about the school

---

[1] Katherine Andrews, Wynne Lackersteen.

and participating in the cooking gave them the necessary opportunities of a social nature. Seven years of experimentation with activities for this age resulted in a choice of present day occupations as the most suitable subject-matter. The general method of procedure was the same with all groups. Ten to fifteen minutes were always given at the opening of school to group conversation. What had been done was talked over and the reasons for success or failure were brought out; plans for the day were made; jobs were distributed. Each child served in turn as leader. The written program was pinned to him. This was for the guidance of adults in a case of a temporary change of rooms. The children usually carried the program well in mind, although there were interesting individual variations and ability to lead was often used as a test of maturity and judgment. At this age (six years), the characteristic attitude is still that of play. Therefore, the greater amount of time was given to active pursuits, only about two hours a week being devoted to things intellectual, the stories and conversations about the social activities of the group. The amount of concrete number experience in connection with constructive work in the shop, cooking, and number games was unusual for children of this age. This frequent use of number symbols, combined with the gradual introduction of the symbols of measurement throughout this year and the next, was considered the explanation of these children's rather unusual understanding and later use of arithmetical relations and expressions.[2]

Many excursions kept the balance between the children's observational attitude and their constructive expression, including music and all forms of art. They were encouraged to look in order to use; to return to actual situations and to pictures

---

[2] A mother of one of the boys in this group recently wrote to the authors of this book: "The work done in the school by my boy in arithmetic, history, and English especially pleased me. Because they were taught arithmetic concretely, not abstractly, they were able to accomplish feats in mental arithmetic which to me were phenomenal. They added, subtracted, and multiplied fractions as easily as I did whole numbers. Their history was made a living thing to them, and the good literature which was read to them was suggestive to their mother, as well as very helpful in forming in them a taste for good literature."

for information. In other words, they were encouraged to research at a six-year-old level.

Beginning with blocks and floor games where social organization was necessary to carry work through, the children developed an astonishing technique in the use of the sand-table
and all sorts of materials for observed or imagined scenes. One
objection to a restricted use of the sand-table was that such
representation often became static. Hence recourse was often
made to dramatic representation by the children themselves in
outdoor meetings. For example, the sand-table was transferred,
in the spring, to the side yard, and fields and gardens were laid
out on a larger scale and with a greater sense of reality.

The study of present-day occupations, with its emphasis on
those supplying the food necessities of life, led this group to
spend much time in the study of food. In the kitchen-laboratory
many opportunities occurred for the children to try things out
for themselves, to handle and manipulate materials and combine them, and to see and criticize the results of their handi-
work. At this age, they began also to go to the art studio, although the impromptu drawing and designing done in the
group room were often still superintended there by the art
teacher or her assistant. Two years of games and other activities
had deepened and widened their knowledge of their immediate
physical and social world. Each child recognized the similarity
of his own to other homes, and in some measure, the dependence of all upon the larger world through the service of
the many persons who brought letters, food, clothing, or other
fundamental necessities for daily living. Interest had centered
primarily in the individual who brought things, not in the
things he brought. Always it was the person, what he did, how
he did it, and what came of it that excited their curiosity. People, and only incidentally their occupations, had been the subject of his study, his conversation, and his play. Gradually,
this interest in people had enlarged, and plays had extended
to activities that took them out of the home and the immediate

neighborhood. With this change, the interest which earlier was primarily personal, centering largely in action and the feeling induced by action, passed over to an interest in the objective results of action; from the milkman carrying the milk to the milk, where it comes from, and how it is made. Ideas are now best conveyed to the child by the story form, which is also his own favorite method of expression. The story at this period is the intellectual counterpart of the child's interest. It must have go, movement, the sense of use and operation. It must be a physical whole, holding together a variety of persons, things, and incidents, through a common idea that enlists the feeling of the child. The latter is seeking "wholes," stories that are begun, continued and ended, that are varied through episode, enlivened with action, and defined in salient features. The study of corn, for example, as something he has seen growing, has himself husked, shelled, and perhaps ground is highly interesting and exciting to a child of six. Without this background of personal experience, a study of corn separated from the story of the farm and the farmers, the miller and the mill, becomes divested of the glory of its use, the part it plays in life and living.[3]

The material selected as the basis for this stage of growth, existing social occupations, was designed to meet and feed this attitude of this period of development. The typical occupations of society at large is a step removed from the child's egoistic, self-absorbed interest and yet deals with something personal, something which touches him, and which will therefore lure him on. Experience proved there are great advantages to be gained from a study of natural objects and processes placed in a human setting.

ILLUSTRATIONS OF MATERIALS USED IN STUDY OF OCCUPATIONS

The study of occupations as carried on during the year involved observation of seeds and their growth, of plants, wood,

[3] "Inspection of things separated from the idea by which they are carried, analysis of isolated detail of form and structure, neither appeals to nor satisfies a little child." John Dewey, "Introduction to the Work of Group III," *The Elementary School Record*, 1900.

oil, stones, and animals as to phases of structure and function of parts or habit of performance, of geographical conditions of landscape, climate, and arrangement of land and water. The pedagogical problem was to direct the child's power of observation, to nurture his sympathetic interest in characteristic traits of the world in which he lives, to afford interpreting material for later, more special studies, and yet to supply a carrying medium for the variety of facts and ideas through the dominant, spontaneous emotions and thoughts of the child. No separation was made between the social side of the work, its concern with people's activities and their mutual dependencies, and the scientific side, its regard for physical facts and forces. Such conscious distinction between man and nature is the result of later reflection and abstraction and is, therefore, far beyond the mental ability of this stage of growth. To force it, at this time, will not only fail to engage the child's whole mental energy, but will confuse and distract him. To make the child study earth, air, or water, bird, beast, or flower apart from environment and out of relation to their use by other factors in the environment, their function in the total life-process, cuts the tie that relates and binds natural facts and forces to people and their activities. The child's interest fades for he misses the way. His imagination finds no avenue of connection that makes object, fact, or process concrete to him. He loses his original open, free attitude to natural facts. Nature herself is reduced to a mass of meaningless details. In contrast, however, when a natural object is clothed with human significance and human association, a road lies open from the child's mind to the object through the connection of the latter with life itself. The unity of life, as it presents itself to the child, thus binds together and carries along the different occupations of living. The diversity of plants, animals, and geographical conditions; drawing, modeling, games, constructive work, numerical calculations, are ways of carrying certain features of it to a completed mental and emotional satisfaction. It was found that such interaction of the various matters studied and of the powers that were acquired by the children avoided waste and maintained unity of mental growth. The problem of correlation, therefore, often solved through devices of instruction employed to tie together things in themselves disconnected, was not present in this school because of the community and continuity of its subject-matter.

In addition, the study of the often observed, well-known, everyday occupations of living satisfied two recognized demands and principles of primary education: (1) the need of the familiar, the already experienced, as a basis for moving upon the unknown and remote; (2) the important claim for the part which the child's imagination plays in the process. Each day the child had occasion and opportunity to get from and exchange with others his store of experience, his range of information. He needed continually to make new observations, correcting and extending them in order to keep his own images moving and find mental rest and satisfaction in definite and vivid realization of what is new and enriching.

DETAILS OF METHODS USED

Children in Group III (age six) were beginning their third year of school. The first week was usually full of talk about the experiences of the past summer. These were related by skilful direction and suggestion to the work of the previous year and the attention gradually focused on the extension of these interests to their present and future activities. The group went outdoors every day and noted the changes taking place in the woods, fields, and parks. Insects were found going into winter quarters, and many kinds of seeds were collected. The question of seed distribution came up, and the children thought of various agents—the wind, people, and various sorts of animals. Talk and interest centered for some time on seeds, and excursions were taken to the park and the woods twenty blocks away, where several seeds that were good to eat were found. This suggested others also good for food, and finally, each child made a list of such seeds and with help, classified them as (1) those where the seed house was good to eat, (2) where the seed house was not good, (3) those fruits such as the tomato, the bean, and the cucumber where both the seed and seed house were good for food. The next point developed was that certain seeds are cultivated for their food value by people who are called farmers. This took the children's thoughts into the country and back to their previous year's experience and the various farms they had visited. Some one suggested, "let's make a farm," and they were then started on a project similar to that of the previous years. There are, however, several points of difference worthy of notice. Although the same use of materials continued with these children, more definite forms of control were established. Desirable means were considered with relation to desired ends. This is well illustrated by the way in which the seeds that are good for food, the cereals, were studied in cooking. The preparation and cooking of the cereals brought out their constituents. This led to an additional classification of foods with relation to their source, whether the seeds, the stalks, or the roots of plants.

The possibilities found in the gardening and indoor occupational work possible for this year increased so rapidly with the increased capacity of the child that the choice was almost unlimited. All the problems connected with plant growth recur in the care of plants and animals, but now definite experimentation, planned by the child, began. The storing up of food by the plants either in seeds, leaves, stems, or roots can be taken as a problem in itself and linked with the care of the schoolroom bulbs or garden seed. Another link made in the child's mind during this year was the dependence of animals (and human beings) upon plants and of plants upon the soil.[4]

GENERAL PROGRAM OF A TYPICAL GROUP

The general method of the classroom, for the most part, followed a certain daily order. At the beginning of the period, the children were given time for the exchange of the amenities of the day usual to a group of persons meeting after an absence. This general conversation was soon directed by the

---

[4] While too much emphasis should not be placed upon the child's dawning interest in discovering for himself appearing at this age, yet it can be utilized in finding new ways of getting old results.

teacher to the business of the day. The results of previous work were reviewed in a group process, and plans for further development were discussed. Each child was encouraged to contribute, either out of his past experience or his imagination, ways and means of meeting the problem of needs that might arise under new circumstances. These suggestions were discussed by the group, and with the aid of the teacher, the plans for the work of the day were decided upon and delegated. At the close of the period, there was again a group meeting when the results, if successful, were summarized, and new plans for further work at the next period suggested.

The first project of the year started off with the building of a farm-house and barn out of large blocks varying in size up to six inches. In order to find the dimensions of their square houses, the children added the lengths of the blocks on one side and found the sum to be twelve inches or one foot. A plan for a chicken coop of manilla paper was then discussed and was finally marked off in two- and three-inch lengths, a rough approximation to keep in scale with the house. In the meantime, attention was centered on the farm itself, and the decision was made to raise corn and wheat and to have sheep and a dairy. The land was divided into fields and pastures, which were then fenced. For this they gathered twigs (to take the place of logs in making a rail fence), cut them into six-inch lengths, and built the fence three rails high. Around their pastures, however, they decided to have a stone fence, as they thought this was stronger. Work continued to some extent on the farm-house. Boards were cut to proper lengths, with spaces for the door and windows. A chicken coop was started. In planning the back part of this, when laying off spaces for the windows and doors, it suddenly struck the children that the door was wider than it was high. One of the children went to another table and measured the door already laid off for the front of the farm-house, and came back with the correct dimensions. This was an encouraging indication of a developing power of initiative and judgment. The square, the triangle, and the ruler were used freely. Although they had used the latter only a short time, they were very apt in its use. They knew the inch and half-inch, but hesitated on the quarter-inch. In general, it was found that they all took manual directions very well and showed great ability to plan and a high degree of independence in the execution of their plans, doing all the measuring and sawing themselves. As the project developed they suggested many of the things necessary in the making of a suitable house. The interest was well-sustained. In the kindergarten these children had been accustomed to making things that could be finished in one day, but they worked on this for almost two weeks without any loss of interest.

Early in the fall the group measured off and cleaned a space in the school yard five by ten feet for planting their winter wheat. A method of plowing was discussed and at one child's suggestion, a sharp stick was used and the field prepared in which the wheat was sown. In their sand-box farm their imaginary crop had come to fruition and, like the sheaf brought in from the farm, was ready for threshing. The various parts of the whole plant and their uses were discussed with the conclusion that the seed was of most value to people. A list was made of the wheat foods they had eaten—breakfast foods of coarsely ground wheat, and bread and cake from the finely ground flour. They played that they were farmers and discussed the best means of getting the seeds from the hulls, as they called the process of threshing. At first they picked it out by hand. This was too slow, so they suggested beating it with a stick and found that only the edge of the stick struck the ground. The problem was taken to the shop director, and with the help of some questioning, the children decided that if the farmer had two sticks joined together, more of the stick would hit the grain and thus the work would be done more quickly. The handle of the flail was made twice as long as the part that hits the grain. The next stop was to experiment with the wheat they had threshed and winnowed. Accordingly, it was pounded in a mortar and compared to some fine, white flour. They saw that the inside of the grain was soft and white like the fine flour, but that it was mixed with coarse, yellow particles. A child suggested putting this meal through a sieve to separate the coarse from the fine. This was done, but although the meal was a good deal finer, some of the yellow particles still remained. They then wanted to put it through a still finer sieve, but as there was none convenient, the process of bolting was explained to them, and the flour was sifted through some cheese cloth. This took out all the yellow particles and left the flour fine and white. They had in the end about three tablespoonsful of it, which was used in making a cake.

The experimental work with the food products of the farm and the effect of heat upon them as demonstrated in the cooking bulked large in the daily activities of these children. The interest in this phase of their occupational work was keen and assumed great importance in the development of the whole project and particularly in their use of numbers. When they talked about grains in the classroom, they cooked cereals in the kitchen. For this they needed to learn to measure, to know how many teaspoons equal one tablespoon, how many tablespoons equal one cup, and so on. They discovered that two halves make a cupful, just the same as three thirds, or four quarters, and they came to talk about ½, ⅓, or ¼ of a cupful, with ease and certainty. It was easy for them to see that ⅔ of a cup of water is 1 and ⅔ of a cup.

Much also of the number work was related to the construction work done on their farm or in connection with it. When their sand-table farm had to be divided into several fields for wheat, corn, oats, and also for the house and the barn, the children used a one-foot ruler as a unit of measurement and came to understand what was meant by "fourths and halves"— the divisions made, though not accurate, were near enough to allow them to mark off their farm. As they became more familiar with the ruler and learned the half-foot, and the quarter-foot and inch, finer work was naturally expected of them and obtained. Their use of this tool made it easy to distinguish those children who had had a kindergarten education from those who had just entered the group. When building the farm-house, four posts were needed for the corners and six or seven slats, all of the same height. In measuring the latter, the children frequently forgot to keep the left-hand edge of the ruler on the left-hand side of the slat, so the measurements had to be repeated two or three times before they were correct. What they did to one side of the house, they also did to the other and naturally worked more rapidly and more accurately as the work was repeated.

A new game of dominoes, invented by one of the teachers,[5] did much to interest the children in the composition of numbers. Each domino had lines in place of dots. These when joined make numbers. A child is asked to take eight blocks. At first, he takes one block at a time, eight times. He builds his eight and is asked what he sees in it. He may see four and four or five and three. When all the compositions of eight are exhausted, he is asked how he can take eight blocks more rapidly than just one at a time. He may say: "Take six in one hand and two in the other," or "four in one hand and four in the other," and then proceeds to demonstrate this, by building an eight with a six and two, a four and four, and so on. This was done with all numbers up to twenty. When they came to the number ten, a child was asked to count the fingers on both hands and when he answered ten, was told that he had counted "once around his fingers," and a symbol for that was "1 (once) O round." The children agreed this might have been the development of our "10." Twenty was then twice (2) around and so on. In making eleven, twelve, and the "teens," they built their ten and began again to build another ten, but the blocks gave out (purposely). One of the blocks from each child's set was marked with a blue chalk line, and this marked block represented ten. So when they made eleven, twelve, etc., they made it with the ten block and one or two more. They were interested and understood quickly. The report comments "the children of these two groups seem to be mathematically inclined, and numbers are a pleasure to them."

An interest in reading also developed during these weeks, starting in a game which necessitated it. All the things they had found in their outdoor excursions were placed on a table. Sentences were written on the board, such as: "Find a cocoon," and the child who could read it was allowed to run and get the

---

[5] Clinton Osborn.

cocoon. After playing this game a few times, the same sentences were shown printed in large type, so that they would get the printed form simultaneously with the script. They seemed very eager to read and decided themselves to make a weekly record of their work. This record was printed from time to time in large type and was reread with undiminished interest. One of the children brought David Starr Jordan's *The Story of Knight and Barbara* to school. Knight and Barbara were children of three and six, who retold and illustrated the stories that had been told to them. The children were so pleased with the book that they thought they would like to make one like it and at once set to work on the fable of the Hare and the Tortoise as the first story for their book. The story was told to them and they retold about one half of it at one sitting. This took some time as considerable discussion was necessary to make their story logical and clear. The story was written on the board and, when completed, was printed in large type on the charts, and later in small type for their books. The group seems to have shown the same sustained interest in reading and in finishing these books that they did in the making of their farm and, in general, exhibited a rather remarkable ability to concentrate on all phases of their work.

DETAILS OF EARLY DRAMATIC PLAY

Dramatic play frequently helped initiate a new phase of the activity and as frequently was the means of summarizing the result of a period's work. The distribution of the threshed or milled wheat started off with such a play. The setting for the play, the farm and the mill, was constructed of large blocks; some children played they were farmers; others were millers. The farmers carried wheat to the mill; the millers ground it. The farmer paid the miller by letting him keep some of the flour and carried home the rest for bread in sacks already prepared for this purpose by the children. Wagons were needed, and in a day or two these outnumbered their horses. Day by day the idea grew, helped on by timely hint or suggestion.

It was explained that times had changed, that now there was

no small near-by mill where a farmer could take his grain. It must be sent many miles away to a large mill, which ground the wheat of many farms, and when each farmer wanted flour, he bought it at a grocery store in the nearest town. It took some time for them to get a clear idea of the modern transportation of wheat from the farm to the big mill and the distribution of the flour from the mill. Here again, their first ideas were worked out through dramatic play. Some of them were to be farmers, some trainmen, some mill hands, and some grocers in different towns. The farmers were to take the wheat to the nearest small town where it could be put on the train and sent to a large city mill many miles away. Here the millers would receive it and, after making it into flour, would put it on another train and send it to the grocers in the different towns where it would be sold to the farmers when they might want it. In order that the play should be a success, much preparation was required, and the little farmers were again busy in the shop, making miniature bushel, peck, and other necessary measures. These, through the careful planning of the teacher, were circular; all had bottoms of the same size and varied only in height. Incidentally, but logically, they then saw that to be good actors, they must learn how to use these tools in order to measure out their grain.

It was necessary to help them in the logical arrangement of the rather complicated series of acts necessary in their play. Early in the process of making the plan, each child was given a large piece of paper and a pencil, and diagrams were made representing the ideas previously worked out. Circles were used to represent towns and cities, squares to represent farms, lines for railroads, and a pictorial representation of the events of the play was thus worked out.

Other cereals such as corn and oats were studied in the same manner as wheat. The developing activities in each case furnished opportunities for close correlation between the shop, the sewing, and the textile and art studios. Needs were many in these miniature living projects. Groups of children or individuals frequented the shop for help in making wagons, fence pickets, house lumber, or furnishings. Others besieged the textile studio for bags for their grain or to make rugs on their looms. Thence to the art studio for design ideas for either rugs or book covers or illustrations for their written records. There was much need to know what to use and how to use it in their never ending activity. It had the qualities and possibilities of real living; it was genuine and linked to desired ends. It was not too easy nor yet too hard, but was of such a nature that the child was alternately satisfied with his accomplishment and lured on to greater undertaking.

The study of the farmer's life now took up the animals on his farm. The cow and the dairy products seemed of first importance to the children. A list was made of all the foods given by the cow—milk, cream, butter, cheese, the flesh which is used for food, and the skin for leather.[6] The group talked about the habits of the cow and watched those in the lot across the street. They concluded that most of a cow's time was spent in eating grass. It was explained to the children that grass contained very little nourishment, and the cows had to eat great quantities of it in order to get enough for their needs. It was noticed that when the cow was biting off the grass, she did not stop to chew it, but ate it very rapidly. The children then observed some of the cows lying in the shade, chewing. Again it was explained that long ago the flesh-eating animals preyed on those which lived on grass. The latter, always in danger when they went out into the open grassy places had to eat quickly. Out of this grew the habit of rolling the cropped grass into balls and swallowing them into the first stomach, where they lay until these animals could return into the comparative safety of the woods. Here, while resting, the muscles of the throat brought these balls up into the mouth again, where they were thoroughly chewed and then swallowed into the second stomach.

The winter quarter was begun with talk of the sheep-raising business on a farm. The kind of land was considered that a

---

[6] The work in cooking was in close correlation. In the science laboratory an attempt was made to tan leather. The various daily products were studied, and butter was made by each child in an improvised individual churn.

farmer would use for the pasture for sheep. After much discussion supplemented at the right moment by bits of information and timely reference to maps on the part of the teacher, the group finally decided that a temperate climate would be the best. The cold winters would make the wool grow well, and the sheep would not miss their warm coats in the summer. On the globe, they found the principal sheep-raising districts, which were located midway between the equator and the poles. The raw wool was examined and its agency in seed distribution was noted. The natural oil in the wool of the sheep was discovered by dipping the wool into water and noticing how it shed the water. Wool was compared with duck feathers that also shed water; wool was burned to get the odor, which the children compared with burning fat and burning hair. They then tested different kinds of cloth to see if they could tell those made of wool, first by feeling of it, then by noticing its absorbent qualities, and then by burning. As a next step, the wool was pulled out and twisted to show how easily it could be made into thread. The manner of shearing, of washing, and of transporting the fleece to the factory was discussed. Through picture, song, and story this age-old occupation was surrounded by and linked to some of its many esthetic connotations.

EXTENSION OF INTEREST TO OTHER CLIMATES AND PRODUCTS

The children now seemed ready and interested to go farther afield and think about the farming crops of other climates than their own. Accordingly, a study was made of cotton. The plant was drawn and finally pulled to pieces to find how many seeds the ball contained. As these seemed more than were necessary for replanting, the question came up as to what could be done with the excess. As the children did not know and had no suggestions, it was necessary to tell them. They opened some of the seeds and saw that the inside is like a little nut, which they thought might be good to eat. They were told that, ground up, it made an excellent food for cattle and saw for themselves that the inside of the seed is very rich and oily. They then learned more of the characteristics and uses of cotton-seed oil. They wanted to plant some of the cotton seeds and raise cotton themselves. As it was too cold for this out-of-doors, some was put in flower-pots in the house, and at the same time corn and wheat were planted to see which would be the first to germinate. In this connection, the question of climate came up, and the children found the places on the globe where cotton could easily be raised. A cotton plantation was described to them, and they were told of the old-fashioned way of separating the seeds from the cotton. An ounce of the cotton was weighed, and ten children took ten minutes to remove the seeds. They saw that this was a very slow and impossible process by hand and suggested the use of machinery. When told of the invention of the cotton-gin, they readily understood that this would make the cotton much cheaper. They then spent some time in removing the seeds from a quarter-pound of cotton and making it into bales. A small quantity of picked cotton was then ginned and with much speculation and interest was again weighed, and found to have lost one half its weight. Their written conclusion was that the seeds made up half of the weight of the boll. In the process of weighing the children became familiar with the pound, half-pound, and other weights and grew able to tell how many ounce weights are equivalent to a pound, how many quarter-pound weights to the pound or to the half-pound, and how many ounces there are in each of these weights. They also spent a little time counting by two, three, four, and five.

The ginned cotton was finally baled and prepared for shipment to the factory. For this they first cut four-inch squares of paper, working out the problem for themselves, which served as patterns for the cloth squares in which they sewed the cotton. This was then tied with string. Some was shipped to a cloth factory in the north and some went to be made into thread. To help them summarize the whole process, they were shown a case of samples of cotton in its various stages of manufacture from the raw cotton to the finished product. After talking about it, the children were asked to describe the process without looking at the samples. As they could not do this the whole lesson was repeated until they were able to give a consecutive description. They then commenced to make little combs for combing the cotton, as this is the first step after it reaches the mill.

During this period at the close of each step of the process, a written record was made of the work. Often this was put in the form of a drama. Toward the close of the quarter, and after the carpenters of the group had finished the train of cars which was to transport their cotton crop from the factory to the wholesale stores, the complete dramatization was undertaken. Parts were assigned and the different steps in the process were clearly outlined so that each child would have a definite idea of the part he was to take. The children made a list of the places to be represented in the play, such as the plantation, the factory, the wholesale and retail stores, and so on. This was written on the board and opposite each place was written the names of the children who were to be in that particular part. Some hands on the plantation, some trainmen, some factory hands, and so on. It took quite a time to organize this play, and several rehearsals on different days were necessary before things went smoothly. Each child soon realized the part he must play and was able to act out the steps of the different processes in their right order. The written story of their work was finished. It recorded the chief facts they knew about cotton and was read in an assembly of the whole school.

The next development in the story grew out of the past experience and led them on into a new experiment. When trying to locate the places on the globe where cotton might grow, they had noticed Egypt and the adjoining desert of Sahara and could not understand why cotton would not grow in the desert. The conditions there were explained, and they realized that cotton needs water as well as heat. One of the children immediately asked what farmers do when they cannot get water on their farms. On looking at the globe they saw the great stretch of country in the western part of this continent where there is never a sufficient water supply.

In talking over the causes for this, they said right away that the water would have to come from the Pacific Ocean, which is the nearest large body of water. It was explained how the winds blowing across the lands would strike high mountains and would lose their moisture. Some of the children said that the wind could still get over the mountains, but that it would be a dry wind. Then, looking from the eastern side of this dry district, they saw that the east wind after traveling over the land such a great distance would also be dry. One of the children had been in Lower California and spoke of that as a dry country. Another child brought up the question of why it is a dry country when it is so near the sea shore where it can get such a supply of water. One boy suggested that the wind might blow from a different direction, but it was decided that the wind from any direction other than the west would be dry because of the mountains. In another period the same topic was discussed and the same conclusion reached.

Again they studied the barren district in the western part of this country and again noted the mountains to the west with the understanding that the western sides of the mountains would be places of great rainfall. They suggested that if they could get the water from the mountains for these dry regions, it would be "all right." It might be carried by train in carts; but they soon saw this was impracticable, and the problem was left for solution until the next period when they launched into the methods of irrigation. This involved a good deal of experimentation on the sand-table. After much questioning as to the best method of irrigation, they thought that the natural flow of water from a high place to a lower one could be utilized, and by means of ditches the water could be taken into the different parts of a farm. Their idea was that the supply of water from mountain streams would be small at certain seasons of the year, but could be stored in large tanks. They then went to the sand-box and built farms on this principle. They poured water into their lake in the hills, but some of them found that they did not get a supply of water on their farms because they had made their ditches without any regard to the natural slopes. A talk followed about the conditions under which water would flow from one place to another. A good many experiments were necessary, but finally, they decided that the supply tank must be on a hill and the ditches must extend down a

slope, or the water would not run in them. They next decided
to use pipes instead of ditches, as the ditches might get clogged
up or the water might soak into the ground, and some mentioned the loss from evaporation which would take place from
ditches in a warm country. None of the children, however,
realized that the water could go up the hill as high as the
place it started from. A high tank was therefore arranged with
an outlet of bent glass tubing, and the children found that the
water in the tube rose as high as that in the tank. If they
raised or lowered the tank, the water would also rise or sink,
the water in the tube staying at the level of that in the tank.
After this experimentation it was decided that the best system of
irrigation would be to place the tank on the highest hill and
put the pipes on the slopes. The next problem was raised by a
child who asked how water could get to a second story that
was higher than the level of the lake. A little city was built
of blocks in the sand-box, and the problem was how to get
water to a point higher than any of the houses. The children's
solution was a water-tower. Water was pumped from the level
of the lake to the level of the tower, and they proved to their
own satisfaction that it would rise about as high in the pipes
as its level in the tower.

The next separate enterprise was the lumber camp. Out of
their own experience and needs, the children realized that great
quantities of wood are needed for houses, tables, and chairs, and
their curiosity was aroused as to where the supply came from
and how. Lack of space, however, renders it impossible to
quote these records of the lumbering process, the development
of the sawmill, and the transportation of the finished product
to the retail dispensing houses; nor is it possible to include the
succeeding project of coal and ore mining and its transportation.

As previously indicated, each occupation was often initiated
and usually concluded with a dramatic play. The children thus
demonstrated to themselves their gain in power to image and
to execute. Their first efforts to dramatize the play of "Miller"
compared with the later detailed and complicated drama of
"Cotton" showed a decided gain in power to plan, to carry out,

and to consider the end in terms of the means available to reach the end.

The written record of the work continued at regular intervals and was printed for the group from time to time on the school press and then read by them with great interest. Some work on phonetics was slipped in with the reading of the records, and the children learned easily the sounds of about eight consonants, were able to give the sound of the latter when they saw it written, and could write it when given the sound. As their ability to read increased, more time was given to collateral reading both to them and by them, until toward the end of the year a half-an-hour a day was devoted to reading and the writing of connected sentences. The reports comment that "they read with intelligence, have a good idea of phonics, and show great independence in forming new words."

SUMMARY OF THE FIRST THREE YEARS

Thus in the first three years of his school life the child's play enlarged from the mimic games of his home people to those of the persons who contributed to the daily life of the home. His interests gradually extended to their activities and the things they did, made, or bought. Foods were traced to their sources, and finished products of wood or clothing to their raw materials. So far as he was able, he reproduced these activities and himself learned to shape materials and means to reach his ends or to fashion his ideas. In the shop he was shown from the first the right ways of handling the saw or the plane, as he made from the wood of this tree or that something to use in expressing his ideas. In the textile room he fingered the raw wool, the cotton, the flax, or the silk and compared it with the cloth of his coat or the shining luster of his mother's dress, and the old lure of "the how" and "the why" began to stir. In all the activities which filled his day, spinning, weaving, cooking, shop-work, modeling, dramatic plays, conversation, story-telling, or discussion, he was vitally interested and constantly absorbed knowledge of materials and processes. His activities were always fundamental and typical and, therefore, related and recapitulated his similar previous attempts, enriching and enlarging them into more definite purposes and plans. Thus experience, was an onflowing stream continually enlarged from all sides by the pouring in of useful knowledge.

As life flowed on, the child became conscious of his social relationships: that there were others in the group like him who had rights and privileges; that it was far more fun to play games with them even if he must renounce somewhat his own way and consider the way of others in relation to his own. It was more pleasant to work with them, even if he must think of the consequences of what he did in relation to others' plans, and he soon came to see that his consideration of and work with others was to the advantage of all, that by pooling his effort with that of the group, larger and more interesting results were obtained. There was a noticeable difference between those of the children who had been trained for three years in the discipline of the school's activities and those who had but recently entered. The former took hold of new situations much more competently than the new comers.

All along the way the function of the teacher was to assist and further, by direction and anticipation, to remove the too difficult elements of the situation such as search for material and too detailed preparation of material. At the same time she must see to it that the way was not made too plain, that there was enough hindrance to his plan to stimulate his faculties of resourcefulness and judgment in directing the choice of ways or means so that the meaning of his plays, his games, his activities continually grew. New needs constantly arose in process, and new responsibilities were as constantly assumed by the child. The effect of discovering, of inventing, of using facts and processes to further his activity, enlarged his ideal of it, gave an increased confidence in his ability to handle materials and a deeper appreciation of their worth. Most important of all, there developed unconsciously a habit of acting that made him an essential human factor in his environment.

CHAPTER VI

PROGRESS THROUGH INVENTION AND DISCOVERY

GROUP IV (AGE SEVEN)

GROUP IV averaged fourteen in number. The group was divided for its activities, which centered around the historical development of the fundamental occupations with special emphasis upon the progress made in methods due to invention and discovery. The headquarters for this group was a northeast room which had a large eastern bay-window, fireplace, and closet and was also used as part of the chemical and physical laboratory. The room was large and was furnished sparsely with a sand-table, a smaller table, and the necessary chairs. The school session was from nine to twelve, and about one and a half hours of this time were spent with the group teacher. More time than with Group III, however, was given to conversation and the discussion necessary to the organization of the dramatic occupational work. The textile activities in this year overbalanced those of the shop and the kitchen. The time spent in the art studio was also increased, and the first steps in technique were undertaken in this year.[1] The group teacher in charge of the group was trained in science and was helped by the assistant who also worked with Group III.[2]

Two years of experimentation with subject-matter for children of seven and eight years had given indications that this is a transitional age. For three years the children had been interested in and busy with the occupations of the various

---

[1] There was a division of opinion as to whether the introduction of conscious technique thus early was advantageous.

[2] Katherine Camp, Wynne Lackersteen.

persons through whom food or clothing came to the home and with the sources of the materials from which the home itself was built, was lighted, or kept warm. Each child had been helped to imagine, to express in some tangible form, or to dramatize his own ideas of these occupations. In the process he had stored away many useful facts, had learned some skills of hand and eye, and had become familiar with the folk lore and ways of his own people. As a result of what he had done and seen, he had come to know something of the value of his own impulses through seeing what they can effect. The emotional satisfaction such expression gave led him to think about and experiment with better ways to express and thus discover the use of the scientific method although at this age not yet formulated as such. He had also gained from experience an idea of the moving character of the present, in the life of which he was a factor. At this age a child's activities are still for the most part direct from idea to action by use of the physical environment, but he is willing to develop an idea to a certain extent before expressing it. He is not content, for example, with a one-act play of "Miller," for he sees that a real miller goes through a series of acts and dimly perceives that there is an end in view. The new realization of and interest in the ends and aims of action go hand in hand with an increasing willingness and ability for longer periods of mental concentration. His best loved materials for play are still sticks and stones, dirt and sand, fire and water. Social situations interest him, persons using and controlling their environment in getting food, clothing, shelter, and gradually, comfort and satisfaction. Life is still a unity to him. Facts and skills are interesting and worth while only as they help in his activities. It makes no difference whether the occupations he is reliving are those of the present time in the forests of Michigan or those of primitive man or of Greek and Roman days. His interest is in carrying on his play.

CENTERING INTEREST ON PRIMITIVE LIFE

Less and less often is his question "What does he *do?*" Wonder has begun to stir his imaginings as to the whence and the where. The lure of the how and the why begins at this age to leaven the questing mind. The child is less and less content with endless imitation and likes more and more to experiment and, after the fashion of his own thinking, to originate. The spirit of inquiry is opening the door to investigation, to discovery and invention. These and other signs along the way seem to show a changing, an enlarging, and increasing purpose.

The aim of this year's study, therefore, was to make sure of these enlarging interests and awakening impulses to action and to carry the child, by means of them, into an ever enlarging understanding of his moving stream of life—whence and how it comes, whither and how it goes. The dawning psychological consciousness of a relation between the means and the end suggests that the interests of the child of this age are ready to extend to persons in situations different from his own. In response to this awakening interest in other times and situations, the work for this group became historical in character. It was still concerned with what *men do,* but the factors of men, their environment, and relationships were stretched out longitudinally, as it were, into the characters, environment, and social situations of primitive times. Continuity of subject-matter, the fundamental activities of getting food, and providing shelter and clothing, was thus preserved and at the same time the physical and social settings of these activities were so simplified that they permitted and required the greater detail and definiteness of treatment that the child's present environment denies. It was necessary for him to lift himself and his images out of the complexity of his present life and gradually people the situation and environment of an utterly different period of time. This required a certain power of abstraction. Farming, as studied the previous year, had shown what certain people do, what things they come in contact with, how they use them, and how the farmer serves other people. Agriculture taken in historic perspective, however, while reviewing much of this material, throws emphasis upon the peculiar needs in man's life which call forth this occupation, and the way in which it reacts upon the make-up of society. In one case, the matter is taken up as a situation to be realized; in the other as something whose typical motives and effects are to be discovered and traced. Used in this way, the historic statement as Mr. Dewey suggests, "is a method of *analysis of existing social life,* not mere information about something past and gone."

The historic approach also requires attention to the sequence and order of progress in *its larger* and more obvious features. The child is led to consider imaginatively the needs of other times and places which call forth certain kinds of occupations and the devices and inventions that gradually take place in them. He sees the advance made in ways of living through control of tools, fire, and directed uses of wind and water. He understands the greater feeling of security that results from a more constant source of food and from the combination and coöperation of individuals and families in a clan organization. He recognizes that the qualities of leadership demanded in war and hunting cannot take away the control of affairs from those of the clan who are wise in tradition, the old, both men and women, and thus comes naturally to a respect for age and experience. He learns that it is necessary to know both how to follow and how to lead and that there is adventure *under* as well as *of* leadership. This sort of dramatic play cannot fail to make clear the way invention reacts upon life and calls into play new powers of both individuals and groups, new ways of coöperation and association, and leads to the use of natural objects and the control of forces hitherto unmastered. "The orderly and cumulative narrative of history *is* logic in its concrete form, a form which appeals to the child mind of this age."

This type of material uses the interest in the primitive and the savage so characteristic of children of this age. It could be said with truth that the fundamental interests of a child at this stage of growth and of a savage are the same, food, comfort, shelter, although with the child these interests are multiplied and refined. It could be said that the child is like the savage in ability but not in capability, for behind the former lies the great heritage of civilization. It follows that the activities of primitive peoples are in line with the child's interests and under wise direction this study can provide the avenues for his best effort.

The dangers attendant upon an unwise use of the primitive life approach were fully recognized, but the advantages apparent in the results of repeated experiment with such a study seemed far to outweight its disadvantages. The dramatic use of its incidents utilized the interest of the child in the primitive way of living so as to minimize the sensational or merely picturesque features and bring out its defects. He came to realize the motives that otherwise lie hidden from the modern civilized child, and the hard conditions of primitive life that forced men to work their way to a better and better life of a kind that gave a sense of peace and security. When the child realizes the reality of primitive problems, he wants to rediscover and reinvent for himself the better ways and means of living. He thus finds the secret of advance which has resulted for the race in an upward spiral of progressive action.

Finally, and most important of all, it was hoped that if good practice proved the method true, there would crystallize in the child as a by-product of this directed activity, a similar habit of considered and considerate behavior which would carry over into his present situations. Certain rather sensational incidents proved there was basis for such a hope. A child of eight who had carried such a program was playing in the attic of his home with his sister of thirteen and his brother of four when he suddenly saw his brother's clothing in flames. The sister ran shrieking for adult help, while our boy wrapped a blanket about his brother, threw him to the floor, and smothered the flames so quickly that no serious injury resulted. When praised for his quick work and asked how he knew what to do, the boy, very simply and with no apparent feeling that he had done anything unusual, replied that his teacher the previous year had told them the different ways of putting out fire with earth, heavy cloths, water, and so on and had shown them just how to act in case clothing caught fire. In another group where the teacher had not sufficiently emphasized the right choice of a place to build a fire, a little child went home and started a fire on the wooden floor of a closet.

METHOD OF STUDYING PRIMITIVE LIFE

The starting point of the study for this year was varied, depending upon the background and experience of both teacher and children.[3] Sometimes the journey back to the long ago was made by the old, old road of "Let's pretend," dropping along the way, one by one, all the comforts and conveniences of present foods, clothing, and shelter which the children thought they could do without.[4] By this process of eliminating the nonessentials they were reduced to water (always mentioned as the first essential), food, and the necessity of protection from the elements and wild animals. They found difficulty, some groups more than others, in imagining any life without fire and guns, while clothing was easily cast aside as immaterial to comfort. They told various stories of the possible ways in which fire was discovered, although the one which seems perhaps the most obvious, lightning, had to be suggested. They had heard of making fire with flint, by rubbing sticks together, and suggested that it might have been first taken from volcanic sources. The value of fire for protection from the dangers of primitive times necessitated some elaboration of the abundant animal life then existing. After much individual experimentation each child learned to make a fire and formulated the chief things requisite to the experiment: (1) a supply of air, (2) use of inflammable material such as kindling, (3) proper arrangement in stacking sticks for the admission of air. They decided that as it was very hard to start a fire in those days, it would be well to find some way of keeping it from going out. They discovered that hard wood burns slowly and that by partial covering from air fire can be kept for a long time.

---

[3] The study of primitive life was always present in the curriculum at this stage of growth, but by reason of its imaginative nature it varied widely from year to year. Each year it was the outgrowth of a particular group of children and teacher by whom it was planned and enacted. Other material was also tried—Indian, Eskimo, African savage tribes, but the course described seems to have been the most fruitful in its results.

[4] The ability to reconstruct such scenes varied with the experience of both children and teacher.

It was difficult [5] for one class to carry out dramatically even the simplest imagined scenes in the daily life they were discussing or to construct adequate images of the physical surroundings as the setting for a story. Neither could they suggest incidents which might fit this setting. Much time, therefore, was spent in experimental work with the materials which primitive peoples would use, and then the children could more easily originate and dramatize the story side of the study. In addition to their work with fire, they carried out in detail (as far as their physical limitations would allow) such things as the selection of stones for making weapons, cooking by roasting and by boiling with the aid of heated stones. They talked about the sort of place early man used for shelter, trees and caves and their comparative merits, and how the discovery of fire had made the cave a more comfortable and safe place to live. The questions of where caves would be found and how they were formed were considered very slightly. The kinds of rock in which some of the children had seen caves, limestone and granite, were compared with a view to the probable shape and size of the caves in each. The various foods that could be found by men of this period were thought of and grouped by the children under four main heads: berries, fruits, roots, and animal food. The sort of weapons used and the ways of getting animal food were talked over. One child said that if they once found nuts, they could make a trap baited with nuts for squirrels, and when they had a squirrel, they could bait a larger trap for bear. The first inventions suggested were improvements in weapons. Shape was suited to purpose. The club with its inserted stones developed into the spear and axe with a sharpened stone at the end of a handle. A question as to the kind of stone suitable for weapons brought out the idea that it must be such as would break in sharp edges, and that these edges must not crumble or flake off easily. Various stones, such as limestone, granite, slate, soapstone, and flint, were examined for cleavage and friability and were tested by the children to

[5] The failure of the story and dramatic approach caused the substitution of experiments with primitive materials.

find out which possessed these characteristics. They were, one by one, rejected with the exception of granite, flint, and the harder limestone. When making their clubs and spears the children were told that guitar and violin strings had the same characteristics as the sinews and skins, and these were used for binding arrow-heads onto sticks. After soaking and drying, the sinews would readily split and, when soaked again and wound closely around the arrow-head, would shrink in drying and hold the arrow-head tightly in place. The invention of the bow and arrow was described, and its advantages for the tribe which possessed it were brought out by showing that men now had a weapon which could be used from a distance, thus lessening the risk to the user and increasing his chances of success in hunting or defense.

Cave life as a whole, with its weapons, utensils, and clothing, was worked out in tangible form by the children. Much other, detailed preliminary work gave background and a setting in which the children, in fancy, could become a tribe of primitive people. Caves were constructed of various shapes and sizes on the sand-table. Into them were put the necessary utensils and weapons. When this was done, the class discussed the merits of each cave, each child selecting the one he would prefer. Their talk brought out various improvements, such as blocking up the doorway and the proper placing of the fire beneath the smoke hole. Each cave, when finished, contained a rude spit for roasting, a stone pot for boiling, chipped out of rock, weapons, huge stone axes and spears, a bed, and skins of beasts that had been slain for use as clothing. In discussion they came to see the use of the stone pot for cooking meat and nuts in water heated to boiling by hot stones. They then heated different kinds of stone, limestone, sandstone, slate, and granite over bunsen burners and threw them into water to see how this was done.

It was only after this preliminary work that one group could appreciate Stanley Waterloo's *Story of Ab* enough to act out dramatically such incidents as the meeting of the two boys and their plans for the capture of some grazing animal by the construction of a pitfall in the plains below their homes,[6] could imagine and carry out more easily the autobiographical account of their own tribe, could state their problems and discuss intelligently ways and means of solving them, and thus develop an attitude of mind that was alert to discovery and invention.

In these various ways the children passed imaginatively through different stages of living. Their tribe, more independent through the invention of the bow and arrow, migrated to homes nearer the open plains in the lower part of the river valley, where the grazing animals, which were now their special dependence for food, were most abundant. The necessity of hunting the mastodon was suggested by the children as the reason for a combination with a tribe near-by. Such a hunt required many people, and its success depended upon some degree of coördination under a leader, whose position had been gained by acknowledged ability and whose commands, for the time being, all must obey. Another possible reason for a combination defense might be an appeal for help from the raids of a cave tiger upon an isolated community. Skilful direction by leaders was recognized as essential to success where large numbers were concerned.

The temporary combination for a specific aim brought the children logically to the consideration of how a permanent combination might develop out of the need of a change of residence, necessitated by the migration of the animals, their chief source of food. The children were helped to develop the situation and physical setting out of which the need for such a migration would probably arise. They gathered together all the physical characteristics of their present home, the high bank and river valley. They were told it was the time of year when the days would begin to shorten, and the birds and animals move southward. The experience of a bad winter the previous year was given as a reason for moving southward with the animals. They discussed the plan of going and, with a good deal of help, decided that the river was the easiest route to the

---

[6] Some classes preferred the *Story of Ab* as told by the teacher; others demanded the book to be read in serial fashion week after week.

south. They quickly suggested a raft as the easiest plan for transportation. They then organized a party, naming the things they would take with them and the way each thing would have to be carried.

They agreed that their leader would have to be one who had at some previous time followed the river and found the animals on the plains near its mouth, and they discussed the qualities that would make a man a leader. They said he would have to be brave and willing to meet danger, and that he must know a great deal and own a great many arrows. They then elected as leader one from their number. One of the children said, "Just like voting for President." The question was asked what name the chosen leader would have, and how people would be named in those days. As they had no suggestions ready, they were told the story of how each young Indian earned his name by what he had done. Instead of suggesting a name for their leader from the exploits of one of their own tribe, they promptly transferred the name of a young Indian to their leader.

The children had several times proposed finding and using clay, but were not able to suggest how or where it could be found. Upon starting down the river in their migration to the plains, one child suddenly recalled the fact that he himself had found clay in the banks overhanging a small river and proposed that the party should have that experience on their way down the river on rafts. In order to find out in what sort of a place, plain or hill, high bank or low level, the clay would be found, they experimented with clay and sand on the sand-table and found how both would settle when the water became still. Their surprise in finding the water perfectly clear above the clay was very pronounced. They decided that as the clay settled only in the glass that was kept still, the clay would be "dropped," as they called it, in quiet waters, or "ponds." They proposed that their party camp out on flat lands near the river, where the clay bottom of such a pond was drying in the sun. They made a map of this part of the river valley and a lake in the flat plain. They put water (into which they had stirred clay) in the hilly part of the sand-table map, so that it flowed down into the lake below, settled, and formed a clay bed.

The making of clay vessels has been so often and so successfully worked out that for brevity's sake it seems best merely to list the outstanding things gained by the children in the rather long series of experimental activities incident to this phase of the study. They worked out:

(1) The principle that the shape of a vessel should be controlled by its use
(2) The length of time necessary for drying before firing
(3) The change of the color of ochre to red after firing
(4) The source of the black used by the Navajo Indians, soot
(5) The type of the first form of potter's wheel, a flat disk of wood or stone turning on a smooth surface. (They made one. This was used by some of the children in making their vessels.)

These results suggest the way in which ample time was given the children to play and experiment with the various raw materials used in their activities. The simplicity of the things they played with was enriched by frequent visits to the museum to see the results of the perfected technique of primitive peoples. Their own lack of it never seemed to bother them. Although all this experimental work took some time, the children did not lose their sense of identification with the tribe. They frequently discussed the individuals they were impersonating, some choosing names for themselves. One called himself Clay-finder.

About this time also the children began to show a more alert interest in the tribe's doings and were able to realize and picture the physical features of its setting much more intelligently than before.

They went over the uses to which they could put the different parts of the animals the clan would kill, the flesh and marrow of the bones for food, the bones and horns for weapons. Wool was studied to see the use to which the hair of an animal could be put; the inside fibres of the bark of the basswood were torn out and woven into mats; and the children tried dyeing the fibres with dogwood and berries gathered in the lot. Their plan in doing this was to select the number of basswood fibres needed to make the mat and then dye half this number for making a design in weaving. They experimented with border designs on paper and first drew these with curved lines. When they tried to weave the design into the mat, however, they found that they had to remake their pattern in straight lines to accommodate it to the stiff material.

While these developments in making utensils of pottery and other material were taking place, there was talk of how certain animals might have become domesticated. Their own idea was that people would bring home wounded animals for their children to play with. It was suggested that young animals would be even nicer, for they would grow up with the children and gradually become tame. The fact was brought out that in a herd of animals one of the pack often signals to the others when an enemy is near. This suggested to the children that the dogs might signal to men in the same way and so be good watchers. Dogs might also be of use in aiding the hunt. Talk then continued of the flocks people would accumulate after they once began to domesticate animals. This led to conjecture as to the difference this might make in the home of the tribe, as grass would be necessary for the flocks. In addition, they thought the sheep would need a great deal of light and air, and that water would be required. They accordingly decided to migrate.[7]

Arrived at the grassy plain, they decided to be a small tribe of about twelve people with thirty sheep. They thought it not unlikely that another tribe would come to the same place, since the plain would feed more than thirty sheep. When this happened, the two tribes consolidated and arranged to unite their forces, since less men would be needed to watch the sheep and it was desirable to have some of them at home for other work. In first planning the consolidation the children thought it would be very bad, because it would be the surest way to bring about a fight. They said that if the two tribes ever wanted

---

[7] For their migration they needed tents and began the construction of one large enough to hold the "tribe." This was made of unbleached muslin and, when finished, was taken to the field and set up where they encamped for the morning.

to separate they could not tell which sheep belonged to each tribe.

In one year the experience of Abraham and Lot was one of the stories told them to illustrate the character of shepherd life and the conditions and situations likely to cause difficulty. These stories, rewritten by the group either working together or as individuals, were often printed by the older children in large size type on the school press and became the basis of their study of language, while they also served to vivify the story they were dramatizing.

STORY OF ABRAHAM AND LOT

THE LORD THEIR GOD TOLD ABRAHAM TO GO OUT OF THE COUNTRY. ABRAHAM TOOK LOT WITH HIM. HE WAS ABRAHAM'S BROTHER'S SON. ABRAHAM AND LOT WENT OUT OF THE COUNTRY. THEY STAYED TOGETHER FOR A WHILE, THEN THEY PARTED. THEY WENT ABOUT TOGETHER, FINDING PASTURE FOR THEIR HERDS. THEN THEY PARTED BECAUSE THERE WASN'T ENOUGH FOOD FOR BOTH HERDS AND THEY COULD NOT TELL THEIR ANIMALS APART AND SO THEY QUARRELED. THEN ABRA-HAM TOLD LOT THAT HE COULD CHOOSE WHICH WAY HE WANTED TO GO. HE CHOSE EAST. THEN ABRAHAM WENT UP ON THE MOUNTAINS. THEN GOD TOLD HIM TO LOOK EAST AND WEST AND NORTH AND SOUTH AND SAID, "I WILL GIVE TO YOU ALL THE LAND THAT YOU SEE."

The roving shepherd tribe now settled down for a space and after its consolidation and subsequent readjustments chose for the site of its permanent village an island in a river, a situation thought advantageous because of the protection afforded by the river. The children thought that the animals they were hunting, cattle, horses, small deer, would not frequent a settled place. As this village was on an island, the habits of the animals feeding on the adjoining plains would not be much disturbed because of the broad expanse of running water between the village and the plains. On one side of the river island the land was low and the children called it "Riverland." The fact was brought out that the island was formed where the river deposited the fine soil that it carried during flood times. Here wild wheat was growing, which the women of the village gathered and threshed and ground for food. The method of grinding was left as a problem to be worked out after they had done more work with various cereals in the kitchen, so that there would be a present reason for its solution.

The earliest differentiation of labor was brought out in the occupations in the new homes. The old hunters confined their energies to bringing in small game from near their homes. The young hunters were the main dependence of the tribe, and the women and children gathered moss for beds, nuts and fruits for food, made the fireplaces, and kept the home fires burning.

The children asked who would be the most powerful people in a settled agricultural tribe and considered the question important. In the hunting tribes the old men had given place to the younger men when they were no longer able to take the lead in a hunt; but now it was concluded that the old men would have the most influence, as they would have the largest experience and could best direct the younger people.

In order to enable the children to comprehend to some degree the length of time which elapsed between even slight improvements in the ways of living of primitive peoples whose lives they were relating, they were told something of the changes of climate during the glacier period and of the migrations of the animals. The length of time was made clear by referring it to the successive generations of the Ab family, for the children were so much attached to the name that it was continued from age to age. The increase in the number of the tribe during the successive generations was calculated, adding by threes, fives, and tens. The children added up to one hundred and twenty by tens and were then shown another way of saying it, i. e., twelve tens equal one hundred and twenty. Most of them knew this, but it was a starting point for further number work, and they then added together numbers of flocks of sheep, or tribes of people.

The next advance toward civilization was the making of

cloth from wool, a step beyond the clothes of skin or feathers with which, until now, the tribe had been clothed. Raw wool was given to the children to examine and decide how the fibres could be made into yarn. When they had pointed out the crinkles which would hold the fibres together, they spun wool with their fingers and wound it on a stone. The weighted thread twisted round their fingers, and this, coupled with what they had observed about spinning, led one or two of them to suggest something that would spin like a top. They then were shown pictures of a spindle, a spindle whorl, and so on. Thus the primitive way of spinning and its gradual development became clear to them as they reconstructed and gradually improved the primitive tools. Information about a process became knowledge of a process because it was the result of experience. The primitive method of weaving was also taken up. The way of carrying on this experimentation varied with teacher and year. Where there was keen interest and an inventive spirit, the children were given the raw wool, and the beginning stages of carding and spinning were carried through in the classroom. Otherwise, the spinning and the weaving were left for the period in the textile room. This flexible and helpful coöperation between specialist and group teacher made quick adjustments easy. It was possible to "strike while the iron was hot" or to leave an idea such as the spinning or weaving to be worked out more slowly and in detail in the textile studio.

The children now pictured freely other tribes than their own, living near and far, and dramatized meeting with them and the first exchange of goods such as wheat for baskets or wool, etc. In this exchange which the children were told was called "bartering," the articles made by them were used.

In the on-going story different groups worked out the discovery of metals, in various ways. One year there was a discussion of all the metals known to the children, together with their uses. Iron, lead, tin, copper, and zinc were compared as to their hardness, weight, and the amount of heat required to bring them to the melting point. Tin, zinc, and lead were melted over a bunsen burner and poured into water to cool. Since all the children had handled shot, they were interested in the spherical form assumed in cooling when the metal was poured from a height. In heating the metals they noted the time necessary to melt lead and tin and learned that copper and iron wire did not melt, but became red hot and could be flattened easily by hammering. They were shown metals in the natural state and given the word *ore* as a general term. They discussed how metals were probably discovered. It was suggested that people may have found melted copper in the charcoal on the hearth, and they were given the various stories about the discovery of iron.

The next step was the construction of a smelting place of clay or stones. The chief problems for the children to solve in this undertaking were the position of the chimney and the arrangement for proper draught. They found by experience the advantage of a steady draught, how to protect the fire from sudden changes of wind, and that hard wood makes a hotter fire than soft. Further experimentation was necessary before they could understand the principle of draught. With the help of a taper, they investigated the currents of air in the room and found the current of cold air from the windows sinking to the floor and a current of warm air leaving the room at the top of the door. They then appreciated that the hot air in their furnace would rise and understood the necessity of a chimney for an intake of a continuous supply of cold air. Tin and zinc were melted successfully in a few of the best constructed smelters, and the group, now quite intelligent as to the principle, pooled their experience and labor to construct a larger one in which ore was to be melted for the tribe's arrow-heads. Discussion of their plan for this made it clear that in order to form the melted ore, it was necessary to have molds. More discussion followed as to the material from which these would be made, resulting in the making of molds of clay and sand into which the molten lead was poured.[8]

So much of the work assumed the form of play that the children were not conscious of the knowledge they were gaining. They handled several kinds of metals, both in the ore and in

---

[8] Copper was melted for them from the ore by means of a blow pipe so they would understand how it could be done.

the pure state, and gained a knowledge of the processes by which apparent "heavy stones," as they first thought them, became changed into articles of great utility. Incidentally, they learned how the metals unite as in the making of bronze. They heated copper in the furnace and then, in order to make it plastic, submerged it in water and learned that copper unites with the air in the process of heating and forms a black scale which comes off in water.

While working with metals, many stories were told illustrating the advantages of metals and the value that would be attached to a knowledge of them by a tribe ignorant of how to work them. In order to demonstrate this, the class was divided into tribes, each tribe selecting what seemed to be a desirable location for a special occupation. One tribe, interested chiefly in raising wheat, selected a fertile plain near a range of hills where they could get some ore when necessary. This tribe naturally became interested in the way in which various foods, such as the wild cereals found, were "domesticated" (the word cultivated was given them) and the relation of climate and natural environment to the raising of these foods. The resulting effects upon the living habits of the people were brought out. These occupations were naturally closely related to the preparation and cooking of food and the changes · that developed.

Another tribe, interested in sheep raising, chose a valley with grazing plains and made a study of textiles and the sources of clothing. The metal workers picked out a site in the mountains near a river, and a fourth group selected the seacoast for its abundance of fish, shells, and pearls. Each tribe, after imagining themselves settled in their new homes, began to perfect the one line of labor chosen and to decide how they could obtain other necessities of life. The tribe along the seashore needed boats and endeavored to think out some method of making them. The tribe raising wheat used first a bent twig dragged over the ground as a means of loosening the soil, then thought of taming oxen and training them to drag an improved plow; they also worked out a flail for threshing grain. The shepherds decided on the shelter for themselves and their flocks and discussed the raising of sheep. Each tribe decided the number of families they would have and the number of persons in a family. Most of the class objected to having any children in the family, only one announcing his intention to have a "nice comfortable family of five."

The various tribes next sought some method of trading, or bartering, in order to secure the products of others. They attempted to find some standard of value, but found it difficult not to rate highest some rare shells which the people from the seashore brought to trade for wheat or sheep. A few children showed some skill in driving a bargain.

Intercourse between tribes for the sake of barter involved the subject of transportation. Most of the children had so little idea of distance that it was necessary to build up something of a background of experience. They were asked how long it would require to walk the longest distance they knew definitely —from the school, downtown. After much discussion of their own and their friends' experience, they finally arrived at the distance that could be walked in an hour and calculated the distance that might be covered in a day or in a week. With this idea of average distance reckoned in time, the children returned to their tribe and its situation. After more thinking they found that, with burdens to carry and a way that led not over smooth roads, but over mountains and plains covered with vegetation, a new estimate of how far the tribe could carry their produce for exchange would be necessary. Of course, the idea of animals as beasts of burden occurred to all the children, and they spent some time investigating the different types of animals that could be so used. The typical burden-bearing animals were cut from paper, and a study made of their habits. As a result, they concluded that all burden-bearing animals are "grass-eating ruminants."

A dramatic summing up in story form of the social organization of the Bronze Age completed this year's work. It may not be necessary to remind the reader that at the same time that this dramatic study of primitive life and experimentation in its ways of living were going on, the same materials and similar though modern tools and ideas were being used in the shop, kitchen, studio, music room, and garden. Here also, emphasis was laid on the relation of materials to their uses, the value of the inventive attitude, of designs and plans, and the rôles of the different forms of communication in all their activities. Museums and books were constantly used as sources so that the children in no way felt out-of-joint with their present. Instead, they gained a new point of view as to how the present had come to be. The relation of the sort of place they lived in to the type of thing they did grew clear and definite in their minds as they pictured the physical setting needed for raising sheep and cattle, or as a source for their clay or coveted metals. As each phase of industry developed, attention concentrated upon its natural habitat, and as one occupation succeeded another, the children traveled in imagination till they found the locality especially suitable. Meantime in their sand and clay maps each new environment was added to those previously brought up, until all the main features of physiographic structure were both introduced and placed in their relationships to one another. The child thus had a picture of a typical section of the earth's surface, of the way in which its various features—mountains, uplands, river valleys, and seas—connect with one another and with the activities of human life. The large amount of imaginative abstraction and arrangement of the natural features of their self-constructed sand maps, so that they were suitable for the changing sequence of their activities, proved an intellectual exercise of great importance.

SUMMARY

This natural setting of man and his occupations, the basis of their future, was clothed with human significance to these little actors of primitive life as they imaginatively wandered in the sand-box hills and valleys of their tribal habitation. In the process, many scientific facts of geology, of chemistry, of physics, or of biology, found their way into the sinews of their intellectual wings.

In addition to such a view of geography in a human setting gained through constant dramatization of imagined situations and behavior, these children had an early glimpse into the beginnings of the social organizations of tribal life, in its various stages of development. Certain definite associations were built up between people, their social life, and the land they occupied. Ideas were gained as to a gradual progress in man's way of living—his forms of shelter, his clothing, and kinds of food as well as of the part that invention and discovery had played in this development.

As the year drew to its close the children summarized in written records and dramatic plays what the experience had made real to them. Facts about the gradual development of better ways of getting food, finding shelter, and the making of clothing, of tools, of the means of defense, and the attendant discoveries and inventions were thus brought out. The records specified many of the different materials found on the earth which could be used in their natural state, also those which must be made over or refined. The general conclusion was that man's necessity was the cause for change, and "using your head" was the means of invention.

The long stretch of time between the imagined scene of the study and the actual present seemed to cause no difficulty. It was not difficult for these children to doff their rôles as members of a primitive tribe and don their parts as children of a Chicago school in 1900. The needs and therefore the interests and the duties of the wood-gatherer, the fire-tender, the shelter or clothing-maker, or the cook remain the same from one age to another. It is the *art* of living that changes and progresses. This the children seemed to recognize in all phases of their work and play, whether constructive or experimental. Their activities were real and continuing, because they answered the genuine, ever present needs of life.

The beginnings of many kinds of activity challenged each child to experiment along lines of his own interests and choosing, to make, to decorate, to contrive, and to invent. There were rafts and dugouts to be made for the migrating tribe; bows and arrows or other weapons must be strung and fashioned or traps made for the sabre-toothed tiger or other dangerous animals. A way must be found to harvest the good wild wheat of the river land and then to grind it. A use had been found for the newly discovered clay, and ideas were many for making bowls and utensils of all kinds. The potter's wheel was redis- covered. The coöperative effort of the shop director and the young inventors produced a rude, first potter's wheel. New dis- coveries led to new needs and these to new inventions, and made increasing demand for skill—skill in the arts of construc- tion and communication. What each one did was never fully appreciated until it was passed on to others, and what one received from others frequently had to be tested to be ap- proved. Language was useful. One must write as well as speak, must read as well as listen in order to share more widely and in turn profit by such sharing. It was necessary to know how to count and measure and use the necessary tools in order to put ideas into concrete forms that were satisfactory and beau- tiful.

All this was true of the fine as well as of the useful arts; the beginnings of the former naturally grew out of a finer and deeper appreciation of the latter, and a basic and fundamental relationship between the two was established. In their creative work in music, as in art, the influence of this imaginative life of primitive times was most marked and was used as far as possible. The function of time in producing melody grew plain to the children as they listened to the rhythmic beat of the tom- tom and caught the meaning of a metrical succession of notes all on one pitch.

This imagined and dramatized story of man's long climb to better ways of living brought the children, at the end of the year, close to the period when authentic history begins. Through being actors in their own retelling of the probable story of civilization they had gained a background of experi- ence for the next year's continued study of the actual records of specific peoples.[9]

There is now perhaps too great emphasis in many schools on the "Here and Now" principle in selecting the constructive

---

[9] Much of the material in this chapter is taken from John Dewey, "His- torical Developments of Invention and Occupation, Central Principles," *Elementary School Record*, 1900.

work of small children from the confused and complicated modern environment. Unreflective selection in reproductive play may include modern sky-scrapers, ocean liners, part of a National Exposition, or the ferry-boats of New York harbor. This chapter points out in detail that a skilled adult mind must operate in such selection. It also presents an approach which will leave the child in full possession of his inventive ability to be used in developing the simple activities and undertakings which he sees have been and are essential in social relations and organizations.

CHAPTER VII

PROGRESS THROUGH EXPLORATION
AND DISCOVERY

GROUP V (AGE EIGHT)

THE homeroom for Group V, medium in size with southern exposure, was equipped with a geographic sand tray, blackboard space, table, and closet. Because of the constant stream of visitors each room was supplied with extra chairs, and the mental picture of every classroom should include a number of adults looking on.[1] The group was under the direction of one of the instructors in science, with a teacher in history coöperating.[2] The occupational work centered around the trading and maritime activities of the Phoenicians, their exploration of the Mediterranean basin, and commerce with its various outstanding settlements, and then moved on to the larger topic of world exploration and discovery. It must be remembered that as each group passed from home room to shop, to laboratory, to studio, to music room, the things they did or expressed, related to or illustrated as far as possible the activities that went on in the historical study they were dramatizing.

In previous years these children had gained a working knowledge of some of the occupations and social relationships of present life and an idea of how the present had come to be, through their study of primitive life. They had seen that any change of the physical situation of a tribal group necessitated and conditioned a revision of its social program and a redistribution of individual duties. Further, it was only through the invention of devices which made for better living conditions, more efficient weapons for defense and the getting

---

[1] As a rule the children were astonishingly unconscious of being observed.
[2] Mary Hill; Laura Runyon.

of food, that man had come to a more settled and secure way of living.

The choice of subject-matter for this year had been, as for all years, the result of much experimentation in order to find the type of civilization which possesses a progressive quality, an on-going, out-flowing, and developing way of living which gave a "go" to the story, linked it with the previous study, carried it on to the next step, and at the same time satisfied the spirit of romance and adventure which is rife at this age. In one year a detailed study of the American Indians, their inventions and customs, was followed by a study of the discovery of the Indians by the white men. Then came some of the explorations which made known the form of the earth and its larger geographical features and forces. While satisfactory in some respects, the Indian civilization is so highly static in its type that an advance into the next era of culture was not easily made.

THE STUDY OF THE PHOENICIAN CIVILIZATION [3]

The Phoenicians were finally chosen for the study of this year because the fixed habitat of this people was similar to the imaginary location of the tribe of metal workers of the previous year, and yet presented conditions that were different from and unfavorable to the earlier life experience of the tribe, up to this time a nomadic pastoral people living on a plain beyond the mountains. New problems would have to be met and solved in this unfamiliar environment. In this year, also, when the children began a serious use of the symbols of reading, writing, and numbers, a study of the Phoenician civilization that had spread these conveniences through the then known world (the Mediterranean basin), seemed particularly appropriate. It also furnished the link between the life of primitive man, as developed in the previous year and the following age of discovery in the world's history, when knowledge of the earth's form and some conception of its physical forces were gained.

---

[3] Laura Louise Runyan, *The Teaching of Elementary History in the Dewey School*, University of Chicago, June, 1906. This account is indebted to Miss Runyan for extracts.

For a tribe of people like the Phoenicians, with the sea in front and mountains behind, agriculture and flocks and herds were impossible as a means of support. The conditions had to yield a means of subsistence, however, if this tribe were to continue. How this could be done was the first problem given the children. Out of their past experience with ancient peoples, they themselves suggested that the sea might furnish fish and the mountains, metals and timber, and that these, if means of conveyance were found, might be exchanged with other tribes for wheat or wool. After much further discussion the group wrote out a description of their physical situation and plans for the future. This took the form of a recital by various members of the group, telling how they had come in their flight from some unfavorable situation to a physical situation similar to that of the Phoenician coast.

The children, in their rôle of Phoenician traders, met the problems and inconveniences similar to those found in the earliest form of trade by barter. As indicated in the children's own records, a need arose for persons able to make usable articles from raw materials and for those who exchange these articles for others needed but which cannot be produced. In such relationships the child sees the need of the middleman. A dramatic picture of these early bartering relationships and of their development into trade was imagined by the children. They imagined themselves Phoenician sailors landing at some barbaric settlement of the African coast, and they saw the probable events which took place. The sailors, laying down their goods, would retire to their vessels. The barbarians would creep out of the bushes, inspect, and then place on the sand their produce, shells, ivory, or whatnot, and in turn, withdraw. Then came the inspection by the sailors of the offers made and acceptance or refusal of part or all of the exchange and, in case of refusal, the second chance given the natives to increase their offerings.

Such a scene carries with it a spirit of adventure, a tang of excitement; it can illustrate how cupidity or generosity would develop, how gradually the confidence necessary for a permanent trading relationship can be established. These transac-

tions also little by little establish the reputation for probity
of the sailors at home with the merchants who had entrusted
them with goods for sale.

THE PRACTICAL APPROACH TO MATHEMATICS

To carry on their work successfully the first merchant and
trader would need to invent, adopt, or adapt a system of measurements and weights. He would need a numerical system and
a system of records; he must plan how to utilize the labor of
others, how to combine with others, and how to exclude others
from his field of labor. Through enacting their rôles these children came to appreciate the tasks of these first carriers of the
world's commerce, and how a system probably evolved by which
the products of a people could be measured and valued, and
the records of such transactions kept. This gave reality to the
point of view that the origin of writing, of number, and of the
system of weights and measures grew out of an attempt to solve
the problem similar to this imaginative one. This problem was
formulated by asking, How could a merchant trader from the
Phoenician tribe tell the value of his merchandise as compared
with that of other merchants? How could he record future exchange of merchandise? Only a word is necessary to link this
situation with the rôles of the salesman, the commercial trav-
eler, or the advertising agent of the present.

The question of records seemed easiest, and the child who
acted as trader at the time devised his own system of records.
This was usually a picture of the article exchanged with marks
by each to indicate the number. Thus a trade of fish for wheat
was indicated by a bag and a fish opposite each other, with
marks to indicate the number exchanged. When, however,
other products were used in quantity, and it was necessary to
select and name a part from the whole quantity, a more definite system was demanded.

The ability to initiate solutions of the problems which thus
arose varied with different groups of children and with the individuals within the group. Parts of the body as means of measurement were suggested. The distance from the end of the

thumb to the first joint and the span of the hand were used as units of measure. The full length of the fore-arm and the pace were also used. The transition from a somewhat irregular unit to an adopted unit could usually be obtained from the class. For example, the distance from the tip of the middle finger to the elbow was used as a unit for measuring cloth and called a "cubit." After this had been used in many measurements, a story was told of a Phoenician who went to trade in cloth and, noticing that the men in the market place were of different heights, selected the man with the longest arm from whom to purchase cloth. The other merchants noticed this and called a meeting to decide what should be done. At this point the class was called upon for suggestions. One child thought that the shortest man's arm might be taken as a standard and others stop short of the elbow in their measurements; others thought that the tallest man's arm might be used and the little man measure above the elbow. When, however, some one suggested that a middle-sized man be selected, and the rest get sticks just the length of his cubit, all agreed that this would be the best plan. The next most apparent need was a unit of weight. In group discussion they decided that water would make the most convenient and common thing to use and talked over ways and means of making a standard. Each child finally made and paraffined a square box the size of his smallest linear unit—the distance from the tip of the thumb to the first joint. This was filled with water, weighed, and taken as the standard unit of weight.

At this moment of partial solution of their immediate problem as traders, namely, that of developing a practical method of barter, the children's interest was easily directed to the standards and tables of measurement used today. For the shop they made their own foot rulers and yardsticks. Many spent spare time at home devising scales which were then tested, improved, and reconstructed in the shop. The laboratory scales were in demand to get the proper amount of clay for ounce, two-ounce, half-pound or pound weights. These were molded to the form that each child thought most serviceable. Liquid measures—half-bushel, gallon, quart, pint, and gill—were constructed and their relations determined by measuring. The numerical symbols were improved from time to time. The children were shown primitive systems of counting. One child introduced a diagonal line across four vertical marks to indicate five, the common method of tallying in their games. Another child came one day and said she knew a new way to count and put on the board the Roman numerals to X. The class was then interested in seeing how IV could indicate one less and VI one more, than V; that X was two V's, and that less or more than X was indicated by the position of the I to the right or left of the X. The pleasure of the class when they comprehended the significance of this device proved how much a matter for thought a number system had been to them.

INTEREST IN WRITTEN AND DRAMATIC EXPRESSION

Concurrent with this construction of a number system, the need for a more accurate method of written record than that of rude pictures was felt. The use of a part of a picture to stand for the whole, then a sign to stand for a sound resulting in an alphabet was worked out with suggestions from the teacher. The arbitrariness of this system was reflected in two alphabets invented by the children. All this gave meaning to the reading and writing which were emphasized in this year. The symbols of social intercourse worked out naturally centered about the trader and his experiences. The child, at this stage, still chiefly interested in himself, was, of course, the trader. The method adopted was that of imaginary travels for exploration and trade. Story-telling and dramatization were used as in the preceding year. The events narrated at the beginning of the year were chiefly confined to the experiences of the past year: the trader had met with strange peoples, friendly or hostile; he had had to make his wants known by signs; he had asked only for things he knew about, and hence his increase in knowledge had been slight. As the year went on, however, more and more content was apparent in the stories of the children, and accounts of new processes and devices of manufacture were related or demonstrated. The physical features of their play country were pictured in map or sand-box. The high, rock coast with its stretch of shore along the sea was planned and built; lead and iron ore were cleverly hidden in the clefts of the mountains to be discovered later; and miniature forests of oak, pine, and other trees were set up for the forests. The aid of the art teacher was sought in developing the background and setting for the scene. To give an impression of distance to the region, plain blue wall paper was tacked on a frame as large as the sand box. On this the children drew a landscape showing a continuation of that they had planned in the sand box. The blue background served as the sky, clouds were added with chalk.

MANUAL TRAINING

The main purpose of the work was to stimulate the children's minds to study and, so far as they were able, to seek solutions for certain of the problems of the Phoenician type of civilization that must be solved in order that progress in comfort and convenience in living might be made. Thus the children carried out inquiry into the origin of products and the development of processes which have transformed modes of living from primitive crude forms to the present. The sort of houses that they as a Phoenician tribe should build was discussed, and it was decided that stone might be used, since there was such an abundance. The question of how it could be made to stick together was brought up and led to a discussion of lime in its native state and its use as mortar. The children then turned into masons, made mortar boxes, trowels, and a sand sieve in the shop. Lime was procured, and experiments were carried on to demonstrate the effect of water upon it. Mortar was made and used to build the walls of a typical house of that time and region. A bridge was necessary to cross a ravine; bricks were made from clay; and the bridge built in the form of a keystone arch.

Some difficulty was found in making the sides of the stone walls straight. How this could be done in real building was the next inquiry, and the principle of the plumb-line was worked out. The globe was used to show how the plumb-line appeared with relation to it, and it was found that "right angles to the surface" would describe it. "Up" was then defined as away from the center, and "down" as toward the center. This was connected with the study of weights, and gravitation was defined by the children as a force pulling toward the center of the earth. Weight represented the strength of this pull on the substance. "But hot air goes up" was brought up immediately as a contradiction of the law of gravitation. After discussion and experimentation it was concluded that those things that are heavier, such as cold air, force others, such as hot air, out of their way. Liquids, which move easily, are pushed aside by moving air or by liquids of greater density. The children were helped to relate this fact to the currents of air and water on the earth and to develop something of a conception of air pressure. They were reminded of the weight of still air and their frequent experience of leaning against a strong wind.

Gravitation was taken up from different points of view. The earth as a whole was compared with a magnet. The attraction of all things toward the center of the earth was defined as due to gravitation, and the effect is weight. A barometric tube was examined to show that air has weight, and that its pressure is its attraction to the earth by gravitation. Some of the children seemed to doubt that it was air that supported the mercury in the tube. They were allowed to experiment. A small tube was exhausted by filling one side of a "U" tube with mercury. The end was then sealed and the mercury allowed to flow out at the open end until the pressure in the pan sustained the weight in the closed tube. They were told that mercury was about fourteen times as heavy as water and asked to calculate the height of a column of water that could be supported by air. A water wheel was discussed and its use seen to depend upon the weight of water and the weight referred to as the attraction of gravitation.

One year the children made a large map as an aid to story-telling. The Mediterranean Sea was painted in blue enamel on the bottom of a galvanized iron pan. The surrounding countries were then built up in plaster of Paris, papier-mâche, and putty, and were covered with enamel paint in shades of brown and green to distinguish the mountains from the plains. The sea was filled with water, and each trader loaded his boat with merchandise and sailed it to the place where he expected to trade. Each captain must know his country and something of its people. As a search for tin took these Phoenician sailors as far as England, the development of navigation was discussed so far as the interest and the ingenuity of the children seemed to make it worth while.

In the shop, a rude boat was made. The principle of how to overcome friction as much as possible by a pointed bow and stern was worked out, and the boat contrasted with the flat one made the year before by burning a dugout. The question of how a sail worked, especially in sailing against the wind, was solved. In the science laboratory the constructive imagination of the children was stimulated to suggest ways in which the difficulties of these first wanderers might be overcome. They saw that keeping an accurate record of a route for others involved all the difficulties of map making by observation and instruments and the problem of how to secure a record of distance traveled on the sea. For the latter the children first suggested anchoring a buoy to which a string was attached which could be measured on the way back. From this they were led to the idea of measuring space by rate of speed and then to the idea of *logs* and *knots* as indicating the number of leagues traveled per hour by a sailing vessel. Sounding, as a means of finding the right depth of water, introduced the fathom or the full stretch of a man's arms.

In one year under another teacher the study [4] included a migration (by the class) to Greece, where a highly different civilization from the Phoenician was in progress. Here, the agricultural conditions and peasant life were described as given by Hesiod in *Words and Days*. The relation of the mountainous character of Greece to the individual development of states

---

[4] *University Record*, Vol. III, No. 32, Nov. 4, 1898, p. 201. Teacher, Katherine Camp.

was noted. The early Cretan civilization also holds possibilities to show the growth of early communal and political life. In contrast to the dynamic character of this and the early Greek civilization, the Chaldean, Assyrian, and the Egyptian, while containing many possibilities, were by reason of natural geographic situation too static in character to make the story of the entire human race continuous and swiftly-moving enough to hold the attention and interest of this age.

The constructive work of the group was in accord with the many activities of the historical drama they were reconstructing. In his study and reproduction of typical industries or occupations, constant use was made of the child's power to initiate, to take crude material, and to find, as the early peoples did, the way and the means of fashioning needed results. He became familiar with the typical forms of all materials used by or about him, wood before it is dressed into lumber, ores, or stones, wool, and food. In carrying out some industrial process, chosen for its interest to the children and its typical social nature, general ideas of the relation of heat to the solid, liquid, and gaseous state of matter were developed. Crystallization and the beginning of the study of combustion, because of the necessity for its control, were carried into the form of questions to be answered by definite experiments. From this time on, the child can realize that an experiment is a definite question, the answer to which is to be used in the process out of which it arose. Science, therefore, for this group was connected rather than differentiated. It was taken up as involved in the study of cooking, or of history, and not as a subject by itself. In cooking, the child learned to recognize food in its natural forms, to classify these roughly as to plant or animal, or as to their nature as part of the plant—root, stem, fruit, or seed. In history, as he journeyed with his chosen explorers, he was helped to observe how life—plant, animal, and human—has adapted itself to climate, to soil, and to physiographical structure; he sees what part the large physical forces and processes have played and are playing in the evolution of the globe, and how they were and are related to the problems of navigation and of commerce and have been used to solve these problems.

THE STUDY OF WORLD TRAVELERS

Chronologically, there is an impossible gulf between the early Phoenician explorers and the world travelers who first brought the whole round world into ken. Psychologically, however, the child passes swiftly across the gulf of time on the wings of his imagination. Eager to get on in the fascinating story of discovery, he accepts brief outlines of the intervening years as a base for his thinking and finds it easy to go with Marco Polo on his voyage of world discovery to the East, with Prince Henry of Portugal to the coast of Africa, or with the Spaniards to America.[5]

The starting point again varied with the interest of the children and grew out of their class discussion. Sometimes incidents in the life of an explorer were told or read by them. As a beginning of the study of Prince Henry of Portugal, the children were asked to pick out on the globe the largest masses of land. As each child decided on what he thought was a continent (the word was given to them), he wrote its name on the board. In this way they located the six continents and then agreed on a definition of a continent, incidentally defining an island and an isthmus in the process of discussion.

The question was then asked if any child knew which were the first parts of the globe to be explored and inhabited. Most of the children agreed on Europe or Asia by eliminating North and South America and Africa. Those who had studied the Phoenician civilization were the first to develop this idea and pointed out the region around the Mediterranean which had been explored and settled. They looked at the curious map of the early cartographers, showing strange animals in the unknown regions and the encircling, whirling sea which was supposed to surround everything. These and other early notions

---

[5] In some years this was followed by Magellan, Sir Francis Drake, and Captain Cook. Books used by the teacher for biographic material were: C. K. Adams, *Christopher Columbus;* Geo. M. Towle, *Magellan,* Hezekiah Butterworth, *The Story of Magellan;* Geo. M. Towle, *Drake the Sea King and Prince Henry the Navigator;* Captain Cook's description of his voyages; Edward R. Shaw, *Discoveries and Explorers;* and Daniel Defoe, *Robinson Crusoe.*

of the form of the world interested them and gave them something of a feeling of superiority or at least confidence in their own vantage point of superior knowledge.

The limits of Prince Henry's route were pointed out on the map—his observatory at Sagres in Spain, and India. Selected anecdotes to show his desire to find his way to India around Africa gave the children a sympathetic understanding of his motives. They then speculated on how he would go about it. Most of them wanted him to go through the Mediterranean Sea and Suez Canal, finding the names of seas and countries as they pointed out the way.

Digression was made here to tell the story of the hostility of the Moors to the Christians, the lands held by each, and the efforts the Christians had made to recover Jerusalem. The effect of the Crusades in making known to Western countries the rich products of the East was pointed out.

Some of the children thought Prince Henry might build a ship like Nansen's, and this led back to the kind of ships that were used in that day and the few instruments available for guidance at sea. Some of the children had dwelt enough on Nansen's thought in arranging for his voyage to see that study and planning were desirable. They could therefore understand why Prince Henry built an observatory where he gathered men for study on the problems of better instruments and methods of recording. This brought up the subject of map making, and each child was asked to bring in a map showing how he came from his home to the school. These maps, finally made by all the children, showed a great difference in accuracy. Only one child thought of representing the distance by a scale. The experience, however, made them appreciate to some degree the series of maps in *Henry the Navigator* by C. R. Beazley, which well illustrate the evolution of map making. The children were then given a certain amount of detailed instruction in map drawing. This was only enough to meet the needs of the moment. At the same time the shop director, the art teacher, or the special number teacher also coöperated by developing to some degree beginning notions of ratio, proportion, and symmetry.

The length of time spent in preparation was dwelt upon in order to impress upon the children the meagerness of equipment and knowledge that handicapped these earliest explorers. The slowness of the actual start was explained by a description of the strong northeast trade-winds and the ocean currents they would encounter on the west coast of Portugal. The belief that if one went far south he would find that the sea was boiling, that men would turn black, and if they got caught in a whirling current they would never return, was used to begin an investigation of the larger physical forces and relations of the earth. They took up the reason for wind and water currents starting near the equator and followed them to the poles to see how and where they would affect travelers. The value of lines of latitude was appreciated when the effect of winds and currents upon the ship was understood. The method of locating lines of latitude was worked out, first by finding the number of degrees in any circle, then in a semicircle, a quarter, etc. This was done geometrically. The children also took up the use of longitude in reckoning time. They made compasses by magnetizing sewing needles and suspending them by silk threads in a box on which the points were marked. The attraction of a magnet and the fact that like poles repel and opposite attract were noted while working with the magnet.

Most of the children thought that when Prince Henry's men landed anywhere in Africa they would meet with negroes and were surprised to find that this was not the case, that the black people were south of the point reached. Many difficulties were met in passing the dangerous coast of Cape Mogador because currents from both the north and the south meet here. It was only because one captain was brave enough to venture far out to sea where the water was more smooth that he was able to pass the point. The others followed and thus the explorations were continued.

An account of the capture of some of the natives followed. The children's own ideas of what could be done with these prisoners were elicited, as this was the beginning of slavery and the slave trade. They were told of Prince Henry's desire to make them Christians and how the children were often adopted, of the early attempt to teach the adults trades and its failure because their ineptitude made them unfit for any but the most laborious work. The children also noted what might be expected in the way of trade with the natives. Certain periods each week were given to special study of various forms of communication and expression, in particular, that of writing the records of their journey or of collateral reading. This "journal" was at first dictated to the teacher by the whole class and agreement reached as to its form. The hard words were put on the board where they could be found when needed, and the children really enjoyed the writing and worked hard, but without conscious effort. At one time, one or two could not form certain letters, and when the piece of work was done, time was spent in practice to attain better skill in the mechanics of writing. Parts of several periods were given to number work. This was concerned with reckoning the log-book of their voyages and computing the total distance traveled in a certain number of days. In this process individual problems and tasks were discovered, as, for example, certain children of the group could not add by threes up to thirty-six.

Much time was given to the making of individual relief maps or to the sand-box picture of the physical features of the country being discovered. Discussions were resumed as to why Prince Henry's expedition did not get into the interior of Africa. Two were emphasized—the lack of navigable rivers, and the desire to pursue the discoveries by sea. Mountains were picked out on a small paper relief map, and the effects of these on the climate of this country along the coast was talked about. Eventually the desert of Sahara was explained to the children's satisfaction. As a good deal of experimentation was necessary to explain the causes of climate and the various and characteristic forms of life of the different zones, the science work of this group took on the nature of an introduction to physiography. To understand how heat affects climate, they investigated, with the aid of a taper, the currents of air in the room. They found the cold current from the windows sinking to the floor and the warm air from the register rising to the ceiling. From this they were led to see the effect of the heat of the sun's rays in the equatorial zone in producing the trade-winds. They first described the direction of these winds if the earth were standing still, then the direction because of its revolutions. With a thermometer, they found the temperature of water and of sand in the room. They then heated the water and sand over the same gas flame and noted that while the water soon had the same temperature near the source of heat and at the surface, there was a great difference in the sand, that at the bottom becoming very hot and that at the top showing only a slight change. From this experiment they drew inferences as to the amount of heat absorbed by land and water and the ease with which each would give up its heat and the resulting effect on climate. The motions of the earth about the sun were discussed in order to understand the changes of season and the contrasts in climate which the explorers met. The points dwelt upon here were the demonstration of centrifugal and centripetal forces and the inclination of the earth's axis. A star was placed on the blackboard on the north side of the room, a Bunsen burner was used as the sun and a ball as the earth; and the children were asked to show the rotary and revolutionary motions and to explain the effect on climate. The children drew diagrams on paper to show these motions, and then watched the Tellurian to see especially in different continents how far north and how far south the sun was vertical and at what times of year.

Trade beginnings between the Europeans and the Africans were then taken up. Connection again was made with the familiar, past trading experiences of the Phoenician sailors and its helpful results, and they were reminded of the glowing account of the riches of India brought back to Europe by the survivors of the Crusades. The possible and probable routes by land were worked out: that across the Suez and through North Africa was studied in detail with special reference to desert travel. A few pictures of deserts and camels helped out. The group listened with interest to stories of Egypt and the ancient monuments still to be seen. This was review to some, but new to more than half the children. The fact that deserts surrounded the valley of the Nile was pointed out as the reason that the culture of the Egyptians had not spread among the native Africans. The connection of Egypt with the story of Moses and Joseph was reviewed. Space will not permit the continuation of this voyage, of the slow advance along the coast until Diaz finally rounded the cape and made the discovery of a route to India.

The children also followed Livingstone in his trip up the Zambezi, read selected portions of his diary on the character of the community and of the plant, animal, and human life. The dramatic story of Stanley's search for Livingstone, their meeting, and the illness and death of Livingstone, faithfully attended to the end by his native attendants, concluded this biographical tale of exploration. Far away Africa grew real for it also was the home of men. The study of the physical setting —rivers, mountains, plains, the jungle and its plant and animal inhabitants—took on human significance because of their relation to the journeys of a man. Livingstone's motives, springing from desire to stop the slave traffic, to establish trade relations with the natives, to extend Christianity, and to add to geographical knowledge, became the qualities that made him a leader, a missionary of better ways to live, a discoverer of new frontiers. These, together with his devotion and his zeal, stood out concretely in his deeds of bravery and sacrifice. The spirit of children of this age is in tune with adventure. They thrill to its dangers; they understand something of the satisfying fervor that attends heroic effort.

Records of their work were faithfully kept. For the most part these were dictated, but a regular period was now set aside in which each child wrote his own account of Prince Henry. Many words were misspelled, even though they had been put on the board and the children had been able to look at them when writing. These were such words as *world, because, boat, about, built,* etc. A new list of the words which gave trouble was again placed on the board by children who volunteered. This was corrected, and the whole list of twelve was dictated to them, making the third time of writing. Even then, none of the children got all right; two or three were unable to write a third of them. In spite of the necessity of repeated effort, the children showed a good deal of interest in writing and even volunteered to take things home and copy or finish them. It may not be inappropriate to emphasize the importance of recording such observations as these. They are the straws that indicated that there is a time and a place for the practice of skills, a period when such necessary drill is not distasteful to children, when they see its logical necessity and crave facility of expression that it gives.

THE STUDY OF COLUMBUS

With the beginning of the spring quarter the children of this group began the story of Columbus' journeys, resulting in the discovery of the American continent. The origin and motives that actuated Prince Henry's discoveries were reviewed and included the accomplishments of his undertaking. The children were asked to suggest what led people to question the idea that the world was flat. To the reasons they gave was added the discovery of the reason for an eclipse of the moon. The nature of this was made plain with object and globe. All the children seemed to know that the earth goes around the sun, but very few knew of the revolution of the moon.

Where and how Columbus lived as a boy and something of the geography of Genoa was studied. The nature and names of land forms, such as a peninsula and isthmus, a harbor and a cape, were discussed and were added to the children's vocabulary. The children mentioned what they thought would be of most interest to a boy who lived in the town of Genoa in those days. They compared his liking for the wharves and sailors to that of Robinson Crusoe.[6] They told their ideas of what he would learn at school, talked a little of why he learned Latin,

---

[6] The collateral reading matter for some time had been the story of Robinson Crusoe. "Only two of the children in this group have difficulty in reading—one who cannot read at all, and one who is gaining, but very slowly. In writing, the same two children have difficulty. When this work was done from 11:30–12, they were often almost incapable of doing any thinking. When this fatigue was general and pronounced, the daily lesson in reading or writing was put aside, and a story was read to them. This rested them and had an additional value of reënabling the children to think and feel as a group in a constructive way."

and whether he would be likely to follow his father's trade, that of a wool comber. Some of the new children had had no experience with the processes of preparing wool. This was carefully explained to them by the other children. The first sea voyage Columbus made at the age of fourteen was taken up, and the limited geographical knowledge of this time was described. They recalled that Prince Henry's explorers had gone far down the African coast the year that Prince Henry had died and, from the base of this familiar fact, were able to surmise that the early voyage of Columbus was probably only in the Mediterranean. They learned of his interest in navigation, of his careful collecting of books and charts, of his study, of his inheritance of the maps and papers from his wife's father who was a captain under Prince Henry, and of his final determination to seek means to prove that the world could be circumnavigated. This was supplemented by further detailed study of Columbus' birthplace.[7]

The children named the countries whose people might have been seen at Genoa in Columbus' time. This number was compared with that possible to be seen by the children in Chicago. Chicago was compared with Genoa as a town to which ships come, and the differences of present experience from that of Columbus' day were noted. The children were told that Columbus thought the world was 14,000 miles around, but that it is really 25,000. They were asked to find out how much greater it is than Columbus thought it was. They also determined how long it would take to go around it if one could go at the rate of 5,000 miles a day, and at other rates. H. volunteered that he knew "the earth is 8,000 miles through from *Alice in Wonderland.*" The children were asked, "If you knew the distance of the circumference, how could you find the distance through the earth?" Several of the children thought it would be half the distance round and measured it to find their error. They then measured different circles to get an idea of the relation of the diameter to the circumference. None of them seemed able to make the generalization, but apparently under-

---

[7] A present study of Columbus might find some of this material labeled apocryphal.

stood the ratio when it was given them. A certain amount of time was given each week to writing a record of Columbus for their books.[8] The facts which appealed to them as worth recording were those which were, to some extent, either within their experience or were of a sensational character. In the story of the boyhood of Columbus, all the children remembered that on one occasion he was sent on an errand and stayed all day, playing on the wharves. The places he would probably visit in his first trip around the Mediterranean had little interest, but the statement that once in a fight with a pirate vessel, both ships caught on fire and Columbus sprang overboard with an oar and swam six miles to shore was remembered and thought important enough to be recorded.

It took some time for the children to realize what a long and difficult task it was for Columbus to secure the help he needed. These children had an idea in common with many adults that Columbus merely presented his case to the queen, and she pledged her jewels to have the plan carried out. In order that they might realize the real difficulty in getting support for a new idea, emphasis was laid upon his repeated attempts, at the court of the King of Portugal, at Genoa, and for seven long years in Spain, all of which took fourteen years of his life. This elicited from the children expressions of great sympathy. They then tried to imagine in what form help could come. Perhaps some of the money came direct from the King and Queen, and two of the ships were levied from a town.

The group followed Columbus' first voyage in some detail. An account of the departure was read to them, and the general direction they took through the Sargasso Sea was followed on the map. The story included the discontent of the sailors, their alarm at finding that the wind blew constantly from the east and in the belt of the trade. They learned of Columbus' fear lest they might be missing Japan by sailing too far north and

---

[8] These books were started the previous fall and contained their records of the voyages of Prince Henry of Portugal and of Livingstone. They were in printed form. The printing was done by older groups on the school press. The fact that their own story of Columbus was to be included in this book added incentive to the keeping of the record. It also helped to keep up the needed emphasis on writing during the quarter.

the consequent shifting of their course to the southwest, which took them among the Bahamas instead of to Florida. The children gained some idea of how the speed of a vessel was estimated in knots, and how Columbus himself always took the speed on this voyage to let the sailors think they had come less far than was really the case. Otherwise they would have become discouraged and insisted upon an immediate return. On reading that they "shifted two points to the starboard," one of the children who had been on a sailing vessel drew a sort of diagram on the board to show the others what was meant. The map was followed very closely in this voyage, both on one such as Columbus was supposed to have had and also on a modern map. The children made out the direction Columbus was sailing at every step up to his landing at one of the Bahamas and later to Cuba and along its coast. This was charted from day to day from observations of latitude and longitude.

His return landing near Lisbon, in Portugal, because of the severity of the storm was related, and the children suggested that he would send a messenger to the King of Spain telling him of his arrival. The route was traced by which Columbus would then go to Palos where he had started, and up to the King at Barcelona. Bayonne was found where Captain Pinzon landed with the *Pinta*. The children were told of this captain's feeling that Columbus was lost and of his attempt to take to himself the glory of the new discoveries and of his message concerning this to the King. In order to see how the moral side of this action appeared to the children, they were asked what they thought Pinzon would do when he landed. They suggested that he would send a message to the King telling him that he had returned and that Columbus was lost. When told of his real action, they considered it "mean." Some suggested heavy punishments, some light because he had been of service in the beginning. A description of the reception given Columbus by the King was then read to them from *The Makers of America*.

The course continued with the study of Columbus' second voyage. At a suggestion the children proposed writing and staging a play of Columbus' life. This meant an unpremeditated (by them) and systematic review of the work done. A bright interest lit up the old material and gave a new motive for a fresh attack. Under this renewed inspiration it was possible to correct many false impressions and to emphasize without undue effort the attainment of necessary skills in the construction of many types of the communicative and expressive arts. It also did much to help the children review and evaluate the significant events of Columbus' life and of that period of history.

The latter weeks of the quarter and of the year were spent on the story of Balboa. The series was finally rounded out by the voyage of Magellan. As a start for this, the children surmised a way for his voyage to the Pacific, of which he had heard from Balboa. They suggested that he would look for a waterway through the land which he had found. Some of them thought this would be a river, and discussed whether the way between two oceans would be fresh water or salt. They were told of the discovery of the Straits and of Magellan's determination, when he found himself in the Pacific, to circumnavigate the globe. The children from previous study knew that he must expect to meet air and water currents near the equator, and that the calm would have to be endured. They were told of the distress from the lack of food and water that did occur and of the arrival at the Philippines where Magellan was killed. They were reminded at this point of Prince Henry of Portugal's explorations, that he had gone around Africa and found India and that the Portuguese were, in Magellan's time, engaged in making settlements on the coast of India. The Edict of the Pope at that time, was also recalled, by which he divided the world giving the east half to Portugal and the west to Spain. The story was continued until finally the home-seeking ships rounded Africa and returned to Spain, and made the exciting discovery that a day in time had been lost. The last period was spent in talking over what they had studied during the year and in a character comparison of the men.

The group teacher [9] at the close of the year's record comments as follows:

---

[9] Laura L. Runyon.

The different spirit of the two sections, *a* and *b* of this group has been interesting. *a* was made up of children of such decided personality that the spirit of the group was conflicting and critical. The only time when a semblance of coöperative spirit ruled was in play. In group *b*, on the other hand, a congenial spirit ruled with the result that they progressed faster and accomplished far more than Section *a*. I have been impressed with the way in which the adventurous spirit has grown in this class during the year. They seem to have gained a vivid image of sea conditions, of tropical lands and natives, of possible adventures on sea and land, and an awakened interest in recognizing differences between what they know of their own environs and the new images resulting from the imaginative study of going out by sea into different climates and conditions

When they take up a new country, it might be of value for the children to taste the native fruits and products and attempt the manufacture of certain products, such as the making of rubber from the caoutchouc, or chocolate from the cocoa bean. This would make the work more permanent and valuable; would serve to keep in mind the true motive of most explorers, the wealth to be acquired for an individual or a country; would help to a better understanding of the contact between the civilized and uncivilized, and the results of that contact; and would give a meaning to the search for short land waterways in and through a country. It would also seem a wise plan another year, that early in the fall the children be sent, in school time, singly or in twos, on short exploring trips, and be required to report on their discoveries. The report should include a map of directions as well as the things seen.

From the point of view of getting a rational idea of the explorers and their aims, the work of this year has been very satisfactory. The children seem to have a fairly correct idea of what made Columbus and the other explorers great, and on the other hand, to recognize that some of their deeds were not commendable. They also seem able to contrast their own times with those of the men they study, and also to compare different countries.

CORRELATED ACTIVITIES

A hasty reading of this account of the activities of Group V in its historical story form may give an impression of a very academic school. The balance of this group's work was so arranged, however, that there was plenty of time for activities which engaged the whole body as well as minds and hands, eyes and ears. The children were on the playground and excursions, in the art and textile studios, in the kitchen-laboratory, in assembly with the rest of the children, back and forth in a round of natural and highly correlated social living.

As heretofore, the number work was largely incidental to the carpentry, cooking, sewing, and science. The children formulated their own problems involving multiplication and subtraction, or measurement of surfaces. The reading and writing was, for the most part, of their own records. In art, the subjects for representation were those of their history, done on the sand-table, in clay, colored chalk, charcoal, and water-color. The scenes and backdrops for their play, especially the Columbus drama, were done by the children. The aim was self-expression and more skill in visual observation.

In their music the children were given note-books with lines for writing music, and began this year to make copies of the songs they had composed. The key in which the song was to be written was determined from the piano, then the time was noted from what is called the "strong pulses" and was indicated by putting a bar before each in writing the notes. Last of all, the stems of the notes were marked, designating the time assigned to each. In the shop work also, emphasis was placed on getting the child's idea constructed and comparatively little was placed upon technique or finish. Instruction was given in the first principles of machines and in handling the materials such as lumber, reeds, cane, or bamboo, and in making the articles necessary to illustrate their history or for use in their experimental work. Cooking, as always fitted into the program of the weekly luncheon, and emphasizing an experimental study of the proteins of eggs, meat, or milk.

SUMMARY

Certain educational implications of both the subject-matter and method of the study of this year seem worthy of emphasis. The conditions for learning, and, therefore, for thinking, were well set up. For each child of the group the whole experience was inherently personal enough to stimulate and direct his observation to the connections involved. It led him to inference and then to its testing. As he followed his chosen explorer in the various laps of his voyage, when problems arose, the child was stimulated to forecast possible results—things *to* do. This entailed some inventiveness, for he must jump in thought from the known to the unknown, from the old to the new. Such imaginative forecasting was for that child creative thinking. It had the quality of original research. It fulfilled the essentials of true reflection. These essentials are also those of scientific method in all research whether of the kindergarten or of the scientific laboratory.[10] *"They are first, that the pupil (or research worker) have a genuine situation of experience—that there be a continuous activity in which he is interested for its own sake; secondly, that a genuine problem develop within this situation as a stimulus to thought; third, that he possess the information and make the observations needed to deal with it; fourth, that suggested solutions occur to him which he shall be responsible for developing in an orderly way; fifth, that he have opportunity and occasion to test his ideas by application, to make their meaning clear, and to discover for himself their validity!"*

---

10 John Dewey, *Democracy and Education* (New York, The Macmillan Co., 1916), p. 192.

CHAPTER VIII

LOCAL HISTORY

GROUP VI (AGE NINE)

Two years of experimentation with the school's curriculum demonstrated that there are dominant interests and attitudes which characterize definite stages in a child's development. These stages are not sharply defined. There are periods of transition when one merges into the next. The first of these stages is one in which children are largely occupied with direct social and outgoing kinds of action, with a progressive increase in the complexity of work undertaken and responsibilities assumed. At about eight years of age they are ready for and feel the need of getting skill in the use of tools and knowledge of the rules and techniques of work. While the children in Group V exhibited many of these characteristics of the second stage of growth, the year was markedly one of transition. By the time they entered Group VI, however, they were well launched into the second stage.

Some of the important theoretical statements lying behind the work of the school were developed through faculty discussions of the practices of these two groups. In the first stage of growth there is always motor activity, and there is always a story, a drama, an image—a mental whole. But the two are not separate from each other. Acts are not, to the child's consciousness, means for realizing ideas; they are just spontaneous overflow and exhibition. The child's thoughts are not something to be realized; they are the living meaning and value that saturate whatever he does. Hence this is called the play period. The activities of the first four years of the school were based upon the working theory that the child's attitude is predominantly of this sort and that it is premature to force upon him work where there is a separation of means and ends in psychological essence, a divorce of elements, steps and acts from the idea for which they exist. This theory accounts for the relatively slight and incidental attention given to reading, writing, and numbers in the sixth and seventh years and for the attempt to introduce geography and science in a synthetic and living rather than an analytic and morphological way. It was not supposed that conscious relating of means and ends is wholly absent in this period or that in school work there is no need of anticipating the next stage of growth. Even with six-year-old children, consciousness of somewhat remote ends begins, and there is interest in regulating behavior so as to reach results. The change to one of conscious direction of action comes easily and hence earlier in activities with a tangible result, such as making a box to use or cooking cereal for lunch. This working hypothesis of the school by no means blocks out the possibility of greater use of symbols in what might be called free reading and writing during the sixth and seventh years in the form of labels, proper names, and brief records of work, when such efforts by the child do not divert his energies from the more fundamental activities involving the larger muscles. There will always be individual children ahead or behind chronological age, but readiness to read must be determined by the psychological attitude described above, namely, a willingness to work out means for deferred ends. A child who has reached this stage of mental development will see in learning to read, write or figure, means that will often help him reach his desired ends more quickly and efficiently. Too much emphasis cannot be laid upon the fact that undue premium is put upon the ability to learn to read at a certain chronological age. The child who cannot read at seven or eight is considered retarded. The fundamental wrong done young children by the large classes in the public schools has of necessity given rise to endless series of "readers," so-called work books, which are supposed to direct activity on the part of the child. The entertainment plus information motive for reading conduces much to the habit of solitary self-entertainment which ends too often in day-dream-ing instead of guided creative activities, controlled by objective success or failure.

In the Dewey School the active and constructive work for children of six and seven held an immediate appeal as an outlet for energy. It also led on in orderly fashion to the next undertaking and enabled the child to form a habit of working for ends and a method of controlling present activities by a sequence of steps so that they grew into larger ideas and plans. This method of thinking and acting was gradually transferred to the accomplishment of ends more consciously conceived and more remote. In the eighth year, or that of Group V, such transfer was marked. By the ninth, the average child showed an evident dislike of attempting to reach results for which he felt the means at his command were inadequate. For example, he objected to the kind of drawings he had made formerly with delight, apparently because he was beginning to see them as results which appeared crude and even absurd.

From observation and discussion of the early work, three fundamental working principles were formulated. First, growth is gradual; it comes in reading before in writing, and in both before in numbers. This does not mean that the child may not have used numbers with great interest, as distinct from analyzing them and learning the rules for their use. Growth in the use of science comes even after that in numbers. Children of eight or nine were found to be interested in experimental work in science, but not because they conceived a certain problem and regarded the experiment as a way of solving it. They took hold of experimentation as they did of constructive work; it was the active performance of a series of steps; and it was "seeing what happens" that occupied their minds. Second, at the psychological level of six and seven years, children are not yet ready for analysis, for attention to forms and symbols, since interest in technique demands a background of experience. A stretch of positive subject-matter must come first, enlarging and deepening the child's world of imagination and thought until he gradually becomes ready to analyze an experience he has not yet had, to learn rules that have no immediate outlet in action and whose appeal is remote and imaginary. Third, the introduction to technique must come in connection with ends that arise within the child's own experience, real or imagined. It is not enough for the teacher to see the end. The prime psychological necessity is that the child see and feel the end as his end, the need as his need, and thus have an inherent and impelling motive from within for making the analysis and mastering the rules of procedure. The faculty of the school found that these principles could be put into effect only as the formal work was in connection with active, constructive, or expressive activity presenting difficulties and the need of meeting them. The technical exercises were selected from such material. Additional concrete material or occupation supplied opportunities for using the newly acquired power and realizing its value, and the spiral course of the circuit of experience rounded the next ascending curve.

SETTING OF GROUP

Group VI, the nine-year-old children, was divided into two sections on the basis of their previous experience in school. Their headquarters were in a rather inadequate room, but their study of local history and physiography took them into the laboratory of the outdoors. In fact, with this group and those above it, the home room and the group teacher assumed less and less importance because of the growing physical and mental independence of the children. The children were under the direction of one of the history teachers and her assistant.[1] In order to secure more time for practice in reading and writing, the school day was lengthened to include an hour in the afternoon. The year was characterized by the children's growing ability in control and self-direction. They often asked for extra work to do at home, and when they showed a desire to carry on a piece of work alone, they were allowed to carry it to completion independently.

The study of the great explorers and world discoverers the previous year served as a transition in the story of social life

---

[1] Laura Runyon, Margaret Hoblitt.

to the settlement of local adventurers and pioneers. The starting point for the study grew out of discussion. As was customary in their first meetings, the general possibilities for study the coming year were talked over. Thoughts naturally reverted to last year's work, and a quick review was made. The adventures of Phoenician sailors and traders, of the explorations of Marco Polo, Prince Henry, Balboa, Magellan, Captain Cooke, Drake, Nansen, Livingstone, or others who had become familiar figures to the group were passed in rapid review. At the close, emphasis was laid on the English, the Spanish, and French settlements in America. The motives which led to all exploration were discussed. Love of adventure, the lure of El Dorado, and in some cases freedom from oppression were mentioned. Of all these the children decided that the search for a short way to India and her riches was the most powerful.

THE STUDY OF LOCAL HISTORY AND GEOGRAPHY

The group decided they would like to know more about the United States and how it began, and finally agreed that the place where they lived would be a good place to start, that they would like to know how the Chicago they knew had come to be. This had been the teacher's objective; but because it was obtained by means of a group process, the children regarded the plan as their own. Local museums and historic spots were at hand and easy of access. They could even talk with persons whose memories still held something of the fact and flavor of early days. In such a study definite activities of a particular people would be prominent and could be developed according to the children's power to deal with limited and positive fact. In the study, also, they would use what they had thus far gained in understanding of the origins of occupations and the beginnings of social organization outside the family group. From the teacher's point of view, the problem was to introduce the children to new situations requiring constructive action and then help them to analyze, plan, and forecast the various steps which might be taken in working out the problem. In other words it was hoped that when confronted with the new situations of early American frontier life, the children would be interested and stimulated to size them up, calculate the resources of the settlers, and from time to time reformulate the probable solutions and the courses of action taken.[2]

Local history and geography, therefore, in this year were begun with the study of the Northwest and especially of Chicago. This was considered in three stages: (1) the period of the French explorations, (2) Fort Dearborn and the log-cabin age, (3) development of the city of Chicago. In general, for this course in localized history the choice of a locality would be determined by the local environment and experience of both teacher and the group. In this school other experiments than this were made. One group studied Roman history. This was not altogether successful, as it seemed too remote from the present interests and aims of social life. It presented too many abstract problems of a political nature which a child of this age is not interested in and with which he is unable to cope until a later period.

THE PERIOD OF FRENCH EXPLORATION

In the first period the children were told stories of the lives of Marquette and Joliet, La Salle and Tonty, with the reasons and aims which led them into the west, and their routes of travel were traced on maps.

The related geography was the finding of the great lines of travel from the Atlantic through the St. Lawrence and the Great Lakes to the Mississippi and the determination of where forts should be located. In all cases the class first found where the man went and then the later names of the rivers and towns with which he was connected. The antagonism between the English and the French, and the territory claimed by each were

---

[2] "Knowledge of the past is the key to understanding the present. History deals with the past, but this past is the history of the present. An intelligent study of the discovery, explorations, colonization of America, of the pioneer movement westward, of immigration, etc. should be a study of the United States as it is today: of the country we now live in." John Dewey, *Democracy and Education* (New York, The Macmillan Co., 1916), p. 251.

explained. The way was then sought by which the French would enter unprotected territory, and the points where conflicts would arise. The hostility between the Iroquois Indians and the French, the locality of the Five Nations, and the diminished fur trade of the east helped to make plain the route the French fur traders must take to reach the Indians of the western lands. With the occupation of new territory went the necessity for forts. The location of these at points commanding entrances of rivers and portages of the heads of lakes was noted, and the reasons given. Politically, these were strategic points of vantage from which to carry out La Salle's desire to found a new France; commercially, they held the same advantage as points for reaching the fur trade of the West. Father Marquette typified the religious zeal of the times, so that it was possible for the children gradually to become conscious of the various motives which lie back of all exploration and progress.

Beginning with the boyhood of Marquette, as a typical missionary of that period, the general trend of the French explorations in Canada and the Lake regions was traced by means of incidents in his life. The story of the part the fur trader Joliet played, as an explorer, in opening up the West then followed. That of La Salle and Tonty and their various journeys were sketched more briefly.

The records note that there was little freedom of language in the group, but as the work continued, the children developed a great interest in reading and writing, asking to have all new words and important names put on the blackboard to copy. They began to suggest of their own accord the available sources for looking up additional material and spent much time voluntarily finding the meaning and pronunciation of Indian names. It became a pleasurable game to have new and difficult words used in conversation or reading aloud, put upon the board. This growing conscious demand for something hard, something which would last and call out power, efficiency in selection and adaptation of means to end, was a frequently noted characteristic of this age.

FORT DEARBORN AND THE LOG-CABIN AGE

In trying to discover why Fort Dearborn was built, Group VI-*b* had followed with intense interest the story of the George Rogers Clark expedition. At first they could not understand why Clark should think it worth while to make so long and dangerous a journey. They were reminded that the capture of a few forts meant the accession of a large tract of valuable land. One child suggested that perhaps Clark saw it would be more easily won when few people lived there than when it was thickly settled. The return of a pupil who had been absent through the most interesting part of the work was made the occasion for a review. This the children seemed to enjoy more than their first study. There was scarcely a detail which they were not able and eager to tell. They took particular pleasure in relating what a hard time Clark had to take Vincennes and how it actually was accomplished through the persuasion of some friendly Frenchmen without the firing of a gun. After finishing the story of Clark they were anxious to write their own story of the expedition on the blackboard.[3] Each child tried this experiment by himself, the teacher aiding with the spelling. The difficulties of composition became very great, however, and some of those who had been most eager found that they had little to say. As time went on, each week there were two periods of drill in reading and writing. In one the children did individual work; those who were able read by themselves; others wrote sentences from their history on the blackboard; and one child who was behind the rest had the teacher's special attention. The second period was given to blackboard drill in word building by the entire group. On the whole their ambition outran their power of accomplishment to such an extent that it was difficult to hold their interest in the writing.

---

[3] Careful planning was necessary on the part of the teacher in order that the desire of the children to express themselves in writing should not be unduly checked by their lack of skill. When, in her judgment, interest flagged to the point of failure, she usually stepped in with a proposal that she write at their dictation, or in some other way diverted their effort into channels affording a flow more in accord with their desires.

THE DEVELOPMENT OF CHICAGO

The beginnings of localized history, such as that of Chicago, have since been so well worked out in so many places that many phases of this year's work have been omitted, and only those which show how the continuity of the story was maintained are kept. Much time was spent in discussion of the reasons for the choice of the site of Chicago, on its importance as a strategic point in the fur trade as well as the natural meeting place for the North and the South, the East and the West. Its importance politically was brought out by locating the territory of the English who now held Canada, and that of the Spanish, who for a time were holding the west bank of the Mississippi.

During all this detailed study, much time was spent in reading from *Stories of Illinois*. The children were delighted to have a book which they could use by themselves. Several read a good deal at home. This particular book proved a great spur to one child who had been discouraged over his reading and up to this point had insisted that he knew he could not read and did not care to have a book.

A large map of Fort Dearborn had been made by the group, and the interest of the children carried over into the making of small individual maps of the Fort and the surrounding region with which, from constant reference to their book maps, they had become tolerably familiar. One section of the group was much more interested in the map drawing than the other; nearly all were dissatisfied with their first attempt and wished to make a second map. Some volunteered to work on them at home. One period was spent in making an outline of the work of the quarter. This was done by asking the children to suggest the titles for a series of stories on the history of Chicago. By this means a sequential statement of topics was secured rather than the disconnected details which children are prone to offer in such a review.

In a subsequent year, the early settlement of Chicago was given over to a trained science teacher [4] who abridged the dis-

---

[4] Harry O. Gillett.

covery period and introduced other stories of explorers, which brought out the actual geography of the Lake region. This was worked out in a detailed sand-map, by assigning a lake and the adjoining country, or a river and its basis to each child. Natural competition, as well as interest in each other's work, gave the children a much better conception of the relation of different parts of a lake system to each other and of the kind of country bordering on each lake or river, than if they had worked in rotation upon different parts of the country. In the construction of these lakes the teacher discovered many erroneous notions of geography, such as the general idea of a lake as an immense, slow river. They thought the water ought to flow right through the lake and only gradually worked out the notion of a basin holding a large amount of water only a small portion of which, relatively speaking, flows quietly into the next lake at its outlet. The idea of the great importance of the animal life in early times was already theirs, so very little emphasis was put upon the dependence of the pioneers on this source of supply. It was necessary, however, to spend time in developing the idea that the Illinois Indians possessed a great asset in their fertile fields of Indian corn and to bring out the practical point that the two industries of greatest extent and value for the early settlements were farming and fur trading.

The study of the past was finally linked to the present by a discussion of the formation of village government when a charter was granted by the state. The children formulated the various functions of such a city government. They then took up those things which were left to individual initiative and were surprised to find that they far exceeded the others in number. In connection with the organization of the waterworks, they recalled what they had studied about the sources of water and the means of conveying it. Most of them understood the relation of the cribs and the pumping-stations to the present water-supply, but only one or two were able to suggest ways of pumping water with such simple materials as a hollow tube and leather for a piston. The principle of a pump was connected directly with the action of water in the siphons which they used to carry water to and from their sand-table lake and river. Although they seemed at the time to understand the theory of the working of a siphon, it was not until the end of the half year that they were able successfully to fill and operate a rubber tube as a siphon.[5]

One year much of the time for construction work was spent in the building of a model of Fort Dearborn. This gave interest and incentive for the development of skills, in the handling of tools and the use and manipulation of numbers, but proved lacking in movement and too difficult an undertaking for this age. In another year the village of Chicago and its environs were constructed in sand. The first stage-coach route, organized after the completion of the river-bridge, was incorporated. Along this first road the children saw the beginnings of the trade in cattle, wheat, and other food staples, which have since made Chicago a commercial center. In the construction of the sand-map of this locality such points as the formation of a sand-bar at the mouth of the river were made clear. The extreme flatness of the country around Chicago brought out the explanation that the locality is the original bottom of an old lake which had its outlet into the Mississippi through the Des Plaines river, and that the portage over which the early explorers dragged their canoes was a part of the divide upon one side of which water flowed through the Lakes into the St. Lawrence River and the Atlantic Ocean, and on the other side down the Des Plaines and the Illinois Rivers into the Mississippi and the Gulf of Mexico.[6] This work demonstrated to

---

[5] This seems to reënforce the theoretical statement that children of this age are not yet able to apply easily any large generalization or abstraction.

[6] "The reason for the placing of any settlement on the Chicago river at all was developed over and over again without seeming to have much meaning to this group of children, whereas another class had found no difficulty in seeing the logical conclusion. The former group seemed to show less power to invent or reconstruct probable situations or events; and imaginatively to continue a story beyond the point to which discussion had proceeded. They possessed, however, in contrast with the other group, much more skill in written expression and, with the exception of one or two individuals, could, without much effort, rewrite in story-form any interesting part of the actual narrative." Report of Group VI, 1902–1903, Harry O. Gillett.

the children the strategic position that Chicago held geographically, and they were easily helped to suggest a canal to connect
the Chicago River along the old portage with the Des Plaines.
They also suggested ways in which the canal might be paid for,
prophesied the boom that would result from the demand for
cheap land in so promising a place and, with knowledge of
what had happened, anticipated the collapse that would follow the boom. In this the facts learned were regarded merely
as the means for the development of correct judgment.

The importance of Chicago as a commercial center was
viewed from the side of geology by reading and discussing an
article in a current magazine. This was made the starting point
for a somewhat different treatment of the study of geography.
Up to this time this subject had been considered as incidental
and in close connection with the relation of people to a locality. Following the parallel of latitude of Chicago, around the
world, the children located and named all the lands through
which this parallel passed. The zones were then considered in
their relative position to the sun, and the countries in each
zone were learned. In this way they became familiar with the
names of the continents, their relative sizes, climates, and the
oceans separating them.

CORRELATED ACTIVITIES

The question of the means of transportation and of representing it on the sand-map routes led one group to the construction of a typical prairie schooner such as brought the families of the east to Chicago. The work in the textile room received many incentives from this study. The development of
the loom and weaving was studied. Each group worked out
special problems such as finding a way to stretch the warp
strings for regular weaving. One of the children invented a
heddle although he had never seen one, nor so far as could be
discovered, the picture of one. The sewing, like the shop work,
was to supply school needs in the kitchen or sewing room.

Because of lack of space and opportunities, little of the experimentation along the line of pioneer industries which had

been planned was carried out. A number of experiments in constructing the kinds of ovens used in early days proved successful in holding the children's interest and carried over into an understanding of the various principles of draft, choice of material, etc. in the modern furnace and fireplace.

The character of the plant and animal life found by the explorers in the Lake region was constantly emphasized. Almost all the children possessed a large amount of information as to what animals live now or have lived in this region. They knew something of their habits, much more of the uses of their skins, and although a sensational account of fierceness, courage, or the reverse was always told first, an account of the animal and its habits soon followed. The beaver was chosen as an animal for special study because of its importance in the fur trade. The children made a list of all animals belonging to the beaver family and decided that the common characteristic of all was the habit of gnawing. The teeth were examined and their chisel shape noted. The use of the tail was discussed, whether as a trowel in plastering the dam, or as a rudder.

Part of the time given to cooking during this year was spent each week on experimentation with the particular food prepared for the class luncheon. The children investigated the nature of the plant material, both as to its use to the plant and its use for food. This, in the course of the year's work, brought out the functions of roots, stems, and leaves, and the forms in which the plant stored its reserve material, starch, oils, and albumen. The children were given the ordinary tests for starch and for oils. Albumen they identified as something similar to the gluten which they had extracted from wheat. The character and uses of the acid and mineral salts in certain foods were not dealt with experimentally, as the points involved were too difficult for them to grasp.

The program was rounded out by opportunity for expression or representation of ideas in finer forms of activity. The subject-matter sprang out of and was in line with the main idea of the course and took on the color of its general atmosphere. The music was a further study of harmony practice in its recognition and in composition, and the expression of ideas of harmonic phrases. In art, some of the best work of the school grew out of the group's visit to the monument in memory of the Fort Dearborn Massacre. Three children posed as the figures of Mrs. Helm, her Indian assailant, and Black Partridge, the rescuer. Each member of the class also chose a subject from the life of Marquette to do in clay, which was cast in plaster and hung on the studio walls.

The records give evidence of a growing recognition by these children of the possibility and the desirability of obtaining more permanent and objective results than had heretofore satisfied them. Each child had also begun to realize that skill in control of means was necessary to achieve desired ends. The previous vague and fluid unity of his life, when mere play satisfied, was broken up.

Subject-matter was chosen to meet and satisfy the needs and demands of this developing attitude. From an historical point of view it also differentiated the more vague and fluid unity of the race life into typical phases, when individuals and groups of men and women, actuated by various motives, met, conquered, and controlled the specific conditions of frontier life. The child followed in deed and fancy these actual accomplishments of mankind and realized the importance of a command of method and of skills in thought and action. The problem for the teacher was to use selected subject-matter so as to help each child recognize his own needs and secure practical skill and intellectual control of methods of work and inquiry which would enable him to realize results and make contributions to the group. In this way learning and increasing ability were by-products of purposeful, helpful, and self-directed activity. As these particular children felt the need of a better method and more skill in picturing the routes their adventurers traveled, they were given a cursory but helpful study of two or more types of map projection which involved the use of numbers and the tools of measurement. The need for accuracy in navigation was easily understood, and the children were helped to think out an appropriate method to use in making a dead-reckoning. Their rather unusual ability to do this was without doubt due to their unusually varied experience. Again and again it was found that, at this age of development, children are not only willing but anxious to attain facility in writing and number work, in order to carry on a project to a desired conclusion.

They began also to be somewhat self-conscious in art and found free expression most easily in modeling where the material lent itself with fascinating ease to the formulation of an idea. The bas-reliefs of scenes from the life of Marquette were produced by this group. Comments in the records reveal what are perhaps general characteristics of this stage—a tendency to attack big enterprises without sufficient planning and to drop quickly before completion something which proved more difficult than expected. Increasing ability to abstract and to formulate processes made the children impatient of very detailed experimentation, and yet they found such detailed work as printing exceedingly satisfactory.

The additional afternoon hour gave more time, approximately two hours a week, for studying technique in reading, writing, and number work. In the latter the method of a process was worked out, and the rule formulated and used in practice until familiarity gave ease in performance. The balance of added time was given to experimental problems in science, either springing out of or related to cooking or history. These nine-year-old children also spent more time in listening to reading, due to the addition of literature as a separate subject with a special teacher. The English, or literature, had two forms. In one, emphasis was on esthetic appreciation of stories and poems; in the other, help was given in oral expression. German or French was also introduced.

The study of the settlement of the Northwest and of Chicago occupied half of the school year. In discussing the work of the second half year the same group was easily led to feel that a next logical step would be to study the settlement of part of the United States that was unfamiliar to them. A brief review was made of Columbus and other explorers, and the story of the first settlement of white people in America was sketched. The English claim to North America and the story of the papal decree which for a time had compelled England to keep her hands off the continent were retold. The children were then asked to suggest probable motives for American colonization. The desire to find gold was the only reason first suggested, but when the old-time search for a northwest passage was recalled the children thought it probable that this would be an additional argument for settling in America. They were reminded of the hostile relations of England and Spain and of the Spanish trade in America, and they saw that it would be a great advantage for England to have a hold in the new country. One child also suggested that perhaps England had not land enough at home and wanted more. When told of the economic conditions in England due to the growth of the wool industry, they concluded that the farmers driven out of their farms in England ought to come to America and have farms of their own for sheep raising.

THE STUDY OF VIRGINIA

Raleigh's efforts at colonization were taken up.[7] On concluding them, the children decided that the best plan for such future attempts would be the formation of a company to furnish the money. The East India and the Muscovy Companies were touched on in this connection. The children were greatly interested in Captain Barlowe's account of his exploration of the coast of Virginia. In their opinion the best argument for colonization was the opportunity for new homes in this fruitful land. The story of Captain John Smith then followed, and a week was spent on the history of the first year at Jamestown. The children were able to anticipate in large measure the directions given by the London Company with regard to the choice of a site and the precautions with regard to the Indians and other possible enemies. They were surprised that Smith was not chosen for leader and were sure that he would be later on. They condemned the "common kettle" in advance, saying that the men would be even more lazy if that plan were carried out because they would think some one would provide for them whether they worked or not. This expression of opinion

---

[7] Course taught by Margaret Hoblitt.

came from VI-*b*; VI-*a* was inclined at first to think that the "common kettle" would be a good thing. The children felt the value of Smith's early experience and his self-inflicted discipline as a preparation for leadership. In VI-*a* this led to a conversation as to the children's plans for the future. They decided that it was a good thing for a boy to look ahead to the life he expected to lead when a man and prepare for it.

The story of Smith's return to England was discussed briefly and was followed by the administration of Percy, Lord Delaware, and Sir Thomas Dale. The children were surprised to find that even after Delaware had established a new order of things and restored order in the settlement, Percy in his second attempt was unable to enforce the laws and control the colony. They asked whether he had not had the same power which Delaware had possessed, and why, if he had, he did not make as good a governor. They were reminded that in their group they found one child a better leader than another, although the conditions under which they acted and the authority they possessed were the same. They were led to suggest the abolition of the "common kettle" and the establishment of a system of land tenure before they were told of the institution of this same reform by Sir Thomas Dale.

The cultivation of tobacco, the story of its introduction into England by Sir Walter Raleigh, and the growing demand for it there were told. The necessity in Virginia for some development of the country's resources in order to satisfy the expectations of those interested in England entered the discussion. Some time was spent on the administration of Argall and the events which led up to the establishment of representative government in Virginia on the basis of a new charter. The opportunity for a new form of government offered by the revision of the charter was presented, and when asked what kind of government the people of Virginia would choose if they had their own choice, the group proposed that form in which the people themselves could have a voice. They were asked if this meant that all citizens were to vote directly upon the laws that were to be made, but they said, "No, each settlement ought to choose some one to vote for them, just as we do now." The actual plan was then presented, and the coming of Governor Yardley and the first meeting of the assembly described. The children suggested some of the matters which would be probable subjects of legislation; the amount of taxation and the treatment of the Indians were among these.

The study continued with a detailed consideration of the house and life of a Virginia planter and his family, the relations of the colony with the Indians, its subsequent political history, and the changing status of its relations with the mother-country. Many questions were asked with regard to contemporaneous English history. The children were jubilant over the death of James in time to save Virginia from the kind of charter which they felt sure he would have made and agreed that under the new conditions the colony would be more independent than it had been under the Company. They then passed to the period of Bacon's Rebellion, taking up the Navigation Laws, the arbitrary rule of Berkeley, and the Indian troubles as the causes for popular discontent. In Group VI-*a* party feeling ran high, the sentiment of the majority being that the governor was right. The similarity in the character of Bacon's declaration to that of the Declaration of Independence, just a hundred years later, was noted, but the significance of the earlier rebellion seemed to make little impression on the children. At the close of the study a general summary was made by the group and teacher, followed by a review in which the children quizzed each other with considerable rivalry as to who could ask the hardest questions.

THE STUDY OF PLYMOUTH COLONY

The study of the Plymouth Colony was then begun.[8] The children had already learned something of the religious differences in England, and of the religious freedom which the people of Holland had won for themselves. When the story of the Scrooby Congregation was taken up, they were accordingly ready to suggest that the people go to Holland to live

---

[8] Course taught by Georgia F. Bacon.

when they no longer felt safe in England. They also suggested the departure from Holland to America. The question was asked as to how they could obtain the necessary funds, and finally it was suggested that they borrow money and promise to pay back the value of it in timber and anything they could find in America that would be of value to the merchants in England who would lend them the money.

The story continued with the settling of Plymouth. Bradford's account was read to secure a description of the country and the first experience ashore. The children asked what the women did while the men went ashore and were told of the first wash day on Cape Cod. They planned the division of the company into families, allotting the single men to homes with some one else, and asked eagerly for the men with whose names they had already become familiar. They decided also that the first building would have to be a fort and after that a common house for their supplies. In this connection, they expressed the opinion that the idea of having everything in common was a bad one, but it was more likely to succeed here than in Virginia, on account of the difference in the character of the two companies. When asked to plan for the distribution of land so that no one should be favored more than another, they proposed first that the governor make the allotments, and then the best places be set aside and not used at all. This seemed a needless sacrifice and far from solving the problem. At last, one of the children proposed that the Pilgrims draw lots for their plots of land.

The children were asked if they thought people could be found now-a-days who would be willing to endure the hardships which the Pilgrims encountered for the sake of their religion. Some said no, and some said yes. The lad who was on the negative said that "people are too much hothouse plants now-a-days." The others were to support the other side, but failed to do so. They were then told briefly of the "spirit wrestlers" who have come to Canada to find a home where they can be free—or hope to be—to live as they think right, and of Tolstoi's sacrifices for the sake of a principle. In the latter they were much interested, asking many questions.

The usual periodic review was given for the benefit of a long absent member and proved to be the best thing they had yet done. One child who had never before been able to offer anything but detached statements was able to carry the story along without hesitation and with a good grasp both of the general sequence and details. Formulation of what they had done had at last ceased to be unpleasant to them.

Reading was continued from various texts. The children were anxious for more details than could be supplied. Names of people and ships, those who died, and others who were married were among the things eagerly sought after. Among other things the question of the common house was once more discussed. The children had long anticipated the time when the common store would be given up, and were ready for the trial of an individual allotment of land in order to encourage better effort in the trying times of 1624. They said they thought that men would work better if they had a chance to keep the results of the work themselves, and that there would be some who would not work at all if they could live without it.

DEVELOPMENT OF THE TOOLS OF EXPRESSION

A period was given to finishing their written stories and one to reading them aloud. This exercise gave an opportunity for a review of the work on the Plymouth Colony in which the children were asked questions suggested by their papers. Later each child chose some topic from the story of the Pilgrims. One began at the beginning; another chose the first encounter; and some could not choose without help. The papers were much better than those that they had composed as a group by dictating to the teacher and then copying from the blackboard. The children worked much more industriously, tired of their work less quickly, and showed greater freedom of expression. The work was continued through the second period at their own request, and one period was given to spelling a list of words which they had needed in their writing.

Subsequent periods were spent in reading aloud the story of William Blackstone and the coming of the Puritans from *Pil-*

grims and Puritans. A list in writing was made of the principal events of this period of history, with the dates. This was the result of a discussion in which some of the children had shown rather hazy notions of the sequence of events, and they took great interest in straightening things out and, when the papers were finished, declared that they must be taken care of, for they "were worth saving."

The story of the coming of the Puritans, introduced a discussion of the settlements made by Roger Williams, Thomas Hooker, and others who found the rule of the Puritans too oppressive. The departure of Blackstone in order to free himself from the "Lord Brethren" was the starting point of the discussion. The children were divided as to the amount of religious liberty which ought to have been allowed. One said that the Puritans had a right to any plan they chose and ought to be allowed to make church membership a condition of citizenship if that seemed the right thing to do. There was plenty of room, so that those who did not agree to this could find another place and live in their own way. The same question came up again in connection with the story of Roger Williams. There was also a similar division with regard to his criticism of the settlers for dispossessing the Indians of their land. One said that there was room enough for the Indians and the white people too, and that the Indians did not care very much where they lived anyway—this inference being drawn from the fact that they were in the habit of roaming from place to place. It was, therefore, all right for the white people to take all the land they wanted, if they did not drive the Indians from land which they were actually occupying. The children saw that the religious intolerance of the earlier settlements was an aid to the growth of the new country, since there would be less reason for people to scatter if the terms on which they were admitted to the older settlements had been less severe. Before leaving the history of the New England colonies, the children worked out the formation of the Federation of '43, with the causes which led to it, its advantages, and its weaknesses.

The children read accounts of the early settlement in New York. They were told something of the Muscovy and the United

States India Companies, saw the opportunities for trade opened up by Hudson's discovery, and were led to suggest a West India Company. *Young Puritans of Old Hadley,* was read aloud. The book proved rather too difficult for the children to read by themselves. They later proceeded to work out the probable course of events in the settlement of New York.

A study of the physiography and geography of the coast colonies was carried on with the history study and was similar to the study of the environs of Chicago. It was supplemented by experiments in plant physiology. The topography of Virginia furnished topics for the study of the formation of a river system and of a mountain-range and was also considered in relation to the gradually developing social life of Virginia. At the beginning of the study an attempt was made to get the children to eliminate, one by one, the conveniences of civilization with which they were familiar until they began to realize how it would seem to live in America without a single railroad, steamboat, or road of any kind except Indian trails and rivers; to be dependent upon England for every yard of cloth not brought with them, for salt, pepper, sugar, vinegar, tea, coffee, and so on; to have no fuel except wood, no means of lighting a fire except flint, no oil for lamps, no lumber but hand-hewn logs. When the children had sufficiently imagined the conditions of pioneer life, they were able to picture the English settlement of Virginia, as they had that of Chicago, in its physical setting and could then reconstruct more easily the typical industries that would occupy the people of each colony. As they followed the development and progress made in these activities, the growing organization of social life became more clear.

In their study of the probable equipment of a colonial house the use of pewter dishes was mentioned. In response to a very evident and real curiosity an experiment was arranged to help them discover for themselves the constituency of pewter. When the children found that it would mark paper, they at first pronounced it lead with which they had worked the year before. The next test suggested was the melting point. They found this to be higher than that of lead. It was then suggested that it must be mixed with some harder metal, such as zinc; and zinc and lead were fused, cooled, and melted again to determine the time required to melt a given quantity. While the melting point of zinc or lead alone was low, when combined it was found to be high. It was then suggested that tin be added to see its effect upon the combination. Zinc, lead, and tin were then fused, and the combination found to be nearer that of pewter. Bismuth brought the alloy still nearer. The children were then told that sometimes antimony and copper were also added and were given the approximate formula that was used in colonial times: 80 per cent tin, 7 per cent antimony, 2 per cent copper, 2 per cent bismuth, 9 per cent lead. The pewter made was pressed into thin sheets between smoked pieces of zinc and then hammered into miniature dishes. While working with the different metals, many questions were asked and answered concerning tests for various metals and methods of preparing them for use. Other work in science was divided between the actual work of planting and caring for gardens and the experiments connected with an understanding of plant life.

In art work the children were able to express their ideas in clay and were given their first instruction in modeling large pieces. Their models of the Baryé lion and tiger were each fourteen inches in length and were cast in plaster of Paris when finished. The responsibility of keeping the clay moist between lessons was placed upon the children, and their interest in making good reproductions kept up to the end. As these pieces were large and took a good deal of time, they were occasionally laid aside for a lesson in sketching or designing.

Some of the children in this group were tone-deaf and received individual instruction in music. It was found that they could most easily recognize and imitate the G above middle C, and could then go to B or D above. These notes were then combined in the time of a trumpet or tally-ho call. From 'these notes the more difficult intervals were taken up. Considerable success attended this method, and the children who before had not beeen interested in the composition of class songs or class music were able to help as well as enjoy.

Physical culture for this group was, in pleasant weather, outdoor games under the direction of the instructor and, at other times, indoor drills. Special attention was paid to planning movements and acquiring quick perceptions.[9]

In this year a beginning was made in differentiation of studies. In addition, therefore, to the number problems that arose in connection with other subjects, a special time was given to drill in number work. In connection with cooking, problems arose which could be solved by actual measurement. For example: if one-fourth of a cup of wheatena (the right amount for one person) requires one-fourth of a cup of water, how much cereal and how much water will be needed to cook cereal for six (or more) children? The child to whom the duty of cooking the cereal was given could measure the quantities, but this was easily seen to be a tedious process, so the question of finding a quicker way was taken up in a separate hour. The process used was that of adding small units and then grouping them in larger ones, as the children had not studied multiplication or division. The addition was also seen to be a slow way, and the shorter process of multiplication was explained.

SUMMARY

Group VI had now completed their sixth year of the study of social life as mirrored in its occupations. The first three years their interests had been in persons—their actions and the products of their activity. The view of society had been a static one. It had not been actively concerned with how these had come to be, although curiosity had been gradually awakening. The fourth year's work centered in the study of early civilizations and the gradual development of social life through discovery and invention. In this year the children also began to see in a dim way that the physical world and all its life are the result of the evolutionary process. In the fifth year, by following a few of the great migrations and explorations that opened up the continents of the world, they built up an idea of the world as a whole, both racially and geographically. In their imaginary travels they acquired some knowledge of the place

---

[9] *Elementary School Record*, October, 1900.

of the earth in the universe and its large physical forces and of the means that man has used to meet or employ them. They then settled down to the study of a specific people in a specific way and learned how, through the agency of individuals, groups of persons have subdued the untoward elements of their physical environments and have utilized the favorable ones. By a more or less differentiated study of the physical setting (including its biological aspect) they came to realize something of the effect of environment upon the occupations of a group of people, and the resultant type of the organization and character of social life.[10] At the same time, through an ever greater participation in the general social activities of the school (printing, assembly, outdoor and indoor games), these children consciously or unconsciously utilized their subject-matter in their present community living.

---

[10] Georgia F. Bacon, "History," *Elementary School Record,* November, 1900. This section contains the substance of the above article.

CHAPTER IX

COLONIAL HISTORY AND THE REVOLUTION

GROUP VII (AGE TEN)

ONE of the sections of Group VII was under the direction of the head of the textile department, and the other of the director of history.[1] These groups met in one of the dining rooms and in one end of the kitchen laboratory, which was also used for discussion and recitation. Their study centered around the activities of the colonial period. The study of the development of the textile industry set the trend of their interests, which were mainly in the invention of mechanical devices and the discovery of processes. There was an increasing amount of individual research at the ten-year-old level and a corresponding gain in the power of self-direction.

It had been assumed, up to this time, that the interests and attitudes of boys and girls were similar, as no marked differences had been observed. One of the first instances of a difference, probably reflecting the study of the colonial period, was the division of labor which naturally developed in the construction of the colonial room, one of the projects undertaken as a group. The boys, of their own volition, chose to build the furniture for the room, and the girls undertook the making of the bedding, rugs, and other fabric equipment. However, both worked together on the construction of the fireplace, which was an entirely new enterprise and, therefore, highly interesting to all. There was a marked increase in the amount of time given to chosen interests and activities in out-

---

[1] Althea Harmer, Georgia F. Bacon.

of-school hours, which was a happy indication of the good results of self-initiated, self-directed, and increasingly meaningful occupations. There was great inequality in the ability of the group in using the tools of communication. Consequently, it must be kept in mind that the basis of grouping was not skill in the use of any kind of tool, nor chronological age. It was harmony and fitness as revealed in social attitude. This harmony was often disturbed by the introduction of pupils from other schools.

THE STORY OF THE AMERICAN COLONIES

The history for this group was a study of the growth of unity among the different colonies, the resultant growing in independence of England, and the social and political development that followed. One week was spent in reviewing the conditions in America, previous to the revolution. The development in government, the coöperation needed among the colonies, and the growth of the home industries were discussed. The group talked of the various ways that the colonists became acquainted through the growth of the longshore trade and the increased travel on the improved main highways, such as the road from Boston to Philadelphia. Correlative with this, they studied the geography of the colonies and the development of agriculture, how the homes and towns and villages were organized and governed, and the various industries that occupied the people.[2]

As class and teacher grew acquainted, many in the group were found deficient in ability to read or write with ease and proficiency. In consequence and after discussion, the group decided to give, for a period, much time and attention to collateral reading. This reading was planned to give a review of work previously covered and to lead up to the period immediately preceding the revolution. Writing lessons were also begun, supplemented with drill exercises on words or construction that troubled them. Most of the children entered into

---

[2] Course given by Georgia F. Bacon.

this arrangement with whole-hearted acceptance of its being the best way out of a bad situation. They recognized that they could not go on with the term's work until they could read the books that held the necessary information. Each day they asked for a lesson to prepare at home, and at the end of the three months, with the exception of two children, they were able to read independently enough so that regular historical work was again resumed.

In reviewing the work of the previous year on the Virginia and Plymouth Colonies for the benefit of the children who had not done that work, the social differences between the two colonies seem to have made a great impression on the group. Their work on the products of New York carried them into a discussion of the kinds of occupations which could be carried on in such a country as Holland. They concluded that the Dutch necessarily would be a commercial and manufacturing people, and were told of the commerce of the Dutch with the East Indies and of the length of time it took to make the trip. They looked at the map and concluded that it would be much shorter to go straight west, if only America were not in the way. They knew from their study of the Virginia Colony that the Europeans believed the American continent extended only as far west as the Allegheny Mountains, and that the great aim and end of all discoveries at this time was to find the rumored passage which extended through the continent.

The discoveries and explorations of Henry Hudson, the formation of the great companies, and the necessity of associated capital for the great enterprises of the time were discussed. The group followed Hudson on his trip up the Hudson River, heard of his seizure by the English and his second trip to Hudson Bay under the patronage of the English people. They referred constantly to the map, traced out the country drained by the tributaries of the Hudson Bay, and were interested to know that this territory had since changed hands. They then took up the establishment of trading posts at Fort Orange, discussed the fact that only men came over at first and the company's feeling that they must induce families to accompany them so that the trade with the Indians might be permanent.

For a better understanding of the manorial relationship, they were told of the old feudal system of Europe and were much amused by the fact that, after it had been discarded in the old country because it did not work, people could be so stupid as to establish it in this country.

The home life of the colonists on the manor in New York was taken up, and the construction and furnishings of their log cabins, the clothing they wore, and the food they ate were all imagined. They then discussed the crops raised, the necessary preparation for market, the mills which were run by wind power, and the markets to which the grain was sent. Each day one child reviewed the work of the day before, the rest supplementing. To this story the teacher added enough material to keep it moving.

THE FURNISHING OF A COLONIAL ROOM

In connection with this rather extended and detailed study of the home life of colonial times, the group planned and carried through the furnishing of a colonial room.[3] The first decision was for a fireplace large enough for an actual fire, and stones were immediately collected and sorted. A four-post bedstead was planned, a colonial chair, a tall clock, and a spinning-wheel. The girls said they would dress a colonial doll for the room and weave a rug for the floor. Work was begun on the furniture, and in fourteen days they had finished the bedstead, the feather bed and bedding for which were made at home. The stone was ready for the fireplace and work had started on the clock, the spinning-wheel, the table, and the chairs. In this process all the suggestions originated with the children, who also brought in drawings of their plans. The fireplace was a group undertaking. The pattern was drawn; the chimney and the hearth were lined with asbestos. In their first attempt at mortar, the lime had not been slaked, so they pounded and wet it and used it immediately. This seemed to work all right

---

[3] This project was under the supervision of the shop director, Elizabeth Jones, although the coöperation of the textile and art departments was much solicited.

at first, but the mortar when dry, crumbled, "So," the report reads, "we shall have to do the work all over again." The tall clock, one chair, the center table, and the rag carpet for the floor were completed. This took two weeks, then they started rebuilding the fireplace. The old mortar was cleaned off and more stones collected. This time the water was put on the lime at night and allowed to stand in order to slake adequately, with the result that the mortar hardened properly. The whole group of children worked for a half-hour period, and two remained to finish it. Bent iron was used as a frame to hold the stone work of the flue, and the crane they had made was placed in the fireplace as they built it. There was great excitement upon the occasion of lighting the first fire and great joy and satisfaction at finding that the flue drew well. One of the boys, quite unaided, contrived a little spinning-wheel on his own scroll-saw at home. The window spaces were cut, window casings made, and the glass fitted to place. One of the children brought a small mirror; a circular frame was made for it; and a picture of George Washington was hung upon the wall. This group spent more time in the shop than any other one group. The children worked as individuals as well as coöperatively and discovered for themselves the use of mechanical drawing in making their plans. These were well drawn and exact and were found good guides in cutting the wood. The place in their method of an exact working drawing, therefore, was more secure than if they had been required to use it through all the previous years when exactness was not a fundamental necessity, and the formation of a habit of the use of an exact method was weighted with an emotional pleasure which made it a permanent acquisition. In addition, they also constructed a large loom and shuttles for use in their textile work and caned a number of chairs for the school.

The time and labor which the group expended in furnishing this room brought home to them something of what it meant to the pioneer families to be dependent upon themselves for shelter, for food, and for clothing. They saw how the beginnings of many occupations and industries rose out of real and pressing need, how certain individuals and communities became experts in making certain things or in raising certain crops, and how trade began. As the means of communication improved, the exchange of various products, the growth of agriculture, the home manufacture, and commerce with the mother country also increased. The children compared the social life of New England with that of the Southern colonies and discussed the products that would probably be exchanged. They decided that New England would lead in the manufactured products, and the South in farm produce. They saw that this rapidly growing trade between the colonies would do much to knit them together, to make them more dependent upon each other and less dependent upon England, and would lead to jealousy and interference by England.

To make this a concrete experience each child became an imaginary captain who described his home, telling what longshore cargo he carried, where he unloaded, and what he took with him on the return journey. They were told the current point of view—that the colony existed primarily for the good of the mother-country. Then followed much discussion as to how England would be able to make money out of the colonies. This introduced the Navigation Laws, and each child pointed out his idea of the effect these laws might have on the prosperity of his captain. The development of the home industries, which resulted from restrictions put upon trade by the mother-country, and worked out in great detail, the wool industry being chosen for special study. The children were expected to do most of their own reading. Reference was made afterwards to the map, and helpful geographical facts were explained. The usual procedure was to draw a quick map of the eastern part of the United States with strong characteristics of the coast line, and on this were located the places and incidents discussed.

THE STUDY OF THE REVOLUTION

The study of the French and Indian War was then reviewed. The children saw that this war had taught the colonists their own power and had given them military ability and training. The question then came up as to who should pay for the war, and the children read the story of the Stamp Act and its results.

The logical sequence of the events that followed were seen as the results of the Stamp Act. The Molasses Act was reviewed and the revenge the colonists took in refusing to import goods from England. It became clear how the navigation acts resulted in smuggling by the colonists, and how it came about that the English gave their officials authority to issue writs of assistance. An imaginary individual case followed. They were told of James Otis, who resigned his position as attorney under the King in order that he might try a case of this sort for the colonists.

Collateral reading dealt with the results following the Stamp Act, its nullification, the taxing of tea, and the Boston Tea Party. Two or three days were spent in this reading in order that the children might secure a detailed picture of the times and thus sense the intense feeling that was rife in 1775, especially in Boston. The story of Paul Revere was read, and four of the children who had been east described different places in and around Boston. Most of the children had read many stories of this time and were delighted to find the historical setting of these stories. M. told of the boys in Boston who remonstrated with the British officer over the interference of his soldiers with their sports. When the group heard of the Quartering Act and the placement of British soldiers in Boston, M. was much delighted to find that her story had really happened at that time, that it had a genuine setting in both place and time.

The children read the accounts of the battles of Lexington, Concord, and Bunker Hill out of school hours. They were far more interested in planning the campaigns and surmising and forcasting the movements of both the British and Continental Armies than they were in the gory details of the battles. Class discussion brought out why the battles were fought in these places and the preparations made for them by the Americans. The account of the capture of Ticonderoga which supplied the Americans with ammunition and arms, the siege of Boston, and its evacuation by the British then followed. The children were much interested in how Washington accomplished the reorganization and drill of the army and amused that the northerners thought Washington a "dude." They were much impressed with his character and especially his patience while waiting near Boston for munition supplies. When asked "What are the qualities of a great general?" they decided that one highly necessary characteristic is the ability to imagine what the enemy will do and prepare to frustrate that plan.

The class was asked to forecast what the British would do after leaving Boston. At first they were at sea, but finally agreed that the best plan would be to try to divide the colonies. After the reminder that there was an army of British soldiers in Canada, and with the relief map of the United States before them, the group decided that the British would attempt an approach to Lake Champlain both from the north and from the Hudson River Valley. The children then realized that a forest would be an impassable barrier for the army and were told of Howe's plan for Burgoyne and St. Leger to come from the north, while he advanced up the Hudson River, with a meeting near Albany. This accomplished, the colony would be divided.

The aim of this course was to emphasize the geography of the country rather than the sensational features of warfare. To this end much time was spent on map work, and the children were encouraged to plan the campaigns of the war themselves, to select important strategic points, and decide what moves would be made, on the one hand to capture, and on the other to defend. The children grew so interested that a large relief map was begun, and the various campaigns of the war were worked out under the direction of a leader chosen by the group.

THE STUDY OF TERRITORIAL EXPANSION

Two periods were spent in the discussion of the Declaration of Independence and the attitude which the different colonies took toward its acceptance. The terms of the treaty at the close of the war were discussed, and the United States territory in 1783 was traced on their map. The remaining time was spent in a brief study of the territorial expansion of the United States after the war, and of her gradual growth in unity. They were told how Lousiana, then extending from the Mississippi to the Rocky Mountains, came into the possession of the United States; they reviewed the Lewis and Clark expedition down the Ohio River, up the Missouri, and across the mountains into Oregon and the claims of the United States to this region, based on this exploration and those of its early settlers. They did much collateral reading and spent two periods a week in writing a story of the Revolution based on one that they had heard read. At this time they became much more conscious of the looks of their papers; several even voluntarily copied them in ink.

The topic of territorial expansion finished, they took up in more detail the current trouble with Spain; the children themselves furnished a good many of the pertinent facts. The resulting treaty, which involved the question of quelling difficulties in the Philipines, the acquisition of Porto Rico and one of the Ladrone Islands, and relevant discussion included a critical survey of how the Hawaiian Islands came into the possession of the United States. A short sketch of their discovery by Captain Cook was given, of the subsequent migration thither of missionaries and speculators, of the gradual, general immigration of foreigners, and of the final request of the white population that Hawaii be annexed to the United States.

The story of the purchase of Alaska from Russia by the United States then followed; its climate was reviewed; and the reasons why it was valuable to the United States. The gold of the Klondike was first thought of, but on thoughtful consideration the children found that its gold resources were not known at that time. They then suggested sealskin as a valuable product and were told something of the trouble between England and America over the seal rookeries and of the boundary dispute between the two countries.

THE STUDY OF COLONIAL INDUSTRY

The introduction of industries necessary to provide food, clothing, and shelter for the early pioneers naturally brought many changes, changes which did much to shape the subsequent political history and the social life of each community. Each house at first was its own producer, but even here there was a division of labor. The study of social life was largely one of the gradual development of its industries, the increased efficiency through invention of machines, and the social reorganization and adjustments that follow the introduction of labor-saving devices. The textile industries in particular offered much material and opportunity for individual investigation and reinvention. The processes carried on in the home industries of the period suggested much study and experimentation in the cultivation and preparation of wool, flax, and cotton. The group, after examining the different fibres, took flax for special study. They agreed that so fine a root would need a light soil and searched the map for river valleys which would furnish the right conditions. The valley of the Nile, together with Belgium and Ireland, were found to answer the requirements. Methods of sowing the seed were then discussed, and the children decided that flax sown for seed only should be scattered more than that to be cultivated for the fibre. Some were sown in a window-box for observation, and that which had been grown the year before was used for experiment. This was soaked to soften the fibres and heckled with a heckle designed by a member of the group. The spinning of flax was demonstrated for the class by a German woman, and some of the children tried to learn, but the time available was too short to allow very satisfactory results. There was some experimenting with dyes. Various combinations of madder, fustic, Brazil wood, alum, potassium bichromate, and copper sulphate were tried. (Group X later chose, from the mounted samples of these dyes, a color to be used in a screen they were planning.) Two of the group made soap, using lard and caustic potash. Others attempted to bleach a piece of linen, which had been woven by a member of the group, but without much success.

There was also weaving of Indian mats on the looms that had been constructed in the shop. Designs in color were made for these mats in the art studio. The children also worked in clay and water color, choosing from their history such subjects as were adapted to their purpose. In making a relief of Washington taking command of his army, they studied the costumes of the time and the face of Washington himself in order to reproduce them to the best of their ability, and took turns in posing for the group. The work in water-color was designed to emphasize arrangement, color values and relations. A study of perspective was also begun.

The aim of the study of the period of American colonization was not to cover the ground, but to give children of this age some knowledge of how social processes were used to secure social results, how obstacles were overcome and means contrived to attain these results. The ulterior problem was by this method to bring the child to recognize his own need to secure practical and intellectual control of such methods of work and inquiry as would help him attain desired results in his own life situation. Pioneer life afforded many illustrations of patience, courage, ingenuity, and continual judgment in adapting means to ends, even in the face of great hazard and obstacle. The material is so definite, vivid, and human that children of this age can readily imagine and reconstruct situations and forecast results and solutions. The method involved the presentation of a large amount of detail, the minutiæ of surroundings, tools, clothing, household utensils, foods, modes of living day by day. Social processes and results thus became realities. When younger, the child had identified himself in dramatic action with the persons of his interest. Now, there begins an intellectual identification; the child puts himself at the standpoint of the problems that have to be met and rediscovers, so far as may be, ways of meeting them.

The same general standpoint, the adaptation of means to ends, also controlled the work in science, now differentiated into the geographical (in its relation to social groupings and to industry) and the experimental. The child learned to appreciate that the natural environment affords resources and presents problems, and was helped in his understanding by field excursions, planned that he might make his own observations. These observations of a local situation, of what certain people have done in a particular environment, furnish the data which the child's constructive imagination uses to image more remote environments. Out of it all, he abstracts his own general statement of the probable relationships between physical characteristics, the soil and climate of any locality and its natural and commercial products, its typical industries and social groupings. The idea of the physiography of North America, and in particular that of its eastern coast, gradually became related in the child's thinking to the doings of the various groups of colonial settlers. It took on a concrete dress of meaning and gradually extended into a large truth which the child found could be used in his thought about more remote situations. This idea of the relation of habitat to people, gained in the study and discussion of a relief map of North America, became more significant as the children set about constructing their own map. They found many deficiencies in their method and skill in drawing maps. In order to get an idea of proportion and of drawing to scale, they took up the relative sizes of different bodies and met with the problems of dividing a whole into its parts and the process of factoring. Individual experimentation went on with the drawing and dividing of rectangles into any number of parts, one or two children discovering that if they doubled the divisions in one direction, they could halve them in another without changing the number of parts. They also learned to use a compass and how to measure a circle. After measuring the home room and making a drawing of it, they made a map of the school grounds and were then ready to start on their map, which had now extended to one of the whole world.

INTEREST IN SCIENCE

In the meantime the geological history of North America was being studied. The children learned the difference between old rocks that had been subjected to heat and those that had been laid down by water, and examined specimens of granite and of limestone. They pointed out the Laurentian Hills as part of the original skeleton of the continent. They talked about the effect of glaciers upon soil, compared the soil of New England with that of Virginia, saw the difficulty of clearing the former because of the glacier action, and decided that it would take much longer to settle this part of the country than to open up the West. In talking of the easiest ways west across the Appalachian Mountains, some thought of the Potomac, others of the Mohawk Valley and were pleased to find that the railroads in New York State were along the Mohawk.[4]

In the experimental aspect of their science, interest centered in how processes yield results. Their work in physiology, therefore, began from the functional side. After a little study of the mechanics of the various types of levers and a talk on the use of muscles in the body, they began by moving the arm to discover the muscles by which this is done. They knew, of course, that the upper arm must have one bone and the lower arm another, and that both were moved by muscles. By feeling and with the help of diagrams they worked out the places where the muscles were attached, bringing out the fact that it would be of no use, were both ends of the muscle attached to the same bone. The function of the nerves was then taken up, and the concept developed that the nerves are the paths of the "feeling and moving messengers" which go to and from the brain and make the muscles move. Ingoing nerves from the muscles make us aware of what is happening.

A study of the eye was begun by seeing that the image of a candle passing through a small roll of paper is inverted. The children were also shown the way a ray of light passes through a convex lens and from their own observations drew the conclu-

---

4 From typewritten records of Group VII (ten years). Teacher, Mary Hill.

sion that to have a correct image on the retina of the eye something corresponding to a lens would have to be in front of it. They then set up and carried through the experiment of the image of the candle flame through a pinhole in a paper. They tried putting a lens in front of the pinhole, found the difference it made, and decided that the chief difference was in the focus.

The physiology of digestion led to some experimental work with foods in the cooking laboratory. This began with the determination of the different amounts of water which would be needed with six different cereals in different quantities of whole and fractional cups. In the work of the three previous years, the children had found that in cooking, flaked corn would take its own volume of water, and that by weighing each cereal against the flaked corn they could determine the amount of water required for that cereal. This was done for a fraction of a cup and then for larger quantities. They then weighed twenty grams of wheat flour, let it stand for a time in water, and filtered off the water. This water was then heated, and the children saw that it became milky and compared it with heated water containing some white of egg. They had previously tested the filtered water with iodine for starch. This water was then reheated and refiltered three times in order to remove all the albumen for weighing. The object of the experiment was to find the proportion of soluble albumen in wheat flour. Comments on the experiment were that the result obtained by two in the class was a good deal below what it should have been, owing to the number of handlings the materials had to undergo, that the class as a whole had improved very much in the way the apparatus was handled, and that this should improve the results of the next experiment.[5] This quantitative analysis was repeated with a number of flours, with milk, and with meats. The class had difficulty in translating the results of the experiments into percentages, so the experiments were temporarily dropped, and percentage was taken up. The children formulated their own multiplication tables and drilled on them, changed measures of the English

---

[5] Typewritten records of the school, 1900. Teacher, Mary Hill.

system into those of the metric, and solved and wrote problems involving these processes.

At the beginning of the next term teacher and group discussed the work of the preceding term. The children felt they "had changed around a good deal." They had "begun with the body, after that experiments, and then a good deal of number work." They were told that this term they were going back to physiology, that it was necessary to know something about foods before studying physiology, that it was also necessary to learn how to make experiments, and that it was easier to experiment with flour and milk and meat than with animals. They were also reminded that when they did make experiments, the results were of no use to them because they did not understand how to use numbers, and this was the reason for dropping the experimental work and studying numbers.

This explanation seemed satisfactory to the group, and discussion then began about the differences between plants and animals, one boy suggesting that, "they had different foods and different ways of taking them." Experiments followed on the conditions and food necessary for growing plants. These led to a discussion of the differences between plants and animals in this respect. Many excursions were made to Jackson Park for specimens of plant life and for toads' and frogs' eggs which were placed in the aquarium. As the course went on, the group became much interested in biological problems and asked many questions about different species. The monkey and the descent of man aroused the most curiosity. One period, therefore, was spent on an account of the Darwinian theory of the origin of species. The discussion then turned to the different classes of animals. The vertebrates and the invertebrates were given them as the two great divisions. Under the vertebrates the group discussed the amphibian, since they had been studying the toad, and under invertebrates the insects, with which they were all more or less familiar. The class also made a study of the earthworm.

Records were written by the children of their excursions, of the dissection of the frog, and of the material read aloud to them on the habits of toads. They learned a good deal of the technique of making drawings of their work. These, toward the end of the course, were of quite excellent quality. In connection with their experiments with plants and the making of a nutrient solution for their plants, they had had need to use metric measurement, and time was taken to study this system and to make cubic centimeter measures.

In addition to the number work which was incidental and necessary to their laboratory work and other activities, the group spent a great deal of time mastering techniques in the various number processes. This was done willingly and often with evident enjoyment. The work began with the four fundamental processes. The children worked out their own tables, and made up problems of their own. Some of these were long and complicated, involving several processes. "A woman had 40 hens; each laid 8 eggs; she gave away 24 eggs; she sold the rest at 2 cents apiece; she has $80.00 in the bank. How much did she have altogether?" Every night each child wrote out a problem and brought it to school for the class to solve. They then asked to have these printed and decided that they would write an arithmetic. When learning the multiplication table they also tackled division, C. volunteering the information that if the division tables were the opposite of the multiplication tables, you could prove the answer of multiplication by dividing it by the multiplier. All the children tried it to see if it would come out as C. said and thereafter were never satisfied until they had proved every example. They wanted to go on immediately to long division so they could prove the multiplication problems where the multiplier contained more than one figure. This group experience demonstrated clearly that this year is the peak point of interest in a skill just for sheer pleasure in manipulation. Children of this age thoroughly enjoy playing with numbers. This interest, when added to an increasing desire to acquire skill because of its use in some other activity, makes this year an important one in which the child can easily and happily acquire many of his skills and techniques.

SUMMARY

In their earlier years these children experimented just to see what would happen. At ten years they experimented to find how materials or agencies must be manipulated to give certain results. Since the predominate interest is still in practical results, the study of this period is a study of applied knowledge, of applied science. In cooking, the child learns the general principles of cooking by means of experimentation. He analyzes typical foods and observes the effect of heat and other agencies upon the component parts. He classifies the food according to its constituents and deduces his own rule or recipe for its approved treatment. At the close of his study he is able, in a guided group discussion, to make certain large classifications of food, to arrange his cooking recipes according to these classifications, and to state the general principles governing the right treatment of these so that they are suitable for digestion. His study of food, therefore, through his own guided experimental handling of it, becomes linked, in his thinking, with the digestive processes of his own body and thus brings him back by the route of logical thinking to the subject of physiology. In sewing also, methods of cutting and fitting dolls' clothes were gradually accepted as good means to get desired results. Certain designs could be adapted to certain fabrics better than others; certain dyes gave more pleasing colors. In art, the relation of means to end was seen in the practical questions of perspective, proportion, spaces, masses, balance, and effect of color combinations or contrasts. In music, melody and rhythm were beginning to be used as the means to get a desired result in composition.

The French for this group was taught by conversations about topics of everyday interest, an occupation they were carrying on, or a picture they were sketching. Special attention was given more and more to forms of speech and to pronunciation. Individual needs in voice training were met in connection with reading aloud, and the children developed considerable interest in the correct use of their voices. This was in many cases extended to correct bodily posture and linked to special apparatus work with individuals in the gymnasium.

This age often is characterized by intense activity. With proper laboratory facilities and proper organization of subject-matter into topics, a group of ten-year-olds, that are shielded from distraction and waste of energy, can make much progress in many directions. In the school, it seemed to those directing the work that the children of this age grew by leaps and bounds in their facility to handle all kinds of social situations, as well as those demanding intellectual ability. Individual differences, especially in interests, began to show clearly. The children were also more conscious of each other. Comparisons began to be made. While there were no overt symptoms of inferiority aside from those in one or two of the exceptionally slow pupils, the children, in planning the division of work, were discriminating in their choice of individuals who had ability to carry to completion any part of an undertaking.

At the end of this year the children showed the effects of their practice in experimental method. They had grown quite skilful in abstracting the meaning of one action with regard to the next. They had exercised their imaginations and stretched them to larger objectives which had such interest for them that they were content to wait and work for necessary skills, the lack of which presented a practical difficulty to attainment. They began to conceive of the end as something to be found out and had had some experience in controlling their acts and images so as to help in the inquiry and solution.

In history there had been a change from the biographical method of approach to discussion of general social problems, the formulation of questions that arise and possible solutions. The children still needed a mass of detail in order to get an adequate background of living and social situations before they could appreciate the problems or foretell probable solutions. Points about which there was a difference of opinion, matters upon which experience and reflection could be brought to bear, were always coming up in their history, as in the discussion of the common pot of the Virginia Colony. The frequent use of such discussions, however, to develop the matter of doubt and difference into a definite problem was necessary to make the child feel just what the difficulty was. Again and again at this point, it was necessary to throw him upon his own resources in looking up material and upon his own judgment in bringing it to bear on the problem or in getting its solution. When the question in a child's mind was formulated by himself, was his own question, it became a doubt that needed his reflective attention; it had a halo of interest which enlisted his undivided attention. He needed no prod or spur, no memorizing of ready-made answers. He actively sought and chose relevant material with which to answer it and considered the bearings and relations of this material and the kind of solution it called for. The problem was his own, hence the training secured by working out its solution became his own. This was discipline in the school. It was self-discipline; it resulted in self-control and a habit of considering problems.

CHAPTER X

EUROPEAN BACKGROUND OF
THE COLONISTS

GROUP VIII (AGE ELEVEN)

GROUP VIII was divided into two sections on the basis of previous school experience. Section *a*, the larger, contained the children who had been in this school but a year and a half, and section *b* those who had been longer in the school.[1]

Both divisions studied the European backgrounds of the nations that had established colonies in America. Understanding of these backgrounds would naturally help the children appreciate the motives which sent the early explorers on their migrations and lured permanent settlers to the new lands. What these nations of the old civilization took to their new colonies, what they brought back for use or trade, and how and where they established the trade routes: these were some of the points to be solved by the course.

SUBJECT-MATTER MODIFIED TO SUIT EXPERIENCE

The differences in the previous experience of the two sections made it necessary to use two quite different courses of study. Group VIII-*a*[2] had not had the study of the world discoverers. Their work, therefore, was analogous to that of Group V. They imagined themselves living in Europe in the middle of the thirteenth century. With a globe before them, they noted the parts of the world known at that time and then took

---

[1] Group teacher, Marian Schibsby, Latin and German; assisted by Margaret Hoblitt, history.
[2] In charge of Margaret Hoblitt.

185

up the adventures of Marco Polo in Asia to see how Europe became acquainted with the wealth of the Far East. They learned how Venice and Genoa developed and the effect of the introduction into Europe of the many products of India and China on commerce. When the Turkish pirates cut off the Mediterranean route to the East, these pioneer commercial nations were forced to look for a new way, which led to all the discoveries and explorations of the fifteenth and sixteenth centuries.

The method used was to study the lives of the great men of the period and thus gain an idea of the industrial and social problems of the country and its political status. Prince Henry of Portugal was first taken for study. The children then went with Diaz around Africa, with Vasco de Gama to India, with Columbus on his four trips to America, studied the settlements of the Spaniards in the West Indies and Central America, rediscovered the Pacific Ocean and the western coast of America, conquered Peru with Pizarro, Mexico with Cortes, and finished with the discovery of Florida and the lower Mississippi.

The language, both English and foreign, literature, and the various other arts and constructive activities closely correlated with the history study. In science, too, the interest and emphasis was on the discovery of the world as a whole through a study of physical geography and of the formation of the earth's crust. The science teacher thus built up the globe physically at the same time that the history teacher was giving its social and political development.

The fall work in science began with a general survey of the earth, its shape, size, relation to and in the solar system, and the effects of its different motions. Day and night, summer and winter, the tides, and so on were considered. This introduced the subject of gravitation, and the class quickly got the meaning of weight. To show how weight varies with the mass of the attracting body, the weight of a man on several planets, the moon, and the sun was roughly estimated and compared with that on the earth. The effect of this increase or decrease on running, jumping, or climbing was a matter of much amusing discussion. The numerous questions asked and the various conjectures stated indicated that the children were not lacking in one kind of imagination. Various phenomena of gravitation were brought out by supposing that the force did not exist and imagining the difference this would make in everyday life. The effect of the Japan Current on the climate of the western part of North America was also studied. The aim was to help the child realize the significance of a great physical force.[3]

THE STUDY OF THE ENGLISH VILLAGE

Group VIII-*b* made a different approach both in history and science. After a quarter's intensive work in English literature, a study of English village life was undertaken. This was made to provide a background for the work in literature and also for a better understanding of the social life which preceded and led up to the emigration of the first English settlers. As a study for children who had done the work in Group VII it proved almost ideal. In the first place it is real history. It has to do with the lives of the people—what they did, how they lived, how they acted, and what forces influenced their actions. It is a stage of social life or culture which is typical of all developments. It was of special interest to these children because it was English, and because in it could be seen the beginnings of most of the present industries in America. It is especially adapted to study at this age because it is simple, and because it lends itself readily to constructive work. It gives a chance to reason, to conceive of a village in its simplest and earliest stage, to see its growth and organization, and to watch its development into a feudal organization.

The dividing of village lands into that which was arable and that for pasture and the old systems of measurement and notation were taken up. The children discussed the sort of

---

[3] The children were eager to make thermometers, and as this fitted in well with the work, a little time was given to this construction. There were many accidents, of course, and many failures, but finally, nearly all succeeded in getting the bulbs filled with mercury, and some of the children started to mark the scale on the tubes. This threatened to take so much time, however, that the children were asked to finish the work out of school hours, which several did.

land it was, the tools used, the seeds available and their sub-sequent treatment as articles of food. Occupations were also studied, that of the milkman, the shepherd, the swineherd, the plowman, and the ironsmith, and what each contributed to the village by reason of the value of product produced. The qualities of personality which continued work in one trade might develop in a group of people, the effect of this develop-ment on their conduct in social situations, and their social status as individuals in community life were brought out in group discussion. This emphasis on the occupational side of the study led logically to the conclusion that the classes of people in the village, the villeurs, the cotters, and the different kinds of workmen, were the products of their various occupa-tions. The children grew able to distinguish or picture individ-uals of one class from another. The lord of the manor would be picked out by his dress. They would then add the details of his life, his duties, the kind of house he lived in, and his social status in the village. This would be in distinction to the next lower class, the villeurs. Thus there grew up a clear pic-ture of how the hard and fast class lines were drawn that even now hold in the social life of England. Constructive work was correlative; primitive plows and hoes, or mills and water-wheels were made.

The general survey of the village industrial life extended itself to a study of the political relationships of the social and civic life of the village and to the conditions of England in the tenth century. A rather intensive study of the feudal system centered around the story of William the Conqueror and his conquest of England. Richard and Philip were followed across Europe in their crusade to the Holy Land. Certain chapters of *Ivanhoe* revealed a picture of social conditions and the rela-tions of the Saxons and Normans. The story of Sir Lancelot was read and discussed and contributed something of the real spirit of the age and the ideals of the knights.[4] A general sur-vey of the geography of Europe, of the British Isles, and finally

---

[4] The *Boy's Froissart, Mort d'Arthur,* and *The Age of Chivalry* by Bulfinch were used as sources of information.

of the world followed. Outline maps were drawn. On these were traced the great land and water routes of trade, and the different nationalities who had made settlements in America were located with emphasis on those of the Dutch and the extensive claims of France, England, and Spain in America. As the children seemed unable to express in written form what they talked about with such evident pleasure, time was given daily for each child to develop skill in formulating clearly and correctly and in written form their knowledge of the English village community. There were drill lessons in spelling, writing, and those language forms which they were unable to use because they were unfamiliar.

The life of the English people at the beginning of the seventeenth century was briefly reviewed to help the children discover for themselves the reasons for exploration and why the early colonists left the old and sought the new. Again these children were carried far afield and once more traveled the world around. They went to India with the English and established the East India Trading Company (contemporaneous with the settlement of Jamestown), compared the products of these East Indian colonies ("nearly everything that can be raised in any country grows in India") with those of America, and understood the deadly rivalry that grew up between the English and the Portuguese who in the days of Vasco da Gama (1497) had established factories in this far-away land. They thrilled to the destruction of the Armada, rejoiced in the resultant freedom of the seas, marveled at the high-handed division of the world by the Pope, and realized how this affected the settlements of the Dutch and French in India. The work as a whole enabled the children to place the history of their own country in some adjustment to that of other countries. It also supplied the romantic and adventurous interests of children of this age with the best cultural expression the races have to offer.

ELEMENTARY SCIENCE IN HISTORICAL SETTING

In science, VIII-*b* studied elementary physics and physiology.[5] After reviewing the principles of electricity covered in the fall, they went on to a study of simple machines. A seesaw was made in the shop, and each child drew the plan for and made a pair of scales. They began their study of physiology with a study of the leg and arm movements. The general subject of body-movement as involving a series of joints was discussed. They found the nature of the hip that of a ball and socket, the knee joint that of a hinge; while the ankle possessed a more pivotal motion, and the toes could be moved in all ways. They worked out the mechanism of the forearm, locating the biceps muscle by feeling, and the tendons that attach this muscle to the shoulder and below the elbow to the forearm. They tried to move a door on its hinges by a string attached in a way similar to the attachment of the biceps and found it very difficult to do. They thought it queer the arm should be attached in a way so difficult to move. In the shop at this time they were making models of each class of lever.

In working out the principle of the lever involved in the movements of the forearm, the children reviewed the metric system of weights and measures. In order to take their thinking from the English system of linear measure to that of the metric, they were asked to indicate in the air their ideas of the lengths of an inch, three inches, four inches, one foot, and a yard. The children who had been in the school some time were very correct in their ideas of these distances. The others were quite inaccurate. Their remarks showed much interest in the metric system as a rational method in comparison with the arbitrary measure of the English system. The importance of this in being able to emphasize volume of cubic contents in terms of weight of the standard unit, water, seemed to impress them.

At the end of a week devoted entirely to work on the metric system, they had formulated all the English measures and had

_____

[5] Katherine Camp, assisted by C. E. Marks and continued by Harry O. Gillett.

contrasted them with the metric system. In doing this they worked out a statement of the meaning of mass and the way in which measure of weight differs from all other measures. In this discussion it was brought out that we do not know what the so-called force of gravitation is. They were struck with the convenience of having the measure of mass and of cubic measure so constituted that one can be readily converted into the other. Much of the time was spent in actually making the cubic measure in pasteboard and tin, for they seemed to have no clear idea of the comparative size of a cubic centimeter and a cubic meter.

As the work went on, it was found that this group preferred manual manipulation to numerical calculation. Two of the children were to make a half-gram by taking a decimeter of silver wire, finding its weight, and then calculating how many centimeters they would need for a half-gram. For some reason, probably to make the multiplication easier, they found how much it would take for a whole gram. Then, instead of dividing that amount by two, they measured the whole amount and then tried to weigh backward to the half-gram on the scales by actually removing the wire piece by piece without measuring. As this indicated a real need to understand the use of the numerical symbols in this operation as well as a lack of skill in their use, much time was given to number work in connection with those units of the metric system which they had been making. As originally planned, they were to use the units of both the English and the French systems in a study of the arm, as an illustration of a machine, and in some other mechanism, such as a clock or a steam engine. Most of the time, however, was spent on the different processes needed to work out the experiments.

With the weights and measures they had made before them, the children next were asked what could be used as a unit of work. After about ten minutes discussion one child suggested that the kilogram would be the unit in the French system. Later on, the same child volunteered that if a pound were raised a foot in a certain time, that could be used in the English measure. The other children had already given the horsepower unit without knowing how many pounds or what rate it represented. In all the examples they at first ignored the question of rate and simply used the total amount of work done. Their first problem was to show what would represent $\frac{1}{1500}$ kilogram of work. This was accomplished, by choosing $\frac{1}{1500}$ of a kilogram for a weight. They were then asked to do this problem in another way, and in most cases without suggestion, they divided the distance moved instead of the weight. They here had occasion to use the fractional parts of the foot and pound and to reduce them to their simple forms. Time was taken to develop familiarity and skill in such manipulation, and the group then passed on to the use of the pulley, the wheel, and the axle and formulated the laws involved.

After reviewing the main points in the machines constructed, the question of the source of power for each was brought up. Muscular energy was referred to food, and food to the light from the sun. Then the power of the steam-engine was carried back to the same source. The heat obtained in burning coal brought up two questions. What happens to the coal in burning, and what is meant by heat? The first was answered in part by one or two of the class and then postponed for further consideration. The second was touched upon and then eagerly discussed after an interval of four days. All the class gave instances of the effect of heat on various substances; three declared that heat was friction, several others that it was heated or hot air, but were unable to state what they meant by hot iron. One boy said that hot iron was full of hot air or hot gas or something, i. e., heat. The subject of weight was reviewed as a measure of the amount of matter in a definite amount of iron. Three of the class declared that hot iron did not weigh any more than cold; therefore, heat was not "something," i. e., matter, added on or taken away. One thought that as iron expanded in heating it should weigh less when hot, that is, be more buoyed up by the air replaced. Then followed a long discussion of the ways matter of various kinds could be measured by taking a certain unit of each substance. Through the difference between the solid, liquid, and gaseous forms of water, iron, and air, the conception of the molecular constitution of matter was developed. "Heat as a motion of the molecules of the heated body" was a definition contributed by one child, but was not comprehended. As soon as they understood the theory of the different states of matter in elements, the children asked questions about compounds. They then worked out with some illustrative experiments: (1) the change of state of an element such as mercury, lead, or tin; (2) the combination of two gases—hydrogen and oxygen; (3) the measure of the unit of mass—specific gravity.

An opportunity was given in the shop-work to use the facts that had been learned. The class tried to construct a clock from a pendulum, bicycle sprockets, chains, and other necessary equipment. They were able to work out the theoretical part by themselves, but some of the mechanics proved too difficult. They then constructed a set of balances which were more sensitive than the first rude ones they had made. These were for the school's use in weighing small packages.

The work in physiology was continued by a study of the circulatory and respiratory systems. The class dissected the lungs and heart of a sheep, and each child made a careful examination of the circulatory, respiratory, and digestive systems of a frog.[6] The gills of the tadpole were compared with the lungs of a frog. This led to a brief study of the metamorphosis of an insect, consisting of a summary of the various stages of development and the determination of what constitutes a complete as compared with an incomplete metamorphosis.

The main trend of the work of VIII-*b* was to build up the physical and social backgrounds out of which the early colonists of America had come, to get an idea of their occupations and how far they had progressed through the use they had made of the resources of their natural environment, of the social relationships that had resulted, and finally, of the motives that had led certain of them to exploration and a pioneer life in a new land.

At the close of this year these children were ready to under-

---

[6] One child was chosen to buy the heart and lungs at a butcher's, and each child provided his own frogs and tadpoles.

stand next year's detailed study of the revolt of the American colonies against the restraining hand of old custom and ancient usage. They could sympathize with these early colonists who in freedom had molded their new environment to their own desires and had tasted the wine of purposeful and creative action. They could understand that this wine could not be bottled by old laws and selfish traditions.

INTEREST IN TEXTILES

Details of living and the industries of both colony and mother-country filled in the background and contributed to the mental picture that was gradually build up by the children. The different methods of spinning and weaving fibres and their preparation were discussed in detail. The children wrote brief but complete histories of the development of the textile implements used in carding, spinning, and weaving up to the colonial period. They learned that the invention of machines had brought many improved ways of living, had changed the organization pattern of many industries, and had left many industrial and social problems for later generations to solve. The invention of John Kay's fly shuttle had brought about a scarcity of yarn and made spinning a more lucrative occupation than weaving. An impetus was thus given to inventions in the spinning industry, and the social and economic conditions of the subsequent transition period were discussed. The children realized somewhat the position of the spinner and weaver, the beginnings of organization in several branches of the industry, the misunderstanding of the value of machines and the benefit of machine work to the community, the unfortunate position of the inventor, and the riots which followed any invention replacing hand-work. They took up the problems men struggled over two centuries ago when the supply and demand for yarn were so unequal that weavers travelled the country seeking yarn. They understood the mechanics of intermittent and continuous spinning and were asked to invent a machine in which a number of spindles were rotated by the revolution of one wheel, that is, by power. This problem was given, not so much to stimulate the inventive power of the children, as to make them realize the problems faced during the transition period. A little research work was then done on present-day methods of spinning in different parts of the world. Each child investigated a country, and the findings were tabulated as follows:

SPINNING

Machine	Wheels	Distaff
United States Patterson Philadelphia	Kentucky Mountains Tennessee " Carolina " Canada, French Inhabitants	Arizona California Alaska Mexico } Indians

They also found that in a city like Chicago all methods of spinning were still used due to the presence of newly arrived emigrants from older civilizations. Some of the group had traveled and from personal experience could describe primitive forms of spinning in Italy, Switzerland, France, Germany, and California, as well as the more advanced forms of factory work in New England. Foreign helpers in some of the children's homes supplied much information. Others used the encyclopaedia. This piece of work gave the children some idea of the overlapping of different periods of civilization. The class also constructed a Navajo loom for pattern weaving, making the loom frames, battens, and shuttles.[7]

The experiences of the previous year in dyeing, including indigo dyeing with copper in the vat, were reviewed quickly and developed in one or two shades of blue and in white. Lamp wicking was used. The colors were limited so the children might realize the beauty of good spacing with two tones. Most of the children made looms at home. Some made small looms and wove with fine mercerized cotton dyed with aniline colors. The children gave most of their attention to the design of their weaving, comparing and vying with each other. In nearly

[7] An interesting connection was the coöperative attempt to work out the beginnings of a labor museum by the teachers in the school and the residents and foreign neighbors of Hull House.

every case, the design was modified after it was first made on account of the weaving, the criticisms of other children or because of a development in their own critical faculty.

They next constructed a roller beam loom in which the method of warping is intermediate between the Navajo and the colonial method. This enabled them to trace the development of warping as definitely as they had that of carding, spinning, and weaving. Six children in the group purchased spinning-wheels and spun flax thread to use on the roller beam loom. Those who did not spin used flax hand-spun by an Irish woman. An accurate heddle was made in the shop from a careful drawing, also made by the children. Small table mats or doilies were woven on the loom—a type used in colonial times for weaving such articles as tape and braid, The study of the textile industry was reviewed and summarized by papers on the history of carding, spinning, weaving, and warping, on the original invention of the spinning machine, by a map showing the present methods of spinning in different countries, by designs for weaving on a Navajo loom and the tape loom, and by the drawing of a heddle. These were bound together by each child in a portfolio, decorated by an original and appropriate design.

CORRELATED ACTIVITIES

The experimental work in cooking, which was a study of meats for both sections of the group, took up the effects of moist and dry heat on meat fibre. An analysis of meat and a comparison of different cuts in order to discover the reason for the superiority of some over others were also made. This, with a review of their work on albuminous foods, and an analysis of eggs and milk completed the elementary course in cooking.

In this year the character of the work in physical education changed. More time was spent in apparatus work than in the younger groups. Emphasis was put upon the group's learning to work and play together. Two periods each week the children played games and gradually came to realize that it was not what each individual did, but what they did as a whole that made for a victory. The quality of this work in the gymnasium was excellent; good team-work and considerable individual proficiency were developed in basket ball.

Much of the number work was connected with problems arising in various studies. One of these developed in connection with the work in physiology. It was desirable to know how much ventilation was necessary in two (a large and a small) rooms of the school. The children first measured the rooms and estimated their cubical contents. As one of the rooms was irregular, they had to deduct the cubical contents of a jog which complicated the work somewhat. They found, from a physiology textbook, that the amount of carbon dioxide permissible in a room was two parts in ten thousand. In order to use this in decimal form they were shown how to reduce fractional parts to decimals of per cent and worked enough problems to gain facility. The proportion of carbon dioxide given out per hour by an adult and by a child and the time it would take to reach this limit for the rooms under consideration were then found. Next they estimated how much air must be admitted to give perfect ventilation and found the average velocity of wind in Chicago from a weather-map. These figures were reduced to meters, and taking the area of the windows in meters, they estimated the amount of air that would pass through the rooms in a given time.[8]

The plastering had fallen from the ceiling in one of the school-rooms, and the group wanted to find the cost of replastering. With some help they were able to make allowance for the closet. They found out the price of plaster and estimated the entire cost. They also solved other problems which came from their work in other subjects. As a result of their study of the history of Chicago the previous year, they found the amount of taxes paid by certain individuals and estimated their property holdings. The school tax bill was worked out, and taxes in general studied. Some time was also spent in explaining and balancing the budget of the school. The children then added up the tuitions to see if they corresponded with the

---

[8] *University of Chicago Record*, September, 1899. Teacher, Georgia F. Bacon.

account in the budget. They figured out how much material the children would use in a month, in a week, and in a day. A great deal of work of a formal character was also carried on. The children developed their own multiplication table and drilled on it, and on multiplication and division of two or more figures. They studied fractions, square root, ratio, and proportion. In the spring, for the first time, a textbook in arithmetic was used, and each child systematically undertook a review of the various number processes that had been covered.

The language expression of this group was varied. The study of Latin and English grammar, parts of speech, and sentence analysis was taught as a unit by one teacher.[9] The method of teaching in Latin, like that in French and German, was by conversation and drama. Words were always associated with the appropriate object, action, or quality. By writing from dictation and answering questions on a Latin story, the children grew familiar with the story in Latin before they attempted to translate it into English. In some cases they were able to tell the story in Latin without having made any conscious effort to commit it to memory.

In the study of English literature made by one of the sections of Group VIII during the fall months, group and individual instruction in vocal expression was given by a teacher especially trained in this work.[10] The children were asked what they would like to learn to read well. One child brought *Miles Standish*. This was read in dramatic form so that they learned to differentiate characters and to read description. In the beginning they were very faulty in breathing. Some concentrated well, others did not. Some lacked an average use of English, but all showed a good spirit and worked hard. A few had a very limited vocabulary, which the teacher tried to enlarge. Later the children worked on poems selected for them individually. These children, more than any other group, showed interest only when they were reciting. Each was anxious to recite his own poem, but the rest were not interested in hearing him and did not listen. The children were also given

[9] Marion Schibsby.
[10] Minerva Butlin.

practice in reading their reports to the weekly assembly, instruction which was welcome as each child wished to deliver his own report or that of his group with credit.

After hearing a series of readings from Howard Pyle's *The Merry Adventures of Robin Hood* [11] in their study of literature, the children discussed a figure and an image. They also talked about three pictures of deer, Landseer's "The King of the Forest" and "The Monarch of the Glen" and Bonheur's "On the Alert," and found, or were guided to find, the words for the deer, the epithets to describe them, and terms appropriate to the chase. They memorized Shakespeare's "Under the Greenwood Tree." This work was designed to give the children power to read fluently and with expression. They had an excellent background for this work. Texts with plentiful notes gave them opportunity to look up all the references and to prepare the lesson before they came to class. Each child first read his passage slowly, then he reread it to gain fluency and natural expression. The class drew a ground plan of a feudal castle on the board, read a description of a castle from Viollet de Duc's *Habitations of Man in All Ages,* and did some written work in connection with the reading.

Music and the graphic arts all had a place in the weekly program, and were knit into the daily activities, illustrating and refining them. They were always regarded as of peculiar value, for by means of them the child's appreciation of his experience found its best and highest expression.

SUMMARY

Toward the close of the year the children in this group had gained in power to hold problems before their minds. They could keep themselves from action for longer and longer periods in order to consider that action in the light of possible consequences. Ends were more often not just the overcoming of practical difficulties, but something to be found out in order to reach further ends, and in reaching them the child himself learned to control and direct his own acts and images.

---

[11] Mrs. L. M. MacClintock.

CHAPTER XI

EXPERIMENTS IN SPECIALIZED ACTIVITIES

GROUP IX (AGE TWELVE)

THE experience of a twelve-year-old child in this school had been a continuously developing one. His activities had constantly extended in scope and significance. They had involved much positive and detailed subject-matter that had enlarged and deepened the world of his imaginative thought. The ideal, not always fully realized, was that the subject-matter in science, geography, history, or any subject should relate to the child's activities and should suit each phase of his experience. For him, therefore, geological, geographical, or other scientific facts were part and parcel of the historical story and, introduced in a synthetic and living way, thus became an integral part of the stream of his experience. The mere beginnings of large and fundamental concepts of the first early years were enlarged through the later years, either by themselves or in relation to still larger and more inclusive concepts. Widening areas of activity frequently supplied occasions for introducing supplementary lines of study which still further enlarged horizons and increased the dynamic power of individual effort. In the process real problems and difficulties often arose in the midstream of action, obstructions which the child himself must remove or circumvent. He saw that skill was essential to this, and that repetition was necessary to skill and the attainment of a finished result. His need for skill thus became sufficient to engage him in its acquisition; he had an impelling motive from within for analysis and mastering rules. This was found to be possible only as formal work was kept in connection with active construction and expression which presented difficulties and suggested the need of an effective method to cope with them.

THE GROWTH OF SELF-DIRECTIVE POWER AND JUDGMENT

The conscious recognition of the relation of means to ends steadily increased with the child's growth. Indeed it came to be the specific unifying principle of the second stage of growth —the measure of the child's development in thought and action. Activities were planned to center around projects of longer and longer duration and thus took on the nature of occupations. Shop work with wood and tools, cooking, sewing, and work in textiles reproduced or ran parallel to some industry carried on in social life, whether in the past or present: In such work the child utilized the intellectual and the practical phases of his experience; for, in addition to skill and technique, it involved constant observation of materials and continual planning and reflection to carry out effectively the practical or executive side. Mind, hand, and eye were needed. There was, therefore, a continual interplay between ideas and their embodiment in action. The great stress laid upon personal experimenting, planning, and reinventing required that the child be mentally alert and quick if he were to do the outward work properly.

Aside from its peculiar educational value to a child at this stage of mental growth, the evolutionary study of the different textile occupations, paralleling as it did the social history of Colonial times, had brought him a deeper interest in and a keener appreciation of the social life of the period, its problems, and its contributions to the later life of the nation. The industrial and economic progress of a colony of people was seen in its proper relation to intellectual growth. The reciprocal value of each for the other lay in the dependence of the one upon the other, and the whole of experience was deepened and enriched by the fact that they geared into and reënforced one another.

By reason of the nature of their school experience, therefore, in the years from four to twelve these children had built into the fabric of their consciousness an intimate knowledge of materials of all kinds. They had traced many of these materials to their sources or to their simplest forms. They had the easy attitude toward them which follows in the wake of familiarity and intimate knowledge. Each child was accustomed to take raw materials and manipulate them to the form of his idea. Lead in native ore, through controlled use of heat and the child's own labor, became weights for his balance. He had washed and scoured the unclean oily wool of the sheep with soap of his own making, had carded it with a hackle of his own invention, spun it on a spindle and wheel of his own construction. He had dyed the yarn with self-mixed color and on his own loom had woven it into the self-designed pattern of his rug. The genuineness and importance of his work had sunk deep into his consciousness, for he knew it had paralleled that of his own forbears. His way had followed their way; their problems from start to finish had become his, for he knew something of the situation and circumstances out of which they arose, and of the methods and means used in their solution. Many facts were thus easily woven, by the child's own effort, into the web of his experience. A method of thinking was gradually adopted which from daily use became a method of action, and it was the constant hope and ideal that new significances of action, new appreciations of beauty, of goodness, and of worth in every field of endeavor might develop out of these habitual ways. For these children, it can at least be said that out of the years' activities was born the consciousness that there was need to do what they did more quickly, more effectively, and more perfectly, and with due consideration for others.

With the close of the tenth year the second stage of growth draws to a close. Just as in the first stage, the change is gradual. The eleventh year, while it has been grouped with those of the second period, was markedly transitional in character, and at twelve years, the average child in this school was fully awake to values of larger purposes and further objectives than those which had heretofore absorbed him. His observations of nature had led him to carefully guided but self-directed experimentation. He had thus gained some command of the secrets of nature and a measure of control of a few of her forces. In the process he had exercised, to a greater or lesser degree, his power to think logically, to initiate, and to execute. Out of such an accumulated background of experience was born an understanding of the wonderful transformation in methods of production and distribution that has taken place in the history of the race. His eyes had been opened to how it had all come about, because man had tried and kept on trying; it was the fruit of experimental science, of a scientific method of putting knowledge to use in all areas of living. While still a child in a highly plastic stage of growth, he had imaginatively companioned man in the simplified physical and social situations of ancient living and had experimented and invented to meet exigent circumstance with immediate and adequate action. He has seen how, with the lamp of his own mind, man had operated in and worked on his situation with the result that there was a better understanding both of the attendant difficulties and of the way out. In the story of changing civilization, it had been brought continually to his attention that it was always science and scientific method that had broken down physical barriers, conquered disease, and eliminated evils once thought insurmountable. He came to have a sensitivity to the difference in the quality of living in the "then" and the "now," and of their contrasting values. Accompanying this was an increased appreciation that scientific method was more than a tool for the extension of his arms and legs, that in it lay the possibility of using past experience as the servant, not as the master of his mind. In varying degree it was true of these children at this age that constant use of the test-and-see-for-yourself method had developed in them a belief, greater than in most children, in their own ability to direct their actions. As this belief deepened and became apparent, each child felt himself freed more and more from the necessity of guidance from without and tasted of the true freedom resulting from inner direction and control. At the age of twelve such a child was often able to crank his own engine and keep going under his own power and guidance for longer and longer periods.

This growing self-directive power was accompanied by better judgment in selecting and abstracting from the subject-matter of his former experience that which he thought would be helpful in the new. Abstraction thus came to be the artery for his thinking, for by it he intentionally rendered one experience available for guidance in another. Soon his conscious use of abstraction to clarify and direct new situations, brought him to discover how to generalize, to make his own rules, to formulate a general principle, and to draw his own conclusions. A term's work always concluded with a review and a summary. The children did this with pleasure. In a long course of cooking, cereals, meats, and many different kinds of foods had been analyzed and classified according to their predominating constituents as carbohydrates, proteins, and those valuable for their mineral salts. While finishing up their cook books, the children were astonished and delighted to find how few general principles covered the cooking of so many different kinds of food. This summary or review was always done both by individuals and by all the children working together. In addition to the stabilizing effect of a knowledge of inner power and control, there was a sense of security born from years of working in and with a group, a trust in the efficacy of coöperative action for the reconstruction of experience.[1] This conscious use of abstraction and of generalization, added to an increasing sense of reliance on his own ability to find a way out of any situation by trying what had helped before, brought a child, in this school, to a forking of the ways at the age of twelve when the individual interest and personal preference of one child may see a beckoning down this path and another may see it along a far different trail. From now on, for each one

---

[1] The present sense of insecurity is exaggerated in many persons by the lack of experience in the use of a tested method of reconstructing individual situations and social conditions through coöperative action. With no habits of acting with others many of the younger generation professing high social ideals fail to see that they themselves are not social in their personal relationships.

and for the school and teachers, the way of the group became more difficult. Mere play of activity satisfied less and less. It must accomplish more and must move on to an increasingly definite, a more perfect and abiding outcome.[2]

The historical subject-matter, chosen with the growing child in mind, had paralleled, as closely as possible, the phases of his rapidly differentiating experience with those periods which were characteristic and typical of similarly growing phases of social life. By study of the *work* of the American colonies— by following the road of their industrial and economic history—he had came to a real understanding of two of the most fundamental aspects of social life. First, he saw how present social life has been made more prosperous and secure. The successive inventions and discoveries by which theoretical science has been applied to the control of nature are thus seen as the causes of social progress. Second, through participating in similar work, he himself had come to grips with the things that fundamentally concern all men, namely, the occupations and values connected with getting a living. His conception of history thus deeply embedded in actual experience and supplemented with timely second-hand information, was colored with a human, a democratic, and hence a liberalizing point of view. It may be truthfully said that these children at twelve years had a conception of history that was dynamic—it was moving and progressive social life.

In their school life, the children of this group were active in school assemblies, newspaper work, and all club activities. They were so individual in what they undertook that at times it seemed more difficult than ever before to carry on new group plans. Four years of experimentation led to the development of a curriculum for children of this age in which geography, while connected with the history of the people studied, was

---

[2] The physical and psychological tests on the children were conducted by F. M. Smedley, A. D. Wood and Dr. D. P. MacMillan. Mr. Smedley and Dr. MacMillan later shared in the testing of over six thousand public school children. The results of this investigation were published in an article by Dr. U. S. Christopher. "The Relation of Unbalanced Physical Development to Pubertal Morbidity as Shown by Physical Measurement," *The Journal of the American Medical Association*, September, 1901.

concerned with larger wholes. It was the study of the growth of the whole continent of North America rather than just that of the eastern coast of the United States—the scene of their previous historical study.

STUDY OF COLONISTS AS PEOPLE

With the experience gained from a knowledge of the European backgrounds of the American Colonists, the children resumed their study of the developing life of their own country during the Revolution and the later period of westward expansion. In the light of the previous year's experience the historical facts, the growing industries, and the resulting social and political reorganizations became meaningful. With their new point of view and enlarged appreciation of the colonists as people—English, French, Spanish, Dutch—they had a more intelligent understanding of the French and Indian War, the Revolution, and the problems that arose in the subsequent period of westward expansion and gradual acquisition of territory. This study was carried through more or less successfully for the majority of the group.[3] The same classroom method was used as in the earlier study of the colonial period. The rest of the work of the group, science, manual skills, communication, and the arts of expression, correlated itself to the historical program through appropriate activities and related studies.

ACTIVITIES IN SCIENCE

The science for this group grew out of the material they were using in the laboratory and included a detailed study of sedimentary rocks. The illustrative experimental work in science was planned to illustrate some of the more general properties of matter and to bring out the fundamental principle that change of form involves expenditure of energy. Work began, as always, with discussion; here it was concerned with the things that are necessary to life. The children suggested food, clothing,

---

[3] Taught by Margaret Hoblitt.

shelter, water, air. They decided that some of these were more essential than others, but of all, air was the most essential to life. In answer to "What is air?" they responded with several of their own ideas. After a preliminary attempt at an explanation of the difference between a combination and a mixture, a series of experiments were undertaken to demonstrate the make-up of air. Oxygen was separated from the nitrogen in the air by its combustion with phosphorus, and the action of phosphorus in combustion was contrasted with that of oxygen and hydrogen. These experiments involved some discussion of the molecular constitution of matter and were constantly compared to similar reactions taking place in nature. The abstractions involved in the experiments illustrating the chemical action of gases upon solids seemed too remote for most of the class, although a typical example of a gas becoming part of a solid was demonstrated by putting away weighed portions of iron filings to rust for a number of days. The children had been told many times that rust is an oxide formed by the contact of iron with the oxygen of the air, but all but one or two failed to appreciate what this meant. They thought that a union of a gas with a solid would make the solid lighter, that either the filings would not gain in weight at all or would lose. After a few days the filings were again weighed and the percentage of gain found in each case. This type of experiment was then dropped, and a series with liquids and gases was begun.

As an introduction, an hour was spent in summing up all the elements of the earth with which they were familiar and in grouping them according to their state—solid, liquid or gaseous. The state was seen to be dependent upon the amount of heat and pressure. This was made much easier by the group's keen interest in liquid air; two of the class had heard Tripler's lecture on the subject. The aggregation theory of the formation of the earth was explained to them. They themselves contributed the idea of the original gaseous form of the earth, but did not go on and suggest the cooling of the earth to a temperature where life was possible, so a new start was made from another approach. They were asked what temperature they could endure and live. Discussion of this point in relation to plants and animals brought them to the conclusion that there are certain limits of temperature which limit the presence of life. Two sets of experiments illustrated the change from a liquid to a solid or to a gaseous state. An experiment with mercury showed the change from liquid to a gaseous and back again to the liquid state. The melting and cooling of type metal illustrated the change of state during solidification and the processes of crystallization, expansion, and contraction. The necessary proportion of the metals used in this experiment were looked up by each child and were reported to and checked by the group. Finally, each child was asked to carry through, without asking any questions, the whole series of experiments and to report on the amount done at the end of three periods.

During the previous year these children as Group VIII, had made a study of the electric bell and motor. An account of Faraday's experiment with an iron core and a coil was the starting point for their construction of a dynamo-motor. As a preparation for a visit to Armour Institute they had reviewed the things they would want to see. These were, in their preferred order: a motor, a dynamo, a galvanometer (which they called a tester), a storage battery, and an apparatus for telegraphy.

In Group IX, these same children had another opportunity to visit Armour Institute and revive their interest in electrical machines. They saw three kinds of galvanometers and, while looking for them, asked for the first time for the name of the unit of electric measurement. They already knew that the method of measurement was the work done. A powerful electric magnet gave them their first conception of magnetism as a real force. They could feel the force on a steel screw-driver as it required all their strength to prevent its moving between the two poles of the magnet. One of the children asked in great excitement, "What is happening between those two pieces of metal?" They also saw alternating and direct dynamos and electric motors with two kinds of armatures and understood that dynamos can be used to generate current and also as a motor. One of the children went home and made his motor into a dynamo with a small steam-engine as the source of power. The girls showed little interest as compared to the boys, but all came home with the determination to make a galvanometer in the shop and, if they could find the parts, a motor and a dynamo. At Armour they were taken to a shop where a motor was used to run a planer and a jig-saw. This aroused great interest and the repeated comment, "How much we could do if we only had one!" They also saw a portable testing ammeter and voltmeter and asked what each measured and were told how the two instruments could be made to read in different parts of the scale by the amount of wire wound from one cylinder onto another, thus making, as it were, the resistance visible.

The opinion of the director of the course [4] was that a visit of this sort should be made at the beginning of the course and again at its close. They then could have carried the conception of the force they had seen acting on a large scale over into their own experiments of force on a small scale. The conception would have been clearer than the reverse order of occurrences. The second visit could then have been made to review and to give them some conception of methods of measurement and the value of the units used.

After this interlude on electrical machines, the group returned to their study of the change of matter and started a series of experiments to illustrate these changes as they occur in the making of various alloys, such as type-metal, solder, pewter, and fusible metals. Each child worked alone, wrote his own record, a process which often involved study in composition to achieve clarity of statement. At the close of the work each child with guidance summed up and formulated the general principles he had learned.

The spring term work began with a review of what the class knew about the formation of the earth. The children were intrigued with Mr. See's theory of the cold nebular mass as opposed to the ordinary La Place nebular theory. Their interest in change of state, from gas to liquid or solid by heating and cooling at critical points, was keen and carried over well

---

[4] Katherine Camp.

to the story of such changes occurring in the earth's formation. When the children had grasped the idea of the earth as a ball covered with a rocky crust and surrounded with an atmosphere, they went on to changes which have taken place on the earth and can now be seen. After some questioning and discussion they stated that there were three kinds of rocks: (1) lava, granite schists; (2) rocks like marble, which have been changed; (3) water-formed rocks. In discussing metamorphic rocks, they said the gas around the earth would change rocks directly forming crystals without the action of water. They used the word oxides and described the iron sulphides although they did not know their name, placing these in the second class of rocks which had been changed by heat and pressure. The teacher gave terms *igneous, metamorphic,* and *sedimentary* during the discussion. The children recalled from previous work that slate was formed like clay and had been changed by pressure, that granite was the oldest unchanged rock they knew, and that sandstone and limestone had been laid down or made in the water, and gave other evidences of remembering this work well. Part of the class then made experiments illustrating the formation of sedimentary rocks and the action of carbon and sulphur dioxide upon these rocks. Some time was spent formulating the proper order of important points in the records of the work. The children wrote their summaries more successfully this year than they had those of the same work the previous year. Examples follow:

The Story of How Limestone Was Made

A long time ago when the earth was new, when it was lava, there was no water on the earth, and there was steam all round the earth up in the air, as there were many gases in the air. One of them was carbon dioxide. The steam became clouds, because the earth began to cool off, and after a while it began to rain, and the water came down and dissolved the carbon dioxide from the air. When the earth was cooling off, calcium was in the rock lava. The water ran down in the rocks, and the carbon dioxide takes the calcium out of the rocks and makes calcium carbonate. Calcium carbonate dissolved in the water. The little animals eat the calcium carbonate and make their shells—corals, snails, oysters, etc. These shells are pressed down by other shells, and at last they are all made into limestone.

Calcium carbonate comes from all little animals that have shells. Coral, having such a great many little animals, so that when they die there is a great deal of calcium carbonate left by the skeletons.

The other way of making calcium carbonate is in caves. The water leaks through and leaves calcium carbonate in the form of crystals.

Marble is calcium carbonate under great pressure and some heat. The next experiment is to find out if there is calcium in lava.[5]

I took some lava and put on some hydrochloric acid (strong). There was no action that could be seen except when I heated it, and then a vapor came off.[6]

When I evaporated it, it left a little bit of dark stuff in the bottom so that shows that there was some action and the acid did take something out of the lava. Then I let it stand for a few days. After I let it stand I rubbed a small piece of filter paper on the bottom of the test-tube. The dark stuff had absorbed some moisture. Then I heated it until it turned to a dark red color—which I don't know anything about—but the dark stuff absorbing moisture shows some of the dark stuff on the bottom of the test tube was like calcium chloride.[7]

The science work for the rest of the year consisted in following out the geological history of the United States which was now clearer since this experimental work had illustrated some important natural facts and processes. The children were given their choice of illustrating Shaler's *Story of Our Continent* with maps and diagrams or of working out and illustrating one topic of special interest to each pupil. These, one of the children immediately suggested, could all be put together and made into a book. Two of the topics chosen were the history of the Mississippi Valley and of the lake region as showing the location of the great limestone, clay, and metal deposits in the United States.

After a period of arithmetic tests, plans for detailed individual maps showing the location of a mineral or other natural product were begun. The fact that these maps combined would give a complete map of the country aroused much interest.

---

[5] Lava meant igneous rock before it had weathered. The lava used came from the Hawaiian volcanoes.

[6] One or two of the class heated hydrochloric acid without any lava, and found that the same vapor came off as when the lava was in it.

[7] The children had made calcium chloride and seen it dissolve in water absorbed from the air. *University Record,* Vol. III, No. 49, Teacher, Katherine Camp.

The children decided that all would have to use the same scale and system of marks. What these should be was decided by a vote on each suggestion. They voted to show the outline of the country by a black line, to outline the states by a dotted line, to show large cities by circles with radiating points, seaports or towns important because of their nearness to mines or quarries by small squares, canals by a double line with cross marks, railroads by a single line with cross marks, lakes by blue washing, rivers by a double line, mountains by the usual conventional curved lines, and to mark the area of occurrence and production of the natural products by distinctive colors. Methods of scaling and how to make a flat map of a curved surface were reviewed, and each child traced his outline map from one in an atlas. The finished maps were transferred to cloth paper. A large map of the United States was also made in the school yard.

In the meantime the children read at home Shaler's *Story of our Continent*. They were especially interested in its author's summary of the relation between living things and physical environment. Each child then wrote a report of his work after some class instruction in how to make each paragraph carry the story along a few additional steps. At first many of the class tried to write their reports by copying from references. One report written in this way was read aloud and discussed from the point of view of the audience, Group VI, for whom it was intended. This discussion gave the class a new understanding of what the reports might be, and they set about the work of rewriting, with renewed interest. Two reports were rewritten three times. During the writing, reports were frequently read aloud and criticized as to subject-matter and treatment. At the closing session of the course the general physiographical characteristics of North America were reviewed, and new details were given about parts of the country where members of the class were to spend the summer.

The science work of the group, as that of all the school in the spring, turned to the outdoors for illustrative materials and excursions and as a setting for experimental work with living things. A series of experiments on plant life was used. One hour a week was devoted to this laboratory work. The length of time between meetings was too long. A constant review was necessary, and the experiments failed for lack of attention.

During the year's course in what was fundamentally geological science, there were at least two astronomical holidays. The class spent the one occurring at the time of the spring solstice in watching the tellurian. They got a vivid idea of what the equinox meant and of the relation of the sun and earth during the longest and shortest days of the year. The children were reminded that in the northern winter the earth travels that portion of its elliptical path which is nearest to the sun, and that for this reason the winter of the northern hemisphere is slightly warmer and about six days shorter than that in the southern hemisphere, while the northern summer is slightly cooler and about six days longer than the southern summer. It was explained that this is due to the fact that when the earth's distance to the sun is shortest (the northern winter or the southern summer), the earth must move more swiftly along its elliptical orbit in order that the space swept over may be the same as that covered in any other interval of time. To illustrate this the children drew ellipses with exaggerated eccentricities by inserting the point of a pencil in a loop of string of which the ends, fastened by pins, were the foci of the ellipse. They were reminded of the fact (long familiar) that the water vapor in the atmosphere retards the earth's loss of heat derived from the sun. This is illustrated by frost on clear nights and a great difference in temperature between day and night in high altitudes. The intense cold of high altitudes was explained as due to the fact that the rarefied atmosphere of the mountaintops holds in its thin blanket less water vapor and thus allows the earth's heat to escape more quickly.[8]

The year's program was carried through successfully with the majority of the children in Group IX. There were in this group, however, and in several of the older groups a number of boys who were irked by the historical approach and who seemed to require a shift in method. Their interests were not

---

[8] The second event was an eclipse, which was explained to the class and discussed both before and after its occurrence.

in line with those of the rest of the children; their attention was divided or entirely lacking; and their efforts, in accord with their interest, either retarded or interfered with those of the others. These boys were finally taken out of the class and allowed to follow their own diverse and individual lines until the general trend of their interests could be determined. This interest proved to be along scientific lines closely related to things the boys were making in the shop such as pile-drivers, stands for their microscopes, heat engines, or the simple astronomical or surveying and navigating instruments of the early discoverers and inventors. As some of the boys had had the science of Group VIII-*a* in the previous year and the others the science of Group VIII-*b*, it was necessary to begin their work together with a simple, general topic and gradually lead back to their individual choices.

CORRELATING SCIENCE AND MATHEMATICS

This topic was the measurement of time, day and night, and the passage of the seasons. Starting with an ordinary clock as the present instrument for the measurement of time, the relation of the earth to the sun in its daily and yearly revolutions was studied. The place of the earth in the solar system and the relative distances of the planets were used as the basis for number work. The earth's change in position with reference to the sun's rays as the causal factor in the varying length of day and night and the changes of the seasons were worked out in two ways: first by geometry, second by observation. For the second, the boys made a series of daily observations of the time of sunrise and sunset, checking by the times given in an almanac. The first involved a good deal of geometrical construction. The idea of the plane of the ecliptic and the constant angle which the earth's axis maintains with reference to that plane was developed. It took some time for the boys to realize that the plane of the observer's horizon is perpendicular to a line drawn to the center of the earth from the observer's standpoint. The boundary line of that plane was then taken as the starting plane for their measurement of the sun's altitude.

When they had accomplished this and its diagrammatic representation with much suggestion and direction, they were able to construct two instruments of different types for the measurement of the sun's altitude. One, like the old astrolade, was a circle with an index hand at the center. The other, and usual method, was by the measurement of the shadow of a perpendicular stick at noon. The making and the interpretation of the readings of these instruments involved much geometrical construction and the development of new measurement concepts. For two months the time was equally divided between practical construction and the making of geometrical diagrams with the mathematics in their drawings. In measuring the sun's altitude it was necessary to construct a perpendicular to a line representing the observer's plane. Discussion brought out that two lines are necessary to locate any plane. However, when representing this on paper, the boys discovered that one line would serve if the construction were kept in the plane of the paper. They worked out independently at least four ways of constructing a perpendicular. Incidental to this construction, two or three discovered and used the construction of an angle of sixty degrees, the bisection of an angle, the construction of an angle equal to a given angle. They also developed the idea that angles formed by any line cutting two parallel lines, i. e., similarly placed angles, are equal. No demonstration was attempted. All these constructions were used in a final diagram which represented the observer's plane, the plane of the equator, and a line representing the direction of the sun's rays at the equinox. The final step in this construction was to get the angle of a plane cutting a cylinder so that the shadow of the axis of the cylinder might describe equal spaces over this plane during the twenty-four hours of the sun's revolution. This cylinder would then be cut by a plane whose angle would represent any latitude, and this section would give the surface of a sun-dial for that latitude. In order to understand the problem and construct the cylinder, however, many geometrical constructions were necessary. In the process the boys worked out the following original propositions: the bisection of a line, three methods of erecting a perpendicular, the construction of parallel lines and angles, the bisection of an angle, the method of finding the center of a circle, the construction of the hexagon, and the use of terms in defining *line, point, circle, angle, zenith, latitude* and *declination*. The interest and vigor with which the boys worked out these problems was such that for two weeks it seemed best to drop all other experimental work.[9]

Each boy then constructed a cylinder on which he traced twenty-four lines to represent the twenty-four hours of the earth's revolution with axis parallel to the earth's axis. A sun-dial for use in the latitude of Chicago was begun. This problem required that the cylinder be inclined to make an angle equal to the altitude of the polar star and then be cut by a plane parallel to the horizontal plane. The intersections of the hour lines of the cylinder with the parallel plane would be the hour points of the sun-dial on March 21st or September 21st. On the 21st of March the boys all took observations of the sun's altitude. They used these to find the latitude of Chicago and then attempted the last step of the problem, namely, the construction of a plane cutting the cylinders at this angle. This required more knowledge of geometrical construction than they possessed; time was taken to work it out; and the sun-dial was finally completed at the end of the spring quarter. Owing to the crowding in the school building, the boys were handicapped by the necessity of putting away their material each night and by frequent losses. They met this problem by asking if they might equip their group room in such a way that each boy might have his own desk and thus be responsible for his own material. Each week one boy assumed responsibility for the apparatus in general use. This plan worked very well. Fewer losses and accidents occurred. A greater respect for school property as well as for each other's was evidenced after they had purchased a portion of their own supplies.

A study of the various theories of the nebular hypothesis, of the position of the fixed stars relative to the earth's yearly motion, and a brief summary of the theory of the comets, me-

---

[9] The time spent on this geographical measurement amounted to about an hour and a half a week for three quarters.

teorites, and the character of the larger planets were correlative with this work on intuitional geometric construction. The boys were much interested in parts of a lecture given by Mr. Chamberlain at the University, and a few attended a lecture by Sir Robert Ball. Many of the technical terms were beyond their understanding, but they were able to give a fairly good account of Mr. Chamberlain's meteoric theory and the formation of the continents and ocean basins.

The plan had been to follow the review of the nebular hypothesis with regular work that the rest of Group IX had been doing on the geological history of the North American continent. The experimental science correlative with this was to have illustrated the formation of sedimentary rocks. However, these boys' vivid interest in their first taste of astronomy and the concentrated attention given the geometrical construction seemed to make it worth while to go on with this work. The main interest was in the great stretches of time involved, the conceptions of motion and space. They also showed an appreciation of the orderly sequence involved in what had before seemed to them very irregular phenomena.

The boys' grasp of the use of geometrical construction in their experimental attempts to reconstruct instruments of measurement which had been of such untold value to men illustrates the educational import of the experimental method. Knowledge or skill that is tested and found useful is slipped into the sequence, the context, the category where it logically belongs. It, therefore, fits into the intellectual pattern and fuses into the emotional satisfactions of active experience which flows on with more energy because of it.

This work with a difficult group of boys also illustrates the necessity of great care and insight on the teacher's part in the choice of subject-matter and the use of methods that are in accord with the individualized interests and varying abilities and attitudes of children. In summarizing the results of this experimental course in terms of the development of its individual members, the report comments: Three out of this group of ten needed constant assistance in their experimental work with the gases and liquids and with the construction of the pump, syphon, etc. Three had a good grasp of what they wanted to do, but little skill in carrying it out, and four were able to make an intelligent plan and carry it through without suggestions. The latter also were resourceful in meeting difficulties encountered in the material or the process.

SUMMARY

A change of attitude in the approach to scientific facts and in his use of scientific method is noticeable in the average child of this age, and a corresponding change in the presentation of subject-matter is essential. At the end of his twelfth year a child in Group IX was familiar, in a general way, with many aspects of scientific knowledge, for he had experimented and observed to a certain extent in many of its fields, in horticulture, ecology and zoölogy, in geology, physiography, astronomy, and physical and commercial geography, in physics and chemistry, biology and physiology. All this study and all these experiments had been in connection with activities in social life; hence few, if any, of these facts discovered and learned had been dislocated from their logical places in experience. A child in this school constantly saw natural facts or forces in relation to actual situations where they worked or functioned usefully. In consequence his idea of a fact or a force was often clothed, so to speak, with a concrete dress of use. Just as their study of social life—its occupations and relationships—had made them at ease in a world of men, so familiarity with beginnings of natural law and scientific method made them unafraid and able to follow the gleam of native curiosity—grown in many cases to an eager and intelligent interest. This interest was gradually extending itself to causes and farther objectives. Coupled with an increased ability to abstract natural fact, material, or theory from its place in experience, to handle it, to experiment with it, to analyze it, and to formulate statements or principles with regard to it, the child's thought began to play around a problem, just because it was a problem, to hypothecate premises with regard to it, and to attempt to prove by experiment the truth or falsity of these premises.

Some of these children had almost caught up with the adult point of view. They were beginning to see science as knowledge logically arranged (or possible of such arrangement) for the purpose of searching out more knowledge. This was not true by any means of all, nor of some all of the time. Such insight came irregularly and most often at the heels of eager interest; it often took flight as the result of dismal failure in technique.

This same attitude was apparent and had extended itself to a method of proceeding in all the forms of activities of this period. In history, the average child of this group had a concrete background and an intellectual appreciation of social life, which enabled him to follow political history with a degree of interest and to understand something of the contribution that various civilizations have made to the sum total of the present day. He was able to stand an increased emphasis on the analysis of language forms, whether English or foreign, and could find the synthetic use of such analysis in his own efforts at composition. In his number work, the same attitude was shown in the ability to formulate for himself definitions of numerical processes such as ratio and proportion and to state the method used in solving a problem. In music, a genuine desire to compose a song that expressed the highest musical consciousness of the group was proved by the slow critical work of an entire quarter. In art, he was ready for a conscious attention to esthetic elements. He was led to think of art as appealing to the sense of beauty and, in his own work, to regard beautiful arrangement as well as the mere telling of a story. He could in some measure appreciate that difference in effect is accomplished by difference in arrangement of line, mass, and color, and his critical sense was cultivated and exercised by study of classic examples of different effects gained by various methods and by his own attempts to sketch from memory some chosen painting. At the end of this year these children had a start in their own use of knowledge and search for it, and some skill in using the method of experimental research.

CHAPTER XII

EXPERIMENTS IN SPECIALIZED ACTIVITIES

GROUP X (AGE THIRTEEN)

THE programs for the older children of the school, and in particular for Groups XI and XII, were highly experimental in character. The life of the experiment was too short to revise these tentative beginnings for the close of the elementary and the beginning of the secondary periods. The worth of the results, therefore, lies in what they suggest for other experimentation of a similar kind, rather than in what they prove or disprove.

REVIEW OF THE COLONIAL PERIOD

The average number in Group X was ten.[1] Most had been in the school since its beginning which materially helped the successful accomplishment of the program. The centralizing factor in the work, aside from club activities, was a daily discussion of current events. Young as they were, these children had an understanding of how social life is conditioned by and organized around the industrial life of a people and, in turn, sets the trend of the subsequent type of governmental policy and political thought.[2] They, therefore, had gained a comprehensive viewpoint which enabled them, at thirteen, to cover the early colonial period of United States history far

---

[1] Teacher, Georgia G. Bacon.

[2] "Government was presented not as a static thing, but as an organization for the regulation of the industrial and social life of a people, changing to meet changing needs." George F. Bacon, "History," *Elementary School Record*, Vol. 1, No. 8.

more quickly and intelligently than they had in their first study two years before. They were able to picture the various types of social life, the special significance of each colony, and the particular contribution which each made to the whole country's history. A number of topics on different aspects of a situation or period were suggested. Each one in the group read and reported on a subject of his own choice. The children were thus encouraged to make their own investigations; at the same time they were directed in their reading and in the organization of their material. A large number of books were listed, and each child was urged to seek out his own sources and to get the help of parents and friends in writing up his topics. The questions and topics given were of such a nature as to lead them to make use of their experience in thinking out the answers. To gather together what they had learned, a general outline was made of important events, with sub-groupings for the subordinate. This outline was used by each child in writing his own report. This was not a memory test, but a logical arrangement of those facts which might be useful. Books were freely consulted during the writing.

With the completion of the first quarter's work in history, the children had come in their continued story of the stream of time and the accomplishments of man, close to their own period and conditions of living. The text of the story was always the way different groups of people had dealt with, used, and subdued their environment, how they had wrung from it the means for its further subduing and more adequate ministering to their rapidly increasing needs. In following the details of this oft repeated story, these children saw that as man's needs increased in number and kind, so did his appreciation of the value of satisfied senses, of convenience, of comfort, of beauty deepen. Each child saw and often reënacted the part that activity played in all this moving and dynamic drama. Ideas became deeds and brought about results that changed current ways of living and gave incentive to a further quest. When the mental image of the bow and arrow first found form and use and brought down food or the beast of prey from afar, it made of living a less tortured thing and brought satisfaction to appetite, release from fear, renewed confidence in ability, and increased desire for the struggle. These children, sailing their tiny ships along the Mediterranean coast, realized the release to sail fearlessly into the wide ocean brought by the discovery of the compass. Into the small rivulets of each child's experience, therefore, flowed these tricklings from the great stream of human endeavor, the doings of man, his inventions, his discoveries, his accomplishments in the physical world, his method of thinking, and the growing fabric of his social relationship. Impelled to action by the same fundamental desire to express, and again to re-express, to invent and then to re-invent, to do once and re-do under the spell of the reward of ever better doing, these children of the present followed the fast moving life-stream of the past. Through his power of imaginative thinking, each child became, to a greater or lesser extent, one of its currents and was swept into and carried on to a more sympathetic understanding of the dynamic story of the race. Little by little the idea was born that the use of thinking is to manage experience. This idea, through use of it, grew into a consciously formulated principle that guided daily activities with the result that out of repeated successes and failures these children gained the ability to think logically and to the point, to plan, and, in varying degree, to decide judiciously and execute effectively. Many of them, confronted by a dividing of the ways, an ambiguous situation presenting a dilemma or proposing an alternative, were less and less often disposed to conclude that the solution or decision was beyond them. Both as individuals and as a group they recognized that a forked-road situation required thinking and were willing to consider before leaping into action. Steadied and inspired by the desire to find the best way out, they were ready to discuss a plan and the steps of a plan. In case of failure they were not so easily discouraged as most children, for they generally had an alternative, or by eliminating the factor which might have caused failure, could thus revise the original plan and bring it to a successful completion.

At thirteen years, therefore, these children, as a result of experience, were able in some measure to abstract facts for use in activity, to generalize on the basis of repeated use of these facts, and to formulate principles on the strength of substantiated generalizations. In consequence, their viewpoint was gradually changing, particularly in the more extended fields of their experience, from the psychological approach of the learner or mere observer of facts to the logical one of the adult, who observes to an end and classifies what he has observed with the purpose of its further use. For the most part each child began to see the value to him of reviews, of summaries, of the analysis of a problem or a situation, of the classification of facts into their categories, or the logical arrangement of knowledge to facilitate its further use in any field of activity. This appreciation was shown in various ways, for example: the agenda of their club meeting or program for assembly was prepared so that it had logical sequence. This was true too of the preparation of the points of a debate or assembly paper, or the arrangement of the data of an experiment.

Out of the increasing ability to observe, to analyze, and to select that which might be adapted to use, emerged a growing sense of power in self-expression, of ability to link observed facts in new combinations or to fashion raw materials into the more finished product that satisfied the growing and increasingly critical mental concept. This budding desire to put things together after taking them apart and the appreciation that the purpose of analysis is a re-synthesis which may be better than the former whole marked a new stage of growth. Power to conceive, to evaluate, and skill to execute were indications of the birth of individual creative power. The heretofore intensely satisfying story of what man had done paled before the exciting and fascinating thing that each boy or girl felt he might do. For each the present, his own experiments, his work in shop or studio, his own social position in his class, his club, his school, his family, became of paramount importance. The study of history became far less important than the making of his own history. His own activities, and in particular those which had become particularly significant and useful because of the consequences they had accomplished, took on a continuous character with a growing purpose. Because of the social character of the school, the distinctive capacity of each child found an outlet through his preferred activity. This individual expression often proved of service to his group or to the school. Because of the unique nature of the school's organization, these children had greater opportunity than most, not only to find out what each liked best or was fitted to do, but, so far as possible, opportunity to do it. They, therefore, earlier than most children, learned what their preferred occupations were and received training for them by training in them. Their individual needs and interests were the clues, the sign-posts, that constantly indicated growing capacity and special aptitude.

PHOTOGRAPHY, THE BASIS OF SCIENTIFIC ACTIVITY

One of the vital interests of Group X was photography. As Group IX they had made pin-hole cameras in the shop and were anxious to perfect these and go on to the actual taking, development, and printing of pictures. Many of them had carried on their own experiments during the summer and were all ready, therefore, so far as interest went, to grapple with the study of light, already planned for their autumn program.

In their work on the growth of North America, the previous year, this group had reviewed and summarized the various theories of the earth's formation, its position in the solar system in relation to climatic conditions, and the main physical forces which have formed and are still forming the continent of North America. It was considered highly important to emphasize the dynamic quality of this study in order that the child might understand the present as but a stage in a long series of changes and realize a link to future ones, and that the physical (and social) forces, which acted in the past to bring about these changes, act still.

In this second imaginative remaking of a continent, much explanation is necessary to secure typical experiences of such things as the action of a gas on a solid, the solution of solids and the change by such action in water, the crystallization of the solid from that solution, the solution of a gas in a liquid, and the conditions which determine that solution. These experiments were illustrations that unlocked the secret meaning of the processes that formed the earth. They were also planned to demonstrate some present use of the material involved.

Through a physiographic first-hand study of local conditions near Chicago the children had gained a series of mental pictures of the action of glaciers, rivers, waves, and the formation of sand dunes. The outstanding characteristics of the chief evolutionary types of plant and animal life were restated. During the year the work was still further differentiated along the physical and biological aspects. Emphasis was successively laid on special forms of energy, gravity, electricity, heat, in relation to their geological study. On the biological side, particular consideration was given to the study of function. This again related to a special consideration of the respiratory system and digestive tract in relation to types of food and methods of preparation. A natural transition had thus been made by means of practical or applied science to a more technical study of biology and physics. The interest in photography also made this transition a natural one from the children's point of view.

Group X's work in science [3] during the first quarter, therefore, related itself to a use of the camera and a study of its parts, the meaning of laws of focusing and of perspective. Other instruments such as the microscope, telescope, the magic lantern, and the primitive methods of signaling by means of mirrors were included in the course. Many excursions were made to the University laboratory to see perfected instruments, such as the interferometer and spectroscope, for demonstrating what they could only roughly approximate or estimate. This connection with the University and adults who were studying and working on the same problems steadied and heightened the children's appreciation of the importance and reality of their

[3] Arthur Taber Jones, a student of Professor A. A. Michelson's. Mr. Jones came each day fresh from his own laboratory study and was unusually successful in his experiment of recalling the course of the college laboratory so that children were able to carry on simplified experiments demonstrating the same principles.

work. The actual work was a series of experiments on light, bringing out the principles involved in the construction of an image in a convex lens. The children began by working out the laws which govern the size of a shadow. Two sets of experiments were carried out which required careful work and covered a number of periods. At their close, the children were ready for the construction of an image in a convex lens. This was worked out four times with dimensions given by the teacher.[4] Some work in reflection was also undertaken, the relation between the complements of the angles of incidence and reflection being worked out by a diagram. Some part of the class periods was given to a discussion of instruments in which lenses are used. The class made out lists of all the instruments they could think of that used lenses, and had some fifteen to talk about. The one of greatest interest was probably the spectroscope. The group visited Ryerson Physical Laboratory and saw a spectroscope and a few spectra.

The children were then ready for simple photography. In preparation they had been making pin-hole cameras in the shop and frames to form a dark room. As a first experiment, a piece of leather was moistened with a solution of silver nitrate, as Thomas Wedgewood did. A design in paper was then pinned on the leather and the whole exposed to the light. After a time it was noticed that the part of the leather not covered by the paper had darkened considerably, while that covered was not noticeably darker than when the paper was put on.

A brief description of the daguerreotype followed, and the work of Fox Talbot was taken up. For illustration by experiment, some silver chloride was precipitated from a solution of sodium chloride by pouring into it a solution of silver nitrate. The precipitated silver chloride was then spread on a paper in the light and darkened rather rapidly. The mechanism of different kinds of cameras and the uses of the parts were studied,

---

[4] The results of individual children agreed about as closely as could be expected. A comment is made that the children evidently enjoy this kind of work. One of them exclaimed the other day in a tone of extreme gladness and importance, "Oh, Mr. Jones, we've made a discovery."

but any further work in the development of pictures was made impossible because there was no dark room. Even space for the construction of one was lacking. Interest in practical photography for the time being, therefore, waned, and the course was discontinued until later in the year.

The science for the winter quarter was a continuation of the study of light, emphasizing the history of the various scientific theories as to its nature. The children first reviewed and stated the four conditions necessary for the sight of an object: (1) the object must be present and within range of the eye; (2) the eye must be directed toward the object; (3) there must be no opaque body between the eye and the object; (4) light must be present.

The various theories of the ancient Greeks and the corpuscular theory of the sixteenth century were then stated. Each of these was tested by the four conditions listed above. The wave theory was considered, and the objections to it discussed. The action of waves of light was roughly illustrated by the vibrations of a piece of rubber tubing. Experiments with the tuning fork and with vibrating strings brought out the principle of interference. The use of the interferometer was explained, and a study of the spectrum and the spectroscope followed. The composition of white light was demonstrated by experiment. The relation of the rate of vibration to tension and length was brought out by the use of the rubber tubing. A brief study of spectrum analysis and of the recent discoveries made by its use was the final work before writing up the record of the quarter. The group all saw that by means of the solar spectrum some idea has been gained of the constitution and temperature of the sun. In view of the prevalent skepticism about the capacity of children of this age to understand such a science course as the above, it must be borne in mind that these children had had five years of experience in this kind of schooling. This meant five years of training in experimental method and practices. Their first attempt in the abstractions necessary in the scientific treatment of their environment had been made four years before when they had learned general scientific principles through the use of what they themselves saw happening around them. They then related this to their previous incursions into geology and thus linked their experiences in the two fields of physiography and geology.

In the spring the children again took up the study of botany, beginning with a review of their knowledge of the functions of leaves. The following facts were formulated: leaves receive light and give off water; they absorb and give off carbon dioxide. Seeds of different kinds were planted in order to have a variety of plants for study. They then began some experiments to show the effect of exposure to light on the amount of starch found in the leaves. Leaves of a growing plant were protected from light by thin pieces of cork fastened above and below, and when it was found that the chlorophyl had noticeably decreased, the part of the leaf which had been protected was boiled in alcohol to remove the chlorophyl and then tested with iodine. No starch was found, and the children concluded that light is necessary to its formation. Another experiment had for its object a comparison of the rate of evaporation from the upper with that from the under side of leaves, and that during the day with that at night. The experiments were supplemented by correlated reading. A study of the parts of flowers in relation to function was also included in the course, using the iris, the nasturtium, and the wild mustard blossoms.

Toward the close of the fall quarter the demands of the very active Camera Club for a dark room grew loud and insistent. Lack of space in the house at Ellis Avenue, which two years before had seemed so large and commodious, was cramping and checking this and other of the rapidly growing interests of the older children, specializing, as many of them were, along lines which called for new equipment and space for individual experimenting.

THE CLUB-HOUSE PROJECT

In response to these many developing angles of interest a number of social organizations had sprung up. The most active enterprise was a Dewey Club for discussion and debate. This group, like the Camera Club and all the others, was sadly put to it for quarters. There was no spot which they could call their own, where their meetings could be free from interruption and under their own control. Out of the actual, pressing, and felt need of the children the idea of the club-house was born— an actual house planned, built, and furnished by themselves. The two clubs joined forces, discussed the idea, consulted with the adults, and decided that the erection of a club-house was a feasible plan. Committees on architecture, building, sanitation, ways and means, and interior decoration were formed, each with a head chosen because of experience in directing affairs. The site for the building was chosen under the guidance of the teachers in the different departments; plans were made and the cost estimated. A scheme for decoration was worked out, designs for furniture made. The choice of a location was prefaced by a study of the formation of soil, the conditions of drainage, climate, exposure to light or wind, which must be taken into account in building a house. The contrast between city and country requirements was noted. Each member of the group was afterwards asked to draw a plan for the house, keeping all the above points in mind.

The choice of the site of the house in relation to the type of foundation was extended into a study of the relation of material and range of soil to house sites in general. This led to a larger consideration of the character of Chicago city sites. The importance to city building of a knowledge of its underlying geological formation in its effect on drainage was the point of departure for the subsequent study of the physiography of the region. This study reviewed the physical geography of Chicago and the city's unique trading situation in the Great Lakes, its drainage problem, the building of the canal. The course in local physiography and geography consisted almost entirely of field trips under a teacher trained at the University of Chicago by Professor Rollin D. Salisbury. These field trips were followed by write-ups of notes and class discussions. Maps were drawn to illustrate the formation of the great lakes and the St. Lawrence Valley by the retreating glaciers. The whole course was characterized recently by one of its members as one of the most interesting studies he had ever had.

In the meantime the children's own problem of a club-house

site had related itself through skilfully directed discussion to large and interesting facts, such as the difficulties engineers had met in constructing the foundation piers of the huge downtown buildings and the direct relation of well drained building sites to health and security. The details of what constitute sanitary conditions, such as proper ventilation to prevent dampness, were worked out by the class. Similarly, the size and proportion of the windows, the relation of the amount of light admitted to health, proportions and proper placing of the fireplace so that it was both pleasing and convenient, all these presented no inconsiderable problems.[5] Moreover, because of the diminutive size of the building, small errors would be important, which in turn magnified the need of accurate measurement and workmanship.

In the studio, discussion went on as to the style of architecture that would be suitable. This was the occasion for a brief study of architecture and the origin of the various familiar types. Among other things the children found that Greece and Egypt were the homes of the lintel, Rome of the round arch, and Europe of the pointed arch of Gothic and Saracenic architecture. The style which they at last selected for their club-house was "just as colonial as we can make it." They discussed house decorations and furnishings and decided that only the beautiful and the useful have any excuse for existence. The qualities judged necessary for use were strength, durability, and firmness of material; for beauty, form, color, quality of material, and consistent style. This study included the sketching and modeling of antique buildings, the study of pictures, and trips to the Field Museum. In addition, outdoor sketching as a basis for the study of perspective was carried on through the spring quarter.

The interior decoration, like the problem of the fireplace and windows, was a subject of many exciting questions and discussions with the art and textile teachers. Mistakes were often made and were permitted. When against the advice of the elders, the committee chose a stain for the walls which proved

---

[5] A mason was secured to help with the fireplace on the advice of the parents in order that all risk of fire from a defective flue might be avoided.

too dark for a small room, the problems of curtains and cushions became serious, for much color was necessary to brighten and lighten the general effect.

A considerable amount of the actual construction of the little house was accomplished by the children with no outside help. Work proceeded rather slowly, however, for Group X only included twelve members. The club-house, moreover, was their own pet project, and they jealously guarded the privilege of work upon it. Pressure of their other classes left only a small amount of school time for the work, so much [6] was done in the children's free time at noons and after school. Complications also arose. The Camera Club insisted upon a stairway to the attic, which was their dark room. This complicated the interior construction. The children, however, met this problem with some help, careful planning, and allotment of tasks according to interest and ability. No part of the interior finishing was attempted until working drawings had been completed. This was true also of each piece of furniture constructed. Many of these drawings were made in the studio under constant direction. Those responsible for them were held to an astonishing degree of accuracy in order to avoid having a drawing turned back by the carpenters with sharp criticism couched in no uncertain terms. The report indicates that on the completion of the working drawings of the stairway, the front door, the window trim, and interior finish, the children so thoroughly understood what was to be done that in the shop all the different structural parts of the stairway were taken charge of by the girls in the class, each being responsible for the part selected. The boys assumed responsibility for the front door, cut the stock, and on its completion considered the difficulties which would be met when they put on the hinges and hung the door. On the stairway, the different structural parts such as the stringers were carefully marked out to show the proper size of treads and risers, and the upper and lower ends labeled to make the proper connections with the adjoining parts, whether the first part, the landing, or the second story floor. The four

---

[6] Preparation for college board examinations had also begun.

stringers were all nicely sawed from 2″ x 12″ planks and put up. The joists, posts, and framework of the two landings were then prepared, and work commenced on the treads and risers. All the pieces and parts were made in the shop by individuals working from the drawings and were then assembled in the club-house by the entire class. Covering the ceiling and walls with flooring was comparatively quick work. Finishing the mantel piece with shellac, installing the trim of doors and windows and a bric-a-brac shelf on brackets extending around the room, made the house ready to receive the furniture, which the children were anxious to plan and make. All the children were increasingly enthusiastic and lent their best efforts as they saw the vision of the completed building. There were times, of course, when interest waned, as with the shingling of the roof. This work, involving much drudgery in the hot sun, was a never-ending job. At last, emulating Tom Sawyer, the next lower class was invited to assist, and in one noon hour, that which had been gapping to the skies for several weeks was finished with the aid of these younger brothers and sisters.

As the work went on, Group X realized that what they had undertaken was beyond their own powers to accomplish, and little by little the whole school was drawn into coöperative effort to finish the building. There was need of careful suggestion and direction by the teachers, both to avoid too much and too little guidance and also of much team-work by the various departments of the school.[7] This enterprise was the most thoroughly considered one ever undertaken in the school. Because of its purpose, to provide a home for their own clubs and interests, it drew together many groups and ages and performed a distinctly ethical and social service. It ironed out many evi-

---

[7] Frank Ball, head of the Manual Training Department, was largely responsible for the successful management of the project which was finally carried to conclusion under the sympathetic direction of Mr. N. and Mr. G. Fowler. Clinton S. Osborn (mathematics) in coöperation with Lillian Cushman directed the plans and helped the children select their materials and make out their specifications. Althea Harmer (Home Economics) directed the work of choosing the site and the course in sanitation that followed, and Harry O. Gillett, its further extension into a course in geology and physiography of the region. The art and textile studios were centers of activity as has been indicated.

dences of an unsocial and cliquish spirit which had begun to appear in the club movement. As the children came to realize the possibilities afforded by the coöperation of numbers, this spirit changed from an exclusive to an inclusive one. The boys busy on the benches and the girls working on the cushions were brought together by a common purpose as they had not been for more than a year. The original club, meanwhile, took on a departmental character, with sections devoted to photography, botany, debating, and science, and was named the *Educational Club*. Members were chosen from the lower groups, and various committees were appointed, not on the basis of personal preference but of fitness for responsibilities. Another value of the project was that the children made contacts with a wide variety of professional people whom they consulted on their problems or from whom they purchased supplies.[8] An hour was spent with one of the parents in discussing parliamentary law in order to learn how to conduct a meeting on house membership. The financial organization of the club caused frequent anxious hours, for a system of dues and fines had been installed which proved far too complicated.

The project also furnished many kinds of activities, and except where it was essential to work as a group, each child was free to choose his sort of contribution. To the great delight of all, the little building was finished and furnished in the latter part of the last year of the school. The clubs used it, but for all too brief a time, as the next year found the children at the University High School, some distance away from the site of the old Laboratory School and their club-house.

THE STUDY OF CURRENT EVENTS

In the meantime, lest the groups should grow too self-centered in their fascinating project, it was deemed wise for them to spend some time on current events. The war in South Africa, the government of Porto Rico, and the transcontinental

---

[8] The educational value of purchasing and accounting was not utilized as fully as it might have been, owing to pressure of time and distance from source of supplies.

railways were among the topics discussed. Their comment upon the state of affairs in Porto Rico was to the effect that if England had treated the American colonies as well as we have treated Porto Rico and taxed them only until they were able to take care of themselves, there might have been no Revolution.

Before taking up the actual progress of the transcontinental railway, the class looked the map over and discussed feasible plans. There was great discussion as to whether it would be better to build a bridge over the Strait of Gibraltar or to tunnel underneath, but the latter plan finally carried the day. They were then told of the plan which had actually been made for such an enterprise. In discussing the railway across China, the children were greatly impressed with the opposition shown by China to the advance of western civilization and asked what China had ever done to benefit the world. One of the children said in this discussion: "Nations are just like people: first they are little, then they grow big and die, and then another nation comes along and takes up what they have done and goes on with it."

SUMMARY

During this year of intense activity the usual attention was given to an increasing use of language. The aim was to inculcate an increasing respect for language symbols as a means for self-expression and for description of individual and joint undertakings. Such use of language brought a deepening realization of the meaning of daily experience in both its individual and social aspects. It involved a voluntary search for new words wherewith to describe the experiment, the excursion, the process, or construction. It extended the meaning of present living and linked it to the doings, the sayings, the happenings, discoveries, inventions, formulations, verbal or written expressions of persons of other times and remote places.

The school was a miniature social group where study and growth were incident to shared activity. Its playgrounds, shops, work rooms and laboratories not only directed the natural active tendencies of these young people but work in them involved intercourse, communication, and coöperation. Language was constantly used to give or get ideas about joint work, and the children quite naturally came to regard the right descriptive words as the best means of getting or giving social direction to a joint endeavor. Their vocabulary, therefore, was built up in conjunction with their use of the physical means. Mental concepts included *thing* or *process* and word or words to describe each. The children, therefore, could talk or write of what they did with comparative ease and could read of what others had accomplished along similar lines with more comprehension than most children of this age. Most important of all, as a result of having shared constantly in joint undertakings, the children possessed the concrete quality of mind that enabled them to understand things in terms of the use made of them. Furthermore, their mental attitudes were consistently social. They understood things in terms of the use to which they were turned in joint or shared situations. They consequently knew how to think, to plan, to act as a group, and there were among them those who had grown into an efficient method of controlling and directing group action by their ready statement of plans or measures.

There were some in the group who wished to read to the school assembly what they had written with the expression that would convey their thought more accurately. They were interested in studying the technique of good reading. The group decided that in order to read well one must have a clear mental picture of what is read. The poem of Miles Standish was chosen.[9] They found that the reading voice has a scale and tone color, that a sentence has rhythmical qualities, and, above all, that self-directed breath is the foundation of vocal expression. They also saw that physical position is requisite to secure this breathing. At the close of the course each child asked for a poem with which he could tell his own story his own way, and special voice work with individual children was undertaken.

In music, these children began a study of harmony. The formal intellectual work went on harmoniously, but in song

---

[9] Course given by Minerva Butlin.

singing and song writing, the boys were very self-conscious. The group finally succeeded in writing a two-part song which they notated upon the board and copied upon tablets, but which they regarded so critically and with so little satisfaction that it was difficult to induce them to sing it before the school chorus, as was the usual custom. The tone of the group was strained and unsatisfactory through the entire quarter.

The group studied algebra and arithmetic, emphasis being laid on the fact that algebra is only generalized arithmetic.[10] Laws were developed and formulated by the children as they went along. Special emphasis was laid on the study of ratio and proportion, each child working out his own statement of both. The number work was used extensively in the shop for the working drawings of the club-house or in estimating expenses and calculating dues.

Although there were some children in this group whose progress in the traditional school studies was retarded, on the whole their school experience fully demonstrated that the more direct modes of activity present plenty of opportunities and occasions for the necessary use of reading, writing, spelling, and number work. It is repeated at the risk of tiresome reiteration that these things were introduced, not as isolated studies, but as organic outgrowths of the child's experience. The additional vitality and meaning which these studies thus secured made possible a considerable reduction of the time usually given to them. The use of tool subjects, especially by the older children, whether in reading, calculation, or composition, was more intelligent and less mechanical, more active and less passively receptive, and gave more evidence of increasing power than is usual with children of thirteen.

---

10 Course taught by Clinton S. Osborn. One quarter Anne Moore taught logarithms and angle measurement, as they were needed in the work on focus.

CHAPTER XIII

EXPERIMENTS IN SPECIALIZED ACTIVITIES

GROUP XI (AGE FOURTEEN TO FIFTEEN)

IN a developing experiment such as that of the school, the work of the oldest children is of necessity highly exploratory and tentative in character. Because of the school's early demise also, many of the courses for this age were repeated but once, or at the most twice. An account of them is, therefore, only suggestive of a way in which the interests and activities of the elementary stage may be guided into the deviating paths of the more specialized interests and subject-matter of the secondary period.

Careful study of the school's brief and very condensed records during the year 1901–1902 seems to indicate that in this year the two older groups were united into one. This was true for at least certain of their studies. The oldest members of this united group (who normally would have been classified as Group XII) were given special tutoring and review courses in preparation for their college board examinations, which were complicating the program. Had the group consisted solely of those who had followed the consecutively developing program of the school, and had it not been hampered by the demands of college entrance examinations, the various courses for the oldest children doubtless would have followed a far different and more logical plan, hints of which appear in the records. Roman history would have been studied from the point of view of the political state; the history of industry and of social groupings would have been developed; and more of the specialized sciences gradually would have found their places in the curriculum. As it was, the theoretical plan for the oldest children was greatly altered by circumstances. There was also lack of space and of proper laboratories and equipment for older children. Many of these difficulties were swept away in the following year when the Laboratory School, for one year, became a part of the School of Education, and moved into its beautiful new building. Records of the work of that year (1902–1903), however, were not available; hence the history of the school ends with the records of Group XI.[1]

THE WORK OF THE FALL QUARTER

For two years the course in general science for these children had been separated into its physiographical and biological aspects. The year before the children had continued the study of the various forms of energy with special emphasis on light. This course had included a fundamental consideration of various theories of energy and had been in the nature of an introduction to the technical study of physics, which would soon enter the program of those preparing for college entrance examinations. The science course [2] planned for Group XI was a continued and more detailed consideration of their earlier study of existing types of animal life. This was constantly related to the evolutionary processes touched upon in the geological study of North America the preceding year. It was characterized by more laboratory work and outdoor excursions than usually mark a study of biology in the secondary period. The aim was to preserve the spirit of individual investigation and rediscovery that had characterized the children's scientific work from the beginning.

The study of mathematics also became more highly specialized. The work in algebra included involution, evolution, the theory of exponents, and operations involving radical quantities. In geometry, each member of the group worked out, for the most part independently, from twenty to thirty propositions and exercises and wrote up his demonstrations with a

---

[1] Group teacher, Alice C. Dewey.
[2] Course given by George Garrey, University of Chicago.

varying degree of care. In addition to that of clarifying the children's fundamental mathematical ideas, three ulterior purposes were kept in view by the teacher of this course: to train each individual into the highest degree of independence and perseverance in attacking new and difficult work, to aid him in developing a clear concept of what constitutes a geometrical demonstration, to attain clear, definite, and concise expression.

THE WORK OF THE WINTER QUARTER

In the second quarter the pupils used Will's *Essentials of Geometry* as the basis of their work and were able to work more rapidly than when they had had to make constructions as well as work out demonstrations from dictated exercises. The propositions of Book I and many other related exercises were covered—in all about one hundred. In order to have time to finish the desired work in algebra, geometry was discontinued in May without reviewing the work done. The remainder of the quarter was spent in the study of radical equations, quadratic equations, the theory of quadratics, and problems involving quadratics. Although all the work usually prescribed for college entrance was taken up, only a few of the group completed the course in a satisfactory way. Some of them were hampered by lack of a ready command of fundamental principles and processes. Others did not put sufficient time on study to acquire familiarity with and ready application of the principles. The work of three was highly satisfactory, but even these needed a month of review before taking college examinations. It was felt that other members of the group would require at least another quarter's work on the important and more technical parts of the subject.[3]

The work in history was also more specialized than in previous years. Six years' study of social living the world over, as well

---

[3] "It is possible a mistake was made in trying to carry both algebra and geometry together during this year. With only three hours, or less, of classroom work and a limited amount of home study, some of the group failed to keep up the necessary amount of momentum to carry two such subjects satisfactorily." Clinton S. Osborn, teacher.

as that of their own present, had more or less adequately prepared these children to appreciate a study of certain thoroughly differentiated and, so to speak, peculiar types of social life. It was hoped that on the basis of their rather thorough knowledge of both the principles and facts of social life they would be able to discover for themselves the special significance of each civilization and the particular contribution it had made to the world's history. The plan, therefore, was to change from the psychological approach to a study of history to the chronolgical, to begin with the ancient world around the Mediterranean and come down again through the European story to the peculiar and differentiating factors of American history. The plan, however, was tried for two years only, and the records of the work of the last year are too meagre for inferences of any value to be drawn as to its ultimate success. In history, much time was also given to making up the lacks in the consecutive study of history required by college entrance examinations.[4]

The shop-work of this group for the quarter was not up to the standard of that of Groups VIII or IX. The pupils chose their own work, and the results were unsatisfactory. Some showed a lack of ambition to undertake any worthy object; some were ambitious beyond their skill; and some lacked decision and perseverance. When careful work was required, most of the group worked very slowly. The boys took some time to complete the tool drawers in their benches, did some repair work about the school and finished a tripod for a camera and a bread board. The girls completed tool boxes, a mail box, two or three book racks, a window seat, an oak table, an oak music rack, and other smaller articles. The whole-hearted effort and genuine interest of other years seems to have been lacking. The cooking as a course had been discontinued with Group IX, but on occasions when distinguished guests were present at luncheon, the older groups were called in to plan, prepare, and serve the meal.

The work in languages, French, Latin, and English, took on a specialized character. In Latin, before beginning Caesar's

---

[4] A number of children had not been in the school from its beginning and, in consequence, had not had all of its history courses.

Commentaries, the class read his biography from *Viri Romae*.[5] In translation, emphasis was laid on syntax. In composition, the aim was to help the children to gain a free use of Latin idioms in their translation of English into Latin and in their condensed historical reports. Sight reading was also part of the program, and in connection with work on the Gallic wars a detailed study of the life of Caesar's times was made, of its outstanding men and the social, intellectual, and political events of the period. In this year the children also started their first formal study of the English language, and English was chosen as the subject for special emphasis during the year. Some intensive work was done on Latin derivatives. The points emphasized were: (1) consonant and vowel changes; (2) suffixes and prefixes, their value and changes; (3) growth and change in the meaning of derivatives. Coöperation with the French teacher was necessary as the Latin element in the English language, while partly derived directly from Latin, has, in the main, come through French, and has been largely modified in the process.

The first piece of work in composition [6] was a theme relating to summer experience. The children's style was clear and fluent, but inclined to be loose and inaccurate in sentence structure. Careful criticism brought out some difficult grammatical points which were analyzed and discussed; considerable logical power was evidenced in attacking these grammatical problems. After this preliminary work, the reading of one of Shakespeare's plays was undertaken. As these children had not the habit of reading aloud, they were very awkward. They had never read a play, with the exception of two pupils. They knew nothing of Shakespeare, nor of dramatic history, so a brief sketch of Shakespeare's life and the prominent social features of his time was made from books which the children read themselves. They had no way of expressing their ideas of meter and in the beginning found it difficult to tell when they omitted a syllable or inserted one which did not belong in the phrase. As their attention had to be continually interrupted to dis-

---

[5] Taught by Marion Schibsby.

[6] Taught by Alice C. Dewey.

cover errors in reading, the work went very slowly at first. They had had Roman History so that they understood the story of the play. They committed to memory some couplets and short passages, and as soon as the study of the first act was completed, they prepared an abstract. By this time they had enough command of method to understand the character of work expected of them, and their interest in the story and the dramatic setting was thoroughly aroused. The play was completed by Christmas time; abstracts of each act were written; and an outline of the entire play given by every pupil in the class. In a general way they understood the difference between the Shakespearean drama and preceding English drama. They were familiar with the versification so far as its use went, although no technical terms were given to them. The class showed particular interest in the character study. Two members carried on a two-day debate over the comparative virtues of Brutus and Cassius. Each member of the class had weighed all the main characters and could give an opinion on their virtues or vices and the relative importance of the part each had in the drama.

This study cleared the way for a return to a study of the village life and history of Shakespeare's time. Notes were made of the many incidental allusions to the commercial changes which were taking place in England. To explain these allusions a study of the Tudor family's position and importance in history was made in the winter quarter. The religious attitude of France, Spain, Italy, and the Netherlands was also discussed. Since the pupils had no idea of the reasons why this period was called the Renaissance of Learning, biographies of the great discoverers in science were read. The discovery of the New World and its commercial importance they already understood. They studied the lives of Copernicus, of Sir Thomas More, Martin Luther, the inventors of printing, and the story of the rise of Protestantism and the settlement of Ireland. Working back in history from Shakespeare and Queen Elizabeth to the Wars of the Roses, they studied Shakespeare's *King Richard III,* following the same method used in *Julius Caesar.* About five or six weeks were spent on the play. The class was much shocked by the evil portrayed, and interest was somewhat depressed by the shock to their feelings. The outlines and abstracts of the acts were prepared, and a very good idea of the historical setting was gained. The class was somewhat critical of the play and inclined to compare it with *Julius Caesar*, which they considered much superior. However, in the end they were all impressed by the intellect of King Richard, as well as horrified by his wickedness.

THE WORK OF THE SPRING QUARTER

In the spring quarter work followed quite different lines. It consisted of a critical analysis of the class papers prepared in science.[7] The subjects of these papers were volcanoes, glaciers, and other physiographical features. The first task was to prepare an outline of what they themselves were to write. They had no idea how to attack this and in the first attempt were quite as likely to put descriptions into their outlines as to separate the headings or main topics. However, as the subject-matter had been given them in logical order in the science class, they soon grasped the idea that the order of composition was simply the logic of thought or subject-matter, and rapidly gained power to prepare clear and accurate outlines. The only details taken up were those of grammar and sentence structure. The differentiation between English and Latin caused them some difficulty. In the former, they had to learn to depend upon their own analysis to determine the relation of a word to the sentence. They were inclined at first to define such terms as subject and object in too restricted a way. They came to see that where no endings existed to place the word, the difficulty of defining its use was increased. The main points in sentence analysis, they soon grasped. Certain forms of diagramming sentences were given, but these were not used for more than two days, although the class showed an inclination to come back to them. As time went on, they improved greatly in definiteness

---

[7] Taught by Wallace Atwood.

of statement and in ability to criticize their own forms of expression. Considerable time was spent throughout the entire year in studying the derivations of words and the historical development of their meanings. At the beginning of the year the whole class was satisfied with a very loose explanation of the meaning of a word, but after the year's study not one was satisfied until he had looked it up in the Century Dictionary. They often followed a word to its roots in other languages.

Group XI also carried on the printing of a daily newspaper for a short time, as did other groups. This did much to interest the children in language expression. On account of the pressure of time, inconvenient quarters, and type of press, the work was more limited than it might have been under more flexible conditions. At one time the press was of great service in printing the reading lessons for the younger children. Developments in later progressive schools have shown that carried out in the same way in which other occupations in the school were pursued, printing might have been an absorbing interest and of great educational value.

The group was active in school clubs and in the club-house project. The Educational Club was under the special guidance of these children. It started out with fine spirit the last year of the school. The constitution of the club allowed any member of the school to become a member, and several new names were voted on. A committee was appointed to attend to the finances of the club-house and to confer with an adviser to consider the best method of raising the money for it. A new president, secretary, and treasurer were elected. The club then voted to take charge of the Friday afternoon exercises of the school. A committee of three members was appointed for this purpose. The children voted to have a general adviser, and a teacher was appointed. At a special meeting the Monday before Thanksgiving, the club decided to raise the dues of club members to twenty-five cents a month until the house was paid for. They also formed an athletic department, and the president appointed a committee of three to decide definitely on the work of this department.

DEVELOPMENT OF EXPRESSION THROUGH THE WEEKLY ASSEMBLY

The weekly general assembly of the older children on Friday afternoon of each week was always a social occasion and was usually directed by the older groups. In the beginning, one of the girls read a story of her own composition. The children were then asked to bring in suggestions for programs. One offered to have a friend come and play the piano. A girl offered the play that she had been writing, volunteering to select the actors and actresses and drill them in it. They all voted to ask Professor Judson of the University to come to talk about the trouble in China, requesting that they be allowed to ask all the questions they wished. Extracts from the records of some of these assemblies follow:

At the general exercises held on the Wednesday afternoon before Thanksgiving, the children sang their songs of last year. Professor MacClintock read a Thanksgiving story—Whittier's *The Pumpkin*. On another occasion, papers written by the children of the various groups on their class work were read. One read a long account of the conquest of Peru, another, an account of a series of experiments carried on in science during the fall.

One week Mr. F—— gave a very informal talk to the children about his experiences in Cuba during the late war. The children were so much interested that they stayed half an hour afterwards asking questions. In February Mr. Jenkin Lloyd Jones was invited to talk on the subject of Lincoln. He accepted the invitation and entertained them for half an hour with stories illustrating Lincoln's characteristics.

At the next meeting the children celebrated Washington's birthday, Group IX prepared the program, in which each child had a part. One played the boyhood of Washington; another, his school-days; another, his part in the French and Indian War; Washington in the Revolution; Washington as president; and Washington at home. One girl said that she knew several stories of Washington which did not come under any of these heads, so she wrote and read a paper on "Incidents in the life of Washington." On this occasion they worked together as a class better than ever before. Another afternoon Miss Harmer talked to the children on the Horace Mann School, and they asked many questions and seemed interested in the subject. At the next assembly Dr. Coulter gave a description of his trip to the Yellowstone Park in 1870 when he went out with an expedition appointed by the government to explore the Wyoming geysers. On one occasion when a speaker failed to come, the children had an old-fashioned spelling contest, Groups IX and X doing themselves credit. On another, to which friends were invited, the program consisted of a German play, the composition of which had formed the basis of Group VIII-*b's* work for the winter quarter; in addition there were songs and English and French recitations.

In the later years of the school the debating society became very active and frequently took charge of the assembly program. It was noticeable that a child speaking to children always got rapt attention, and judgment of points in a debate grew to be very discerning. All these weekly assemblies were productive of good results, but a great handicap was the lack of an auditorium and any stage facilities.

The boys and girls of Group XI were divided for their music periods. The latter sang well and with much enthusiasm. Sight singing was emphasized, and they learned Schumann's "The Wanderer," Schubert's "Haiden Roslein" (in German) by note and spent a large portion of their time in writing a long two-part song which they notated on the board and copied. The boys of the group, having completed the work on key and time signatures, were told that unless they wished to sing, there was nothing further to do, for them, in music.[8] They responded to this by suggesting that they write a song and chose as a topic "La Journée" such as they had seen described in their recent study of *Ivanhoe* in a literature course.[9] The words finished, they were at a loss for the music, and finally decided that the teacher had better write it. Accordingly, she put a phrase of music on the board which they proceeded to change by telling on what line or space each note should be placed. They then listened to and criticized the result. In this manner the song was completed. The three older groups were allowed to learn it. They were then to invite the composers to chorus practice and sing it for them. The latter, however, were not pleased with the result, saying the voices were too high to do justice to the song, and finally decided to learn to sing it themselves.

---

[8] May Root Kern, teacher.
[9] Mrs. Lander P. MacClintock.

This they did and, finding they could, continued to sing for the rest of the quarter.

The work in the art studio centered around the furnishing and decorating of the now competed club-house. All the groups of the school had been drawn into interested participation in the final touches on the cherished project, but the older groups designed and made most of the furniture, hangings, and rugs. At various times the center of activity shifted from the studio to the science laboratory for experimentation on vegetable dyes (aniline dyes were viewed with scorn) or for the right mixture of stain for the woodwork; again the carpentry shop was sought out for some necessary construction of wood or metal; or it was back to the textile studio for sewing and embroidery of the curtains, or weaving the rugs already planned and designed. Through all these activities ran the artistic motive—a genuine longing that the house and all that was to be put therein should be beautiful and appropriate. Interest and effort harnessed as a team, driven by genuine desire that sprang from genuine need, accomplished results of real quality. Although skilled guidance was at hand and irremediable errors were not permitted, the children had great freedom in directing their project. Naturally many mistakes were made, some of which took much time and hard labor to correct, but which taught much otherwise never learned. The groups primarily responsible for the project had organized themselves into various executive committees. The committee on house decoration decided in favor of a dark stain (then in vogue) for the woodwork of the house and, in spite of the advice of those guiding the work, carried their idea through. They were much criticized by the rest for the gloomy effect of their choice, a criticism some of them recall to this day.

SUMMARY

The little house when finished represented the best thought and genuine interest as well as labor of many children, and it grew out of genuine need. Its construction and decoration had been guided by skilled persons, interested in helping the children to conceive and achieve their ideals, and in the process to learn to judge and critically evaluate their own results. With these older children, as with all the groups in the school, the motives for art expressions sprang out of other activities and thus held vital relations for the children. The ideal of the school was that skill in the technique of artistic expression should keep pace with the children's intellectual concepts of the way they wished to refine, adorn, or represent in line, color, or clay the thing they were making. This was an ideal difficult to attain and more often than not failed of achievement. That it was achieved, in a measure, in art, in music, and to a still more limited degree in drama was a real achievement for those in charge. These were pioneer days, and previous attempts to cultivate artistic quality of expression from the kindergarten to the studio were quite unknown. Since these early days great progress has been made in the teaching of the musical and those representative activities usually called the fine arts. There is great value in this type of activity for securing freedom of expression and joyous creative effort. For the child this is what might be called consummatory experience.

In justice it should be said that at all times the experiment was much hampered by its limited quarters and equipment. Because of the lack of library and laboratory facilities especially, many of the things done with the three older groups were second choices as to subject-matter. The very nature of the school also made it necessary for the children to concentrate under difficult conditions of noise and interruption. This was not conducive to the development of the habit of consecutive study necessary to the best expression of individual thought in language or in any other medium. Lack of a library, lack of quiet, lack of beauty, lack of adequate space for club meetings, all made it impossible to carry out many individual and group plans. As was stated at the time,[10] "It was never practically possible to act adequately upon the best ideas obtained, because of administrative difficulties, due to lack of funds, difficulties centering in the lack of a proper building and appliances and in inability to pay the amounts necessary to secure the complete

---

10 John Dewey, "Psychology of the Elementary Curriculum," *Elementary School Record*, Vol. 1, No. 9.

time of teachers in some important lines. Indeed, with the growth of the school in numbers and in the age and maturity of the pupils, it was always a grave question how long it was fair to the experiment to carry it on without more adequate facilities."

Although the school had a number of children who were finishing the third stage of growth of the elementary period, it was not in existence long enough so that many typical inferences as to results for this period could be safely drawn. There did seem reason to hope, however, that with the consciousness of difficulties, needs, and resources gained in the experience of five years, children can be brought to and through this period not only without sacrifice of thoroughness, mental discipline, and command of the technical tools of learning, but also with a positive enlargement of life, and a wider, freer, and more open outlook upon it.

At least it can be said that at fourteen these children had the background of an unusually wide first-hand experience upon which to base their more technical study, not only of artistic forms and appreciations, but of all forms of knowledge, whether scientific or practical, that had come within the range of their activities. Where these experiences had taken root in the good soil of native aptitudes, tendrils of intellectual and spiritual appreciations of beauty of color, line, and form, of harmony and rhythm, of ethical, social, and moral values and responsibilities were reaching out, searching for the light of broader opportunities. They represented permanently rooted motives and vocational interests which, given a chance, would grow into continuing purposes and well-planned social action. This was by no means true of all the children who had come through the processes of the school. It possibly was true only of a very few, but it is not too much to hold that what was accomplished gave those who had eyes to see and ears to hear faith to believe that here lay the way of an education that was also the way of developing life.

CHAPTER XIV

PRINCIPLES OF GROWTH GUIDING SELECTION OF ACTIVITIES

IN the school, education was recognized as a maturing process, in which the young child grows in body and mind and in ability to handle himself in his physical environment and in his social relationships. The conditions for healthy bodily growth had long been recognized, but the idea that power to think depends upon the healthy growth and proper functioning of the mechanism of thought and its expression was, at that time, quite new. The bearing upon education of psychological science as a study of this mechanism, and of the conditions that minister to and promote its normal development in mental power and intelligent action was still for the most part unrecognized.

Two psychological assumptions of the school's hypothesis, basic to its theory and controlling its practices, were radically different from those that underlay the prevalent educational theory and practice. The first of these recognized a psychological and biological distinction between the child and the adult, as a result of which it is neither physiologically nor mentally possible to describe children as "little men and women." The adult is a person with a calling and position in life. These place upon him specific responsibilities which he must meet. They call into play formed habits. The child's primary calling is growth. He is forming habits as well as using those already formed. He is, therefore, absorbed in making contacts with persons and things and in getting that range of acquaintance with the physical and ideal factors of life which should be the background and afford the material for the specialized activities of later life. Recognition of this difference, therefore, conditioned the selection and arrangement of all school materials and methods in order to facilitate full normal growth. It also required faith in the results of growth to provide the power and ability for later specialization.

The second assumption was that the conditions which make for mental and moral progress are the same for the child as for the adult. For one, as for the other, power and control are obtained through realizing personal ends and problems, through personal choosing of suitable ways and means, and through adapting, applying and thereby testing what is selected in experimental and socially acceptable action.

ACTIVITIES OF THE CURRICULUM

The studies in the curriculum, the physical and social set-up of the school building and classrooms, the type of equipment, and the method of instruction all had to be chosen with the idea of the growing child in mind. His changing interests and needs and his ideally increasing power to act, to initiate, to judge, and to accept responsibility for the consequences of his action had to be considered. In selecting studies, it was accepted that a child's present living contains within itself elements, facts, and truths of the same sort as those that enter into the various formulated studies such as geography or other sciences. To constantly develop the possibilities inherent in the child's immediate crude experience was an important problem of the curriculum. It was also recognized as more important, that the attitudes, motives, and interests of the growing child are identical with those that operate in developing and organizing the subject-matter of these studies. In other words, specialized studies were thought of as outgrowths of present forces that are operating in the child's life. The problem of instruction was to help the child discover for himself the steps that intervene between his present experience and these organized and classified bodies of facts known as chemistry, physics, history, geography, etc. Subject-matter was not thought of as something fixed and ready-made in itself, outside the child's experience; nor was the child's experience thought of as hard and fast, but as something fluent, embryonic, vital.

[1] "The child and the curriculum are simply two limits which define a single process. Just as two points define a straight line, so the present standpoint of the child and the facts and truths of studies define instruction. It is a continuous reconstruction, moving from the child's present experience out into that represented by the organized bodies of truth that we call studies.

"On the face of it, the various studies, arithmetic, geography, language, botany, etc., are themselves experience—they are that of the race. They embody the cumulative outcome of the efforts, the strivings, and the successes of the human race, generation after generation. They present this, not as a mere accumulation, not as a miscellaneous heap of separate bits of experience, but in some organized and systematic way—that is, as reflectively formulated.

"Hence, the facts and truths that enter into the child's present experience and those contained in the subject-matter of studies are the initial and final terms of one reality."

Specialized studies are the systematized and defined experience of the adult mind. While not parts of the immediate life of the child, they define and direct the movement of his activities. They are far-away objectives, but are, nevertheless, of great importance, for they supply the guiding method in dealing with the present. As part of the experience of the adult mind of the teacher, they are of indispensable value in interpreting the child's present life and in guiding or directing his activities. Interpretation of the present in terms of the past for use in future activities, and guidance in the performance of these activities are the two essential elements in the instruction process.

[2] "To interpret a fact is to see it in its vital movement, to see it in its relation to growth. But to view it as a part of a normal growth is to secure the basis for guiding it. Guidance is not ex-

---

[1] John Dewey, *The Child and the Curriculum* (Chicago, University of Chicago Press, 1902).
[2] *Op. cit.*

ternal imposition. *It is freeing the life-process for its own most adequate fulfilment.*"

STAGES OF GROWTH

It was necessary to keep in mind that the various stages of a child's growth are transitional, blend into one another, and over lap. His present experience is but an index of certain growth-tendencies. It cannot be isolated from his developing experience. His development is a definite process having its own law which can be fulfilled only when adequate and normal conditions are provided.

The teacher's part in this coming-to-maturity process is that of interpreter and guide as the child reënacts, rediscovers, and reconstructs his experience from day to day. The teacher sets the stage for the moving drama of the child's life, supplies the necessary properties when needed, and directs the action both toward the immediate goal of the child and also toward the direction of that far-away end which is clear in her mind, but as yet unseen by the child.

It was essential that the activties selected for a school life providing this sort of growing experience should be, first of all, *basic;* that is, those that provide for fundamental needs such as food, clothing, or shelter. Such activities are genuine and timeless. Their reality excites the interest of the child and enlists his effort, for they are what his elders do, have done, and must continue to do.

In the second place especially for young children these activities should be *simple.* The early modes of occupations and industries when primitive tools and machines were used such as the child can rediscover, reinvent, and reconstruct or the present small, general farm furnish activities that are both interesting to the child and within his constructive powers. They also introduce the child to raw materials which must be made over by him into the finished product of his imagination. Fear of raw material has been a great handicap of the educational past, in the laboratory, in the manual training shop, the Montessori House of Childhood, the Froebelian Kindergarten.

The demand has been for ready-made toys and materials, which other minds and hands or machines have produced. This is true in academic book-learning as well as in the subject-matter of active occupations. It is true that such material will control the child's operations so as to prevent mistakes, but the idea that a child using such materials will somehow achieve without effort the intelligence that originally shaped or stated this material is false.

Furthermore, these activities are not merely things a child is interested in doing; they typify social situations and involve the relationships which he can feel and understand. A child can no more enter into or understand the present social organization without experiencing the simpler stages of living than he can appreciate a musical symphony without having shared in the simpler forms of music. Man's fundamental common concerns center about food, clothing, and shelter, household furnishings and the appliances connected with production, exchange and consumption. They represent both the necessities of life and the adornments and luxuries with which necessities have been amplified. They tap instincts at deep levels. They are full of facts and principles having scientific, social, i. e., moral qualities and implications. Gardening, weaving, construction in wood, manipulation of metals, cooking, etc., have much more than a bread-and-butter value, and it is for education to reveal their scientific implication and social worth. Gardening gives an approach to knowledge of the place farming and horticulture have had in the history of the race and which they occupy in the present social organization. Scientifically controlled gardening thus becomes the means for studying facts of growth, chemistry of soil, rôle of light, air, and moisture, etc., or elementary botany. These facts are thus seen as a part of life and have intimate correlations with facts about soil, animal, and human life. As the child matures he himself discovers problems of interest which he will want to pursue and thus pass over into more and more adult intellectual investigations.

When the subject-matter of the elementary curriculum is made up of these play and work activities, a child becomes familiar, during his formative period, with many aspects of knowledge in relation to living. With increasing maturity he sees how the sciences gradually grow out from useful occupations, *physics* out of the use of tools and machines, chemistry out of processes of dyeing, cooking, metal smelting, etc. Mathematics is now a highly abstract science. Geometry, however, means literally earth-measuring. The use of number to keep track of things is far more important to-day than when it was invented.

[3] "The most direct road for elementary students into civics and economics is found in the consideration of the place and office of industrial occupations in social life."

Furthermore, social occupations of this fundamental type enable the child to discover and become skilled in the use of the scientific method. They lead his thought and experimental action farther and farther afield. Concrete experiences in living and discovering as he lives, multiply. Horizons lift. Possibilities beckon. Skills improve. Knowledge put to use becomes wisdom, the woof of the web of living. What has proved helpful in a number of situations is drawn off (abstracted) and used in others. Abstraction thus becomes an instrument for intelligent action by which useful knowledge is fed into experience. Facts of knowledge are enlarged in significance, are seen in their human as well as their physical, technical or economic aspects. Little by little the social becomes identified with the moral interest.

This sort of growing experience was possibly best illustrated, in the school, in those groups of children who followed from the beginning the steadily developing course in cooking which was part of the program of all the elementary years. Year after year, as they cooked their luncheons, they tested their foods—cereals, vegetables, meats—for the presence of starch, proteins, fats, and other constituents. At the end of this continued course, in making a summary of these years of experimenting, great was the children's delight to find that they themselves could classify all foods ("a great number") into three great classes, in accord with the presence or absence in varying degree of

---

[3] John Dewey, *Democracy and Education* (New York, The Macmillan Co., 1916), p. 236.

carbohydrates, protein, and fat. Without knowing it, by successive, carefully interpreted, and guided steps, they had come to a realization that their kitchen was a laboratory, and that a certain phase of their cooking was a study of the chemistry of food. Thus appreciation grew of the efforts of the past which had given them a heritage of finesse in the science and art of cooking.

TYPES OF SUBJECT-MATTER

In an article, "The Place of Manual Training in the Elementary Course of Study," Mr. Dewey summarized six years' experimentation with the school program and these types and groupings of subject-matter. He placed the studies under three heads, finding this arrangement both clarifying and of some philosophic value. In the first group are those which are not so much studies as active pursuits or occupations, modes of activity, play and work, which appeal to the child for their own sake and yet lend themselves to educative ends. This sort of play and work gives the pupil command of a method of inquiry and experimental action, leads to inventive and creative effort and gradually to an understanding of the abstract sciences. In the second group is the subject-matter which gives the background of social life, including history and geography, history as the record of what has made the present forms of associated life what they are, geography as the statement of the physical conditions and theatre of man's social activities. In the third group are the studies which give the pupil command of the forms and methods of intellectual communication and inquiry, understanding *inquiry* to include science as the organ of social progress. Such studies as reading, grammar, and the more technical modes of arithmetic are the instrumentalities which the race has worked out as best adapted to further distinctively intellectual interests. The child's need of command of these, so that, using them freely for himself, he can appropriate the intellectual products of civilization, is so obvious that they constitute the bulk of the traditional curriculum. Mr. Dewey points out that in the more advanced stages of education it may be desirable to specialize these subjects in such a way that they lose this direct relationship to social life, but in elementary education he finds that they are valuable just in the degree in which they are treated as furnishing the social setting or background of life.

⁴ "Along the lines of these three groups there is a movement away from direct personal and social interest to its indirect and remote forms. The first group represents to the child the same sort of activities that occupy him directly in his daily life, and with which he is thoroughly familiar. The second group is still social, but gives the background rather than the direct reality of associated life. The third group—such studies as reading and grammar and the various forms of arithmetic—is also social, not in itself or in any of its immediate suggestions and associations, but because of its ultimate motives and effects. The purpose of these latter is to maintain the continuity of civilization."

FIRST GROUP OF ACTIVE PURSUITS

In the school, the studies of the first group included all plays and games, the forms of bodily exercise usually classified as *physical culture,* and the various kinds of manual training or constructive work. There were also a variety of school resources not usually included under this head, such as the out-of-door excursions, and much of the more active observational and experimental work in nature study. In the latter, it was not so much the objective facts, much less the scientific laws, that concerned the child, as it was the direct manipulation of materials and the application of simple forms of energy to produce interesting results. Wide use was made of the various kinds of activities belonging to this first group of studies with children of all ages. It was recognized that physical activity, the use of the bodily organs, is a large part of whatever interests and absorbs a child.

A sound body is a first concern for normal, wholesome growth. Consequently, the play and physical culture program of the school was the result of much thought and careful planning.

⁴ John Dewey, "The Place of Manual Training in the Elementary Course of Study," *Manual Training Magazine,* Vol. II, No. 4 (July, 1901).

Even with the older children, because of the active life carried on at all times, the gymnasium was not thought of as a place to exercise; it was, rather, a place to play in when the weather did not permit play outdoors. It was also the place to deal with the particular weaknesses of children, either as groups or as individuals. A teacher of physical culture in charge of the work for a time describes the work with the various groups: [5]

The work with the young children (Groups I, II, III, ages 4–6) was confined chiefly to marching steps, when posture and rhythm were emphasized. Games came next, in which running played a large part. These served to develop the child's ability to coördinate and control himself, and prepare him for more difficult games requiring alertness, dexterity and strength. . . . It was some time before they learned how to play—how to follow rules and regulations and restrain their whole-hearted eagerness, and it still seems a question, after some months of work with all ages, as to how soon regular gymnastic work should begin with the younger children. The educational value of systematic games and plays for children under eight or nine years is far greater. These, however, should be developed systematically, from the simpler to the more complex, and would then be a great factor in developing the child's sense of coördination and control. This after all is the main object of physical training.

With the older groups (IV and V) more stress was laid on correct posture and regular gymnasium work. The plays, a great proportion of them ball games, were made more and more difficult, thus requiring increased coördination and self-control. Drills took up part of the time, the length of the drill increasing with their capacity, and some apparatus work had a marked effect upon the standing position of the children. Each week, fifty minutes was spent on gymnastic drill, forty to fifty on games, and twenty minutes on marching, running, and similar exercises.

The children of Group VIII spend much time learning to work together. Through their games a great deal was accomplished toward promoting a class spirit, and a certain amount of coöperation in their sports was soon noticed, especially when one part of the class was pitted against the other. Added to this there was a dawning realization that in order to win, it was not so much what each individual did that counted, but what they did as a whole. With the coming of warm weather, baseball revived, and both boys and girls were enthusiastic about it. The boys organized a team, elected officers, collected dues to pay for the outfit, and began practice. The girls took up fencing.

---

[5] Clark Peterson, Head of Department of Physical Culture, 1900–1902.

In Group X (age 13) the emphasis was laid on posture, and a visible improvement in the carriage and general control of the body was noticed, which seemed to show that more should be done in the way of applied gymnastics.

So many of the school's activities involved the child's whole body in such a controlled way that he developed physically as well as mentally. As before stated the limitations of the school's equipment and environment and financial resources handicapped the amount of dramatic and rhythmic expression important to a well-rounded development.

In the spring of 1900 the bad posture of many children resulted in a plan to give each child a thorough examination for physical defects. The age at which such an examination would be of help seems to have been discussed thoroughly. Some specialists held that, as the percentage of children under eight years with slight spinal deviations is great, such examinations under that age would be impracticable. The records show that all the children above Group III (age six) were individually examined. Of the forty-three girls, slight spinal curvatures were discovered in twenty; three cases seemed serious; seven were in poor physical condition irrespective of spinal curvatures. Fifty boys were examined; thirteen were found to have spinal curvatures; five cases were serious; and twelve were in poor physical condition. The examination was a rigid one, and all the slight deviations of the spine were noted, which accounts for the large number of curvatures. The cases were reported to the parents, and when necessary, special exericse was advised. The general conclusion was that a curvature is not a normal condition at any age and needs remedial measures.

In planning the program, preference was given to those physical activities which gave additional control over the child's whole organism through enlisting his social interest in the end or purpose of the activity, whether climbing a ladder, walking a beam gracefully, or playing a game well. The ulterior purpose of the teacher, however, was the development in the child of control, skill, quick thinking, and social attitudes. It is scarcely necessary to add that an essential element in all this health promotion program, and one recognized by all the departments of the school, was the intelligent coöperation of the child himself through his interest in what contributed to his own well-rounded development and the proper functioning of his bodily organs. The place on each group's program for the periods of free bodily movement and play was planned with reference to the type of work that preceded and followed it, but the test of a satisfactory period of play and physical exercise was a quiet, poised, happy child. Such a child went to his next class with a contented spirit, ready and interested to enter into the work.

The department of physical education in this school never fully carried the finer extensions of its meanings to their expression in the art of rhythmic movement as now developed in the esthetic and interpretative dance. In the last year of the school, after it had moved into the School of Education buildings, and there was adequate and suitable space for such experimentation, the first steps toward such a development were taken.

Many of the activities of this first group of studies are part of daily life and minister to daily needs, such as the buying and preparation of food, the making of clothing, and the construction of shelter. They represent to a young child the familiar and yet mysterious and, therefore, intensely interesting things that adults do. They are the present; they suggest the past, and point to the future. They thus provide a thread of continuity in any situation, at any time, which links the child to his present no matter how far afield he may have gone—imaginatively.

[6] "No one any longer doubts the educational value of the training of hand and eye and, what is of greater importance, of hand and eye coördination. Nor is it necessary any longer to argue the fact that this training of hand and eye is also directly and indirectly a training of attention, constructive and reproductive imagination, and power of judgment. For many years the manual training movement has been greatly facilitated by

---

[6] John Dewey," The Place of Manual Training in the Elementary Course of Study," *The University Record*, Vol. I, No. 32. (Address by Mr. Dewey before the Pedagogical Club, October 31, 1896.)

its happy coincidence with the growing importance attached in psychological theory to the motor element. The old emphasis upon the strictly intellectual elements, sensations and ideas, has given way to the recognition that a motor factor is so closely bound up with the entire mental development that the latter cannot be intelligently discussed apart from the former. Even more necessary in present-day society is the social understanding gained by every child who shares, emotionally as well as actually, in all forms of physical labor. . . .

"It is legitimate, therefore, to inquire whether there is not also something peculiarly appropriate upon the social side in demanding a considerable part in elementary education for this group of activities. We must go even deeper in our conception of the educational position of these activities. We ought to see where and how they not only give formal training of hand and eye, but lay hold of the entire physical and mental organism, give play to fundamental aptitudes and instincts, and meet fundamental organic necessities. It is not enough to recognize that they develop hand and eye, and that this development reacts favorably into the physical and mental development. We should see what social needs they spring out of and what social values, what intellectual and emotional nutriment they bring to the child which cannot be conveyed as well in any other way. . . .

"A child is attentive to what relates to his activities, in other words, to what interests him; hence the senses get their stimulus from the motor side, from what the child wishes to do. It is not necessary to make up a set of stimuli to hold his attention or to get him interested when he is using the saw or plane. His senses are on the alert, since he must use them to do something. This is the psychological reason for beginning with the child's activities. On the social side they introduce him to the world of human relationships; on the individual side they reveal him to himself as a factor in those relations."

The carpentry shop of the school was one of its main laboratories. The work there brought the children into relation with the occupations of the outside world. The study of the source of the materials for this work led the children to many countries; its tools and methods were linked to past ways and means, inventions and discoveries. These activities led to study of the sciences, of physics as the study of applied energy and of the methods of commerce and distribution. Much of the constructive work which was necessary and related to the development of the major activities of all the groups was carried on in the shop. For a number of years the head of the carpentry shop contributed more than many others to the worth of this form of manual training in the school's curriculum. From his experience he claims for manual training, as for all other occupations in the school, that it is not just an attempt to teach a child a trade, but is a part of the whole educational process.

[7] Because we teach a child to saw or plane, it does not follow that we expect the child to be a carpenter. What we do wish is to make the child think—to question—to wonder. One day a child was pushing a plane straight on a piece of wood and remarked to his neighbor how hard the plane worked. The small boy thus addressed said: "If you put your plane so (showing how to place the plane at an angle and yet be perfectly level with the edge of the board) it will work easier." When questioned why it worked more easily, he said it was because all of the plane was not on the board at once. The child, knowing almost nothing of friction, had discovered its principle in a concrete applied case, through his own efforts and experimentation.

It is more and more commonly recognized that the best place for manual training is in the lower grades, that the child gets more from it between the ages of four and fourteen than afterwards. Girls profit just as much as boys from this training in the early grades and are often as expert and more painstaking. . . .

Number work is an important skill and is closely allied to the shop-work. Even the making of a simple box calls for a variety of processes. In laying out the five or six parts of a box from a long piece of wood, multiplication and division of inches and fractions of an inch must be used. Subtraction of fractions enters into the cutting of the ends to fit the sides of the box. Addition of inches and fractions of inches is also brought out. In fact, there is no part of manual training that does not use the number processes, and mental arithmetic in various forms is often necessary. . . . Much of the work calls for practical geometry, and a set of small articles to help in demonstrating geometry was designed and made by the children, including protractors, squares bisected diagonally and cut to make

---

[7] Frank H. Ball, "Manual Training," *The Elementary School Record*, Vol. I, No. 7.

forty-five degree triangles, certain forms to demonstrate kinds of angles and to show that opposite angles are equal . . .

In building the club-house, from the carpenter's point of view, many ideas new to the children were brought out. They were interested to find that in house construction as in textile work, we have warp and filling, and that we tie the parts to give strength. The various types of joints were discussed in detail, and models were made in the shop. The bill of lumber for the house involved much calculation and use of number processes. The number of feet of flooring, of drop-siding, the number of square feet to be covered by shingles, the number and length of rafters, sills, and corner posts were all calculated by the children. . . .

It has been said, "Manual Training is a distinct branch of education." Such is not the case. It is part of the whole education of the child, and by working in harmony with the other departments it becomes more so. . . . None of the other branches of the school lose dignity because they are made to dovetail into the other subjects. Why should manual training? Weaving is more interesting to children because they can make their own looms and spindles in the shop, and the shop work is more interesting because they can use their own products. History does not become dull because they have made in miniature the same things the people they have been studying about made. They encounter and appreciate the difficulties that primitive peoples met with, and understand better the labor and cost that has gone into the comforts and conveniences of the present. When a group of children came last year with eager faces and asked if they might make backs for the thermometer bulbs they had just finished in the science department, to them the shop-work was of vital importance for there they could make an essential part of those thermometers. Without the back it would have beeen simply a glass tube, filled with mercury. . . .

This correlation of manual training with other departments is in a state of evolution and will not be accomplished in one year, nor by one man. The results must be accomplished by the coöperation of all the teachers. When the group teacher submits articles necessary in her work and the manual training teacher helps the children to put them into form, bringing out in the process the principles of construction, elements of geometry or of tool practice which the child needs, good results will be reached. Formal number work is put to the test of practical use in the shop, and in countless other ways too numerous to mention, the work of the shop is a part of the complete . whole.[8]

---

[8] Mr. Ball found that ordinary tools were much too heavy for the younger children. He planned and had made a lighter set of tools most frequently used, consisting of a hack-saw, chisel, plane, claw-hammer, and a special

Playing house or building houses and playing at house-keeping in them, after the manner of peoples being studied by the class, were constantly recurring activities of interest to each age in turn. The four- and five-year-olds built houses of blocks and then of boxes or cardboard and furnished them to take home. Much of the constructive work of the children in Groups I and II was carried on in their own room. When they came to work with wood, however, the need for skilled direction sent them to the carpenter shop for help. One year a group of eight-year-old boys, of their own choice and on their own initiative, constructed a large playhouse for the younger children to paint and furnish. Even at this self-centered age the pleasure of working for the kindergarten children carried them through the continued effort necessary to complete the house, to roof it properly, and to leave it in shape for the younger children to finish.

In the succeeding years of their school life, as they relived the story of developing civilization, the children studied the housing people of early times had found suitable to various physical environments. Some of the projects proved too long and repetitious to be worth while. Others were most successful and led the children on into further and related undertakings. When Group VI (9 years) were studying the early settlement of Chicago, they undertook the construction of a model of Fort Dearborn. This proved a long and arduous term's work, but was finally carried through and completed on the last day of the quarter. The next year these same children by mutual agreement planned and furnished the inside of a colonial room.

The building of the club-house, elsewhere described, was the peak-point in the development of the shelter activity program. What was accomplished seemed small even then in the light of what might have been done had there not been so many lacks in the way of equipment, time, and space. Its story, like that of any pioneering in any field, is the story of the blazing of a trail. It is difficult to tell in retrospect to what degree those

---

saw-bracket. These, with the pencil-compass, were all used successfully by the lower grades. There were no serious accidents, and the children gained in strength, skill, and accuracy.

children or teachers who participated in the project realized the possibilities for its extension into the fields of architecture and house decoration, and thence into the world of artistic values and spiritual meanings.[9] It remains to-day only a hint of what might be.

The other activities used in the school were determined on the basis of what would be most constructive in broadening and deepening the child's daily experience into well-rounded wholes from which expression through language and other forms of communication would naturally evolve. Farming, forestry, pottery-making, basket-weaving, gardening, the smelting of metals such as copper, tin, gold, silver, and many other activities carried on sometimes in miniature held the children's interest and gave them a keener appreciation of raw materials, their sources and possibilities, the part they had played with peoples of the world, and their value in our present social organization.

SUMMARY

Technique was not stressed with the younger children. With them the chief interest was in the process. If the result, however faulty, served the purpose they had in mind, it satisfied them. Much of the meaning of the work in the graphic and auditory arts would have been lost if this had not been true. Painting in the early years is merely a putting on of color. If the surfaces of a box, a chair, the wall of a toy house, or just sheets of paper are thus covered, the end of the process, the application of color, for a little child, is a realized idea. He is expressing in color his idea of grass, of sky, of a dog or a man. To enable him by helpful and timely direction to increase his skill that it might be proportionate to the growth of his idea was an ideal that taxed to the utmost the skill of the art teacher.

---

[9] An alumna of the school writes as follows: "The building of the clubhouse, more than all the books I have read, than all the beautiful buildings I have seen, more than any other experience in my life, has helped me to see and appreciate architecture. I got far more out of helping with my own hands in this real and practical work than out of books." Josephine Crane (Mrs. H. C. Bradley).

Little by little, also, in response to need, desire awoke for skill in the more difficult arts of communication, and activities involving the use of the skills of reading, writing, or of commensurable numbers, took their place and time in the curriculum. Thus the list of the needful and useful activities of daily living multiplied. Their educational import became more and more apparent, demonstrated as it was, hour by hour, day by day, year by year. On the basis of this proof by practice of the educational and social value of activity, it is possible to draw certain generalizations which are in turn but a restatement of the original hypothesis.

Social occupations such as these appeal to the interest and powers of little people and at the same time typify to them in simplified and understandable form the general kinds of social activity of their gradually enlarging world. Children willingly enter into the sort of activity that occupies the adults of their world, for they recognize that they are genuine and worthy of effort. Such activities are capable of the utmost simplification to suit the powers of any age; they can also be amplified and extended to meet increasing interests and growing powers. The stream of developing conscious life in a child thus occupied becomes, as it were, a solvent for the absorption of useful information. Interest and effort reënforce one another in the process of learning how to do with increasing skill the things which occupy his larger world and are always just ahead of him, luring him on to better individual effort to meet individual and social needs.

The developing program thus opened up infinite possibilities for the extension of meanings. It aided the child to gain an intellectual constructiveness and a socialized disposition. The play of the first two years gradually took on the character of work, motivated as both were by the same social interest in purposeful activity directed to desired ends. The only appreciable difference between the two was in the child's own idea of the larger result of his work. These occupations of both play and work became direct instrumentalities for the extension of meaning. They became magnets for gathering and retaining an indefinitely wide scope of intellectual considerations. They became avenues along which and by means of which the feeling, thinking, acting child grew into greater power, ability, and sympathetic understanding of himself in relation to his physical and social world; they led to the discovery of the spiritual quality of value that attaches itself to things that are of use and to relationships that are held dear.

PART III

EDUCATIONAL USE OF SCIENTIFIC METHOD

CHAPTER XV

EXPERIMENTAL
ACTIVITIES DEVELOPING
SCIENTIFIC METHOD AND CONCEPTS

IN continuing the discussion of the school's curriculum, it is necessary to remember one of the tenets of its philosophy of growth, namely, that there must be steps in the development of all subject-matter comparable to the stages of growth in the experience of the child. The first knowledge that is important to a child is power to do. The occupations and the arts, therefore, formed the initial stages of the curriculum, for they correspond to knowing how to go about the accomplishment of ends.

This power to do, this familiarity with many things and activities, this acquaintance with skills and tools was constantly extended and deepened through communicated knowledge (or information) gleaned from the storehouses of the past—what man has done and where and how he has done it. To the degree that such information was organized by the child into his experience, was used by him to accomplish his construction, to express his idea and thus attain his end, it became his own; it acted as a bridge for him to pass over from doubt to discovery, from failure to success.

Scientific method was the constantly used tool not alone in the science laboratories. By common consent it was the method at all times and in all situations where processes and activities were such that active investigation, testing out of guesses or theories, imagining possible results of this or that physical or social relation could be carried on. Systematized facts and knowledge (commonly called scientific) were also made available to the child. He was led by the teacher or through access to books to see their use in his activity and was taught how to lay hold of them as real aids in his construction or expression.

Since the time of this experiment in education, an enormous amount of systematized, scientific knowledge has been made available. Largely through the labors of secondary school teachers, chemistry, physics, biology, etc., are taught in favored normal schools and colleges in close connection with the processes of everyday life. The textbooks published for secondary schools contain all details for successful performance of typical experiments. These can be easily rescaled for use by teachers of the elementary age. One of the main purposes of this chapter, therefore, is to point out the psychological and scientific grounds for wise choice of material for this age. The illustrations are chosen to show how the child can be helped to make a habit of forming generalizations helpful in the next step or steps of his plan or project.

GENERALIZATIONS AT LOWER LEVELS

With a young child these generalizations begin as concrete groupings of objects by qualities. For example, he collects stones of certain color, size, or shape, according to his use for them in games such as skipping over water. This develops into grouping objects such as stones according to a character more often recognized as abstract, for example, according to their method of formation. The fact that sedimentary rock such as slate is flat rock becomes a conscious factor in the child's research for skipping stones. Igneous rocks (non-explosive) are chosen for building a fireplace. The child's procedure, therefore, has passed from a color, size, or form grouping to an abstract, geological classification according to method of the origin because that knowledge is of use in his activity.

LATER DEVELOPMENT OF CLASSIFICATION, I. E., ABSTRACTIONS

Such early play experiences are the kind a skilled teacher draws upon to verify and amalgamate new steps in the more advanced activities of a later study of man's use of the earth's rocks in making buildings, cements, plasters, paints, etc. In this later period of school life a child's power of abstraction takes on more and more adult form and grows to an appreciation and interest in the systematized fields of scientific knowledge such as geography, physiography, geology, biology, chemistry or physics. Heretofore, his experience has had, so to speak, a geographical aspect, a historical or chemical aspect. Geographical, historical, or chemical facts were interesting and appreciated, not for their own sake, but largely because they were useful in his activity. With the growing adult point of view he develops interest in and appreciation of the value of organized and classified knowledge, again not for its own sake, but for its classification and organization for use in his more mature investigation and research.

In the formative period of the elementary age these various aspects of knowledge must fit into the child's moving experience as aids to his activities concerned with man's fundamental needs. Geography, physiography, geology, etc., furnish facts about the earth which is man's home and the physical and chemical characteristics of the earth's surface, its formation and the laws of its forces are intimately related to life and living. Biology is the study of living things. A teacher constantly presents to the child such experience in the care of plants and animals that he comes to understand the conditions of growth, ultimately tracing the source of all life energy back to the sun. Through his interest in his own growth and his dependence on light, air, and food, he later comes to appreciate physiology as the study of the way the parts and organs of living things like himself function, and understands what balance and equilibrium in living must be maintained through hygienic habits of exercise, sleep, and food. The linking of the preparation and care of food with these topics insures a favorable conditioning with respect to them that will survive throughout life. In the school, the facts of botany, zoölogy, and bacteriology were taught from the point of view of function and adaptation to environment. In such schooling the teacher is also experimenting in the sense that she cannot foretell in detail just what turn the children's immediate reaction will take. It is her office to see that the children, knowing what they want to do, are helped to solve their problems through recalling what had been helpful in their past experience. In the process she supplied the new vocabulary, symbols, or apparatus needed.

INVENTION AND DISCOVERY TESTED BY ACTION

The method of conducting all classes through the medium of conversation and free exchange of ideas resulted in a uniform daily procedure which supplied the thread of continuity, for it linked the experience of previous days or weeks to the new or continued activity of the present. In all this activity, invention and discovery found their place. In all social situations, the ideas formed by the group were tested in action. When necessary, suggestions were given of ways to act, but a margin of the unknown was always left which the child must try out and so face responsibility in his success or failure. An essential moral attitude, now called *facing reality,* was achieved by the child through manipulating, with varying degrees of success or failure, the brute facts of the material world, as he followed or developed his plan to attain a desired result. With growth in maturity the children came to have more and more remote ends and also became more conscious of what they did. Their group discussions were more detailed, and experiences of their own past more frequently leaped into consciousness. Children of six years remembered playing millers the previous year, but had forgotten what they did as millers. In dramatizing the mining industry they only wanted to be the miners who contributed coal to their own furnaces. They were not interested as to what determined the depth where coal was formed. To an alert teacher the questions asked indicate the amount of detail to be used at any age. In consequence, at six years there was no detailed experimentation with materials used in carrying out play. Each classroom was a social laboratory—a place to experiment with ideas which carried a social import. The children tested the efficiency of these ideas by dramatic action. The teacher was stage director, furnishing the necessary data (how and where coal is really found, where forests grow, how men get the trees that furnish lumber), and when ideas were slack, prompting with suggestion as to ways and means or helping with her greater knowledge of technique. To some teachers it seemed wiser to cover a variety of occupations in this dramatic fashion because of the wide experience of the children with whom they dealt. With those of more limited experience, greater detail in carrying out a few occupations proved better adapted to the children's way of thinking.[1] When the children had acquired enough ease in the skills of communication and had reached the stage of written reports, records, and stories, experimentation with language went on. Everywhere and at all times the teacher's knowledge helped the child to acquire the more formal ways of putting oral expression and inflection into written form. Punctuation was thus wedded to meaning. Dramatization proceeded in the same experimental way from the direct play of reënacting past situations to a definite awareness by the children of the need of preliminaries to enable them to convey their impressions of incident or character to others.

SOCIAL BASIS OF SELECTING MATERIAL

A large part of the art of teaching is to give thinking its proper rôle as "a very present help in time of trouble" without letting the child become confused or discouraged by too large problems. The difficulties in choice of materials which children can successfully use were much lessened as the objective reactions of other teachers who had faced the same problems and had objectively analyzed the reasons for success or failure, became available. But always the value of individual experience and experimentation, whether by child or teacher, furnished the necessary drive to further experimentation. The work which was definitely labeled scientific experimentation

---

[1] This field of experimentation for the teacher is still unlimited. The danger with most teachers seems to be that of embarking upon enterprises which require too much repetition of operations that require no thought to carry one step to the succeeding one, such as the building of a too complicated block-house or the wiring of a play city, in contrast to the wiring of a puppet theater.

was always selected because of its social nature. The children's natural interest was thus made the spring-board to experimental action. With the older children, however, this developed into more and more conscious experimentation, primarily directed to the carrying out of their construction, but, with the ulterior purpose on the part of the teacher, of planting in her pupils' minds the beginning of fundamental scientific concepts. As these concepts were truly fundamental, they concerned practically everything attempted.

EXPERIMENTAL DEVELOPMENT OF SCIENTIFIC CONCEPTS

The way in which these general ideas took form historically was found very helpful to the teacher in arranging conditions for the children's experiments and in choosing those experiences which would help them to understand and formulate definite physical and biological theories in later school years. In all cases man's relation to the physical environment, his control of its forces and resources, led to what may be described as a general scientific interest. The best illustration of such an enlarging interest was the way in which the child's idea of the earth's place in relation to the rest of the solar system developed in spiral fashion, year after year. The history of mathematics deals first with the gropings of the past, and in them the teacher discovers how certain mathematical tools originated. He realizes that fundamental concepts have become familiar to the expert—they are the first tools to his hand. He is, therefore, often quite unaware that the beginner cannot use these concepts intelligently unless they have been developed in the process of individual solving of some practical construction difficulty. If the making of a simple pair of scales has been part of a child's early experience, his mathematics teacher can easily help him build the concept of an equation upon a balance in equilibrium, or of proportion upon the relation of gears. In later years in the more complicated but similar problem of the compound lever, the child will find the equation, here also, a useful tool.

The multitudinous character of present-day knowledge and

the complexity of its processes can only be ordered and singled out for educational purposes by sticking close to the idea that the facts which a child learns only grow into ideas (facts acting), knowledge, and wisdom by means of use in a consciously directed activity. In this school, therefore, scientific subject-matter, both as method and as an organized body of tested facts and concepts, was regarded as the child's means (in experimental play) to a constant process of discovery and accomplishment in all areas of his experience. This is but another name for learning. A brief summary of the science teacher's records of the work in science follows: [2] "The guiding principle, always of great help to a teacher selecting an activity for a course of study, was its use in carrying the child on to an understanding of larger relations. The test question about an activity always was—were its processes such as would relate themselves in the child's mind, as he carried them out, to the great general ideas which represent the controlling factors of all natural processes. Of such general ideas, those summed up in what is called the law of the conservation of energy, the various forms of reversible and irreversible transformations of energy in the concepts of mass, motion, and momentum, are necessarily the most fundamental. . . . In making this choice the teacher must be capable of seeing any process going on as a result of an interaction of forces which can be controlled by analysis, and which are subject to the same laws, no matter how outwardly unlike they appear in manifestation. The first force used by man, gravitation, illustrates the advantage gained through the use of such a concept. It is so continually and everywhere acting. Its very familiarity seems to have bred a contempt which has resulted in ignoring its possibilities educationally. To introduce the child in a natural way to the idea underlying the familiar process of weighing as the process of measuring the pull of the earth is to give him a concept of force which is his intellectual birthright in this twentieth century. In the school, the identity of the notion of weight, which the child already possessed, with this pull or force which

---

[2] Katherine Camp, "The Place of General Ideas as Controlling Factors," *Elementary School Teacher*, February, 1904.

is acting upon him in common with all other things, and the idea of its control and measurement were developed from the very earliest years. . . . Anthropomorphic reasons for the changes which the child sees going on about him were scrupulously avoided. The causes of such changes were stated in terms of such forces or motions as the child already understood, or were not stated at all where such an explanation seemed impossible. This was the first step toward a scientific attitude.

ILLUSTRATIONS OF THE GROWTH OF IDEAS

"In his first cooking the experimenting child found, through his quantitative work with the various cereals, that bulk and weight are not synonymous terms. He further discovered that weight is the only standard by which he could find the amount of water needed for each kind of cereal. This is a great advance. When he carries over this idea of the use of weight in the particular instance, that of finding the proper amount of water for his cereal, into its use as a universal measure he has made another step. He is then ready to gain some conception of the adaptation of this force to man's advantage such as in primitive uses of water power and falling weights. He is able to translate what he sees going on about him, the falling mountain-range, the grinding rocks rolled along by the spring floods as they tear away the land or the waves pounding on the shore, as other manifestations of this same force. When a child recognizes that the wave-motions in a small pond, where he directly controls their direction and amount, are the same in miniature as the wave-motion in lake or ocean, he is ready, though it may be in the form of but a dim feeling, to realize the motion of the earth as it sweeps him past the sun and stars by day and night. He can then intelligibly carry his notion of day and night and the revolution of the moon about the earth over into a comprehension of the yearly journey of the earth about the sun. He will seize with delight the notion of the circling planets as they, as well as the earth, revolve about the sun. The whirling top, the swinging pendulum, and the sling shot will then carry with them such association as will gradually build up a usable concept of force and motion. In the school, children of eight were able to develop a rational system of weights and measures through this notion of mass and bulk. Children of nine carried the same idea farther through some practical application of the principle of specific gravity.

"The notion of the increase of force as proportional to the velocity of a moving mass comes very early in the experience of a running boy, and it is possible, with proper apparatus, early to clarify the concept of this force of impact as dependent upon velocity. Each child's experience contains vivid images of force embodied in a rapidly moving train, in a body falling from a great height, or of the increased danger in motor accidents due to acceleration of speed. Associated with these images is a vague idea that the force possessed by the train is related to the rate and that of the body to the height from which it has fallen. Or, again the ever-present interest of the child of nine or ten in the locomotive can readily be turned by experiment into some idea of the relation of the mechanical energy of the train to the chemical energy stored in the fuel used. This can be further traced to the original source of that energy in the plants which form the coal.

"On the biological side, in the school, observations of the effect of the force of gravity on plants and animals began in the kindergarten. The geotropism of roots, stems, and leaves is an especially good point for experimentation with five-, six-, and seven-year-old children and helps the child to a correct conception of the plant as a living thing, moving and growing under the same conditions as himself. The type of experiment, often given later, which shows the lifting power of germinating seed and the strength of the growing stem and shoot was also tried at this time. The very definite response with respect to posture of some of the lower animal forms to the force of gravitation was one of the earliest ways of helping the child to discriminate between the apparently voluntary and the involuntary motions of animals in his observation of lower forms of life. Later, an analysis of the more ordinary muscular movements was attempted to bring out the principle of use of the force involved. An analysis of locomotion was made to show that it is a continuous forward fall, in which the attitude of greatest security involves the principle of placing the center of gravity with reference to the base of support. . . .

"Experiments which demonstrate the dependence of animal life upon vegetable and of vegetable life upon inorganic material were used to develop the fundamental conception of the dependence of all life on solar energy. The continual repetition of such experiments year by year involved more and more analysis of the forces concerned."

It is important to recognize that the great scientific development of the nineteenth century originated in the need for and development of an intelligent control of the processes of manufacture. This is the clue to the educational value of a study of the industrial processes. The interests of both child and teacher, however, must never center scientifically in the logical use and control of any one particular process. The scientific principle involved must be worked out not only for that process; it must be widely applied also and related by the child to the great natural forces which his tiny process parallels. Thus in consecutive years the child was helped to build up certain concepts of the character of solution. This was begun with a solution such as salt in water. In studying the various uses of salt in flavoring and preserving food the following ideas of solution were developed through the children's observations, questions, and experiments. The first was always the disappearance of the solid in the liquid; that it was divided up evenly throughout the liquid; that it could be recovered by evaporating the liquid; that the weight of the solution was always equal to the sum of the liquid and the solid. They also learned some of the common tests for concentration in solution such as the use of brine strong enough to float an egg. All their experiences in solution found use in the understanding of digestion as the process of making food soluble through the action of ferments so that it could pass through membranes into circulation and be made available to all the tissues. The passing through membranes was illustrated by simple experiments in osmosis. In their later study of plant and animal life many occasions arose for the use of this knowledge.

The growth of this ability to liken causes, that of his own small experiment to that of a natural force and similarly to compare the effects of both, helps the child to recognize that the underlying principle of both is similar, and that it is also the principle which is essential to his desired end. He thus comes naturally into the possession of the scientific method which is the key to intellectual power in any field of knowledge. He will do this without divorcing the play of emotion, and color of feeling from his thinking.

A science teacher in this school had to have at command a conception of the great general ideas of science, and of their function as the factor by which man controls the natural world before she was equipped to select material for a course of study in science with a group of elementary children. The type of scientific material chosen and the method of its teaching were always dependent upon the psychological age of the child. From this point of view two stages of development are recognized in the years of the elementary period, the one differentiated from the other by the child's growing ability to abstract consciously and, therefore, to formulate and classify. As this latter ability increases the child gradually enters the second stage of his development or growth—the period of classification and formulation.

EXPERIMENTATION IN THE ELEMENTARY PERIOD

[8] The objection has been made that until the elementary period is passed, experimental work finds no place in the school curriculum, that science work, or nature study, should be observational in method. The objection seems to hold only when experimentation is regarded from the adult point of view, as a basis for abstract formulation. When an experiment is used as an illustration and a form of expression, it becomes a means of

---

[8] Much of the remainder of this chapter, except as indicated, is taken from an article by Katherine Camp, "Science in Elementary Education," *Elementary School Record*, September, 1900.

utilizing and training the child's natural spirit of investigation, and the above objection loses force. Taken in connection with some social activity in which the child is engaged, experiments serve as valuable illustrations. They are simplifications of the complicated processes he has been observing. Any child who is allowed to play freely constantly constructs his own playthings. Soon he will be found freely experimenting with his materials and environment. It was found desirable to utilize this desire for expression through this kind of constructive activity, and experimental work was included in the curriculum with the youngest children.

In the first stage of growth until the child is seven or eight years of age, the selection of suitable activities, which take advantage of the physical, chemical, and biological facts that constantly come under the observation of the modern child, was found to be more of a social problem than a scientific one. The activities were selected, therefore, primarily for their social, rather than their scientific value. (The term *scientific* is here used in the specialized sense, meaning the formulation and classification of facts from the distinct points of view of the physicist, the chemist, the biologist, or the astronomer.) Scientifically considered, therefore, the main problem during this period is to select and reinforce the fundamental phases of the processes concerned in these social activities by making them concretely visible.

During the latter half of this stage of growth, on the social side, typical occupations were chosen with great care. Similarly, on the scientific side, much thought was used in the selection of those illustrations which are typical of the action of the physical forces studied. A child's interest in plants and animals is in direct connection with their relation to man. The conditions of physical environment should be taken up only as furnishing occasions and material for definite social activities, which a young child carries through with great satisfaction. At this age, however, memory of the process as something to be repeated and adapted to slightly altered circumstances, does not exist. Until children are seven years of age, sometimes older, while there is recognition of objects, there is rarely any distinct memory of process. Such memory comes only with the more or less conscious formulation of the process as a means to an end. The six-year-old children of the school began with an occupation in which conditions were similar to those of their own actual environment. They next took up some specialized forms of this ocupation in which the conditions, such as the changes of the seasons, are in contrast to their own. Only important differences, such as the lengthened day and the greater height of the sun in the sky, were considered in connection with a product of their activity, such as wheat in the North and sugar-cane in the South. The advance in civilization through discovery and invention, as developed in primitive occupations, was the topic for the next year.

While carrying on these primitive occupations, the children naturally passed from the unreflective period, just as the race has done, into a reflective one. They began to be concerned with the consideration of process. The discussion of the Iron Age supplied a demand for the construction of a smelting oven. This was made of clay and was of considerable size. Its construction required much effort. In the first attempt the draft was not right, as the mouth of the furnace was not in proper relation to the vent, both as to size and position. Instruction in the principles of combustion and the nature of drafts was needed. It is of great importance in such teaching that the teacher keep her twofold purpose constantly in view: (1) to provide the child with opportunity to develop and use, thereby learning, great scientific truths, and (2) to preserve, through use, the child's instructive spirit of inquiry, to build in his mind a concept of scientific method as a practical tool and thereby guide him into the experimental, the scientific habit of mind.

It was found that at eight years a child begins to show interest in larger physical and social relations, and the spirit of adventure often flutters its wings. In this school a study of exploration and discovery at this time introduced a variety of social conditions. Curiosity about the whole physical world was strongly manifested, and a brief history of the world from a bare, bald rock to its present condition was the starting point for the consideration of the chief geographical forms. At the same time, in their study of occupations geographical setting was considered in its connection with social life. In the preceding year the children had relived various types of early communal life and had chosen their site as suited to their occupations. In this year actual conditions and historical social events were studied in their geographical location. Stated from the adult's standpoint, the points taken up were the zonal distribution of plants and animals, the trade-winds, and the character of the atmosphere in its relation to life. The main purpose was to build up in the child's mind an idea of the physical world as a whole and at the same time to relate his social interest to definite areas in widely separated parts of the world. About this age the children were able to carry on experiments which they knew illustrated general conditions, or which were in relation to the discovery or use of certain facts or a force of nature by the particular people under consideration. Their approach to the zonal distribution of plants, for example, may have been made through the discovery of wheat by a tribe of primitive people. This led the group to various lines of speculation as to how wheat-seed was first brought to this locality, what sort of climate it required, and other specific questions. These in turn opened up general questions of seed dispersal, distribution of plants according to climatic conditions, and other questions of plant relations and, in response to the alert interest of the children, developed into a course in plant physiology and ecology which had been from the beginning, in the mind of the teacher, a part of the science program.

This alert curiosity about and keen interest in all life, both plant and animal, was the result of a careful stimulation of the child's natural impulses to observe and investigate his world. This desire to know more about the needs of plant life, its preservation and reproduction, led naturally, therefore, into a continually enlarging course of study of plant life and plant relations.[4] The course dealt with the life processes of the plant, especially those of nutrition, assimilation, growth, and irri-

---

[4] Course developed for the most part by Katherine Andrews who worked under the guidance and in close collaboration with Prof. John M. Coulter of the University.

tability, with the plant's relation to animals and to other plants, with the influences of soil, moisture, and other environmental conditions upon the plant, and with the influence of plants upon their environment and geographical conditions. Form and structure were emphasized only where they illustrated the adaptations to function made by the plant. From this point of view the shape and character of leaves and stems were regarded as important only so far as they are related to light. The flower was important only in its relation to reproduction. The use of technical terms was avoided so far as possible, though given the children if necessary.

From a wealth of material for study, choice was made of that which was appropriate to the season, had some relation to the work of the group in other branches, and did not present too many difficulties. One group of children, nine years of age, began the work in the fall with the story of seed dispersal. They first observed and classified all the seeds they found according to their adaptations for dispersal, whether by wind, water, animals, or violent discharge from the seed-pod. Later these same children carried out some simple experiments in nutrition, respiration, and transpiration.[5] The following experiment which proved the weight of air, even to the most skeptical child, was part of a series of experiments to discover the sources of the food of plants. The added inference by the children that air has weight, was unexpected to the teacher: [6]

Each child carefully weighed a pot and filled it with dry loam, weighed the pot again, and computed the weight of the loam. He then weighed a bean seed and planted it in the known quantity of loam. The pots were put in a favorable place for growth and kept watered. Account was kept of the amount of water put upon the plant during the experiment. When the seedling was about six inches high, it was taken out of the pot, and both seedling and earth were thoroughly dried and weighed. In all cases the children found an excess in weight of the earth and the seedling (seven grams) over the earth and bean. This greatly surprised some of the children, as they thought a plant's food came only from the earth; others said

[5] Katherine Andrews, "Experiments in Plant Physiology," *Elementary School Record*, No. 4 (May, 1900).
[6] *Ibid.*

they knew plants took in air through their leaves and that had caused the extra weight. An additional experiment was made to prove to some skeptical children that air has weight by showing its pressure. One child thought that the water put upon the plant might have contained something dissolved in it which would not evaporate. So a quantity of water equal to that upon the plant was evaporated and the remaining solids found to weigh one-tenth of a gram. As this would not account for the seven grams, they considered their original conclusion correct.

In further experiments the children worked out the relations of air and water currents to the varying pressure produced by the expansion of the air by heat. In developing a problem such as the trade-winds, a child of this age takes only general features—the motion of the winds as produced by the motion of the earth, the pouring in toward the equatorial regions of the heavy, cold air from the north and south, and the forcing upward of the broad belt of air heated by a tropic sun. When local weather conditions were studied, the conditions of the child's own environment were taken as a starting point. No detailed or continuous weather observations were made.

By this time the children had a fairly definite idea of the world as a whole. It was to them a rock ball, on which the continents are slight elevations covered with a thin soil produced by the crumbling of the rock. They pictured this ball surrounded by great bodies of water in which warm and cold currents circulate and modify the climates of the shores. It is covered with an atmosphere, a medium of exchange, by means of which the most important conditions of life—water, light, and heat—are distributed. They thought of it as covered with plant and animal life, its kind and abundance being determined by physical environment. For the most part they had a fairly definite idea of the chief causes affecting climate and the zonal distribution of plants and animals, and of man's continuous control and adaptation of conditions about him.[7]

---

[7] Mrs. Alling Aber's book on *An Experiment in Education* will give teachers a concrete illustration of how this work was first carried through successfully with children.

In their experiments with plants these nine-year-old children demonstrated the dependence of both plant and animal life upon these elements and the conditions, and upon each other.

A strong, growing leaf was submerged in a glass of water and put in direct sunlight. Bubbles which the children recognized as a gas were seen to come off from the leaf. They noticed that these bubbles came off faster in strong sunlight and ceased altogether when the glass was placed in darkness. To find out the nature of the gas, some was collected by putting algae in a large beaker of water and a funnel over the plants. A test-tube was filled with water and inverted over the stem of the funnel, so that the mouth of the tube was just under the water. The beaker was placed in strong light, and as the bubbles arose they were led into the test-tube through the funnel and displaced the water in the tube. When enough had collected to test, the children applied a glowing splinter to the gas and found that it burst into flame, proving the gas to be oxygen. A strong, healthy plant was then put under a bell-jar together with a small beaker of clear lime water. Fresh air from outdoors was inclosed in the jar and the rim covered with vaseline so that no air could get in. The bell-jar was covered with a black cloth so that the plant would be under night conditions. The next morning a white coating was found on the lime water, which the children knew showed the presence of carbon dioxide.

From these experiments the children concluded that two processes went on, one a giving out of oxygen and the other a giving out of carbon dioxide. They knew that the air contained oxygen, which was taken in by animals and converted into carbon dioxide, and they saw that the process of respiration was similar in plants. But the quantity of oxygen given off was much greater than the amount of carbon dioxide, for there were many bubbles of oxygen coming from the submerged plant, while the carbon dioxide (which they found to come off in darkness) did not cause bubbling. This excess of oxygen would keep the air in a condition fit for animals to live in. They were told that the process of respiration went on all the time, but only in sunlight could the plant take in carbon dioxide and convert it, with the water and nutriment derived from the soil, into starch and other food for the plant.

The presence of green matter in the leaves, as necessary to the manufacture of food, was emphasized.

At nine years, sometimes as early as eight, the child's attitude toward his work begins to change. Although both generalization and specialization in science come much later, yet the method and spirit of his inquiry are modified at this age, and he has entered upon what may be called the second period of elementary education.

Physiography was chosen as the first subject to be lifted out of its immediate relation to the activities of history. This change in method was partly in response to the children's dawning realization at ten years of the relation of means to ends. It was also in response to their increasing ability to follow one field of interest continuously and to deduce general, uniform principles from their observations or experiments. Physical geography was continued with the eleven-year-old children and covered the general physical characteristics of the whole United States. A change was made to a more definitely planned and, therefore, more formal method of treatment. The children carried on their work by (1) discussion, (2), written papers, (3) assigned reading, (4) construction of putty relief maps of the chosen localities. In the following year the class made a detailed study of the formation of the earth, and especially of sedimentary rocks.

In all of the experimental work of the second growth period the consciousness of the end to be attained was more definite, and the processes necessary to attain that end were more involved than in that of children in the first stage. During this period as in the first, the activities are still carried on for their own sake. They were, however, more consciously used as a means to a result, which may be valuable to the child either because of its social or its scientific interest. At this time the child begins to experiment consciously. He initiates certain conditions to find out what will happen. Instead of "Tell me why this happens," he is apt to say, "Don't tell me, let me see if I can find out myself."

In an article, "Astro-Geography" this anecdote is told which indicates the children's ability to take large and comprehensive views of the physical and social world at the age of eight or nine years.[8]

The members of a class were discussing plans for a year's work on the history of Chicago. . . . A small boy of eight very seriously propounded the following problem which had evidently caused him much thought: "Which do you think," he said, "is the best way to study geography—to begin with your own place and go out, out, out, until you reach the stars, or to begin with the stars and come in and in until you reach your own place again?" He was told that people differ as to the wisdom of either course, was reminded that during the previous year he had studied about people who lived in very different parts of the earth, and the present plan was to study about his own locality. He accepted the answer, and seemed satisfied to begin at home. While settling back contentedly, however, he murmured: "But I shall get a book about the stars, anyway." This story may indicate an unusual state of mind in an eight-year-old child. Experience has proven, however, that children between eight and nine take a large and universal view of their world much oftener than they are given credit for so doing. . . .

The article continues:

A city child has so much of people and their many activities that his naïve attitude of wonder and delight in the heavenly bodies may die still-born. It behooves both school and home, therefore, to give him the chance which only the leisure of youth can afford, for development of his genuine interest in the marvels of the countless stars and immense distances of space. Neither should it be forgotten that there is a great plasticity still inherent in the child's mind, which makes possible the use of material that seems to the ordinary adult mind too abstract or too remote to be suggestive. Furthermore, a child eight or ten has no fear of any subject because of association, no habit of regarding one problem as more difficult than another. Points in astro-geography, as in physiography, which take an hour's work with college students, were worked out by children of this age in fifteen minutes. . . . Occasions often arise with very young children when they note marked changes in length of day and night, and of season. If reference to the causes of these changes is made in a story form, the teacher can keep the ideas plastic and open to the larger universal view, even though at the time the child may be occupied with small results of the same changes, such as autumn fruits, winter ice and snow, the planting of his garden, or the return of the birds in the spring. Seven-year-old children begin to ask

---

[8] Katherine Camp, "Astro-Geography for Children," *The Elementary School Teacher*, Vol. IV, No. 5, 1904.

definitely for the story of the earth. Observation of the days of the equinoxes and the relation of the Christmas holiday to the return of the sun will help make the story of the seasons dramatic. Here again, in connection with something they are carrying on, can be introduced the explanation of the moon's phases, why the North Star only seems stationary, and other stories to identify the guiding stars of the heavens. By the use of globes and a strong light, a real appreciation of the reason for the visible changing phases of the moon may be easily demonstrated, also the periodic recurrence of the eclipse. The detailed working out of the definite position of the moon with relation to the sun and earth, which results in its different phases, might better be left until two or three years later. It was found that the child at this early age will learn to look for the full moon rising in the east, as the sun disappears in the west, and associate that eastern position with its relation to the sun.

Much experimental work, besides that given in connection with the ecology of the lake region, was incidental to the study of colonial industries. The various processes of the textile industries of colonial times were taken up in detail and included the cultivation and preparation of wool, flax, and cotton. In connection with the construction of some machines used in the textile process studied, a most primitive type was studied first to show man's first use of energy. The later forms followed which illustrate a more complicated type involving a change of the form of energy. In such a machine as the spinning-wheel the three laws of machines take concrete form as bringing about some desired end—the thread made. With an understanding of the spinning-wheel as a background, a child easily appreciates each step made in the invention of the spinning-jenny, and its apparently complicated action is intelligently followed. He hails with delight each modification which overcomes a difficulty.

GROWTH OF SCIENTIFIC METHOD IN COOKING

In his laboratory work in cooking, the child at the end of his eighth year had completed a threefold classification of foods. In the succeeding one, in his study of the physiology of digestion, he attempted a more analytic look at each classification. The effect of heat and water on carbohydrates, fats, and proteins was determined by means of detailed experiment. The value of cooking as a preparation for digestion was learned. In this way he made a general survey of the process of digestion and gained some familiarity with it. The points taken up, at this time, were general. The aim was to secure an idea of the digestive process as a series of solutions accomplished by fermentation, of the function of each part of the digestive system, and, in a general way, of the relation of food to energy. The detail of these processes, the particular chemical or physical force at work, did not concern him. All he wanted was a simple illustration of "what happened": hence he was not troubled by the fact that we do not know how it happens, or in the true sense exactly what does happen. This sort of illustrative experimental work seems to fulfil requirements which demand recognition of a problem, initiation on the child's part, and utilization by him of means suggested by the teacher to obtain an end which he appreciates and desires.

It was found necessary to take time each year to sum up the general features of the year's work. Different avenues of approach were used in making this summary. In one year, with children of nine or ten, the geography of the whole world was attempted from the mathematical point of view, the need for the use of latitude and longitude in their historical work furnishing the occasion.

STUDY OF THE EARTH BY TEN-YEAR-OLD CHILDREN

After this kind of preparation the child at ten years was ready to take up the growth of the continent as a convenient basis, on the geographic side, for gathering together all his previous experience. A brief review was made of the various theories of the earth's formation and its position in the solar system as affecting climatic conditions. This was the starting point for the consideration of the physical forces at work in the formation of the continent of North America. As in the fifth year, the child was led to sum up his knowledge and state his conception of the earth as a rock ball whose surface throughout long ages has taken definite shape by the interaction of forces which are still at work. The main purpose was to help the child form a notion of the dynamic character of the changes in the earth's surface, to see that its present condition is but one stage in a long series, and that the same forces which acted in the past act still. In this way, he was led to construct imaginatively the conditions which must have obtained in very early stages of geological history. Here, as in his previous reconstruction of physiographic conditions, his images were of the most general character.

Experimentation accompanied this imaginative remaking of the continent, in order to secure typical concrete illustrations of such things as the action of a gas on a solid, the solution in water of the solids changed by such action and the subsequent crystallization of the solid from that solution, the solution of a gas in a liquid, and of the conditions that determine, roughly speaking, that solution. The physical characteristics connected with the formation of the rocks in the various geologic ages were taken up in more or less detail. The amount of time thus spent was determined by the possibility of actually reproducing some of the conditions which bring about the structure considered.

ADAPTATION OF TOPICS TO INDIVIDUAL GROUPS FOR OLDER CHILDREN

With older children, from ten to thirteen, many such ideas can be worked out. Those which are involved in the construction of a sun-dial, of the day circle, the mapping of the chief constellations, and the making of such a model of the solar system as is suggested in Iles's *Intuitive Geometry*. One year's work of the twelve-year-old children involved a review of the geographical features of the historical setting studied and of the work on general physical forces and zonal distribution, etc., covered when the children were ten. The view of the world as a whole was then dropped and taken up the following year from the standpoint of physical geography and geology. Even in the ninth year of school life, when the child is between twelve and thirteen, the interest in formulation and classification as such was not strongly apparent. True secondary education in scientific subjects could not, therefore, begin. The practical differentiation begun the previous year, however, was carried farther with advantage during the year. Practical considerations, as always, determined whether the differentiation took a physical or a biological aspect. On the biological side the natural sequence was a further study of the existing types of animal life, kept in touch with the evolutionary processes as briefly given the preceding year in the geological study of North America.

Group X, at the age of thirteen years, took their first general course in biology. This was planned to develop the idea of animal life, began with simple forms, and ended with the physiology of man. The course was centered on the function of parts rather than a detailed study of the changes in form of anatomical parts; it was accompanied by some experiments in plant physiology, which emphasized the adaptation of plants to environment, and was illustrated by the adaptation of vegetation to a city's smoke and heat.

The theories of the formation of the earth as a part of a nebulae, once like other nebulae seen today, were repeated from year to year, and afforded an important and clear illustration of the way in which scientific theories are formed only to be replaced by others. The purpose of a theory as a working basis for thought became familiar to the children. For years the study of science had been planned to build up in the mind of the child a mental image of the physical and biological processes of change and growth as a continuous round of the freeing and utilization of energy. The physical forces of gravity, heat, light, electricity were seen as factors in the process, sometimes tearing down and at others building up. During these years practically the whole story of life and growth had been presented in terms of family life and in relation to its requirements for food, shelter, and clothing. Various activities, chosen because of their social worth, illustrated these processes in more specific fashion and made the ideas of solution, evaporation, crystallization, and precipitation concrete to the child. Solids, liquids, and gases became familiar forms of matter. Over and over the story of the earth was told, the formation of the rocks and soil and the parts that air and water, heat and light play in the life of plants and animals. From the very beginning the concept of gravity as the pull of the earth on matter was presented to the children. They rediscovered the use of weights and measures as a way of finding the amount of the pull or gravitation, of the scales as a device for finding equal pulls or for the comparison of quantity as obtained by measurement, and of mass as measured by the pull of the earth. At eight years the child had formulated a rational system of weights and measures; a year later he understood something of the laws of falling bodies and recognized the motion of the pendulum as governed by the same laws. Constant reference of this sort to illustrations of this force acting in the world about him had made the child's idea more and more explicit, until in his work on machines he was ready to use the notion of measuring work by units of weights carried through units of space. Through his own observations he could interpret the effects of the ever-acting gravitational force on animals and plants and as used in the barometer and water-power.

In the same way other topics were taken up in this spiral fashion. The part that plants play in rendering the energy from the sun available to animals was developed. The idea of time and its measurement was related year after year to the rotation of the earth on its axis and around the sun, as the cause of the change of the seasons and of day and night. Each year the concept of the earth as a whole and in its relations to the sun and in the solar system grew in clarity and meaning.

SPECIAL SCIENTIFIC TOPICS

When the school closed, two of the groups had arrived at the point where they profitably pursued special scientific topics. They studied general biology from the evolutionary point of view, and special aspects of physics as well as mathematics were successfully taught them by graduate students in the University. A course in physiography supplemented one in sanitation given in connection with the choice of the club-house site. All of the courses, with the exception of the last, were taught by graduate students who were at the same time doing special work under the many specially gifted lecturers and teachers then gathered in the University of Chicago. All were chosen by the Director because their major interest lay in the particular subject taught.[9]

It was felt that during the nine years of the school's curriculum the use made of observation and experimental activities accomplished certain definite results. Those who observed the children felt they had attained to a measure of skill and readiness in the use of the experimental method of inquiry, had gained a general conception of the dependence of the various forms of life upon each other and upon the inorganic world, had given evidence that their general interest in what happens in an experiment had passed over into an interest in how the thing happens, and in addition, had learned the use of books as sources, not only of information, but also of the condensed conclusions of other men's observations. They were ready, in all respects, for the more specialized work of the secondary period. Such a child would be in no danger of assuming too soon and too rigidly the attitude of the specialist. He would be able to choose a point of view from which to regard any set of natural conditions whether geological or biological, without shutting out the interaction of one field of observation upon the others. The machine with which he would perform experiments in the physical laboratory would never be to him, as it is now to many, a unique and isolated invention of the laboratory, but would find its place as a means of analysis of all the various forms of machines in use about him. Furthermore, his interest in nature would never be that of the collector pure and simple, but rather that of the scientific naturalist whose collections have some specific and definite aim. The children of this school had lived through a continuous series of concrete experiences, in which each used his own acquired method of experimentation and logical reasoning as his guide

---

[9] Biology, George Garrey; physics, A. T. Jones, A. T. Stewart; mathematics, Anne Moore, W. S. Hart; physiography, Wallace Atwood; sanitation, Althea Harmer.

for further planning. There was for them no danger of a too narrow specialization in any subject, for with such training no subject could be tightly boxed off from life. In general, it was felt that the school's use of experimental and observational science accomplished in some measure the training of a constructive and inquiring mind and thus fully justified its place in elementary education. The most important result of all was that these children felt no fear when entering a new environment or attacking a new field of work.

SCIENTIFIC AND EDUCATIONAL USE OF COOKING

The activity of cooking is in itself its own reason for being. It constantly furnishes incentives to attempt new problems and can, therefore, be used to great advantage with children. The choice of the subject-matter for cooking in the school was always in direct relation to an occasion of great importance to every one—the group luncheon. The occasion thus became a natural opportunity to show hospitality to others. The motive for each child's learning how to cook was, therefore, a genuinely social one—to achieve a result which was palatable not only to himself but to others. The clear proof of social gain lay in success as a pudding maker. Moreover, because a good pudding was a desideratum for all, a spirit of free interchange of ideas, suggestions, and results in failure and success, imbued the embryo cooks.

What was cooked was always chosen with a view to its connection with the other activities of the program. Cooking involved fundamental relations to the physical and social environment and gave a reason for the study of geography, of plants and animals. It was the activity around which the child saw all the simple social and economic relationships organize and centralize themselves in his study of primitive ways of living. From a scientific point of view also, cooking as the use of heat and water on food and the physical and chemical changes which result proved a rich source of material illustrative of the various transformations of energy from sunlight to that necessary to human needs and uses. In addition it gave unexcelled opportunities for the use of the experimental method. The necessary facts, technical skills, and ways of doing, charged with an organic emotional interest, were imbedded in experience through continuous use in more and more complicated operations. While cooking was something the child could do in company with others, through the laboratory-like arrangement of the kitchen, he was individually responsible for the success of his own portion, and the social end was not permitted to overpower or befog his joy in discovery by actual performance. Each time he cooked he was guided to find that his method was general to all kinds of cooking. This method lay in the order of the technical steps or was discovered in some principle, such as solution, necessary as a means of control, and which, still later, he found himself using in a more complicated process. With children of six, seven, and eight years, the cooking of cereals was progressively educational in so many ways that it developed into a continuous course of study throughout these three years with no sense of monotony on the part of either pupils or teacher.[10]

"As used in the Laboratory School the activity of cooking supplied the child with a genuine motive and the medium for its expression; it gave him a chance for first-hand experience; and it brought him into contact with realities. It did all this, but in addition it was liberalized throughout by translation into its historic and social values and scientific equivalencies. With the growth of the child's mind in knowledge and power it ceases to be a pleasant occupation merely and becomes more and more a medium, an instrument, and an organ of understanding, and is thereby transformed."

Therefore, cooking held a distinctive place in the curriculum of the school. Its successful use was primarily due to the fact that its program was planned and directed by two teachers [11] whose training in the scientific and practical aspects of household arts was coupled with wide teaching experience. The program began in the kindergarten, and the work was adjusted to the different psychological age periods. At the end of seven

[10] John Dewey, *The School and Society*, p. 20.
[11] Althea Harmer and Katherine Camp.

years it was an adequate working program. A complete series of materials to be used in the program was listed, together with the accompanying and correlating scientific experiments which clarified and illustrated the general principle or process central in any lesson. A great help to this success was the fact that some time previous to this experiment, Mrs. Ellen H. Richards of the Massachusetts' Institute of Technology had worked out in theory as well as in practice what was afterwards called "the free-hand method of teaching cooking." This method presupposed a knowledge of the constituents of food, of the effect of controlled application of heat, and of the processes of solution and fermentation, which should make any housekeeper independent of recipes and creative in her cooking. Through Pratt and Drexel Institutes, where the teachers had been trained, much information and material, as well as detailed results of work with large classes of older girls and teachers, were available. In both, the work had been organized on the technical side and in its bearings on health, hygiene, dietetics, and sanitation. No experiments, however, with children of elementary age had been made. The problem in the school, then, became one of adapting to little children the successful courses already planned and in practical use with older girls. Many persons in the field of household economics were intensely interested in the experiment and were most generous with their suggestions and advice. The experience at Pratt Institute, especially in the adaptation of the equipment to the needs of younger children, can hardly be overestimated.

From the point of view of the teacher of general science, the course in cooking afforded more opportunity for the development of the scientific method than any other activity carried on in the school, with the possible exception of gardening, the general geography of the earth and atmosphere, and some of the textile processes. The equipment, although planned with an emphasis upon economy, was complete and practical. The cooking tables were of the sort that could be adapted by means of stools to the heights of the children.

The experience of the first year brought out certain points on the basis of which the succeeding year's experiment was

altered and improved. It was found there was no need to stimulate the child's interest by allowing him to choose the particular
things to be cooked. Some of the things attempted were beyond
the technical capacities of the children to realize. It is difficult for one who has not shared such an experiment to appreciate how great is a child's interest in the simplest processes
in the preparation of food, and how keen is his observation of
them. Even the ordinary preparation of food, however, proved
so complicated that it was necessary in the succeeding years to
progressively simplify the things which each child did in order
to preserve in him a sense of an effective control of the process.

During the first three years the cooking was done as far as
the child consciousness was concerned for the sake of the immediate product or end. The children prepared some one thing,
each child contributing his proportion to the whole. In this
way each felt the responsibility of the result not only for himself but for the whole class, so that the social end reinforced
the immediate one. This interest in the immediate result so
overshadowed the steps in the processes he was watching that
very little use could be made, from a scientific point of view,
of the important physical and chemical changes going on.
Observation was incidental to securing good results, and the
reasons for certain indications received little attention until
after the first year and a half, when a few general principles
were worked out while the actual cooking was going on. The
children during this period spent most of their time in "science" work on the materials used in cooking.

Somewhere between the ages of eight and ten a change in
the interest takes place, and the thing is done with more conscious reference to technique and to what might be termed
the intellectual side. The child comes to see that if he understands the reasons for what he is doing, he can carry
on a number of other operations of the same general class.
This made necessary a change in the way in which the work
was given. Even the simplest operation in cooking has so many
conditions that it is impossible for the child to select those
bringing about a certain result that is important for him. So
at this stage simple experiments were introduced where con-

ditions were so controlled that he was able to draw a needed inference and get hold of a general principle. For example, the effect of heat on albumen was worked out by first finding out the way in which the temperature of the water could be determined from its appearance—thus were worked out the scalding, simmering, and boiling points. The next step was to subject a little white of egg to each temperature for varying lengths of time—drawing thence such inferences as the following: "The egg albumen had a very few threads in it at 140, at 160 it is jelly-like, and at 212 it is tough." "When albumen is boiling, it is very hard, and at simmering, it is very nice and tender." After these underlying principles were grasped, the work became more deductive, so to speak. It was treated more as applied science. Extracts from a simple clear account of the way this course was taught, written by the teacher who was mainly responsible for its success follow: [12]

For the youngest children foods such as cereals and fruits were selected since these required the simplest preparation and little variation in the manipulation of materials. The children's real interest was in the active work, the luncheon which they prepared and served, after receiving careful direction either in words or by demonstration. The value of the work was in the nice handling and careful use of materials and in the forming of habits of neatness and order. All this helped to create order not only in doing things of a practical nature, but also in their thinking and planning. It was similar to the organized play of the kindergarten in its influence on the social organization of the group. The observations made during the progress of the work were valuable as emphasizing a few regularly recurring phenomena.

In the interests of simplicity, part of the luncheons were brought from home in the form of sandwiches, and a drink of hot dilute cocoa was generally served. The clearing away and dishwashing were as much enjoyed as any other part of the process. This once-a-week school luncheon was the result of close coöperation of the parents with the teacher. In this way the lacking vegetables and meat were supplemented at home on these days.

The cooking had particular educational value for the younger children in giving opportunity for individual work, initiative, and

---

12 Althea Harmer, "Elementary Cooking in the Laboratory School," *The Elementary School Teacher*, Vol. III, No. 10, 1903.

independence. It also called for group work and encouraged a spirit of helpfulness and nice adjustment of personalities to the work of the group as a whole. It made an appeal to children which was immediate and direct and was of such a nature that it could be arranged in orderly sequence. Beginning with the simple preparation of food to be served for luncheon, the children became interested in the material used and in the processes involved in the preparation of these materials. This made it possible to introduce simple experiments previous to the cooking and enabled them to work out the formulae and steps used in the preparation of the food. The logical sequence of this work formed simple and direct habits of thinking and acting. These were built upon and developed in later work where processes were more involved, where the interaction of the work among the children required a finer adjustment of each individual to the social life of the group.

The work as given to six-year-old children changed somewhat in character as regards the manner of its presentation. This change was in accord with the corresponding change in the attitude of the children. The materials were the same, that is, cereals and fruits. Grains were selected on account of their relation to the course on Present Occupations, which began with the study of a typical grain farm. The interest in the cooking started with the desire the child has to carry further the work of the farmer and the miller and follow the food from its preparation to its final use. The grains also furnished the simplest illustration of the effect of heat and water on the starch and cellulose in preparing them for digestion.

At the beginning of the cooking period the class with the teacher gathered in a semi-circle at a blackboard. The various preparations of cereals were examined, and the methods of preparation considered. By means of actual experiments the children compared the different preparations as to difference in time required for their cooking. The reasons for this difference were developed. In cooking each preparation they worked out some new point in the application of heat and water. The work started with the simplest use of fire and water and their effect on the starch granules of the cereal grain. The points brought out were the effect of the mechanical breaking up of the cellulose and of water on the starch granules, so that mastication, taste, and all other processes of digestion were more easily accomplished. The idea that grinding the grains shortens the process of cooking was then introduced. Experiments were made to show in a general way the composition of the grain, the difference in the relative amounts of starch and cellulose in the various grains, and the different preparations of grain found in the market, such as the hulled, cracked, ground, or flaked varieties.

Fruits and vegetables were selected the following year because the problems involved in their preparation grew naturally out of the material as used. From experiments suggested by actual work and formulated in class discussion, the children were led to solutions of the problems as they arose.

The starch and cellulose found in the cereals studied the previous year were now found in varying conditions in fruits and vegetables. The value of water as a food constituent was brought out, as were the flavoring principles, such as the essential oils, vegetable acids, sugar, and mineral salts. These were considered, of course, with the younger children more in the part they have in giving character and flavor to the vegetable than in any nutritive value they possess.

In the experiments made in this year the interest was in seeing what happened and in making discoveries. The purpose of the experiment was often lost in the interest of the immediate program. Therefore the connection was made by the teacher between the purpose of the experiment and the problem to be solved. Though only a phase of the work, this formed a new problem for the children. For example, the potato was to be cooked. The child was led to compare it with the cereals previously studied. This led to an analysis of the potato which completely engrossed him for the time being. After he had discovered all he could about the potato, he was thrown back to the original problem of how to cook it. This at once called for an application of the facts discovered in the experiments. The fact that such experimentation was continuous throughout the year, and that results were always made use of to some practical end, gave added value to each experiment. Each became part of a larger whole. The original problem thus grew larger and showed many sides.

In these practical activities the child also came to have some idea of the real value of number. He used parts of a cup, as units; he then got the relation of these units to a larger whole; and he began to have an idea of simple fractions. From the manipulation of materials, and comparison of these by weight and measure, he got, in a concrete way, a definite idea of proportion which later on was made use of in his study of abstract number. In connection with the balancing of the grains to obtain the amount of water required by each, recipes were made for their cooking. He discovered the practical importance of the recipe: just what it is used for, namely, to give the materials and quantities required.

In connection with the history the children took up primitive modes of cooking out-of-doors. In this connection they considered primitive methods of applying of heat, such as roasting in hot ashes, on hot metal or stones, boiling by means of hot stones in water or buried in the ground. The children had two or three primitive feasts where they cooked potatoes, corn, apples, chestnuts, and some sort of meat. Application of heat under these new conditions served as an occasion for the child to abstract the principle he had been using in connection with modern methods and apparatus. This abstraction was a necessary step in the control of the primitive fireplace.

With the older children the preparation and cooking of proteins was taken up. The cooking of eggs, meats, and fish was followed by a review of the milk and vegetable soups and was concluded with the preparation of batters and doughs by means of the various raising agents.

During 1898–1899 and 1899–1900, the cooking program developed to such an extent that the practical work was turned over to an assistant.[13] The attention of the directing teacher was then devoted to relating the processes of cooking to physiology and especially to nutrition and hygiene. This course was with the older children and, in its experimental approach, was developed and carried on with the collaboration of the science teachers.

Since experience showed that cooking was the activity in which the children most easily learned the use of the scientific method, a detailed account of the way they thought through for themselves the necessary steps in their daily procedure follows. At the beginning of a lesson the proper utensils were gotten out and arranged in order of use and suitability to the cooking to be done. Then, with a view to softening and developing the flavor of the grain cooked, they developed, by

---

[13] Mary Tough.

discussion, the relation of amount or mass cooked to the unit of liquid needed, and of the form of cereal to the time required. Next, through measuring and weighing, volume and mass, or bulk, became practical working conceptions. It was phrased thus by one of the children: "We took two cups of flaked rice to one cup of water because it is so light; one-quarter a cup of whole rice takes one cup of water." Then they learned to distinguish between the different factors which controlled the amount of water needed, the length of time for cooking, the extent of surface of pan exposed to air, and the amount of heat to be applied. Each member of the group followed a different way of preparing the same food. The variable factors were thus sifted out. In one case this would be the amount of water, in another the character of the cereal, or in another the way of applying heat. In all the type of utensil was kept the same.

The technical sequence was worked out by the children as a group. Individual variations from the group plan were made by original children and were recognized and welcomed by both teacher and children. Group discussion clarified the part each one took in the experimental process. The class was held as a group until each individual felt confident that he knew what to do. It was found by observation of the teachers that with the younger children, attitude and expression indicated when the moment had come to cut short the talking and proceed to work. With the older children, the interest in the form of expressing what they were about to undertake increased very rapidly as they became more and more conscious of the need for clarity of method in recording the results of their experimental work. Perfectness of detail came first in acquiring the technique of procedure. This was the same in all classes. For example, two small boys worked out a coöperative scheme of work which enabled them, through elimination of useless motions and combination of effort, to finish ten to fifteen minutes ahead of the others. This time they proceeded to use either in writing up what they had done, or in acquiring skill in number work in which they felt themselves deficient.

The teacher's part was to answer questions and by a skilful

refreshing of the children's memories to insure that plans for the day were workable and also different enough in character to furnish a new experience involving a problem for the group. This was only possible when the teacher's experience already held in conscious readiness the general principles underlying the course. She shared the enterprise of discovery with the child. She functioned in bringing together various results and in assisting the children to trace back effects to causes. She thus helped each child to become conscious of the general principles, however concretely stated, resulting from their combined efforts.

This more or less uniform plan of classroom procedure developed into a method during the second year of the school. The time given to cooking varied from one and a half to two hours a week. The period was always divided into two parts, a half-hour of which was spent in planning and experimentation. With the younger children, this half-hour was on the same day as the luncheon and just before it. With the older children, especially toward the end of each three months, the period was used for formulation of the principles of cooking, which served as a practical review of the quarter's work. The luncheon was never omitted with children under eleven or twelve.

In the four older groups the care and serving of the table was assigned individually, strict rotation being observed, as the privilege of inviting guests was a part of this duty. It was found that children of six and under rarely have ability to converse freely at a table of eight or ten, so that very often a story was told during lunch by the teacher or visiting guests.

One of the outstanding results of the experience with the cooking program was its value in teaching even the youngest children to use fractional parts as easily and intelligently as they did whole numbers. Supplemented as it was by the use of the fractional parts of the foot and yard in their other constructive activities, this work seemed to furnish the needed concrete experience in multiplication and division of whole numbers and fractions. Because it was important to use a third of a cup instead of a fourth, in order to get more to eat, there was no muddle or confusion in the child's mind as to which fraction was the larger. It was easy to understand that if each child needed a third of a cup of cereal, twelve children would need four cups. The use of arithmetical symbols as the way of putting this down for future reference became natural and easy.

The questions of marketing and keeping accounts were frequently discussed. Because of the isolated position of the school little of this work was done except as children nine, ten, and eleven helped keep the school accounts and so covered the cost of the food for the cooking. The children of this school were not cut off from shopping experience at home. With children who lack such experience because of their method of living, it would seem that it might profitably be made a part of the teaching program.

Cooking involves a series of such more or less complex processes that it was often difficult to enable the youngest children to develop independence and initiative in their laboratory periods for they were apt to become far too dependent on direction. The children in consequence were held to a persistent use of general principles in all their preparation of food and cooking. Additional experiments were made which illustrated the kind of processes used and the fact that the amount of time needed for cooking any food was dependent upon its nature. They were taught for example the coagulation of albumen, the character of cellulose and why it should be softened, and how the flavor of food can be developed. This rendered the children confident when confronted with the cooking of unknown foods. They knew how to discover just how tough cellulose of the new food was and the approximate amount of starch in it or of albumen. They were able to judge whether the food was to be used for flavor, for roughage, or as a source of energy. They knew the fundamental proportions for batters and doughs of different consistencies and their relation to the different raising agencies. Such daily experience freed them from a helpless dependency on recipes, which teaching in cooking often gives. When one knows how much baking powder the use of one egg replaces, cakes are no mystery.

When one knows that the principle of making white sauce depends on the separation of the grains of starch by the proper method, that thorough mixing and an even heat will prevent the formation of lumps, and that the addition of one third of the total quantity of liquid needed insures the uniform quality of the product, lumpy gravy and soups never appear on the menu.

To those who saw the alert and vital interest of these younger children in this activity the lack of attention and the usual bored attitude of adult or college students in household economics, even when taught by an expert chemist, stood out in great contrast. It is probable that the college teacher would not find so many inhibitions and would be able to carry her ideal of research in cookery further, had her students had an elementary experience such as that of the children in this school.

To see a class of eight-year-old children produce perfect omelets, using small covered sheet-iron saucepans over gas burners was a revelation of what experimental work could do to curb the natural desire to poke in and see what is happening. They had seen what happened in class test, and their confidence in the control of the heat and knowledge of the correct length of time gave them success in practical application. No failure was ever passed by or covered up. It was critically reviewed to ascertain what conditions had affected the result. Endowed with an unusual combination of scientific and intellectual appreciation and an artistic temperament the teacher, who carried this course to its completion, was able to give the children an unconscious feeling for the artistic side of preparing and serving food and high ideals of efficiency in planning and handling utensils.

The pressure of college preparatory examinations made it necessary to eliminate from the program of the older children the course that had been planned for them in the less used techniques of cooking. Some of the children, however, worked these out at home and became experts in the preparation of certain foods. Almost all of the children used what they had learned with great pride and joy in the preparation of Sunday night suppers for the family. The preparation and serving of luncheons for distinguished visitors went through very successfully. The reports from the alumnae indicate that the understanding and use of cooking principles culminated in surety, dexterity, and confidence in meeting the demands of adult life. This was especially true of the two older classes who had been six or seven years in the school.

MATHEMATICS

Because of the fundamental character of mathematical science the development of that tool was one of the main concerns of the planners of the school's curriculum. During the first stages and the transitional years the problem was to see that the children had appropriately simple occasions to use number so that they saw in it a way to get order and effectiveness into their occupations, whether games or constructions. Measuring of all kinds played its part. It was never assumed that mathematics can be so developed as to control social situations, for mathematical expressions are only of use as formal tools in a special limited kind of experience. Hence number is discussed not primarily as one of the sciences but as a form of communication (see Chapter XVII). In Chapter XVII also is the account of how some children with this practical background were able to think out, to express fundamental mathematical relations such as ratio and proportion and to use freely algebraic symbols and geometric construction.

SUMMARY

The development of the ability to plan ahead, to test, to evaluate results, and to deduce from them the help needed for future action or testing became fully conscious in only a few classes, and in these not with all the children. However, the mental attitude of being objective in sizing up a problem, a willingness to try to see and ability to direct that seeing effectively was so characteristic of the majority of the children who had been in the school for five years that this result seemed to fulfil the hopes with which the science work had been planned. The general use of the scientific method in all lines of the school work had exceeded the early expectations. While the fields of future experimentations have been barely indicated, there is hope that the present crisis will induce educators to experiment scientifically in socially coöperative schools.

Sharing in planning was the secret of the successfully social spirit of this school community. Social experiments must be planned. All concerned must enter into the planning to insure the success of any social undertaking, and all must accept their plan as tentative, to be tested by events. Only in this open-minded coöperative spirit can groups of individuals meet the problems of the shifting scene so as to insure the continuity and therefore the security of experience. Were the present Homestead experiments animated by the same spirit of coöperative adventure in the field of social living as was this school of some thirty years ago, there would be hope of an ever-increasing number of genuine indigenous communities, gaining social security through coöperation.

CHAPTER XVI

EXPERIMENTAL ACTIVITIES DEVELOPING ORIGINS AND BACKGROUNDS OF SOCIAL LIFE

A. GEOGRAPHY AND HISTORY

THE familiar social activities of the child's present, and the attendant manual arts, with their tools and materials, served in the school as a natural introduction to history and geography, projecting and ramifying into these so inevitably that it only remained for the teacher to be alert to these connections and to take advantage of them. The factors in living and the way they function always interest a child, regardless of time or place. In the school the ways of extending these interests and of linking them with the larger world of the past were through familiar activities and tools. Tools and materials, the wood and clay, the needle and cloth, and the processes by which these are manipulated, were used to initiate the child into the typical problems which had required human effort, into the laws of human production and achievement, and into the methods by which man gained control of nature and made his ideals into the good realities of life.

The child himself often made the process of transition from the present to the past an easy one. With something of the intuition of a true scientist he frequently chose an ancient method of historical approach and solved the problem of how to begin his study with "Let's pretend." The group of presentday farmers, miners, woodsmen, cooks or garment makers, craftsmen or artists, sprang with the nimbleness of childhood out of the present complicated and dimly understood ways of present-day living into the ultra simplicity of the past, with its few and crude ways of meeting the same primal needs. It was not a dead past to them; they revived it by reliving it.

The little farmers found that as primitive people they were hunters first or wandering tribes of herdsmen. Their interests were in the way they could get food, the weapons and tools they would be likely to use, the new inventions they made, and the transformations in life that arose from the powers and leisure thus gained. Each child was eager to remake utensils, to reproduce processes, to rehandle materials. He appreciated in a measure the situations of these ancient peoples and vaguely understood their problems and their successes only because out of the reality of his own experience he could picture their difficulties and imagine the resources of their natural habitat. Out of this new play springs a new interest in the fields and the forests, the mountains, the ocean, the plants, the animals about him. He uses his limited knowledge of the natural forces and forms with which he himself is surrounded to build up and reproduce a conception of the habitat of the people he is studying. Their problems became his problems for which he must find solutions, and the story of man—what he did, where, and how he did it in increasingly better ways, what he invented, where he traveled, and what he discovered—became real and worthy. The tale of how things, as they are, came to be, helped him to understand that the problem of how to live is the problem of all time.

Place by place, also, the earth came to be viewed by the child as the home of man, in which he has struggled with untoward conditions and overcome obstacles in a long upward climb. A child's own social world is so rich and full that it is not easy for him to see how much it cost, how much effort and thought lie back of it. Through a study of primitive living, however, he sees man face to face with nature, without tools, without manufactured materials. Step by step he follows the processes by which man recognized his needs and how to cope with them, and learns how new resources open new interests and bring new problems.

The child sees life as a whole in terms of its fundamental needs, its simple relationships, its pure satisfactions. The point of view of the teacher, however, is through the bifocal lens of training and of adult experience. There is constant need for her to be agile in her change from one to the other. At any moment of her teaching she must lift her head for far-sighted vision. Like Alice, she must step with her children behind the looking glass and in this imaginative land she must see all things with their eyes and limited by their experience; but, in time of need, she must be able to recover her trained vision and from the realistic point of view of an adult supply the guide posts of knowledge and the skills of method.

It was essential, therefore, in this school that a teacher, whatever her specialty, should have had the fertile life experience that is the result of experimental living guided by intelligent thinking. Thus while she saw history from the psychological point of view of the child as the story of man, working on and changing his environment, from the point of view of a trained teacher she saw it as the classified facts of history or science. From the child's viewpoint she selected material concerned with the lives of persons or races who did interesting things that led to still more interesting and helpful living. Such selection oftentimes, especially during the years of the elementary period, did not coincide with the chronological arrangement of a curriculum chosen by a disciple of the older school of learning. A teacher who held that the end in view was to give the child, at an early age, an understanding of character and social relationships in their natural dependence, found it impossible to follow the development of civilization through the successive steps in which it actually took place. The chronological order in historical instruction is logical to the adult mind, but because of its complexity and remoteness, is alien to the interests and understanding of a child. Experiment indicated that the young child's interest is much closer in spirit and understanding to the typical conditions, activities, and relations of the social life of a prehistoric people than to the complicated and artificial life of ancient Babylon or of Egypt.

THE CHILD'S INTEREST IN PRIMITIVE LIFE

The history of this early period—anthropology—was, therefore, indirect sociology—a study of the occupations of men as affecting intellectual growth and social advancement. It was believed, and the results justified such a belief, that in such a study the child would find a key to unlock the meanings of his present complicated social life. He would also discover the method of progressive living. As the children relived the drama of early man's active occupations, they found that he always learned by doing. His method was a trial-and-error one in the beginning. Then, by intelligent experimenting, he discovered, he invented, and brought to bear contrivances of his own fashioning upon his physical environment. What better introduction to the experimental method could any child have than that of the first discoveries of the power of mind over matter? As a child of this school he relived the activities of primitive days, he was introduced to much scientific truth and unconsciously absorbed a method which increased his intellectual constructiveness. As he approached maturity he came to see how all the sciences have developed gradually out of the occupations of living; and this is also true of the social sciences. The child realized, out of his own experience, as he followed both actually and vicariously the story of man's climb on the ladder of living, how all the various activities in industrial occupations have developed from the simple to the complex. He followed the wool from the sheep to the rug, patiently contriving his own spindle, his own dye, his own loom: when older, he reviewed the same process more carefully in the developing industries of Colonial days. He saw, that while successive inventions of machines have led to the eventual betterment of social life, the immediate results have often been at the bitter cost of the discarded hand-worker whose plight illustrates an ever-present social problem caused by technological advance. Industrial history thus taught on a background of actual experience with materials and processes will always have more than a materialistic or merely utilitarian meaning. For the children of this school it carried many social and moral implications of unsolved problems of human relationships. Thus taught, the history of work becomes the record of how man learned to think, to think to some effect, to transform the conditions of life so that life itself became a different and less tortured thing and gradually took on, for some at least, comfort and beauty. Here, for all thinking and socially minded persons, logically follows the goading query—Why not comfort and beauty for all?

History, thus educationally considered, was for these children a study of society which lays bare its process of becoming, and its modes of organization. In primitive living social relationships and organizations are reduced to their simplest terms. The quality of an individual or the value of an act stands out clearly in a situation. A child can see in imagination the forces which favor and permit men's effective coöperation with one another, can recognize the sorts of character that help on or hold back, can appreciate the motives which draw men together or push them apart, and understand that quality of character is the same now as then. The organization of the tribe is plain to a child. He sees that every one *must live,* and that the life of the group is dependent upon its members. The law of individual right and social justice is simple and clear. To most of the pupils, studying as a group about coöperative living, a social way came to mean the right way. This penetration into the ethical significance of social acting showed results in their own actions. They were willing to work together and had more concern for fair play. To those who watched and guided them, this augured well that in their later lives the social, ethical, and moral ways of living might become synonymous in meaning. This by-product of an intelligent and sympathetic understanding of the ethics of a present situation might be called an indication of the moral value of history, when taught in this fashion.

As pointed out in a description of the method of teaching history in the school,[1] three lines of historical development

---

[1] Georgia F. Bacon, "History," *Elementary School Record,* Nov., 1900.

were followed, the social, industrial, and political. The social and industrial were emphasized first and the political phase later, although at all times attention was directed to the simple beginnings of government in the organization of primitive tribes for protection and other purposes. Only at a later stage of growth, at eleven or twelve years, was it found that the child is able to appreciate political institutions, to understand what special institutional idea each historic nation stands for and what factor it has contributed to the present complex of institutions.

History for the younger children was of a generalized and simplified type. It was hardly history at all in the local or chronological sense, but aimed to give the child insight into and sympathy with a variety of present and fundamental social activities. The first years of the school these courses were highly experimental in character.

SOCIAL OCCUPATIONS AND HISTORY IN PREFERRED ORDER

One year a combination of social occupations, such as coal mining, cotton growing, and general farm life, with stories of early Greek life and primitive life was tried. The class visited farms, modeled them, made a comparison of the houses in their own city with those in Greece, Japan, China, and Greenland, and worked out the evolution of the home from cave periods. The following year, the course in social occupations was continued. Here the main idea was the interaction of country and city life in maintaining existing conditions. An effort was made to select occupations closely connected with food, clothing, and shelter. In another year this group made a study of child life in Holland, Africa, Greenland, and Japan, with some work on climatic conditions. As a result of the experience of these experimental years the regular course of study for Group III (six years) was present-day occupations of people in country and city. This course was called *Typical Existing Social Occupations*. The differentiation of city and country life, their interaction, and mutual dependence were emphasized.

The later reports show a wide variation in detail of treatment of and in points of emphasis on this topic by different teachers and even by the same teacher with different classes.

The work of Group IV, seven years old, was outlined as: *Development of Social Life; Discoveries and Inventions of Industry,* from the most primitive beginnings to the opening of authentic history. This subject-matter was used for the activities of the children of this age throughout the life of the school. It also varied much each year in details and manner of treatment, but at all times the present and the past were related to one another.

The work of the eight-year-old children, Group V, who were on the borderland of the second period of growth, passed through an experimental period (1896 to 1898). In the first year of this period the work with this group on inventions through discovery had been passed over rapidly, and Homeric Society taken up in historical detail, since it afforded insight into a simple, natural life which expressed itself in a rich, artistic civilization. The Iliad and the Odyssey were used as vivid, interesting pictures of the society of the times. The second year of the school the children of this age, Group V, had been in the school since its beginning. They had had consecutive work in present-day social occupations and in the evolution of inventions and their effect upon life, and were given a course which related their ideas of the development of an imagined primitive tribe to a definite place and people. This course carried the development of civilization to a form in which the symbols and conveniences such as a written language, number system, weights, and measures approximated their own. The Phoenicians were chosen to typify this stage. As they were traders and explorers, continuously pushing back farther and farther the boundaries of their known world, the children easily made the transition to the discoveries of another Mediterranean maritime people, the Venetians. The class then followed the explorations of Marco Polo to the East, of Prince Henry of Portugal around Africa, and of the Spaniards to the west in the journeys of Columbus and Balboa to America. The story of Magellan told of the circumnavigation of the whole world. Children of eight years are interested in adventure, and this course dealt with the great movements of migration, exploration, and discovery which have brought the whole world into human ken. The account of the great explorers and discoverers thus served to make a natural transition from the previous year's work, which was independent of historical data in the strict sense of the term, to what is local and specific and depends upon certain specified persons who lived at certain specified times and places. The course was used with Group V for the rest of the years of the school.[2]

A change is noticeable in the attitude toward his work of a child of nine years, and the problem of the teacher at the beginning of the reflective age becomes more complex. She must see that the subject-matter of history is so presented that the child's mind will reach out, question, examine, and analyze the forces which caused the men and women of history to think and act. He must understand also the social side: how their acts aided or hindered progress. History now becomes less empirical and more a matter of authentic record, so that the question of definite recall of what has been studied comes into the scheme. The attack upon the subject-matter is different; it is not so much a question of how a people *might* meet a problem of conditions as a question of *fact* and why things happened as they did. During the previous years the child has gained some conception of space relations in the study of the world as a whole; definite time has meant little. He must now get some idea of the effect of time. This begins vaguely, but as the study proceeds, a knowledge of dates as an aid in comparing events is found essential. The child is still studying indirect sociology, and his study must be one of types in order that he may gain methods of independent work which will enable him to understand other problems of history.

DEVELOPMENT OF CURRICULUM FROM PREVIOUS EXPERIMENTS

The subject-matter for Group VI also developed out of a series of experiments of successive years. In the later years of

---

[2] Course given by Laura L. Runyon.

the school their study centered around local conditions and the definite activities of a particular people. Extracts from the teacher's account of the work follows: [3]

The French explorers and the early settlers in the Northwest and the settlement of Chicago made a good beginning for children living in the Mississippi Valley. It gave an opportunity to enlarge the concepts formed in the study of the Phoenicians and the early explorers. Marquette, like Livingstone, is seen to be actuated by religious motives in exiling himself from his native land; Joliet, as a trader, was motivated by the same impulses which sent the Phoenician merchants and, long afterwards, the explorers of the fifteenth and sixteenth centuries on long and hazardous voyages. In searching for natural highways into the interior of America, the child finds the Mississippi and the St. Lawrence as he found the Nile, Niger, Congo, and Zambezi in his study of Africa. He can, therefore, compare the American rivers with those of Africa, the Indians with the Negroes, and the degree of civilization of tribes in America with that of other peoples he has studied. The isolation of the early pioneer and his means of getting his furs to the seacoast, his tools, weapons, manner of living, etc., are brought out. In imagination the child sees the frontier life develop into a thriving village with need of a local government, system of taxation, improvements, etc. Through this discussion he is guided to comprehend simple forms of civic politics, so that the paved and sewered streets, the policemen, the aldermen, and the mayor, with all of whom he has been somewhat familiar, have now more definite parts in the social world. . . .

The study of the French explorers is followed by a brief account of the explorers who gave England a claim to land in America. Then a study of typical American colonies is begun, Virginia as a southern colony, Massachusetts as a northern one. The church and the state as institutions come in now as parts of the social life, and efforts toward religious and political freedom underlie the life of the people. With the child, as with the colonists, the first question was always how did the people in the new land live. Recognition was always given to the fact that they could not live independently of the civilization from which they came. . . . An attempt was made to get the children to eliminate those conveniences of civilization with which they are familiar; to realize how it would seem to live in America without a single railroad, steamboat, or road of

---

[3] Laura L. Runyon, *The Teaching of Elementary History in the Dewey School*, Thesis, Graduate School Arts and Literature (University of Chicago, June, 1906).

any kind except the Indian trails and rivers; to be dependent upon England for sugar, vinegar, tea, coffee, etc.; to imagine how it would seem to have no fuel except wood, no means of lighting a fire except flint and steel; to have no oil for lamps, no cattle from which to get milk and butter; and to have to build houses of logs, since there were no sawmills. The children discussed the new conditions of life that must be met, then read the account to see if their suppositions were correct. They discovered that England had to learn by experience the art of colonization. . . .

A vivid description of the settlement of Virginia and the motives which led to it was followed by a discussion of why things were as the historian describes them, whether the starving time was due solely to the "community of goods" system and consequent idleness on the part of the gentlemen who came to find gold, or whether it might not be accounted for in part by the lack of knowledge of soil and farming and the difficulties of clearing ground with the inadequate methods of the time. In the story of the development of the first permanent English colony the child learns more than mere facts. In considering the life of John Smith, or any other hero of the early times, he sees a whole life in perspective. He has had little actual experience with people that will aid him in judging character, but in the study of characters in history the motive of action and the results stand out prominently. Youth with its conditions and age as it has worked out its life are brought together. Thus the lives of historical personages bring the child into contact with the experiences of long life. Such character study is made in its natural setting as the child images the life of the people and the times. That these persons studied are ancestors of himself and his friends gives a deeper interest in the work. As he identifies himself with the colony, he appreciates those who help on and is indignant with those who hinder progress; and this helping or hindering, he comprehends, is not a mere question of willing, but depends upon what a man is. Therefore, his conception of his own social world becomes clearer, and he begins to get a glimpse of the close network which binds each individual to every other.

The study of colonial history, therefore, furnished only the carrying medium for the deeper and more universal study of the adaptation of a civilized people to the primitive conditions of a new environment, the study of character, and the training of judgment. In these early days the prototype of our democratic form of government was worked out, and the child who is just beginning to be interested in the city and national elections is able to comprehend how they began. He is studying the life of a people, the problems they had to face and how they succeeded. He constantly contrasts the past with his own life and gets deeper understanding of the present. He finds the meaning for much of his present life in the past and, hence, is constantly reading into his daily life the new value derived from his study. In New England, the colonial question has a different phase from Virginia in the religious reasons which induced the Pilgrims and Puritans to leave their native land and seek homes in a new country. Commercial products in New England were different from those in Virginia, because of the difference in latitude and physiographical conditions. . . .

The general plan was for the class to discuss a situation and decide from their point of view as colonists what would be best to do next, either from the teacher or books, to discover just what was done, then to decide what probably would be the effect of the action or decision, and finally to find out what the actual result was as stated in historical records. This method of attacking history is similar to that of science. There is first the recognition of conditions, an attempt to relate the situation to those previously studied, next an hypothesis as to the effect of manipulation of conditions, then a study of the effect, and then generalization of results. It was found that the physiographical conditions of a country are largely responsible for its industries. The New England farmers had discovered that their barren hills furnished pasture for sheep and cattle, and that cattle and wool were readily exchanged in the West Indies, together with fish, for molasses, sugar, etc. And molasses helped to make rum, which could be sold for gold (a rare article in the colonies) to the slave trade-ships. England had by law prevented this trade. The fact that the laws could only be partially enforced did not remove the irritation they caused. . . . To understand this irritation, it is necessary to recall the stages of development of manufactures before the Revolution. Industries were carried on in the home and gave each family an opportunity to make a little money. In their study of textiles the children worked out the part invention played in the various steps in the manufacture of cloth and were, therefore, able to comprehend the change that would come with the beginning of those inventions which brought in the factory system and made possible the rapid growth of manufactories at the close of the Revolution.

The ten-year-old children (Group VII) in the experimental first years of the school had the same work as Group VI. In the revised program for this age the American history of the year before was continued, taking up the French and Indian War and the Revolution. The amount of ground covered and the method of treatment varied in different years. For two successive years the group spent the entire year on American history and covered part or all of the Revolutionary War period. One year the group spent six months on this work, omitting the Revolution and studying the

connections of American and European life. With this group the
center of thought and study was focused on the ethical and scientific side of the struggle.

Group VIII (eleven years) was in a transitional period. The subject which seemed to fit this period was the history of colonization
by European countries. The attempt was made to give to this
group the same balance and completeness of world view as that
gained by the eight-year-old children in the study of the Phoenicians
and early world explorers. In each of these years the effort was
made to help the children gather together the knowledge of the
two preceding years and grasp its significance as a whole in larger
relations. Accordingly, the development of the American colonies
was considered from an European point of view. England, France,
and Spain were studied as countries which attempted colonization
in the New World, in the East Indies, Africa, and Australia. The
methods and aims in claiming and holding territory, the character
of the settlements, and the connections with the mother country
were taken up. A comparison was made of the colonies established
by one country in different parts of the world (as England's colonies
in America, India, Africa, and Australia). The conflicts of different
countries over land claims, and the working out of some principles
of international law were discussed, and a comparison of the different national methods of establishing and controlling colonies made.
It was necessary to compare climates, to realize the physiography
of the different regions, the industrial products possible, and the
trade routes open for exchange with other countries. The study also
brought out the knowledge of new products and the necessity of
dealing with larger areas, larger masses of people, and new conditions. The settlement by European countries of colonies in America
brought the children back from their excursion into world history
and geography and the study of the backgrounds of the colonists
to America and her problems in the Revolutionary period.

Group IX, at twelve years, took up the colonies just before the
Revolutionary period, the formation of the Constitution, and the
westward expansion of the new Union and its gradual acquisition
of territory.

Group X (thirteen years) was believed to be ready to deal, not
with social life in general nor social life that is familiar, but with
certain thoroughly differentiated, peculiar types of social life, the
special significance of each, and the particular contribution each
has made to world history. The plan, accordingly, was to follow
chronological order to a large extent, to begin with the ancient
world about the Mediterranean basin and the contribution the
various ancient peoples had made to social life, art, and industry,
and to guide the child through European history and the move-

ments of peoples in territorial expansion to the peculiar and differentiating factors of American history. This plan was never carried into practice, however, in its entirety. For two years this group had no history, as they were absorbed and occupied with building the club-house. Another year, because of gaps in history training, the group made a thorough review of American history, using McMaster's *School History* as a textbook.[4]

Group XI (fourteen and fifteen years) in the last years of the school studied Roman history from the point of view of the formation of a political state. The starting point was the play of *Julius Caesar*, part of college requirements.

SUMMARY OF CURRICULA AND METHOD

The children who had followed the regular work of the school had spent one year on social occupations, one on primitive life, one on explorations and discoveries, one on Chicago and the Virginia and Massachusetts Bay colonies, one on the union of the colonies and the Revolution, one half-year on American history from the European point of view, one half-year on the formation of the American Constitution, the acquisition of new territory in the westward expansion, and the industrial development up to 1830, and one year on history review in preparation for college board examinations or on Roman history. The average time the younger groups spent on history was two and one half hours a week; that of the older groups was one and one half hours a week. The successful practices of each succeeding year became the revised program for the next year. Thus each year's work was the produc of repeated experiments and finally resulted in the general plan outlined above.

A report of the work and method of another group and teacher follows: [5]

The method employed in conducting classes was generally that of conversation and discussion. Facts and conditions were presented, making the life of the time under consideration as real as possible. When the children understood the conditions of the life,

[4] These children had studied Roman history at eleven when they began Latin.
[5] Georgia F. Bacon, "History," *Elementary School Record*, November, 1900.

the problems of the time naturally presented themselves, and the class endeavored to find a solution. It was an interesting fact that the more the class lived in the time the more certain it was to find the same solution to the questions of the day as the people who actually worked them out. Young children like the detail which is necessary for this sort of work; they like to dwell for a long time on an event; they like to walk around it, mentally viewing it from all points and asking numberless questions until the picture stands distinct in the mind. The ideal way of teaching history to little children is to allow them to make whatever approach they wish. To do this the teacher must be well acquainted with her subject, well equipped with facts, and must have in mind a definite thing to be taught. Her real opportunity to guide lies in her suggestive answers to their questions, or in helping the children to make their own answers. By this process they gain not only an extensive but an intensive view. One great difficulty in this method is the lack of books that enter sufficiently into detail.[6] Even children feel this; one child complained: "The books don't tell enough about anything so you really know it. They say a little about this man, or that one, and then leave it and take up something else." The books of Alice Morse Earl meet this demand for fine detail in colonial history in a satisfactory manner.

With very young children the teacher furnished the positive information. As soon as the pupils were able to read, however, they were sent to books to look up the necessary facts. Generally, with older pupils each was asked to report on a different point and thus contribute to the building up of the whole. This provided a *raison d'être* to the recitation. Sometimes the lessons were carried on so that the children ran aground until they could get certain information, and the gathering of this information constituted the preparation for the next lesson. At other times the teacher gave out a number of points to be looked up for discussion the following day. In class the interchange of thought, the additions and criticism, cleared up the ideas and fixed them firmly in mind. If a book was found which summed up a period, it was read as a review, after the material had been worked over in class as indicated above. In United States history, Fiske's *School History* answered this purpose admirably with children over eleven years of age.

The interest of children of twelve and thirteen in historical novels led to the belief that biography could be used with great profit. . . . The experiment was tried to a certain extent with a class in United States history. Each child selected a prominent man of Revolutionary times, made a study of his life and reported on the part he played in the Revolution.

---

[6] This is no longer true.

A child is a natural hero worshipper. He begins by placing his parents on a pedestal; later, the school companion who can perform the greatest feat replaces these. As his horizon broadens, his heroes become men of national repute, for the most part military or naval heroes whose deeds he can appreciate. . . . It is well, then, that the hero should be of the right sort to inspire him. This, history can provide, as it deals for the most part with those who have held high ideals and have possessed strength of character to carry them out. In this study of characters in relation to their physical and social environment, the child is impressed with the relative value of different traits and learns to appreciate those which ensure success of the lasting sort. It was often clearly demonstrated in this school that the ethical teaching of history had for its end the development of the child in the three directions indicated by Mr. Dewey in his definition of character: First, good judgment. This is the ability to take the permanent instead of the transient, the important instead of the trivial. It is the power to have perspective and proportion in considering the possibilities of experience. . . . Second, it involves emotional delicacy or responsiveness to what is conceived as worth while or as good. . . . Finally, character means the possession of practical force, the power to assert one's convictions and aims amid difficulties and to persist in their execution against obstacles.

B. THE TEXTILE INDUSTRY HISTORICALLY DEVELOPED

As the school developed, certain occupations displayed greater continuity than others for adaptation to different age levels and were, therefore, of striking help in teaching science and history. The shop-work with wood and metals, because of limitations as to quarters and teachers, never developed the continuity possible with these materials. Cooking proved of enormous value in teaching the scientific method, although its historical bearings were always adequately developed. The textile occupations were found quite perfectly adapted to show the historical development of an industry fundamentally important to daily living. The detailed record of how this occupation was used educationally in the school is therefore given in this account of the history matter of the curriculum.

The history of work, what people did to get a living, was a main theme of the school curriculum. It provided a continuous story, capable of unlimited extension into many fields of knowledge. Shorter projects grew out of it naturally and in turn led on to others, all giving sustenance and value to the whole. The test of a subject for study was the number of its possibilities not only for continuing but for enlarging experience. Did it lead to a next step? Deference to this criterion gave a continuity to the school's curriculum which was one of its outstanding characteristics.

As the result of a good deal of experimenting from year to year, the various activities of spinning, weaving, sewing, the making of clothing or other necessary or decorative household articles grew into a continuous study of various occupations concerned with the making of fabrics, known on the school's program as a course in *Textiles*. All of the activities of the school were occupations or related to occupations which are reproductions of or run parallel to forms of work carried on in all social life, whether of the present or of the past. One of their most important educational possibilities was that they furnished so many things in simple form that a child can do. More, perhaps, than any other household occupation, the course in textiles opened up many lines of interest to children of all ages and afforded more frequently than most courses, opportunity to each child for free practice in thought and action. Many facts of history, of science, and of geography naturally related themselves to its various phases. The how and why and where of developing human life centered easily and naturally around these activities of human living, and through taking part in them the ways of progress in material and social living grew plain to the participating children. It was, in fact, one of the most successful unifying agents of the whole elementary program. It correlated history with science or with geography and stimulated the child's interest and effort to attain mastery of his skills in reading, writing, or measurement.

The fundamental point in the psychology of the controlled educational use of an occupation such as the spinning or the weaving was found to be that it maintains a balance between the intellectual and the practical phases of experience. As an occupation it is active or motor; it finds expression through the physical organs, the eyes, hands, etc. But it also involves continual observation of materials and continual planning and reflection in order that the practical or executive side may be successfully carried on. Conceived thus, as an occupation, it should be carefully distinguished from work which educates primarily for a trade.[7] Its end is in itself, in the growth that comes from the continual interplay of ideas and their embodiment in action, and not in external utility. Great stress was laid upon personal experimenting, planning and reinventing, and upon the parallelism of the children's work with lines of historical and social development of the period. The first requires the child to be mentally quick and alert at every point in order that he may do the outward work properly. The second enriches and deepens the work performed by saturating it with values suggested from the social life which it recapitulates.

INTRODUCTION TO INDUSTRY IN PRIMITIVE HISTORY

The child, with his untried powers, his paucity of experience, is in much the same attitude toward the world and toward life as was early man. Both are decidedly motor in their activity. In both there is a reservoir of motor energy, urgent for discharge upon their environment. Both are interested in objects and materials, not from a contemplative or theoretical standpoint, but from the standpoint of what can be done with them, and what can be got out of them. Primitive man mainly occupied himself with the direct problems of life—food, fuel, shelter, protection. His concerns were the utensils, tools, instrumentalities that secured him a constantly improving life. His

---

[7] Mr. Dewey points out that "wherever the mastery of certain tools or the production of certain objects is made the primary end of manual training, the educational value is lost. When, however, the child is given intellectual responsibility in his work to select materials and instruments that are most fit; if he has opportunity to think out his own model and plan of work, if he is led to perceive his own errors and find out how to correct them so far as he is able, his work has great educational value. Such work may be called an occupation because the maximum of consciousness is put into whatever is done." "The Psychology of Occupation," *Elementary School Record*, April, 1900.

interest in nature was based upon its direct and indispensable relation to his own needs and activities.

This suggested to those directing this experiment that an important educational task might be to get hold of the essential underlying attitude which the child has in common with primitive man and give it such play and expression that, avoiding the errors and wanderings of his forefathers, he may come to the ends and realities toward which, after all, primitive man was struggling. In developing his idea of this task, Mr. Dewey points out that there is a fundamental and important difference between the two. Necessity, the pressure of getting a living, was upon the savage. The child is, or should be, protected against economic stress and strain. The expression of energy takes, in his case, a form of play, play which is not amusement, but the intrinsic exhibition of inherent powers so as to exercise and develop them. Accordingly, while the value of the motor activities of the savage was found chiefly in the external result, in the game that was killed or the fish that was caught, and only incidentally in a gain of skill and insight, with the child the exact reverse is the case. With him, the external result is only a sign, a token; it is just a proof and exhibition to himself of his own capacities. In it he comes to consciousness of his own impulses. He learns to know them through seeing what they can effect. But the primary interest and the ultimate value remain in the culture of the powers of action, obtained in and through their being put to effective use.

Criticism has frequently been directed against using a year of the young child's life in a study of primitive conditions. The criticism has point only if primitive life is so isolated as to be treated as an end in itself, instead of as an opportunity for the study of the joint activity of social needs and intelligence in esthetic industrial invention. Speaking of this matter in connection with the use of textiles as a continuous course throughout the program, the director of the school wrote as follows: [8]

---

[8] John Dewey, "The Psychology of Occupation," *Elementary School Record*, April, 1900.

The study of primitive forms of spinning and weaving is given in connection with the primitive history to illustrate further the life of people whose mode of living is simple and in direct contact with nature. This study also presents a craft which has an intimate place in the daily life of primitive people.

The suggestion has been made that present conditions of manufacture might more profitably present a study of textiles than a return to unused methods. The advantage of returning to these earlier methods, aside from giving a richer content to the period of history the child is concerned with, is that they exhibit an important industry of today reduced to its simplest terms. The existing forms of the industry of textiles are too complex in process, in the forms of the machines, and in organization, for the children to comprehend; whereas in primitive conditions we find only the essential elements of the industry. Non-essentials are eliminated; basic principles are clear and definite; the child deals first-hand with raw materials. With this concrete background of experience it becomes comparatively easy for children to understand modern machine production.

The child realizes the conditions of the period by reconstructing them with materials naturally used at that time. These are of such a nature that the child can reinvent processes and implements used. The dramatic instinct is appealed to in acting out the life and occupations, the creative or artistic desire to carry a project to its end. The child's joy in doing what other people have done finds an outlet, and meanwhile he gains power in handling materials and in controlling processes. These impulses and experiences are realized in the finished product, which holds the child's interest throughout. The spinning and weaving are for the purpose of providing blankets for the primitive family and are done in a manner appropriate to the limitations of its life. The child also realizes in the progress of his work the artistic impulses of these primitive peoples, which are recalled in his own quaint designs and color combinations. Such material is selected as will give pleasing results. In other words, the finished product should be, so far as possible, beautiful. From the child's point of view there should be nothing in it to offend or interfere with his judgment of what is appropriate. Above all it should contribute something to his standard of judgment of things of an artistic nature.

What is here said about conditions of manufacture in one industry is true not only of industry in general, but of forms of social organization as well. In working out the different processes involved in making cloth, in using materials and implements suggested by necessity, and in observing the results reached by people of the past, children realize the advance made in methods of work and can readily understand the meaning of industrial organization in its simplest forms. This step precedes a more fruitful and concrete study of the later phases of the industry; that is, of the household and domestic period which is richly illustrated in early colonial life. This again is followed by a study of the transition period, the era of inventions in England in the eighteenth century, which in turn indicates economic conditions leading to factory organization. The study of each phase of industry is simplified by following its natural development and by its coincidence with history which provides the social setting. It has a further advantage in that it can be adapted to each period of the child's development. He is himself advancing by easy stages of such a nature as enable him to comprehend cause and effect in the organization of the particular phases of the industry he is pursuing.

It was a matter of common experience in the school that when activities were undertaken in the simple crude setting of imagined primitive life, it was possible and natural to put the children in touch with raw materials. They thus learned by experience to prepare them for use in this work. The educational use of this was most apparent in a course in basketry which was given in the school as a part of the textile work:

[9] The children sought for, discovered, and experimented with native grasses and with those of many other localities. This awakened an interest in their own environment and, by contrast, in that of other localities. In such a course the care and preparation of the grasses carry the child to a further appreciation of their quality and beauty than he gets from a mere understanding of their application. In drying them their constant change and variety of color suggests different modes of working toward securing whole series of colors. Through the greens, browns, and yellows which naturally appear, the child may be led to vary his process in such a way as to secure infinite numbers of shades of all these colors. . . . The finished product is, perhaps, crude compared with the basket or mat made with prepared material, but what the child gets from it is infinitely more worth while. The products contribute to an appreciation of nature, and through the control of nature's material he realizes the pleasure of artistic creation. It has brought something into the life of the one who made it, has contributed to his own experience. . . .

[9] Althea Harmer, "Primitive Textile Work in the Laboratory School," *The Elementary School Teacher*, June, 1903.

Continuous throughout the whole elementary period, this course in textiles, like that in cooking, represented the possibilities of such an activity as a carrier for facts. Freighted as it was with innumerable possibilities for extension into the field of the fine arts and of human relationships, it became in the hands of a very gifted and highly trained teacher one of the main avenues for the extension of knowledge, the development of skill in expression and creative ability, and an increased appreciation of esthetic beauty and the meaning of social values and standards. The story of its use in the school, as told by the teacher who guided its developing activities, follows:

[10] A DEVELOPING INDUSTRY AS CURRICULAR MATERIAL

In every community the greater number of people are engaged in the industries of providing food, clothing, and shelter. Industries largely affect the social life of a community, and the social life its history. The textile industries have been chosen as a type of industry which can be studied in the school-room for illustrating this effect on social life and history.

Under primitive conditions the spinning and weaving are in the first stages of development; skins, furs, and matted fibers are used for clothing. At a later period each home becomes its own producer; clothing, from the raw material to the finished garment, is made by some member of the family. Even in this period there is a division of labor in the hand-work, giving to each member of the family the task he can do best. In the making of woolen cloth, for example, the younger members cleaned and carded the wool; the women spun the yarn; the men washed and sheared the sheep and usually did the weaving, while the mother made the cloth into garments for the family.

Out of the household developed the so-called domestic system. A master-workman, with a small capital, bought wool from a dealer, distributed it among the families in the village to be carded, spun, and woven. He collected the cloth and carried it to town to sell at a profit. The merchant was then separated from the manufacturer.

With the introduction of machines and more specialization, the domestic system gradually grew into the factory. Weavers first took

---

[10] Althea Harmer, "Textile Industries," *Elementary School Record*, April, 1900.

their wool to the factory to be carded by machine; later the spinning was done in the factory, weaving still remaining a home industry. The work was controlled by a capitalist and done under
inspection in the homes of weavers. The weavers were, in consequence of this system, obliged to leave the country and congre-
gate around the village spinning mills. The power used in running
the mills also affected conditions of manufacture. Factories run by
water-power were scattered through the country along the banks
of rivers and small streams. With the use of steam-power, factory
life concentrated in large cities near centers of trade. Large capital
was invested; machines were invented and improved; and finally
the present factory system was introduced.

This is a brief statement of the industrial history about which
the work of the children centers. Three stages of development were
selected because of their connections with the history work, and because the materials and implements involved in the different
processes are of such a nature that the children could make their
own deductions from simple experiments. They were able to carry
out the whole process from the handling of the fiber in its natural
condition to the woven cloth.

The value of the child's social education lies in his gradual
growth in knowledge of the meaning of the simplest forms of industrial organization. He can follow each period of development
when he himself is at such a stage of social advancement as to
readily comprehend causes and their effects. A child who is able
to rediscover and carry out from beginning to end the whole material process of an industry is also able to organize it on the social
side. Step by step from the primitive through the household and
domestic stage and, dramatically, even through the factory stage,
he is able to work out its lines of organization. As the course develops, three stages become apparent. In the primitive stage,
working from the inventive side the children get a knowledge of
raw materials, a technical skill in handling them. They see the
value of implements and invent mechanical devices for converting
the raw materials into cloth. Beginning with primitive implements
—the distaff, spindle, and loom—each step made is traced out, and
the mechanical advantage gained in the application of the force
used becomes clear. The household and domestic stage coincides
with the colonial period. Here the educational value is in the
broad, historical background furnished, and emphasis is laid on the
social side. Attention is directed to the influence of occupation on
community life, the growth of trade and trade centers and the
manner in which these have shifted and developed, to the concentration of industries as conditioned by environment, and the climate
and soils of areas where raw materials are produced. A general

view is sought of routes of trade and means of transportation in the development of commerce.

In the factory stage emphasis is laid upon the invention of machines, showing the utilization of the forces in nature which give increased production. A review is made of machines from primitive times to the present. The mechanics of each are worked out, and a mathematical calculation is made of the amount of work done by each.

A study of different fabrics due to the structure and nature of fiber is made, determining texture, hydroscopic nature, relation to warmth, inflammability, etc. Chemical processes involved in the separation of waste material were worked out in the preparation of raw material, the scouring, dyeing, and steaming.

Since space does not permit a complete statement of the whole scheme, the primitive stage has been selected to show the method of work. As an introduction, seven-year-old children gather together what they know from experience of the difference in quality of four typical kinds of cloth—wool, silk, cotton, and linen. They examine their own clothing, pull to pieces samples of similar materials, and get an idea of different types of fiber. They select the fiber which they think was probably used by peoples in primitive conditions (that requiring the least preparation) and reach their conclusions by means of the following process. They unwind the silk from a cocoon, find it fine, delicate, and difficult to handle. They remove the cotton from the bolls and separate the seeds from the fibers—a tedious task. Retted and unretted flax shows the long process of decay necessary to remove the fibers from the stalk. The wool, however, which can be twisted easily into thread with the fingers, is invariably selected. Each step in the process is so dependent on the nature of the material that the children can make the steps logically and independently. A fleece is examined, and methods of shearing talked over. The next step in order would be a visit to a sheep ranch. If this is impossible, the children can substitute photographs and stories of personal experiences. The relative quality of the different parts of the fleece is observed and also the duties of the wool sorter. Feltings, tarred locks, brands, and wool from lower parts of the legs are removed and spun into coarser yarn. The long, clean wool from neck, breast, and shoulders is made into yarn for the finer cloth. The back is usually full of burrs and more or less matted and requires care to get into shape for spinning. The children work out the process in detail by a series of experiments. Each child tries spinning both "scoured" and raw wool for the purpose of comparison. The oily fibers of the raw wool slip apart easily; the harsh, dry fibers of the scoured wool are matted together and are hard to manipulate. Thus they find from experience the reason for using unscoured wool for hand spinning.

In order to spin wool in any quantity, burrs and dirt are first removed from the raw wool. One child suggested in order to facilitate the process: "If you spread the fibers like a cobweb, the dirt will fall out." Three questions were raised in the course of the work: How would the fibers have to be arranged to make an even thread? How would dirt interfere? How would cross-fibers interfere with the evenness of the thread? At the end of the lesson the children formulated the purpose and method of carding. The clean, fluffy mass of wool was drawn out in a long "sliver" one inch wide. Where thin places occurred, they fitted in loose strands of wool. This gave them a clearer idea of the interlocking of the wool, due to the wavy character of the fiber. Carding implements were worked out. The fleece, as a whole, and even raw wool were new to nearly all the children. Many questions were asked concerning it, such as: "What is the difference between hair and wool?" Wool and hair were examined under the microscope and sketches made of the microscopic appearance of the two, showing the rough, scaly surface of the wool. The children twisted the drawn-out sliver of wool to make a thread by rolling it between their fingers on the knee. When the sliver was too thick, the wool simply matted together; it would not lock to make a hard twisted thread. They tested the difference between matted wool and spun thread, experimented to find the greatest number of fibers which would spin without matting, and finally gathered smooth twigs in an open lot near by and wound their spun thread on it to prevent tangling.

The child easily discovers that when the end of the thread is left free and the twig is dropped, the twist is lost and the thread unwound. He reasons that by twirling the twig in the opposite direction the twig can be made to do the work he had previously done by rolling against his knee. He discovers also that when the twig is weighted with thread it draws out the carded wool and assists in the spinning. So the twig is weighted artificially with clay, stone, or wood, and the wheel is suggested with its use in balancing and giving greater speed to the spinning. The advantage of having the wheel in the shape of a disk is worked out by the children realizing that an uneven distribution of weight interferes with the smoothness of the motion of the spindle.

The distaff and spindle were made in the shop, and each child practiced spinning a fine, smooth thread. They compared this with hand-spinning and showed that it took less time and labor to produce the same amount of thread, many more fibers being made to interlock, and the thread more uniformly twisted. Thus, by comparison, they were brought to realize the use of this first advance step in spinning. The thread was made rather fine for weaving. It was compared with the factory yarn, which was unraveled and found to consist of three and four strands. Separating these strands they found the twisted parallel fibers of wool. After having analyzed the structure of the thread in this manner, they prepared to make "three-ply" yarn of the thread they had spun. They worked out the idea that the strands would have to be spun together in the same manner as they had spun the yarn, that the various strands would have to be drawn out evenly, thus necessitating a frame on which the bobbins could revolve.

The yarn was finally ready to be scoured and dyed. From previous experience the children knew the yarn would have to be in loose hanks to dye evenly. They wound the skeins about the backs of two chairs, one child delivering the yarn from the bobbin while another regulated it. They found it slow work and succeeded in making very small skeins. They decided to make something similar to the bobbin frame upon which to wind the skeins. Colonial reels were examined, and a simple one made in the shop. The yarn from the spindles was wound into loose hanks for dyeing. The yarn was scoured and dyed in the science periods.

As a preparation for weaving, cloth was examined and its structure and texture compared with the mats and baskets they had previously woven. The fact that weaving of materials that did not require spinning must have long preceded the invention of spinning was shown in the following manner. The textile work of the primitive peoples of today was examined and found to consist chiefly of grasses and various other raw materials. The beaten bark or "tapa" of the Hawaiians was examined to show the interlacing of the fibers. The probable discovery of the shepherd who found the cast fleece matted together after the exposure to rain and sun was told as a story. The effect of water and heat on wool was tried and in some cases resulted in a fine piece of felt. The weaving of a rush mat from the chance placing of the reeds, forming a sort of pattern on the clay floor of a primitive hut, was given as a probable origin of pattern weaving. The children gave the cocoon, the bird's nest, and the spider's web as instances of weaving. In the cloth the interlacing was found to be regularly adjusted into two sets of threads, respectively "warp" and "woof." Each child explained his way of constructing a loom. Two rods held the warp in position; two cross-rods kept it stretched; and a weaving needle was used to insert the woof. The woof and warp were made of the thread the children had spun. . . .

The inspection of different fabrics and fibers for the sake of forming a conclusion regarding their adaptability to certain purposes gives training to the children's powers of observation. These are ideal occasions for both sense training and discipline in thought.

The weakness of ordinary lessons in observation, calculated to train the senses, is that they have no outlet beyond themselves and hence no necessary motive. In the natural life of the individual and the race, there is always a reason for sense observation. There is always some need coming from an end to be reached that makes one look about to discover and discriminate whatever will assist him. Normal sensations operate as clues, as aids, as stimuli in directing activity in what has to be done; they are not ends in themselves. . . .

Again this method involves the exercise of judgment. The ability to think and the method of thinking are part and parcel of all the reinventing and the rediscovering. Thinking does not occur for its own sake; it is not an end in itself. It arises from the need of meeting some difficulty, in reflecting upon the best way of overcoming it, and thus leads to planning, to projecting mentally the end to be reached, and deciding upon the steps necessary. The tool and method of going to work are always seen to be dependent upon the material on the one side and the result to be attained on the other. These being given, to find the third term is the problem, surely as logical an exercise as any in geometry. It has the added advantage of being concrete and of calling the constructive imagination into play. . . .

All of the activities correlate with the historical work and give a background which makes the later study of economics much more fruitful and concrete. Similar connections are made with the nature study as regards the materials used and the plants and animals producing them, with physical geography as regards conditions of soil or climate and the sources of the raw materials, and with commercial geography as regards the manufacture and distribution of the finished products.

Manual construction is continuously required. Each child carries out his idea into concrete form. The shop becomes the laboratory where he manufactures his spindle or his loom, and the color or design of the working plan all enlist the aid of the art department.

All of these aspects meet in and radiate from the continuous and direct activity or occupation of the children themselves. From the standpoint of the child there is but one thing going on. He is occupied with making things, with weaving, designing, cutting; he is busy doing something which appeals alike to feeling, perception, imagination, judgment, and manual skill. All of his power and emotions are utilized in an activity which interests him.

CHAPTER XVII

EXPERIMENTAL
ACTIVITIES DEVELOPING SKILLS
IN COMMUNICATION AND EXPRESSION

THE third group of studies in the Laboratory School's curricular classification included reading, writing, the more technical forms of measurement, and the various arts of expression. The children of the school gradually awoke to the need and grew into an appreciation of the use of these various forms of intellectual communication and inquiry. This need and appreciation were met in and developed out of the daily activities of their steadily enlarging program. As the physical organism increases in size and ability to function only as it takes in and assimilates food suitable to its needs, so mental growth occurs only as knowledge is used in action to enlarge the meaning of action and further its end. Judgment to select and skill to use knowledge are essential to its swift assimilation into experience. In the immature child, certain original impulses are available, and the growth of the child depends upon their exercise.[1] The social impulse shows itself in conversation, personal intercourse, and communication. Gesture and language are the simplest form of the social expression of a child. They arise out of need to communicate something about a social situation. Language, therefore, in these early stages of growth, is used primarily as a means of social communication and not for the expression of thought.

The instinct to self-expression in action is one of the earliest

---

[1] These are roughly classified by Mr. Dewey as: (1) the social, (2) the constructive, (3) the investigative, and (4) the expressive. This classification he still further simplifies by finding that, in the process of development, (3) and (4) grow out of (2) and (1).

of the developing impulses. The dawn of social consciousness, however, follows soon, and with it there is born the desire to share, to tell about the results of activity. These may be daubs of color on paper, a weird clay man, a house of blocks, or the story of a day's doings, but each in turn is the concrete embodiment of the child's idea. Under the stimulus of this desire to *communicate* to others he searches for and welcomes all ways and means of letting others know what he has done and of finding out a still better way of doing. This then is the psychological moment to teach him the means for such sharing of his ideas.

USE OF LANGUAGE DURING EARLY STAGES OF GROWTH

Beginning with a hit-and-miss method, the subsequent endless experimentation of a baby in producing sounds is reinforced by the selective response of adults. He gradually eliminates the sounds which are not language and builds up, through imitation, a word vocabulary in which each word is always related to an actual object or situation. He retains those sounds or words which bring him food, comfort, and the condition of play which he desires. Similarly, he later patterns his sentence structure after that of the adults in the spontaneous conversation of the home, and "I" replaces "me" after many efforts.

In this school, which was in character a continuation of the home, each recitation was preëminently a social meeting place where organized spontaneous conversation went on along different lines. It was the social clearing-house in which experiences and ideas were exchanged and subjected to criticism, where misconceptions were corrected and new lines of thought and inquiry set up.

Although the consecutive study of the place and function of language in this school, either oral or written, was never summarized, certain observations as to the child's interests and attainments in verbal and written expression can be made: first, as to the incidental use of all verbal or written symbols as forms of social expression, particularly in the first stage of growth and in the second, as to the gradual development by the child of conscious recognition of need for and skill in the formulation and use of the rules of grammatical construction and of those traits which give literary distinction and form to writing as the expression of thought and emotion.

Continual contact with actual experience stimulated the children to a full and free use of language. Each child always had a variety of material and facts in his mind to talk about, and his language constantly became more refined and full because controlled by realities. Little by little the written symbols for the words already familiar to his tongue and ear were introduced, still in natural relation to experience. By them the child found he could keep track of his work from day to day; by them he could give to others the results of his own special activity; and by them his own consciousness was widened. He thus himself discovered the use of written language in its natural relation to experience.

The occasions in which his attention was directed to form in either spoken or written language were the same as those in actual life, situations outside of the school. They were the reports of work to the general assembly, for the newspaper, or for an individual contribution to a group story or play. At such times of formulation and composition, hints were given as to clarity in sentence structure, as well as the use of climax and interest. The child thus became conscious of the structure of the sentence, of the place and use of modifying words in phrases, and of the position of the latter in the sentence, and of the need for paragraph form. Finally he came to see that a unified structure which has clarity and climactic interest depends upon order and sequence of the material. In the oral delivery of these contributions, help in proper enunciation, posture and interpretation found its natural place. Expert direction was welcome because the children felt the need of being able consciously to correct their faults and gain in ability to express their ideas by voice and gesture.

The teaching of language was at all times a subject of discussion and concern for all teachers. It was of untold advantage that the teaching was never divorced from reality. The children's records were the accounts of their daily experiences and showed unusual clarity and a certain literary flavor. An appreciation of the color quality inherent in words was cultivated and developed by constant dramatization of situations and characters. This was helped on by the enjoyment of good stories, which were used sparingly, as they should be, and were of such character that they reinforced and thus became an integral part or expression of the children's own experiences.

Conversation was the means of developing and directing experiences and enterprises in all the classrooms. The small size of the groups made individual contribution to the group experience possible. Each day's recitation was a debate, a discussion of the pros and cons of the next step in the group's activity. The comparative ease with which these children were able to debate in their subsequent secondary and college experience showed the worth of this type of recitation. Initiative and freedom in any situation were characteristics of the older children of this school. Language was to them all a tool by which they could convey to others the effect produced on them by some fact, event, or social situation. It had come to be more than a means of social communication; it was a medium of expressing thought. In the secondary period, therefore, these children were ready to enter into a conscious analysis of language as such and to generalize and formulate rules which would help them attain the skill demanded by literary tastes and artistic standards.

USE OF NUMBER AND TOOLS OF MEASUREMENT

The instinct to measure by counting, which is also a form of communication, springs to consciousness in response to a felt need in the social situation of a little child. It is continually reinforced by adults' repetitions of nursery rhymes, such as "One, Two, Buckle My Shoe." By the time the four-year-old child arrives at school he has in his own experience a background of contact and acquaintance with social and physical realities. Out of this fertile soil will grow his first concepts of the use of the symbols of language, quantity, or value. Just as he has quite an extensive vocabulary and consciously uses it to supply his needs and express his crude ideas, so he has something of a conception of the use of numbers to evaluate his possessions (in the sense of knowing to a limited extent how many marbles he has). Of the meaning of numbers in its more technical and implicit meaning, that of measuring with measured units, he has, as yet, no consciousness, just as he has, as yet, no conception of the use of language as a medium of expressing thought. The underlying psychology of language and number are, therefore, seen to be similar. Both are forms of intellectual communication with oral and written conventionalized symbols that stand for ideas. The use of both first arises out of the need to get over to some one else something important in the physical or social situation. By conscious design the child met, in the school, a constantly increasing demand for the use of language and number symbols. In the latter, the idea of quantity in concrete form always preceded and accompanied the use of abstract number symbols.

For the younger children the teaching of language and number went on in relation to the daily activities of the child. The sub-primary child of four or five, as he set the table for luncheon, at first laid down one spoon each for Mary, John, and Ellen. His next step, when standing by the silver basket, was to count out loud, "One, two, three, no! four, one for the teacher." When, however, he replied to the teacher's question, "How many persons are coming to lunch?" by answering, "Four," and then, going to the silver basket, counted the right number of spoons, he showed that he had begun to use words as symbols. The importance of this appreciation by the child of the connection between the concrete situation and the symbol, the linking in his mind of the concrete situation to the symbol, cannot be over emphasized. A child who has not made this connection often goes on repeating his "one, two," etc., up to eight or nine, with frequent omission of one or two of the series. This is because he does not comprehend the meaning of the enumeration, because he has never linked counting to a concrete situation where there is a *need* for counting. When "four" means to him not only four people, four spoons, etc., but means, in addition, a way of matching these unlike things through the agency of a number symbol common to both, he may be said to have begun to count.

In his cooking at the school the child learned that one cup of flaked rice took one cup of water. He compared one cup of flaked rice with a granular cereal on a balance and found that the smaller bulk, but same weight of the latter also required one cup of water. When he found by measuring that he had one fourth cup of this cereal, it was not difficult for him to conclude that one fourth of a cup of a certain kind of cereal will take four times its quantity of water to cook properly. He then experimented with another cereal and found that it requires only twice as much. His use of numbers in the two experiments brings him to his first end, the ascertaining of the amount of water that both cereals require. He then compares the two and uses numbers as a means to express this comparison in symbolic form. He has now taken another step, passing to an appreciation of the idea of ratio which is implicit in all numbers.

This concrete manipulation of quantity included comparisons of weights and distances, and so on, and was followed by a more definite use of the symbols of enumeration and relation for the purpose of anticipating consequences and, therefore, controlling results.

From a qualitative judgment of amount the child progresses to a definite control of quantity through symbols. Still another step is made as the child learns the different kinds of measures. Instead of halving the length of string to find half of the garden (the method of the young child), the older measured with the yardstick and divided the number by two. In one activity he uses the ruler. In another he must regulate his action by a unit of time. With the idea that his actions are controlled by a time-unit, he gets his first approach to the sequence of on-going events, in home situations as well as in school. The youngest group visited the baker's shop, saw the oven and the utensils which were used in cooking. The head baker made some little cakes, while the children watched to get some idea of the process. They waited fifteen minutes to see them taken out, which gave the children a deeper interest in time and its measurement by the clock. They gradually discovered there was a time for everything, a time for work, a time for play, a time to sleep, and a time to eat. When the clock in the kindergarten said it was time to begin or stop work or play, it was a universal law to be obeyed by both teachers and pupils. When the question arose, "Can't I do just a few more?" the answer came, "But the clock says it is time to put the work away," and this was accepted without dispute. This conception of what time is functions so differently at different ages that the stage at which he perfects different ideas needs more recorded observations by many teachers. Where activities of a child's environment are definitely regulated by the time seasons, as in rural situations, the latter with their causes will be taught much earlier than with children not so situated. City children, isolated from nature, may get this knowledge through the importance of the calendar to a people whose activities they are studying.

A child becomes interested not only in the origin of the symbols for number, but in measurement units of all kinds. Through his appreciation of primitive man's use of sun and moon as time measurers, he takes interest in his own calendar. This generally happens first in connection with something that intimately concerns him, such as his own birthday or the first day of school. His ability to read the clock, which has been progressing slowly, is usually perfected about this time. His ideas continually enlarge through his daily experience. Whereas once he measured his garden by the number of his own paces, he now begins to use the yardstick or the ruler to find how his patch compares with the length of his neighbor's.

A study of the Phoenicians, who adapted and simplified through use the symbols of the scholarly Assyrians and Egyptians, gave the child of eight the historical basis of our present alphabets and numerical systems. At this age children begin, because of their needs, to grow eager for facility in ordinary number combinations. They gladly submit to drill in order to attain such facility. If they are allowed to discover for themselves such things as the place of digits, tens, hundreds, etc., in our system of notation, they work out their own rules for adding and subtracting, multiplying and dividing. When a child in the school found it necessary to add ⅓ and ¼ of a foot he proceeded in natural logical fashion from the known to the unknown. He knew one foot as 12 inches. He then consulted the ruler and saw that the ⅓ is 4 inches and that ¼ is 3 inches. Their sum he easily calculated as 7 inches or $\frac{7}{12}$ of a foot. Then, if ready for such abstractions, he would himself say that to add fractions they must be the same "kind of parts of anything." He was then ready to add a quarter and a half-dollar, usually by saying that a half is 2 quarters, so he has 3 quarters. He was, however, often able to do this concretely for some time before he was able to state what is done when fractions are added. At this stage, he was given the terms numerator and denominator and understood that the figure above the line tells the number of parts taken, while the one below tells how many of these parts there are in a unit. As the work often involved the use of fractions the child liked this new and convenient tool. He did not have to go back to the ruler or the cup each time and count how much he had. The ability to abstract and formulate began gradually at about nine years of age.

The hard-and-fast distinction between arithmetic and algebra was broken down in various ways, such as the use of letters to represent quantities when writing formulae for examples (base x rate = percentage (bxr = p). In early practice in weighing, the idea of an equation was given as a way of representing the drawing power of the earth on different objects. The earth-pull on an object on one side of the balance is equal to the earth-pull on a number of objects on the other (i. e., the weights) and was represented symbolically in series as x (the unknown weight) = a + b + c.

As the children made simple machines, scales, a wheeled cart, a wheelbarrow, a potter's wheel, small and large looms, a pile-driver, a foot automobile, they formulated and made use of equations of ratios and proportion. This kind of concrete experience enabled them to identify the various kinds of levers in their machines. They studied the principle of the nut cracker, traced the invention of the wheeled cart, and discovered the advantage gained through the invention of the hub. They discovered the advantage of the wheelbarrow and the principle involved in gears, in clocks, and locks; they studied the use and transfer of energy in the treadle and spindle of a spinning-wheel or in the gear of a bicycle. All of this work was used as offering occasions for the child to investigate and discover for himself the everyday uses of mechanical principles involved in the various kinds of balances and pulleys and to point out the differences by the use of diagram and equation. The children continually used ratio with skill and appreciation in demonstrating the relation of the diameter of wheels to the circumference or the laws of the three types of levers. Such use in genuine situations and with simple machines furthers a child's intellectual understanding of the complicated mechanisms and intricate arithmetical formulae used in work with the intricate forms of machines, which he sees and deals with later.

Mechanical drawing was used in making compasses, and a simple astrolade, in calculating the hour circle and distances on a globe, and in finding latitude from the altitude of the north star. These problems served as an introduction to and use of intuitive geometrical demonstrations.

To the mathematician, who has forgotten the way he came, it seems a long jump from the child's use of number in counting out his blocks, or in the control of his game, to the physicist's use of measurement in the construction of a working theory of matter. To the psychologist and to the educator the need of number for control through its function of evaluation is the same for the child in his concrete world, as for the physicist in his.

An historical study of the slow development of arithmetic will give guiding principles to the teacher of little children. Originating as a means of trade control, it passed slowly through the rule-of-thumb period and has just culminated in the most modern of engineering exploits. When the teacher realizes how late in the race development abstraction occurs, he will be content to multiply endlessly the occasions to use number concretely in his dealings with young children. At all times, he must watch for the psychological time and place to introduce symbols and the opportunity to formulate generalizations.

The recognition that the complicated formulae of the physicist as a means of valuation and control have evolved from a simple use of counting by the savage gave important educational implications for those directing this experiment. It gave confidence in the outcome of this approach to mathematical method. It eliminated the too frequent unintelligent and often blind following of historical details without reference to their relation to the needs and demands of physical and social situations. With aid and under direction as he plays his games and makes his simple and more complex machines, a child can be led to understand and use the principles and formulae of control in the more and more abstract forms, which finally eventuate in the various algebraic and trigonometric formulae and, at the college level, in differential functions and calculus. With such mathematical training, based on the appreciation of each step through concrete demonstration, a student, as he passes from field to field in mathematics, is quite aware that he is simply using more and more refined tools to control the heterogeneous miscellany of the physical and social world. Always, at whatever stage, number was taught not as number but as a means through which some activity, undertaken on its own account, was rendered more orderly and effective. In this way it afforded insight into the ways in which man actually employs numerical relations in social life.

On the whole the more direct modes of activity, the construction and occupational work, the scientific observation and experimentation, presented plenty of opportunities for the necessary use of reading, writing, spelling, and number work. These subjects, therefore, were not isolated studies, but were introduced as organic outgrowths of the child's daily experience. The problem was always to take advantage of these opportunities in a systematic and progressive way. When this was done successfully, the children needed to devote much less time to tool study than is usually the case. It was also found that at certain periods of their development the children enjoyed playing with symbols just as babies, learning to talk, play with words. At a later age when given accurate compasses and ruler, children find similar pleasure in the possibilities of geometric design.

There were mistakes and failures made in this new way of teaching the time-honored subjects. With certain groups of children the teaching of writing and reading was postponed too long, with the result that certain children had progressed intellectually so far that the belated learning of the symbols, which at an earlier period would have been enjoyed, was irksome. Such children often marked time, as it were, and only learned to read when a special interest stimulated them to the necessary effort.

Experience repeatedly showed that in those studies where mastery of technique or special method was necessary, there was need for a periodic concentration and alternation in the time devoted to them. When a group, for example, found themselves weak in a certain arithmetical operation or in language expression and, therefore, handicapped in their other work, work on this was emphasized until the children exhibited to their own satisfaction a power and skill sufficient to enable them to go ahead in an independent fashion.

This method of teaching gave rise to the conviction that children should learn that mathematical expressions only cover a part of experience with physical things, that mathematics is a tool which fits only a certain kind of universe, and that its expressions cannot be used as a basis of the whole of experience. They should be aware that much is still unknown of mathematical relations, and that the latter leave other kinds of relations untouched. They thus gain no concept that all experience is mechanical and mathematically measurable, but are left with many open doors through which individual thinking may pass. In conclusion, it is not too much to say that the children of this school used the symbols of language and calculation more intelligently and less mechanically than most, and with a certain sense of power in their expression.

ARTISTIC EXPRESSION

The drama and literature, the music, modeling and painting of the school program, all the expressive activities at all stages of growth, were the child's means of social intercourse, his modes of communication, as well as avenues for individual expression. As he developed in this carefully guided experience, first steps grew into finer and fuller expressions of social and constructive impulses. It was the ideal and the hope of the school that all the developing play of productive and manipulating activities, the play which is not mere amusement or recreation, should become surcharged with joy and satisfaction in its performance and with such social and scientific meanings that this association, once made, should never be lost.

In a recent letter recalling memories of her Dewey School days, one of the older pupils of the school writes:

To outsiders who did not understand what went on, the daily curriculum seemed a grand jubilee. Children apparently played through history and English classes, cooked through arithmetic and science hours, and so on. Surely no real study went on with such antics; surely no essentials of grammar grades and high schools were learned. Then, to a confused amazement, the supposed madcaps entered colleges and universities and acquitted themselves creditably with conventionally prepared students.

This memory seems to indicate that the school work of those days was often like play, a freely productive sort of activity that filled the imagination and the emotions of the writer as well as her hands to such a degree that thirty years later she still thrills with its joyful memories.

Drama played a large part in these activities. In the early years, the classroom work was often a continued play of the unfolding drama of human life. The children handled raw materials of many kinds and had the satisfaction of shaping them to their own planned ends. Under guidance these results grew into more and more finished products of greater meaning and artistic value. It has been well said that: [2] "Art is not

---

[2] John Dewey, "Culture and Industry in Education," *The Educational Bi-Monthly*, Vol. 1, No. 1.

an outer product nor an outer behavior. It is an attitude of spirit, a state of mind—one which demands for its satisfaction and fulfilling a shaping of matter to new and more significant form. To feel the meaning of what one is doing and to rejoice in that meaning, to unite in one concurrent fact the unfolding of the inner life and the ordered development of material conditions—that is art."

The school seems to have had a groping faith that genuine artistic expression in any medium may grow out of the manual arts and carry on to their spiritual meaning many of the processes of everyday life. This did not mean that all art work was to be correlated in detail with the other work of the school, but that there was a spirit of union which gave vitality to the art, and depth and richness to the other work. It recognized that art work involves physical organs, the eye and hand, the ear and voice, however, ideally. As Mr. Dewey has somewhere said, "It is something more than the mere technical skill required by the organs of expression; it involves an idea, a thought, a spiritual rendering of things, and yet it is other than any number of ideas by themselves, it is a living union of thought and the instrument of expression." It was dimly realized, therefore, that the artistic attitude is the ideal attitude of interest, and that if a child could be animated by such interest, he would bring forth results in his activities that would be accompanied by an enrichment of his intellectual and emotional life. As the woodwork, drawing, painting, music, language, or drama proved an aid in extending the meaning of what a child did and gave a motive to develop technique, it also enlarged into the realm of an artistic means of expression.

It was always a hope that each child would enjoy every subject studied at some, if not all, phases of its development and thus grow into something of a sense of its esthetic quality. This appreciation of the quality of a subject depends upon the standards that the child, at one time or another, has formed of its value in his immediate experience. It also depends upon how the range of his inevitably limited direct experience has been enlarged and deepened in its meaning through language and all symbolic forms of intercourse with the similar experiences of others. As these connections multiplied, the children liked more and more to share the meaning of their activities and discovered that language was a good tool for telling about them. They also became more able and willing to listen sympathetically to the accounts of others. Thoughts took form in words. Certain words or arrangements of words expressed thoughts better than others and, when arranged in a certain order, expressed it more clearly and more beautifully. Little by little because its use was daily and hourly related to his living, the child came to realize that language was the medium, *par excellence,* for telling about his actions and thoughts. Step by step he woke to its inherent value and beauty.

LITERARY EXPRESSION

The *need to formulate the meaning* of their activities, either in conversation or in an oral or written report, in recipe or rule for procedure, in mathematics or in the laboratory, in verse for songs, or in dramatic form for formal plays, arose for the most part out of the actual situation of the classroom or the imagined ones of the historical times they were reliving. All actions, involving as they did constant communication of all sorts, developed great freedom of expression and intercourse. Conversations and discussions formed the basis out of which ability to debate developed. Oral reports grew to monologues and took on a vague similarity to the oration, while written reports from words and short sentences grew with enlarging horizons and developing ability and skill to essays, biographies, or stories. These also gradually took on the form of artistic expression. Because they formulated the meaning of each child's actual experience, they were often tinged with the flavor of his own imaginative interpretation and brought home to him, as to others, the vitality of his experience.

Clarity and simple, forceful use of words were ideals sought for the children in their reports which were often reviews of the day's, the week's, or the term's work. Through the use of the school's printing-press by the older children, dictated reports of those children, not yet able to use the written symbols, were made available as reading lessons. These took on such form as:

> We can sew.
> Suppose you had no needle?
> What would you do for clothing?
> Some boys say they would wear a goat's skin.

The youngest children, for the most part, acted out their songs and stories, getting thus a clearer idea of them and a greater sympathy with the characters. These plays and stories continually increased in scope and content. The three- and four-year-olds, in their occupational plays such as that of the dry goods store, were usually content with the mere activity of buying and selling, without specifying what they wished to buy. At five years they carried out their plays in minute detail, and had the cashier, cash boys, clerks, bundle-wrappers, and a horse and delivery wagon, using the vocabulary and characteristic dramatic expressions. They bought only things found in dry-goods stores and often tried them on to see if they would fit. The dramas of Group IV (seven years) were of their history, the study of primitive life.

It was found that when the children wrote their own reading lessons, their reading was purely memory work. So the teacher resorted to composing certain key sentences herself. With these to start from, the children supplied the background of detail, showing a great interest in the composition, changing the sentences when they were not euphonious or suggesting words that might sound better. On occasion, pauses were made to discuss the words under consideration and some for blackboard work in the building of words. When interest in such technique flagged, the composition was continued. The teacher [3] of seven-year-olds reported:

The materials which were chosen for their reading lessons were taken chiefly from their history, with occasional changes to other subjects, shop-work, or cooking. It soon became evident that their

---

[3] Wynne Laskerstein.

power to give a definite account of their work and their interest in doing it were in direct ratio to the degree of activity involved in the original lesson. It was often impossible to obtain a clear statement of their history, even on the day in which it had been presented to them, and frequently different members of the group would give contradictory statements with regard to the most essential point. But whenever hand-work was the subject of discussion they recalled with comparative ease the desired details.

A notably successful lesson was the result of a talk about the making of their looms. Sentences were put on the blackboard by the teacher as the children gave them and were read and reread by the class. A list was made of the new words, chiefly names of tools, and a drill upon these was given by acting out the uses of the various tools. Individual children were chosen to direct the action by pointing to certain words or to find on the blackboard the name of the tool which the others were using. The children were delighted with the lesson. The next day they were eager to write the new words and spent the entire period at the blackboard without signs of fatigue. They called this writing "putting the tools in their shop," and one boy insisted upon buying each tool from the teacher before he wrote its name, gravely proffering imaginary money and insisting that the tool be wrapped up in paper and duly delivered.

⁴ In the next quarter the reading for the group was based on the history work—a study of primitive man. In the beginning much time was devoted to keeping a record of their study, which was printed by the older groups. Book covers were made, and the records were used as reading lessons. They then began to retell the story of *Ab* which one of the teachers had read to them. This extended from day to day. Much of it was dictated by the children. The language of the original story was drawn on freely, but the thought was so padded with their own imaginative thinking that in the end it came to be a new story of their own. Additional characters were introduced who operated in different situations according to the children's original plan. The story speaks for itself, indicating a growing appreciation and increasing skill of expression. In their compositions they were kept to simple sentence structure, but no limit was put on vocabulary. As each child gave his part, it was written on the board for the others to read. Much time was spent each day in picking out familiar words and

---

⁴ Teacher, Margaret Hoblitt.

learning new ones from their reading lessons. The origin and phonetics of these were often discussed.

Most of the children in this group had not at that time reached any degree of ease in reading, but all had a desire to read. Four of them had done a little reading in books, beginning with the simple repetitive stories such as "Henny Penny" and "Cock Robin." They had not yet reached the stage of doing any independent writing, although as a group they wrote two scenes of a dramatic play based on the story of primitive people. Individual children suggested the dialogue, and the others agreed or changed it until they were all satisfied. This work was then written on the board for the class to copy.

As Group V, these children followed their Phoenician sailors to the Mediterranean seaport of Venice and thence embarked on a study of the world wanderings of explorers. The best available story of the life of each explorer was read by the children. They then summed up the chief points and wrote their own records. The books containing these stories were left where the children could get them and read further if they so desired. The life of Columbus came first, and the presence in Jackson Park of the models of the *Nina, Pinta, Santa Maria,* and the convent of *La Rabida* added interest to the story. These written reports culminated in a play about Columbus which was written for and produced at one of the general assemblies. Its production involved much constructive, as well as expressive, effort and finally drew into coöperation most of the school.[5]

At ten years of age, Group VII was interested in arithmetic to such an extent that they undertook the writing of a textbook. The children composed many of their own problems, and considerable attention was given in this group and in Group IX to the formal statement of generalizations in concise and finished English. The latter group was much interested in the logic of the syllogistic statement. Better order in the written work was an aim which seemed of great imporance at this

---

[5] For a statement of the language expression of Group VI, see Chapter VIII.

age to one of the most successful teachers of mathematics, for with the ability to formulate and arrange in exact and logical fashion went a commensurate increase in self-confidence.

In science, too, the most successful statements of the results of observation or experimentation were those that expressed the meaning of things seen or experienced so that they were understood, and became significant and indicative of new possibilities to mutually interested individuals. Knowledge of the right words, of sentence structure necessary to the formal statement of facts observed, problems to be solved, the premises of an hypothesis, or the conclusive evidence of an experiment— all were points of skill necessary for each child in order that he might make his daily observations and experiences in the laboratory or the field excursion successful and, therefore, intelligible and vitally significant to his group. For adequate and successful interpretation of the scientific meanings of his daily life, so that they were progressively helpful in new experiences, both to himself and others, a child must have a suitable scientific vocabulary and an adequate technique in expression. The children planned as a group and talked over their experiments in advance, but each child wrote an individual report of his own work.

This group, dissatisfied with their Dewey School song, wished to write something more dignified and from their study of literature took the subject of the *Adventures of Odysseus*. In the composition of both music and poem they sought to use as many beautiful phrases and expressions as possible.

ODYSSEUS

Land not here! For here dwell the Kine of the Sun,
And Zeus would send a thunderbolt should you in your hunger harm
    one.
Yet they heeded not my words,
But beached their ships upon the shore,
And when I woke from sleep,
I found the roasting flesh midst fires roar.

Hence sailed we on mid storm and wind and wave
And nearer to our Fate we drew—striving our lives to save—
In vain, for I alone escaped,

And drifted toward the fatal rock
Where dire Charybdis sucks the sea
And casts it forth with fearful shock.

Once again, saved by Athena the fair,
I drifted toward a flowery isle, and quietly slumbered there.
Then down the beach Calypso came
And to her grotto welcomed me.
Mid clustering vines and rippling streams
For years I rested peacefully.

At the close of another ten weeks of work (two and one half periods each week and one period of a half-hour of study hour) the individual records of Group VIII (eleven years) were "pieced together" to form a connected story of the formation of calcareous and sedimentary rocks in detail, and of land in general. Oral and written language were given separate consideration only with Group VIII in a course of English. Groups VII, VIII, and IX took over a good share of the printing of songs, poems, reading lessons, programs, records, or plays in English, French, or German for the whole school.

Latin, French, and German were studied in the secondary period. The various teachers coöperated closely, and a correlative study of word derivations and problems of syntax and grammar in each language was developed. At one time the same person taught both Latin and English. Contemporaneous with a study of English village life, an attempt was made to gather together, interrelate, and unify all the previous language experience of the oldest groups in the school. Group XI (fourteen years) had had little formal work in English, most of their grammar having been acquired in the collateral study of French and Latin. Their general reading of the classics had been limited. A critical analysis of one of Shakespeare's plays was undertaken. This was followed by further critical work which included an analysis and study of the history of the period of the play from all points of view, including the industrial and scientific. The results seem to have been suggestive of the weak as well as the strong points in the literary abilities of the children. At their best they showed [6] "consider-

---

[6] Teacher, Alice C. Dewey.

able logical power in attacking grammatical problems and in analyzing characters and situations. This ability enabled them to grasp quickly the idea that order of composition was simply the logic of thought or subject-matter. Analytical work in connection with writing finished reports of their science resulted in a rapid gain in the power to prepare clear and accurate outlines. The rapidity and ease with which they realized their lacks and utilized instruction to perfect their use of language indicated unusual critical ability, and they could analyze, abstract, and formulate conclusions or plans far more readily than the average young person of this age."

The choice of mediums of expression for ideas was rather limited by the school's lack of equipment. It varied, however, with individual children. Clay was early and long a favorite. It was plastic and to some extent durable. A child saw and felt his idea take form, and the result, which he could share with others, survived as evidence and proof of his expression. In music, on the other hand, the structure of melodic sound falls when the song ends, and it is often difficult, except for unusually gifted children, to recapture the fine quality of the first expression. Only when the teacher was a genius were the inventive results of the shy excursions of the unusual child into the field of creative music preserved.

MUSICAL EXPRESSION

The method of teaching music was that of Professor Calvin B. Cady—a musician with the point of view of an educator. He conceived of music as idea, not as the product of sense development—as conceptive thinking and hence a positive factor in education.[7]

The usual test of determining whether a child can discriminate between tones is no evidence of musical consciousness. Music is thought which must be grasped. The musical idea has three elements: melody, rhythm, and harmony, each of which must be conceived and gradually unfolded. Conceptive development may be

---

[7] Calvin B. Cady, "Music in Education," *University Record*, Vol. 1, No. 51.

expressed in two words, analysis and synthesis. Analysis is the individualizing process, synthesis the unifying one. Attention is nothing more than the developing of the conceptive process.

Until simple melodic phrases can be conceived, there is no evidence of musical consciousness. The second step is the recognition of the rhythmic basis of melody, and the third is the development of the harmonic basis underlying the melodic and rhythmic expression. When this conceptive foundation has been laid, the forms of musical manifestation, the voice, or the different kinds of musical instruments may be considered.

Thus music is an expression of the whole of life. Its principles are as fixed as those of geometry and their development as logical. The danger lies in considering music as one sided, as the language of emotion only. True music cannot be the language of discord; it must express the highest unity and harmony.

In the first year of the school, two of Mr. Cady's pupils were in charge of the music department.[8] The musical program was then taken over by another gifted pupil of Mr. Cady's, who developed it with a unique interpretation of her own. Extracts from an article written after two years' experience in the school give her own estimate of the work: [9]

Music is an important factor in the growth of the child's esthetic nature. As early as he is shown beauty in color and form the child should have beauty in tone and melody given him. There are no unmusical children. Interest in musical expression is one of the natural resources of the child, and unconsciously he will awaken to a melodic conception through repetitions, in pure and gentle tone, of melodies suited to his understanding. This process cannot be begun too early. Having understood, he possesses a mental picture which he seeks to express by humming or singing. This expression of an esthetic impulse is as natural to the child as his expression in color. Needing no instrument, it is simpler and would be more readily used were his early environment as full of tone as of color. The more he hears of this music, the more he assimilates, and the more he has to express. And not alone through imitation. If he be given a poetic phrase which touches his imagination, he can give his own melodic conception of it, and the awakening of this creative faculty brings a joy which stimulates the growth of his whole esthetic nature.

There is nothing more precious to a child than his own creation,

---

[8] May Taylor, Miss Whiting.
[9] May Root Kern.

and to preserve his melodic thought he will wish to acquire a knowledge of the symbols necessary to express it. . . .

In the school, a problem to be coped with arises from the diversity of musical attainment in the groups. Children from non-musical environment are to be handled with others who are developed musically. To lessen the chasm, much thought is given to creating a musical atmosphere. The formal side of the work is made as melodious as possible, and all technical exercises are clothed in harmony. The children have weekly opportunity of hearing a short program of music by the best composers, performed by friends of the school, by teachers, or by pupils prepared through outside work. The older children have heard short and simple talks on the lives and work of the great masters, illustrated by piano and vocal selections. A large part of each period of work is spent in song-singing. The school has been divided into two choruses, one ranging from six to eight and a half years of age, the other from nine to thirteen. These choruses have sung melodies learned by rote in their group work, the older chorus having in its repertoire songs by Franz, Schumann, Wagner, Reinecke, Humperdinck, and some of the best English composers. In connection with their work in Latin, they have learned a Latin song of nine stanzas and a shorter Christmas hymn; in connection with French, several *chansons populaires* and two old French rounds. The latter, being very simple in melody, have furnished a valuable exercise in concentration. There being in this chorus a considerable proportion of children unable to sing a connected melody correctly, perfection in detail is impossible. The special aims, other than familiarity with good songs and the memorizing of texts, have been bodily poise, deep breathing, careful enunciation, and a pure quality of tone. A picked chorus of twenty-five voices is now being arranged which will be trained to do some model singing for the benefit of the school.

Owing to the wide differences in musical development, it was difficult to find a common ground for the work of each group as a whole. The technical work, founded on short, original phrases, sometimes failed to arouse interest in those children who but imperfectly grasped melodic idea. The proposition, however, to select a topic and write a complete composite song which should express the genius of the group brought a unity of impulse at once. It was supposed that the unmusical children would devote themselves to the text and leave the musical setting to the rest. But not so; the general enthusiasm awoke them to an overflow of musical ideas and a firm belief in their own phrase as given. Whatever of novelty the song possesses is owing to the odd intervals offered by these non-musical children. It was necessary to harmonize them attractively to gain their acceptance by the musical members of the group, who, left to themselves, would have given only the most obvious phrases and thus produced more commonplace results.

After several successful songs had been composed, a group of children between the ages of seven and eight years, below the average in musical development, but having a strong feeling for rhythm, wrote a song which is saved from monotony by the final phrase given by a boy almost tone-deaf. He offered the phrase, which was repeated on the piano as nearly as possible as he had given it. He objected, however, saying that what was played was not what he intended to give. After repeated attempts, the teacher succeeded in discovering what he had persistently kept in his mind, but could not express. . . .

Composition work with the children has value in proportion to its being an untrammeled expression of their own musical consciousness. The teacher's task is to encourage through beautifying the child's thought by harmonic background. That composition work gives the children a grasp of rhythm is shown by the way they handle it in making their songs effective. A seven-year group completed a Snowman Song in three-pulse measure rhythm and sang it to the school. Later they felt that its flowing rhythm was not suited to the requirements of the words and found by experiment that by using the more energetic four-pulse, the character of their melody became what was desired.

The twelve-year-old children after completing their rollicking Fourth of July song experienced a reaction. They felt they had not expressed their highest musical consciousness and wished at once to begin a song into which they could put their best effort. As the Fourth of July song had met with enthusiastic approval from the school, this impulse showed a normal growth and as such was encouraged. That it was genuine was proved by the children's slow and critical work, lasting through the remainder of the spring quarter, resumed after the summer vacation, and carried on through more than one-half of the autumn quarter. They suggested and directed the piano accompaniment at important points and, after the song was completed and sung to the school, further embellished it by adding a second-voice part.

The group composed entirely of musically developed children was the last to produce a connected song. The original scheme of work, the study of selected songs with their detail and the learning of symbols for their own short melodic phrases, contented them. Emulation, however, urged them to write, and they undertook the task as imitators, thus with less exhilaration than the others showed. Later a second impulse, more genuine than the first, resulted in one of the best of the school songs.

It would be difficult to find songs written by adults which would appeal to the younger children's minds and hearts as do these, in spite of the crudities. The simplicity of thought and expression in the text, the sweetness and vitality of the melodies, exactly suit their needs. Practical trial for over a year has shown their preference for some of the school songs to the best of the child songs written by adults.

[10] ESTHETIC EXPRESSION OF EXPERIENCE

The drawing and painting activities of the school were based on the assumption that a creative attitude of mind is essential to a complete art experience. In order to make such an attitude possible, the pictures which children draw, the objects which they decorate, must be derived from their own significant experiences. They are not interested in acquiring technical skill for which they feel no need, but rather seek fulfilment of wants which dominate their present situations. They approach their work creatively when they make objects which they want for particular purposes, decorative patterns because there are real things to be decorated, or pictures when they afford responses to immediate and fundamental urges.

As it is only through the idealization of their own life and interests that children become creative in their art, it is evident that opportunities for such expression arise from this source. "Things to do" naturally grow out of interests, some of which are common to all children of corresponding age levels, while others are modified by home, neighborhood, and school situations. Our six-year-olds, whose studies centered about the farm, registered in their art expression the extent to which farm life has become real to them. Under their small hands clay turned into figures of farmers engaged in their most dramatic occupations, into farm animals, and even such otherwise prosaic things as fruits and vegetables. An older group, which had been studying the settlement of the Northwest, chose as subjects for a bas-relief, scenes from the life of Marquette. Another group executed in colored chalk on cardboard panels, a decoration for the wall of the textile room, choosing as their theme primitive methods of preparing and weaving wool. These subjects and projects would have held very little interest for a school in which subject-matter is factual rather than living reality. No cut and dried list of projects can mean the same thing to all children. The very perfection of many systems of instruction tends to inhibit creative effort, for in the hands of teachers who lack educational understanding and vision such a system becomes inflexible.

The belief was stressed that the teacher should seek the child's own motivations as a point of departure. It seemed equally important to

---

[10] Written by the art director, Lillian Cushman.

emphasize the second point, that development through learning should begin at once and be continuous. The question was how to secure this result. Is it possible to teach necessary facts and skills as the need arises in the creative process? The art, in common with all other work of the Laboratory School, was conducted on the assumption that these questions can be answered in the affirmative. Knowledge and technical skill are significant to the individual only when they are intermediate between a felt need and its satisfaction.

It is a recognized fact that nothing is more uninteresting or more meaningless to the average child than the subject of perspective. Yet it was a common experience in the school when a child was really interested in drawing something and a difficulty in perspective prevented adequate expression that the teacher found herself giving instruction which was sought by a willing mind. Ten-year-olds mastered fundamentals of convergence, while drawing log houses built by early settlers, spending three consecutive lessons in observing and experimenting before their interest span reached its limit. While modeling subjects taken from the life of Marquette, children of a group averaging eight and a half years of age considered the esthetic problem of arranging the figures in such a way as to produce a harmonious whole. They often checked up on the naturalness of their figures in action by acting out for one another the pose required and also made frequent reference to the various casts of the full-length figures which were kept in the corner of the studio. From the latter, they also sought answers to the questions of proportion and anatomy which occurred during the progress of the work. It must not be inferred that the facts and skills gained in this way were matters of choice. It was, of course, necessary to see to it that they developed as means to an end, not as ends in themselves. It was always within the power of the teacher to select for emphasis those difficulties for which a solution would help the child the most.

A very young child lives so completely in a world of his own creation that he invests his rude scribblings with a meaning, regardless of their outward form. A circle with straight lines attached serves equally as a horse, cow, dog, or man. By the time he reaches his sixth year he observes the external world more accurately and realizes a discrepancy between his crude symbols and the reality. If self-expression is to be sustained, instruction, or rather supervision, should begin as early as this. (We are beginning to carry it back to the Kindergarten.) Technique should not be forced upon a child, but he should be continually and consistently assisted to overcome the simple difficulties of which he is conscious. If there is not a continual improvement in expression, the critical faculty may develop far in advance of the power to execute. If he becomes disgusted with his efforts, a long technical interval is necessary in order to come up to his own standards, during which the art impulse may not survive. It is evident that as the mind matures, the interest span will lengthen, and so the technical effort may be sustained. While the fleeting impulse of six requires immediate expression, the child of twelve works purposively for hours in order to master a difficulty. The degree of effort is commensurate with the intensity of interest.

Aside from the growth which comes through a child's own creative efforts, the artistic inheritance of the race may become an important factor in the development of standards. The best method of using art masterpieces in an educational scheme is a field for careful research. They seem to be of value to the individual in so far as they become, through idealization of his own emotion, an expression of himself, or as they furnish technical standards. The interest, which the adult terms *esthetic,* is only rudimentary in childhood. An attempt to secure clearly defined appreciation of beauty from a child oversteps the mark in so far as it places the matter outside of the limited range of his experience. That esthetic appreciation grows as the child grows may be illustrated by the common tendency of young children to pass through a stage of primitive satisfaction in crude color before they are able to enjoy the subtleties of harmoniously related hue. Appreciation cannot be taught directly, but rather results from a continuous process of reëvaluating experience. This is another way of saying that the growing child is constantly modifying his standards and developing esthetic discrimination.

While the moral effect of art training has not been mentioned, its implications are implied. The only true freedom is that which the individual gains when he comes into possession of himself. Society is pretty much divided into classes of those who think and cannot use their hands, and those whose hands must work under the dictates of other minds. Any experience which contributes both food to the mind and power to the hand should exert a social influence of the highest ethical value. Because art does this, it promises to be a permanent educational factor.

The ideal of the school was that the music, the literary and dramatic efforts of the children, and their artistic expression whether in design, in wood, metal, or fabric, in the graphic or plastic arts—all should represent the culmination, the idealization, the highest point of refinement of all the work carried on.[11] "The school can justly be said to have failed more often at this point than at any other. This failure, however, may be

---

[11] John Dewey, written for the authors.

taken as evidence that the difficulty of achievement in this direction is proportionate to its importance. When artistic accomplishment and its attendant consciousness of satisfying form are treated as something separated from other and more ordinary activities, greater external esthetic perfection in selected forms, as far as quantity is concerned, is easier of attainment. But this apparent, visible, esthetic superiority is the counterpart of the fact that other activities and studies, which occupy much more of the pupils' energy and time, are bereft of that emotional and imaginative quality of personal fulfilment and of realized expressiveness that gives them immediate and esthetic value. Any method of education that strives to introduce an artistic element into all typical school experiences will, accordingly, seem to fail of realizing the ideal more often than those methods which segregate the esthetic experience and confine it to special exercises. But the rare occasional successes will go deeper and leave a more transforming, because more completely integrated, impress."

PART IV

PERSONNEL—ORGANIZATION—EVALUATION

CHAPTER XVIII

TEACHERS AND SCHOOL ORGANIZATION

ORGANIZATION AS SHAPED BY SOCIAL IDEAL

THE school felt and thought out its way as it went along. Its principles and practices were quite unlike those of contemporary method whether in the teaching or administrative area. The school was a social institution. Parents, teachers, administrators were joined in a search for a better way of schooling, where each individual, whether child or adult, could have his chance for normal, happy growth and the satisfactions of creative expression that was social in its character and purpose. In such a school, coöperation must replace competition, and the efforts of each must align, not vie, with one another in a search for a common end. All this meant new planning, new setting of the stage for daily activities which should permit and promote a socially motivated school life. The following statements, made by Mr. Dewey at the request of the writers, help to clarify the theory of the school as it developed in his mind and its method of operation.

"The principles of the school's plan were not intended as definite rules for what was to be done in school. They pointed out the general direction in which it was to move. . . . As the outcome of such conditions and others such as changes in the teaching staff, equipment, or building, the 'principles' formed a kind of working hypothesis rather than a fixed program and schedule. Their application was in the hands of the teachers, and this application was in fact equivalent to their development and modification by teachers.[1] The latter had not only great freedom in adapting principles to actual conditions, but if anything, too much responsibility was imposed upon them. In avoiding hard and fast plans to be executed and dictation of methods to be followed, individual teachers were, if anything, not given enough assistance either in advance or by way of critical supervision. There might well have been conditions fairer to teachers and more favorable to the success of the experiment. But if it had to be tried over again, I am confident that all concerned would prefer to err in this direction rather than in that of too definite formulation of syllabi and elaboration in advance of methods to use in teaching and discipline. Whatever else was lost, vitality and constant growth were gained.

"These remarks are not meant to shift responsibility for the mistakes and defects inevitably incident to a pioneer educational undertaking to the teaching corps. They are made to offset the impression which the formal statement of principles might otherwise occasion, that of a scheme of instruction fixed in advance. In an experimental school it is more difficult than elsewhere to avoid extremes. One of them results in a continual improvisation that is destructive of continuity and in the end of steady development of power. The other relies upon definite presentation of ends and methods for reaching them to which teachers are expected to conform.

TEACHERS' SHARE IN SELECTING SUBJECT-MATTER AND METHODS

"The connecting link between these considerations and the original statements of the principles of the school was worked out by the teachers themselves coöperatively, with consider-

---

[1] "Mr. Dewey had the greatest real faith of any educator I have known in the classroom teacher's judgment as to what children can and should do" was the opinion of George W. Myers, Professor of Mathematics in the Chicago Institute and later in the School of Education. Mr. Myers had an unusual appreciation of the trends in Colonel Parker's and Mr. Dewey's points of view and, therefore, saw more clearly than most where the two men concurred and how they differed both intellectually and administratively.

able use of the trial-and-error method. General suggestions were made by the directors, and of course the spirit of the school, its emphasis upon the connection of learning with active work, almost automatically controlled judgment as to what projects were suitable and what were not. But within these limits, the development of concrete material and of methods of dealing with it was wholly in the hands of the teachers. For each line of work, especially after the school reached a suitable size, there was a head who was primarily responsible. But she worked in coöperation with all teachers carrying out the details in that line, and also with heads of other lines in order to insure coördination.

"While constant conference was needed to achieve unity, the movement of the school as a whole secured correlation of the work in different branches more automatically than would be supposed by one who has not seen the principle of activity in operation. Any large discrepancies of aim and procedure soon revealed themselves in a sort of disintegration in the children's attitudes and thus led to revision. It is very difficult to put in words the extent to which the spirit and life of a school can control, by means of its own developing movement, the work of different individuals and thus effect a reasonable degree of unity in the whole. Of course, the unity came far short of rating one hundred per cent. But experience showed that there are checks upon dispersion and centrifugal effort that are more effective than are the rigid planning in advance and the close supervision usually relied upon. One such check was the weekly teachers' meeting in which the work of the prior week was gone over in the light of the general plan, and in which teachers reported the difficulties met in carrying it out. Modifications and adaptations followed. Discussion in these meetings was a large means in translating generalities about aims and subject-matter into definite form. Almost unconsciously teachers of native ability, even if they were without much previous experience, gained confidence in their own independent and original powers and at the same time learned to work in a coöperative way as participants in a common plan."

TEACHERS' MEETINGS

The rôle of the teachers' meetings is illustrated by the following outline in question form of one of these, which were in fact seminars in method.

OUTLINE OF TEACHERS' MEETING [2]

Questions which suggest problems that are to be considered. These are not to cover the topics in any literal way, but will get your minds thinking along lines that will be of use to you.

1. Is there any common denominator in the teaching process? Here are people teaching children of different ages, different subjects; one is teaching music, another art, another cooking, Latin, etc. Now is there any common end which can be stated which is common to all? This is meant in an intellectual rather than a moral way. Is there an intellectual result which ought to be obtained in all of these different studies and at these different ages?

2. Is the intellectual aim single or multiple? Is there any end which is comprehensive enough and definite enough to mean anything? By multiple I mean do we want to train observation, memory, judgment, etc.? Are these separate ends? If the end is single, how shall we relate all the subsidiary ends, such as memory, attention, observation, reasoning power, to it? If it is multiple, what is the effect of that in practice; is one study especially to reach one end and another another? Do we work for memory in one recitation and observation and reasoning power in others? And if so, how shall we regulate their balance?

3. Is there any normal process of the mind which corresponds to this end which we want to reach, and if so, what is it? If there is a normal process, if the mind actually works toward it, just as the body is working toward health, what is the use of a teacher anyway? Where does the teacher come in? If it is a natural process, why does it not take care of itself? What is the relation toward this movement in the child's mind and the responsibility of the teacher? What is the relation of the different members of the group to the teacher? What is the relation of the different members of the group to the class? What have they to do with each other in working out this end?

4. What is the significance of the various lines of study taken up toward the reaching of this end?

Discussion: Use of past experience to gain enlarged experience through control was arrived at as the aim or common denominator.

---

[2] Led by Mr. Dewey, 1899.

The securing of ability was another reason given, but it was seen that by ability was meant control, and that the experience to be gained was to be gained through utilization of former experiences.

Knowledge was suggested as the aim. and the question asked whether knowledge was separate from experience.

Mr. Dewey suggested that if the end is knowledge, how much knowledge is to be gained? Where will you draw the line? As much knowledge as you can stuff in? And what knowledge? It was argued that the method that brings the desire for more knowledge should obtain.

If knowledge is made the end, have you any assurance that the end is not going to stop when the lesson does? The knowledge that is left in such shape as to give a method for further knowledge is the test of good teaching.

If there is intellectual sympathy between the work of different teachers, must there not be some common end, in order to relate their work to that of the others?

Mr. Dewey: "Is there any way to get a reasonable degree of assurance that we are having the child get experience in such a way as to add to his power of control? If there is any such thing as method in instruction, can it be anything else than that control of the experience which is the teacher's control of the experiences of the child, and this should be such as to add to the assurance that the child is going to get control?

1. Unless there is some general principle that can be got at which gives us some assurance that we cannot only give more experience, but also more control, is there any such thing as a real art or science of teaching?

2. The object is to give the child the experience so that he will get power of control through new experiences. What does this mean in particular? What is involved in the adapting of old experiences so as to get a new?

The child is to get a consciousness of his own power and ability. If he does not get it himself from the realities, the teacher will have to help him make the step from his old experience and then give him a similar step to make alone.

How is the gaining of control and of new experiences ·to be secured?

Through the selection of subject-matter, and method within the subject-matter.

What is meant by bringing in something new? There must be a point of contact, a place where the old experiences comes up to the new, and from the child's point of view, what is the new?

The new is something presented to the child as a problem, a difficulty, something that is doubtful, which has enough connection

with the old to make the thing continuous. Does it make any difference whether this is in arithmetic or Latin or art?

The new is not new because it is new physical or intellectual
material. Unless the lessons suggest a problem, a difficulty, it is not
psychologically new. Would there be any learning unless there was
some obstacle, some effort on the child's part?"

Mr. Dewey's statement continues:

"Those who have attended discussions among parents and
teachers will readily understand that there was a tendency for
these meetings to devote too much time and attention to the
peculiarities and difficulties of individual children. In theory,
the reports on individual children were supposed to connect
with the principles involved in adjustment of subject-matter to
their needs and the coöperative adjustment of children to one
another in the social give and take of daily life. In fact, the
younger and less experienced teachers, who served as assistants, often failed to see this connection and were inclined to be
impatient with the personal phase of the discussion when it
concerned children they did not have to deal with. Experience
showed that 'principles' were too much taken for granted as
being already understood by all teachers; in the later years an
increasing number of meetings were allotted to the specific
discussion of underlying principles and aims. Later results
would have undoubtedly improved had there been more such
meetings as were held in the earlier years. In these earlier years
fellows and members of the faculty of the pedagogical department, graduate-student assistants, and the regular teaching
staff of the school all met weekly with the directors to discuss
the reports of the school in relation to theoretical principles
and to revise future plans accordingly.

DAILY CONTACT OF TEACHERS

"A check of a less formal kind was found in the daily contact
of teachers at luncheon or after school, as they talked over
their work and learned to appreciate the points at which the
activities of different teachers with the same group reinforced
one another or failed to converge. Perhaps the most vital, al-

though the least formal, influence was provided as children moved from one teacher to another. Their attitude and response in a new class furnished an almost infallible index of the quality of conditions of action and learning to which they had been subject in their previous class. Subsequent conversation would bring out a knowledge of the causes of the attitudes displayed and, as it disclosed that such and such a thing worked and another did not, would lead to needed modifications or even to the decision that some line of work must be begun over again on a different basis. . . .

ORGANIZATION

"Coöperative social organization applied to the teaching body of the school as well as to the pupils. Indeed, it could not apply to the latter unless it had first taken effect with the former. Association and exchange among teachers was our substitute for what is called supervision, critic teaching, and technical training. In spite of all defects and mistakes, whether due to external or internal conditions, experience and reflection have convinced me that this principle is fundamental in school organization and administration. There is no substitute for it, and the tendency to magnify the authority of the superintendent, principal, or director is both the cause and the effect of the failure of our schools to direct their work on the basis of coöperative social organization of teachers. The latter method makes unnecessary the grading and judging of teachers by the devices often used. It soon becomes evident under conditions of genuine coöperation whether a given person has the required flexibility and capacity of growth. Those who did not were eliminated because of the demonstration that they did not 'belong.'

"Coöperation must, however, have a marked intellectual quality in the exchange of experiences and ideas. Many of our early failures were due to the fact that it was too 'practical,' too much given to matters of immediate import and not sufficiently intellectual in content. When the school grew larger, there was more definite departmental organization and more definite discussion of programs; in 1901 this tendency was further supplemented by the appointment of Ella F. Young as general supervisor and of Alice C. Dewey as principal. Their personalities and methods were such as to introduce more intellectual organization without impeding the freedom of individual teachers. . . . The use of the word 'departmental' in describing the organization of the school is unfortunate. It suggests a kind of compartmentalizing and isolation of forms of work that should be integrated with one another. But experience has convinced me that there cannot be all-around development of either teachers or pupils without something for which the only available word is departmental teaching, though I should prefer to speak of lines of activity carried on by persons with special aptitude, interest, and skill in them. It is the absence of coöperative intellectual relations among teachers that causes the present belief that young children must be taught everything by one teacher, and that leads to so-called departmental teaching being strictly compartmental with older ones.

"Primary teachers should have the same power, the same freedom (and the same pecuniary recompense that now goes to university and, in less measure, to high-school teachers). Persons selected on the basis of their ability to respond to the needs of an educational situation and to cooperate socially and intellectually with others develop ability to work out and organize subject-matter and methods. Our 'higher' education will not be really higher until elementary teachers have the same right and power to select and organize proper subject-matter, and invent and use their own methods as is now accorded in some degree to teachers of older students. In recollection of many things in our school practice and results that I could wish had been otherwise, there is compensation in the proof our experience affords that the union of intellectual freedom and coöperation will develop the spirit that is prized in university teachers, and that is sometimes mistakenly supposed to be a monopoly of theirs."

This testing in practice of the educational theories set forth in its hypothesis made the teachers of this school also investigators. They were both men and women, who usually varied widely in age and experience. Their previous preparation had generally consisted of a college education or of training in a technical school such as Pratt, Drexel Institute, or Armour. The experience of teaching in a conventional school had been a part of the preparation of most of them, and their own educational upbringing had been full of free activity with a rich childhood experience. They came, for the most part, naturally into the school with a feeling of joy in its adventure. There were some, however, who, in spite of an experience exactly opposite in nature, had won an even greater appreciation of the value and opportunity of its freedom. All were selected as carefully as possible with reference to their social fitness, and the result seemed to suit, in a rather remarkable manner, the needs of the pupils.

GROWTH AND ADMINISTRATION

Unhurried and unhampered as it was by arbitrary requirements imposed from above or by irritating delays in getting necessary equipment or material, the school grew in three years, from fifteen to one hundred and twenty-five children, from two full-time teachers and two assistants on a part-time basis to a staff of fifteen full-time teachers and sixteen assistants. Some of these were salaried assistants, others, as graduate students, received their University tuitions for help given. There were also usually a number of undergraduate student assistants. The amount of time given by these assistants varied from one half to three hours a day.[3]

The increasing demands for administration were met, as the school grew, by a natural division of labor among the teachers according to individual interest and ability. At the end of the third year the administration, so far as the curriculum was concerned, assumed a departmental form, analogous to that

---

[3] While often lacking in finish, the laboratories and studios of the school had good equipments so far as essentials were concerned. The result was that children and teachers of necessity constructed much of the additional equipment needful in the activities.

of the University. These departments were the kindergarten, history, science and mathematics, domestic sciences and industries, manual training, art, music, the languages, and physical culture. Each department was headed by a director qualified by social and technical training, as well as by life experience, to utilize the data of her special field in dealing intellectually with the problems met with in carrying on the activities of her classroom. This director was also a trained investigator, who realized that her intelligent reports of the results of testing certain educational theories in the actual practices of her classroom were to constitute scientific findings for study and revision by other teachers, administrators, and students of educational science. As an investigator she had no fixed or final set of objectives, but each day of teaching enabled her in the light of her successes or failures to revise and better these objectives.

The reports, made weekly in typewritten form, furnished the data of the problems for study and discussion in the weekly informal conference of teachers, as well as in the more formal seminar groups and larger pedagogical club meetings. Thus all the teachers in actual daily contact with children of all ages furnished, in these reports, the data for further inquiries and conclusions. The value of such material to the Department of Pedagogy of the University, engaged as it was with the problems of educational science, became almost like the systematic and cumulative clinical records of medical science.

SUPERVISION OF CHILDREN AND TEACHERS

In the early years of the school, supervision of both the children and the teachers of the school had been informal in character. The children recognized that the teachers were there to help them in their own self-initiated activities. Their energies being fully engaged in these activities there was seldom occasion for "discipline." [4] Responsibility for supervision of the

---

[4] A frequent visitor in the School, Miss Katherine Dopp, writes, "It may not be amiss to mention that at times I heard rumors to the effect that the children of the Laboratory School were disorderly. I had observed sev-

children before and after school fell to the lot of the senior teachers under the supervision of the principal. There was daily and hourly exchange of results of classroom experience; a certain child was ailing and needed rest; another was inhibited by shyness and needed encouragement; certain subject-matter was going well or ill with certain groups; or a science teacher would suggest to the one in charge of number work that the children of a group were ready to mark the Fahrenheit and Centigrade scale divisions on their thermometers, then in the making in shop and laboratory. Accordingly, this topic would be taken up for work in number as opportunity presented.

Such informal interchange, together with the weekly teachers' meeting, performed the function of integrating and coördinating those matters usually called disciplinary, as well as those necessary to the growth of the program. The importance of this continual exchange of news was felt to be so great that the teachers' work was arranged with periods free from class work of twenty to thirty minutes every day for each teacher. In these she could visit and advise with other groups and teachers.

Great flexibility of organization was necessary for the working out of so complicated a program of activities. This was made possible only by the willingness of the teachers to assume, when need arose, extra responsibilities to meet emergencies. In addition to the informal interchange between the teachers, there was, as already stated, the weekly meeting with Mr. Dewey and later with Mrs. Young and Mrs. Dewey present. As the

---

eral groups many times and had not gained such an impression. But to make sure that I was not mistaken I visited the same group for a week from the first morning session until noon. During that time all the children were thoroughly interested in their work and unusually attentive. I observed nothing that could be interpreted as disorder and only one instance of inattention and that on the part of one child for only a few moments. To be sure the children were not required to toe the line, nor was their attention distracted from the work at hand by remarks about the position of feet and hands—remarks which were still prevalent among so-called good disciplinarians at that time. The conduct of these children was above criticism. All eagerly coöperated with the instructors whom they regarded as friends."

school and staff of teachers grew larger, this meeting assumed more formality.

GROUPING OF CHILDREN

The children of the elementary school were grouped according to their interests and social compatibility which implied some correspondence to chronological age. These groupings replaced the ordinary public-school division into grades, where promotion was dependent upon a marking system. There were no comparisons of the work of children, who, with some few exceptions, never asked the teacher for judgments or rankings or even comments on their work. Their activities were such that they could themselves judge of their success or failure, and they were always fairly well aware of variations of ability in the group. Owing probably to the fact that there were almost no children who did not excel in some one activity, however, few overt comparisons by children were noted or can be recalled. Some of the children desired external marks as proofs of their own development. These, at the time, were perhaps not sufficiently met. It might have helped for children to have kept some record of their successes so as to objectify their own advance and thus answer their need of some basis for judgment that should take the place of an ordinary system of marks and grading. As a factor in the general treatment of all the children, however, this lack was possibly more than balanced by the greater happiness of the whole. A sense of inferiority rarely developed overtly enough to present a classroom difficulty. Even in the last year of the school, with the effort necessary to meet college requirements, stimulation by marks was never used. Written or oral review on completion of the piece of work to be done took the place of examination.

The difficulties of adjustment, which arose from having young children under the care of more than one teacher, were met by having one person responsible for the coördination of each child's program and physical care, with whom eight hours or more a week were spent. Intellectual integrity and continuity in the treatment of subject-matter seemed of greater benefit than the hovering care of one person. Just as in homes, children instinctively select certain people as sources for certain kinds of response, the children learned to take their difficulties to those teachers who had specialized in the line where the problem belonged. When manual training, art, science, and literature were all taught, it was found that one person *could not* be competent in all directions, even if this had been desirable.

CLASSROOM METHOD

A successful method of conducting classes gradually developed. This varied with the personality of the teacher, her training, her background of experience and that of the children. It was also conditioned by the availability of the materials and equipment. With all the younger classes, the first few minutes of each recitation were spent in a kind of council meeting with the teacher, picking up the threads of the previous period, planning and assigning the work of the present hour. The children developed their own impersonal methods of distributing important privileges, assigning the waiter at luncheon or the leader of the class for the day, etc., by alphabetical order.[5] The leader's responsibility entailed considerable independence of the teacher in following out the daily program. This was often complicated by unexpected changes of room and teachers. In this way any child who, as leader, was lacking in initiative and executive ability fell naturally into the position of one who must develop both through his own effort and without any insistence from the teacher. In like manner, the naturally executive child, instead of spending all his energy in running the school, as sometimes happens in schools of this freer type, could put it into better planning of his work and forwarding of his skill in techniques.

---

[5] About the age of twelve or thirteen the children voluntarily discarded the custom of following a leader and wished to be allowed to report to their classes as individuals. In case of unavoidable delay on the part of the teachers, the classes of all ages, even the youngest, put themselves to work under the direction of a leader.

Even when accidental delays arose, which were inevitable in a school using the services of graduate students and part-time teachers, the children exhibited intelligence and confidence in meeting emergencies and would go on with class work on their own initiative. When, as often happened, they did care for a situation in this way, it was regarded as a definite indication that the class and teacher were adjusted and the work was proceeding properly. Such rational conduct in emergencies indicated the formation of a thought-in-action method in the presence of unusual situations. It was found that in dealing with such problems of development, in perceiving and meeting the need of the children for right means of self-expression, a teacher's art of teaching was tested to its fullest.

This method in classroom work, the result of the coöperative efforts of teachers and children, had the merit of enlisting the interest and effort of the child both in planning for the activity and in its execution. In this process of directing a self-initiated activity great care was necessary to allow the child freedom to discriminate and select material according to his own idea of its purpose in what he was going to do. For example, in his pottery making, it was desirable that the form of the bowl he was making should be determined by him according to the use that he was to make of it and not according to a pattern set for him by another. His bowl completed and proven useful for *the purpose* which he had forseen, he was asked to use it, and his difficulty in so doing became his new problem. This recalled to his mind the form of a pitcher so that he himself planned and made the appropriate lip on the jar, thus carrying his activity forward. In this way the child gained the method of thinking and planning before doing. The stimulation of a successful accomplishment was the motive for his next act. He became, in this particular instance, conscious that shape was related to the function of use. He formed an image, in advance, of the shape of the jar he must have for the use he wished to make of it and perceived that its use should determine its shape.

This illustrates how general ideas reached the child through the teacher by means of her foresight, wise direction, or suggestion at the right moment. Always bearing in mind that the activity of the child must be self-initiated, the teacher's responsibility was to provide necessary materials and instruction in the technical skills sought by the child to attain his desired ends. There was also need to remember that there is a stage of growth when it is natural for children to acquire their techniques of construction, communication, and measurement easily and with a degree of pleasure, and that activities which were graded and adapted to a child's growing power stimulated his feeling of need and progressively increased his measure of ability. The resulting sense of satisfaction and clearer vision of achievement opened his eyes to the extension of his activity.

There was needed, then, as always in progressive education, a willingness on the part of both teachers and parents to watch and wait for the development in the child of a sense of need for any skill or technique. It was necessary to combat fear of new unproven methods. This Apollyon of progress was always appearing in the untrodden trails blazed by the new psychology. The broad and easy ways of conventional teaching lured the teachers to seemingly pleasant travel. Continually must they be on their guard against the temptation to select the old, easy, and habitual forms of activity for which ready-made materials were at hand, rather than one that required search for new materials and careful thought.[6]

Literacy, interpreted as the ability to read, write, and figure, has laid the responsibility upon the teacher of developing early proficiency in the child's use of these tools. This profi-

---

[6] In many schools this often leads to a misuse of the child's interest in an activity. This is seen when, for example, in the activity of cooking, the whole of a child's effort is steered into the acquirement of a skill in cooking, instead of directing him through his interest in cooking into a further apprehension of the meaning of the activity itself. The latter method develops in the child more and more control of his own share in what he is reproducing—the activities grouped about the production and consumption of food.

ciency was usually considered necessary before the child could help himself from the storehouse of learning in books. The best known way to lead a child to knowledge had been by the wearisome road of the alphabet. In consequence, the efforts of these trail-breaking teachers in the elementary school were often hampered by fear. Their use of these time-honored tools, the "3 Rs," as wholly incidental to their need in an on-going activity was new and untried. What if this way did not prove to be so much more valuable than the old as to justify its use? Was it right to try a newfangled method when it had always been done the other way? Was it right to refrain from making a child learn to read and to wait until he was really ready to do so? "What was good enough for my father is good enough for me," was often thrown in the face of the experimenters by the disturbed parents of a child, who, slow to discover for himself a reason for using his tools, had been slow in learning how to use them, and had not been hurried in the process.

Such disturbed parents are likely to communicate their attitude of anxiety to the child. He feels he is under criticism because he is slow. Desiring to gain approbation instead of criticism, he demands help in school, so that he may the quicker meet his parents' expectations. This is often taken by the inexperienced teacher as an indication that he has arrived at the stage of growth where the use of this tool arises out of a genuine felt need. An observant teacher, however, will recognize this as premature, if in other situations the child gives evidence of immaturity. It was found, for instance, that when a child was interested in an activity just for the sake of the activity, when he played miller without being interested in what the miller did, it was an indication, in general terms, that he was at the stage of growth when he did not separate means from ends. At that stage therefore he certainly would not be interested in learning how to read as a means to an end. If, however, as is characteristic of the seven-year-old, when playing miller he could remember what a miller does and could plan what he must do in the character of a miller, then he would be ready for and would be interested in using language as a means to a specific end.

THE USE OF RECORDS

In the meantime, making records was a necessary part of the classroom process. This, however, was not used to stimulate a child's interest in learning to write. He was, instead, helped with the mechanics of making the record sufficiently to hold his interest in the process. It was found to be good practice, particularly with the younger children, in the council meeting at either the beginning or end of the period, for the teacher to write at dictation the children's story of the work of the hour. This story was arranged and used at the next period as a reading lesson for review. The children, seeing their own experience made lasting and useful to them and others by the written form, gradually awoke to an appreciation of its use. They were interested by skilful suggestion to find that other people had had the same experience and had written it. The desire to read for themselves was often born in children out of the idea that they might find better ways of doing and thus get more satisfactory results. With this interest as an urge, the child himself often freely set his attention to learning to read. A natural need thus became the stimulus to the gaining of skill in the use of a tool.

In such a process, unconscious to him and psychologically right because indirect, the child learns his techniques of reading, writing, and measurement as a means to a desired and immediate end of his own conceiving, and not as something he must learn because he will need it sometime, somewhere, for a purpose utterly unimportant to him. Furthermore, by using his skills to extend his ability to plan and execute his activity, he integrates his experience and furthers his growth.

REALIZATION OF THEORY IN CLASSROOM METHOD

Too much emphasis cannot be laid on the constant and intelligent attempts to put into classroom use, and thereby test, the theory of the school. The success or failure of these attempts occupied to a great extent the weekly teachers' meetings and was the subject of the informal daily discussion that always went on between the teachers in hallways and on the way to and from classrooms. Judgment as to whether there was a right learning condition in the classroom was often based on the attitude (poised and happy, or nervous and irritable) of the child as he went to the next class. A quiet and contented attitude was considered an indication of satisfaction of desire arising from the successful accomplishment of a planned end. Such an attitude also indicated that the teacher was fulfilling her function. Although the immediate decision with regard to treatment of subject-matter and method was left to the individual teacher, each teacher's method was so checked and rechecked by coöperative discussion of results and effect on the children, that changes in viewpoint continually took place. Therefore, teachers and children, administrators and parents, as a result of sharing in the same social process, shared also in the educational benefits therefrom.

ADJUSTMENT OF PROGRAM TO CHILD'S AGE LEVEL

From the beginning, one of the chief problems of those responsible for the arrangement of the program was to get such an adjustment of the time devoted to the different activities as would be in accord with one of the major principles of the school. This principle was concerned with the developing muscular coördinations of the child which determined the type of activity proper for his stage of growth and in relation to his age. The need for the study and investigation of this problem was formulated by Mr. Dewey at the end of the first year of the school. His statement of the problem is based on the findings of the practice of the school during its first year. The time given to different kinds of activities in the accompanying tables was the result of the discussions of the weekly teachers' meetings, of Mr. Dewey's own observations in his almost daily visits to the school and also those of Mrs. Dewey and other parents and friends who kept in close touch with its daily program, as well as of the comments and reflection of visiting teachers, administrators, and graduate students.

This distribution applied to Groups I and II (six and seven

ADJUSTMENT OF TIME IN THE SECOND YEAR OF THE SCHOOL [7]

Subject	Daily Program	Hours a Week	Period (number and and length
Gymnasium	2 days a week	1⅓	2 at 40 min.
Shop	3 days a week	1½	3 at 30 min.
Sewing	2-3 days a week	1½	2-3 at 45-30 min.
Music	3 days a week	1	3 at 20 min.
Visiting Museums, etc.	1 day a week	1½	1 at 1 hr. & 30 min.
Cooking	2 days a week	1½	2 at 1 hr. & 30 min.
Science	2 days a week	2	2 at 1 hr.
Expressive Activities,			
Art, Modeling ...	5 days a week	2½	5 at 30 min.
"History"—Stories,			
Conversations ...	5 days a week	2½	5 at 30 min.
Assembly	1 day a week	⅓	1 at 20 min.
Total	3 hrs. a day	15⅔	

years); with older groups the time was the same in gymnasium, shop, music, and excursions, while the balance between the active work and intellectual work changed so that with Group III (eight and nine years) about three and one half hours a week were spent in each. With the ten-year-olds active work occupied four hours, and the formal intellectual work seven to eight hours a week. The most important principles used in determining the time part of the program were (1) the relative amounts of time to be given to hand-work and the intellectual work and (2) the balancing of the time assigned to handwork of the constructive type such as that of the shop, cooking, sewing, and to the artistic modes of expression such as modeling, painting, etc. The next table shows the allotment for these groups.

GROUP III (EIGHT AND NINE YEARS)

Weekly

A. Cooking, Science .... 3½ hrs.
    Related modes of expression .... 3½ hrs.
B. History, Literature .... 3½ hrs.
    Related modes of expression .... 3½ hrs.

[7] During the first two years of the school there were no children under six years. Groups I and II (six and seven years). The last five years, Groups I and II (four and five years).

GROUPS IV (EIGHT AND NINE YEARS) AND V (TEN AND ELEVEN YEARS)

		Weekly
A.	....	4⅙ hrs.
B.	....	4⅙ hrs.
IV & V Shop	....	2⅔ hrs.
IV & V Geography	....	1 hr.
IV & V Free time	....	1 hr.

In the older groups the necessary balance between the two types of activities became more definite. The total amount of time actually spent by all children of different ages in overt activities was determined. For the younger children this was from nine to ten hours out of the fifteen, the remainder of their time being taken up with expressive activities of an intellectual kind. This general proportion was maintained throughout the seven years of the school. The problem of the variations in this balance demanded by the increasing maturity of the children was ever present. It was complicated by the necessity of using part-time teachers in art, music, and language, and the services of graduate students whose university schedules must be respected.

The resulting practice was contrary to the traditional idea that a little child would attend to one activity for a short time only. After four years' experimenting it was found that six-year-olds could carry on their play in a social occupation from one to one and a half hours. As the result of careful experimentation, the following plan was worked out. A few minutes' discussion of the day's plans, under the teacher's direction, preceded a half to one hour's play and was followed by a summary of what had been done by the group. This summary was necessary to the child because it involved plans for the next day and took place three or four times a week. Later it was found possible to give the class that seemed ready for it to a teacher who had specialized in the techniques of reading, writing, etc. Her time was used in helping the children to make records of the activity. This furnished material for reading at the next period. The one hour and a half previously given to the group teacher was thus reduced to one hour, without interfering with the intellectual continuity of the activity. Development in the technique of numbers, however, was not separately undertaken in this manner until about the middle of the second stage of growth, but was always considered in direct connection with the activity involved and was under the group teacher's direction. Separate teaching of skills in the first stage of growth did not need more than three periods of a half hour each week. It was found that a group teacher's contact with her group could not profitably be less than eight to ten hours a week. This always included one period of an hour and a half each week in the group room, in which the unhurried completion of the integral parts of the class's activity was made possible.

At the close of the first stage of growth (from seven to eight years) the balance in the day's program seemed to be successfully maintained if the longest period was an hour and one half. One hour of this was devoted to the carrying out of an occupation. A half hour was given at least three times a week to techniques necessary to that activity. The following are typical programs for the three stages of the elementary period, during the later years of the school.

TYPICAL PROGRAM FOR THE FIRST STAGE
5 TO 7 YEARS

Subject	Hours a Day	Hours a Week
Social Occupations	1½ or 1	6½–5
Primitive Occupations (History and Science)	"	"
Techniques (Reading and Writing)	½ (3 times a week)	1½–2½
Gymnasium or Games in Room or Yard	½	2½
Music or Art	½	1½
Cooking	½ + 1 (2 times a week)	1½
Excursions, or Assembly, or Shop	½ – 1	1½
Total	3	15

After the age of eight the periods spent in artistic work were lengthened from one-half hour to one hour and occasionally one and a half hours. This work was concentrated in one or two quarters of the year and was alternated with some activity, such as textiles, cooking, or science, while the time spent on history, music, French, and English was kept to an average of two hours a week, in one-half hour periods. With

TYPICAL PROGRAM FOR THE TRANSITION STAGE
7 TO 8 YEARS

Subject	Hours a Day	Hours a Week
History and Geography	1	5
Techniques (Reading and Writing)	½ (2 times a week)	2
Science	1 or ½ (3 times a week)	2
Cooking	½ and 1	1½
Textile	1 or ½ (3 times a week)	2
Shop	½ or 1 (3 times a week)	2
Music and Art	½ (6 times a week)	3
Gymnasium	½	2½
Total	4	20

the younger classes up to eight this division also held, but the work was carried on for an hour with the same teacher in the same room four days in the week. Separate classes in number work or arithmetic began with children of eight or nine years and were never longer than twenty minutes to one-half

TYPICAL PROGRAM FOR THE SECOND STAGE
9 TO 10 TO 12 YEARS

Subject	Hours a Day	Hours a Week
History and Geography	1	5
Techniques	½	2½
Science or	1½	2 or 2½
Cooking or		1½
Textile or Shop		2
Art		1½
Music	1 or ½	1½
Gymnasium		2½
Modern Languages	½	2½
Total	4½	22½

hour. These so-called drill periods were part of the program only as the children evinced the need. Otherwise their number work was occupied with the problems arising in the other activities of the school.

The varying factors in the program for the second stage of

growth are cooking, science, textile and shop-work. The technique periods varied from one and a half to two and a half hours a week. Number work as a separate study was added in the ninth and tenth years, thus increasing the time given to technique and lessening the time given to experimental work. Toward the end of this period, the school day continued to 2:30 P. M., thus giving time for the study of modern languages and Latin. Another modification for this stage was in the time spent in art and textiles. These subjects, alternating every three months, occupied the children three to four hours a week, in one to one and a half hour periods. In the latter part of this period the daily balance was as follows: scholastic, one and a half hours; physical exercise, one and a half hours; expressive activities, two and a half hours.

The first set of programs represents the arrangement of studies during the first two years of the school, the second that during the following five years. Both were planned and changed from time to time to accord with the balance between active and more strictly intellectual work involving discussion and planning found, by experiment, advantageous to the child. In the time given to active work, it was found well to strike a balance between activities involving the larger muscles, as those in the shop, gymnastics, etc., and those of the expressive arts, reading, writing, painting, modeling, etc., which make use of finer muscular control by alternating the periods of each.

One of the characteristics of the school, which in retrospect seems of great importance, was the ease with which changes in the program, both as to subject and method, could be made. Such flexibility and adaptability to the needs of children or circumstances could only have been possible in a school where the informal social conditions and relations of everyday life prevailed.

The condition of the children at the end of the day was usually the test as to whether the learning conditions were right in all respects. This included, of course, the length of time spent by children of different ages in the school building. For the youngest children, four to five years, the school hours were from 9 to 11:30. Six-year-old children were in the school from 9 to 12; seven-year-olds, depending on conditions in the class, sometimes returned or remained at school for an hour's work in the afternoon. All children over nine had afternoon work. It began with an hour and extended to one and a half hours for the oldest children. In general, for children six to nine years of age, the division of the day remained approximately one to one and a half hours in social occupations including active work and discussions, one half-hour in gymnasium or outdoor play, and one half-hour on art or music. The remaining hour was spent variously on different days, in cooking one day a week, in textile work (generally one half-hour period), and a half-hour period in some handwork, either in shop or in work connected with their social occupations. This arrangement was broken into during the week by the assembly, once in two weeks by excursions, and for eight-year-olds by individual work in printing and special work in reading and writing.

During the second period, with children of eight to twelve years the day was extended by the addition of an hour in the afternoon. The same division of time was maintained, save that time was taken from the period allotted to social occupations (varying quarter by quarter) and given to textile work or used in drill in the techniques of number. Toward the end of the second stage of growth, when a larger proportion of concentrated time was given to science, the three subjects, textiles, art, and science, were given successively, one each quarter. In this way longer periods for continuous work were secured in each one of these three lines. Because of the lack of full-time teachers, the assignment of work by quarters of the year was more or less arbitrary. In the second stage of growth, however, when most of the children had become capable of carrying on much longer and more involved pieces of work, this arrangement seemed to suit their interests and attitudes acceptably.

For all the children, gymnasium periods of one half-hour were generally so arranged as to follow work that did not involve the larger muscles. When possible, with children up to the age of seven it took the form of play outdoors. Groups were combined so that about twenty-five children formed a class. Six-year-old children sometimes played with the next older and sometimes with the next younger children. In the stage of growth when interest in organized games develops, from nine years on, the gymnasium periods become more frequent, and more play times, often after school, were arranged. With this change one or two half-hour periods of school hours were spent on the gymnasium floor, in outdoor gymnastics to help posture or in games using the large muscles. The out-of-door organized play was supervised. One of the University coaches helped the children develop their techniques in baseball and basket-ball. The school, as part of the University, was under the University health regulations, in accord with which, as well as because of need, each child received a thorough physical examination. The tests and measurements then in vogue were used. When these disclosed conditions requiring it, individual corrective work in the University gymnasium followed. The school also formulated its own health regulations. One of the records runs as follows:

The boys were convinced by the medical adviser of the University (Dr. Raycroft) that high-school football often formed habits which hindered rather than helped them in their later play of the game. This advice was backed up by the teacher of biology (Mr. George Garrey) whose reputation as a star of the football field (one whose head helped out his feet) gave his opinion great weight with the children.

Two of the students in the Department of Pedagogy (1896 to 1897) were Frederick W. Smedley and Daniel P. MacMillan.[8] Both were members of Mr. Dewey's seminar,[9] where the fundamental concepts basic to the hypothesis of the school were worked out. Both early saw the extent to which these

---

[8] Mr. Smedley was Director of the Child Study Department of the Chicago Public Schools until his death in May, 1902. Dr. MacMillan has been Director of this Department since Oct., 1902.

[9] This seminar was the first in a series which collaborated in bringing out *Studies in Logical Theory*, by John Dewey, with the coöperation of Members and Fellows of the Department of Philosophy (Chicago: The University of Chicago Press), 1903.

psychological principles, with their social implications, would change education.

Mr. Smedley, in collaboration with A. A. Wood, a student in the Department of Psychology, carried through a series of measurements of the sensory and motor abilities of the pupils in the school. These tests were planned in the University Psychological Laboratory with a view to determining the pedagogical value of measurements which could be used as a basis for determining the right balance and distribution of time given to the various types of activity on the daily program. Later a report of these tests was published. In the introduction Mr. Smedley writes as follows:

The school is a pedagogical laboratory where the students of pedagogy are investigating such questions as the correlation of studies, the psychological bearing of the different branches, and the adaptation of the material from the different sciences to the needs of primary pupils. . . . These tests are, I believe, a suitable beginning for a teacher who is to develop an organized, assimilated knowledge of child psychology and become a trained observer of children. It is to be hoped that the schools of the near future will be equipped with such teachers, teachers who, better understanding the natures of the children, will better know their needs and be able to provide for them, and that in those schools pupils will not be promoted simply on account of their having remembered the words of the answers to stated questions. Instead health, strength, quickness and accuracy of intellectual activity, and the acuteness and education of the senses will determine, in part at least, the child's fitness for higher and harder work.

The psychological tests involved much labor, but helped in determining a right balance in the time which could profitably be spent in the typical activities of the program.

The tests were easily fitted into the day's program because of the flexibility of the school organization. There was great difficulty in finding space suitable for them, but an attic room was finally fitted up for the purpose. The freedom with which the children could be sent to the examiners was testimony of the friendly attitude toward adults developed in the school. Only a small proportion had to be taken to the examiners.

STUDIES IN INDIVIDUAL PSYCHOLOGY

[10] The School's beginnings of study of the psychology of individuals were perhaps too informal and qualitative to survive the more definitely organized form of institutionalized school life which reasserted itself after Mr. Dewey left, and the tidal wave of statistical measurements which helped sweep reactionary influences into power. There was nothing in the earlier form of the Laboratory School, judging from the little I saw of it, that was opposed to the development and use of instruments of precise measurement in educational practice. Doubtless these instruments would have come in due course, but applied to the development of values which were unique rather than standardized.

In the last year or so studies were made to discover the stage of growth at which self-consciousness appeared. With so few children no a priori generalizations could be made. The studies, however, suggested that, for these children at least, consciousness of the difference between boys and girls in interests and attitudes did not appear, except in isolated cases, until after eleven years of age. The boys in the older classes, perhaps because they were in the minority, were especially determined not to let the girls, as they said, "get ahead of them," and were not always devoid of the boastful attitude, easily understood, at that time, without benefit of an "inferiority complex" explanation. The girls, most of them excelling easily in many respects, looked with tolerance at this attitude of the boys. There were no major difficulties with precocious sex interests in the friendly association in clubs and work on the club-house. It is probable that there was the usual exchange of dubious experience which is almost universal between small boys and girls. This never amounted to much of a problem, as there were generally activities of much more interest going on.

GENERAL SCHOOL ACTIVITIES

Excursions were a feature of the school's program from the beginning. These were of all kinds, collecting expeditions in

---

[10] Willard C. Gore, assistant in Psychology at the University of Chicago, 1902–03, and later Instructor of Psychology in the School of Education.

the parks, physiography excursions to the dunes and distant regions such as Starved Rock or Lake Bluff on the north shore of the lake. Visits were made to factories and the art museum. They went frequently to the nearby Field Museum where a wide variety of departments offered unusual illustrative materials, useful to the pupil's experiences and experiments. Expeditions to the park, the greenhouses, and occasionally to the University laboratories were a part of the routine of each class as the work reached the point when such visits would be helpful. The excitement and interest of the children over the field expeditions were never failing and always included a keen interest in the scientific purpose of each excursion. The pleasure on the trip, in the luncheon and in being outdoors together never seemed to interfere, but heightened the understanding of what they saw and discussed. The University libraries and those of the city were a never-failing source of books for teachers and children, and the latter early learned how to make use of the reference shelves.

The assembly, in which the whole school except the kindergarten came together, occurred once a week and varied in length from twenty minutes to half-an-hour. It was regarded as a natural outgrowth of the school activities and had both a social and a cultural aim. It afforded opportunity for pupils to share interesting information and to build up habits, emotions, and attitudes which gave social value to information and to artistic expression. It also helped the children learn the art of coöperation, develop initiative, and assume responsibility. It stimulated clear thinking and expression and cultivated the desire to give entertainments of artistic value.

COMMENTS OF TEACHERS AND VISITORS TO THE SCHOOL

There is much of interest and value after an interval of thirty years in the comments of graduate students, visitors, coöperating members of the University faculty, teachers and principals of this and other schools, and the pupils of the school on this experiment in education. A few are here included. One of the teachers in the old Cook County and

Chicago Normal Schools, and later in the Chicago Institute was Flora J. Cooke. In 1900, she became principal of the Francis W. Parker School, part of the Chicago Institute before its removal to the South Side. Miss Cooke wrote: [11]

I believe Dr. Dewey and Colonel Parker had fundamentally the same point of view in education, but Dr. Dewey came to his conclusions from a profound philosophic study, while Colonel Parker came to his through a deep, sympathetic insight into children and their needs. Colonel Parker never lost sight of the child in theory. Both Colonel Parker and Dr. Dewey would have the child work and play in a rich and stimulating environment. Each would have the environment, both of the school and of wider society, give the child educational inspiration and many-sided, wholesome activity. Each believed that if the child filled today with complete and happy living, tomorrow would find him ready to meet the challenge for more difficult responsibilities and socially satisfying work. These two men, working from opposite poles, observing keenly and carefully educational phenomena, came in a remarkable degree to the same conclusions concerning educational procedure.

A young instructor in pedagogy recalls the days when those in the educational process were still quite unaccustomed to experimentalism in education and when the experimental method connoted a laboratory of natural science, rather than a humanistic one.[12]

Mr. Dewey emphasized to all of us the importance of not looking for material results, but to observe carefully the effect of the processes upon the minds, not only of those who were to be "taught," but upon those who were the "teachers" or leaders. The emphasis upon the necessity of *participation* in the educational process and the equally strong and important fact that education is not a state but a process made us look upon this experimental school as something which had a working hypothesis worthy of careful consideration. . . .

My first taste for experimental work in education was developed when Mr. Dewey took me, a graduate student, with him to his school. Coming from a University where the classics still remained the great standard of education, with the sciences standing around

---

[11] Extracts from a statement made by Miss Cooke in March, 1927.

[12] George H. Locke, Instructor, Department of Pedagogy 1898-'01, now Chief Librarian of the Public Library of Toronto and Director of the "Boys and Girls" House of Toronto.

outside or timidly knocking at the threshold or darting in when the door was carelessly left upon for a moment, this was a new atmosphere and it took some time for readjustment. . . . To some of us whose tastes led them to the administrative side of education, the school presented many difficulties, for it is not easy to persuade a democracy which is always shouting for freedom that freedom should be granted to individuals—especially if they are young. Then again progress has been marked out in definite lines with sign posts, and the mode of vehicle, the road to be travelled, and the distance to be covered during intervals of the journey are also marked out. It is expected that there will be little or no deviation. All this was upset by this experimental school. We had been accustomed to *Model* schools or *Normal* schools, but not to *Experimental* schools.

The great work Dr. Dewey did for us, and for all who kept the faith of those early days was to open our eyes, develop our reason, and make flexible our so-called intellect. Indeed, *flexibility* was to me the great word. He sowed widely. He could not tell what the harvest might be. I think he never has known how great a harvest has been reaped in fields he never saw again.

One of the directors of the work with the youngest children in the school writes of her two years' teaching.[13]

These years are among the happiest and most interesting experiences in a rather long teaching career. Naturally, the group of children whose parents would place them in such a school would be deeply interesting in themselves and have much to contribute to one another. These shared experiences we took as the basis of our school life and tried to interpret, deepen, and enrich them through the experience of other children, through our own larger experience, and through the materials used from day to day.

It was felt each child should gain greater control of his body if he would be unconscious of it as it served him in all situations of life. Therefore, his walking, skipping, running, and so on in the home were made more meaningful through the rhythmic plays and exercises in the kindergarten. Partly because music is suggestive and furnishes an element of control which helps to free a child, and partly because in a social group every individual experience gains new stimulus and zest, the individual child's delight in play grew spontaneously, as it took on the new meaning of a game, into the joyous shared activity of the social group—an activity which had a purpose common to all.

It was Mr. Dewey's idea that each child should be free to develop

---

13 Grace Fulmer (1900–1902), now Director of her own school at Los Angeles, California.

his own powers to some ultimate purpose through the guidance of one whose experience was richer. Such also was his own relation to the teachers in his school. I know there were things in my own work of which he did not approve, and yet I always felt free to work in my own way, and all the while his ideals and influence upon my educational experiences have increased with the passing years.

It was with the deepest regret that every teacher who had had the good fortune to be associated with Mr. Dewey's splendid work, in what we learned to call "The Dewey School," saw its doors closed. But that which no door can bar has gone out from that school until its influence has been felt around the world.

Mr. W. A. Baldwin of the Hyannis State Normal School writes of his visits to the school.

During the existence of the Dewey Experimental School I took every opportunity to visit it. I always found it full of helpful suggestions for my own work. We at Hyannis were trying to readjust, to replace the artificiality and mechanism of the regulation public school by the more natural conditions of life. I had read with much interest Dr. Dewey's little book, *School and Society,* and agreed completely with the philosophy of education as therein portrayed. I was, therefore, much interested in seeing how he was working out the principles of progressive education in his own little experimental school. Naturally, I found myself comparing the conditions with which he had to deal with those of our own Training School and as found in the ordinary city school. Usually educational friends were visiting at the same time, and I was interested in getting the reactions of superintendents of schools as shown by their remarks during our visits and afterwards. It seemed hard for many intelligent superintendents to see below the surface and appreciate the real educational development which the children were getting. . . .

My visits helped me to see how much of the industrial-social work in our own school might be looked upon by many of our visitors. As I have since thought about the matter I have come to understand why such educational reforms have met with so little encouragement and even with covert opposition from a large majority of superintendents and teachers trained under the old regime and with the habits of mind and of application which belonged with the old type of education. These ideas, as Dr. Dewey has so well and so often pointed out, are so opposed to those underlying the experimental schools that it is impossible for the conservative to understand what the progressive has in mind. In consequence much of the work of these experimental schools seems to them foolish. We had then and continue to have fundamentalists and modernists in education as well as in religion. . . .

I remember being quite disturbed when I learned that three or four of the older pupils, whom I saw over in one corner, were being drilled up for college entrance examinations in the old way, the regular work of the school having failed to prepare them to pass such tests. As I considered the matter on my way home, I satisfied myself that the fault lay with the type of examination, rather than with the kind of training which these children had received. Here stood out quite clearly the contrasting ideals of the old and the new education—the one demanding that children be drilled up on an established and approved set of facts and laws discovered and thought out by others, the other that children be encouraged to see and to think for themselves each in his own natural way.

Every new educational movement has been associated with and due to some great personality. We think of Pestalozzi and Stanz, Colonel Francis Parker and Quincy, Dr. E. A. Sheldon and The Oswego Normal School, Booker T. Washington and Tuskegee, President Charles W. Eliot and Harvard. Not one of these, however, has done so much for a better understanding of the education of young people as has Dr. John Dewey, who seems particularly gifted in the power to understand the way in which the child's mind naturally develops. More and more the ideas regarding education which he has so long advocated are being accepted, and attempts are being made to apply them often without due credit to their author.

When the true story of the educational movements of our times is written, Dr. John Dewey will, I believe, be recognized as the philosopher and prophet of his age.

CHAPTER XIX

PARENTS AND CHILDREN

IN the first year of the school, a cultivated woman of the neighborhood who had no children of her own was a frequent visitor. Toward the end of the year, she remarked to a person connected with the school: "At first, I was distinctly critical about what I saw. As time passed, I realized that some of the trouble was the standard of judgment I had brought with me from experience acquired in the old kind of school. I finally came to realize that education is not anything that can concern only the children who are pupils. It is also a matter of the education of parents and in the end of the whole community." The life of the school throughout its existence bears witness to the truth of these words.

PARENTS' RELATION TO THE SCHOOL

The parents' relation to the school, like the growth of the school itself, was of slow development. As they grew more and more into an understanding of what was going on and changed their preformed standards of judging, the new sympathy and insight gained reacted not only upon their own children but upon teachers and the whole school life. They brought to the school valuable information and suggestion. The experiment gradually extended and became a large common enterprise which included parents, teachers, and children.

This does not mean that all parents were sufficiently satisfied to continue their children in the school. On the contrary, there were cases of maladjustment sufficiently acute so that children were withdrawn. It does mean merely that there was gradually built up a solid nucleus of actively interested and sympathetic parents who were intensely loyal to the school, and who stood by it in all times of difficulty. Those responsible for the conduct of the school say that without this intelligent and earnest support of the parents, the school could not have begun to accomplish what it did; it could not have continued even to exist. The financial committee of the school consisted of Mrs. Charles R. Crane, Mrs. William Kent, and Mrs. Charles F. Harding. Just as their aid was not confined to financial matters, so many other parents who were active in other respects were also most helpful in giving or raising needed funds. The school demonstrated that parents' interest in their own children is capable of being carried over to the school, so that school and home mutually extend each other. This interest also expressed itself in published statements by a number of parents. Extracts from two follow:

[1] The Parents' Association of the Laboratory School differed from most other parents' associations in that the incentive for its organization as well as its development came almost entirely from the parents. . . . During the first year of the school this group was occasionally invited to come together to discuss subjects related to the home and the school and at the beginning of the second year felt the need of formally organizing. The income from the tuition of such a school was, naturally, far below the cost of maintaining it; there was need for the parents from the start to band themselves together for the support of the school which they so much desired for their children. Outside of this financial need, the main object of the association was an educational one, as its early name indicates, *The Elementary Education Club.*

In such a school, where many of the ideas and methods were radically opposed to the old and familiar ones, the parents especially felt the need of becoming correctly acquainted with these ideas, of knowing the why and wherefore for each change, so as not only to keep in touch with the work of their own children, but to be able to correct misconceptions formed in regard to the school by the outside world. As a by-law itself stated: "The objects of this association are to promote in general the interests of elementary education by discussing theories and their practical applications, and especially

---

[1] Nellie Johnson O'Connor, "The Educational Side of the Parents' Association of the Laboratory School," *The Elementary School Teacher*, Vol. 4, No. 7, pp. 532–535.

to confer and coöperate in advancing the work of the Laboratory School of the University of Chicago."

Organized by the parents, and supported and maintained by the parents, it was truly a parents' association. . . . The program for the meetings was arranged by the executive committee, composed of the officers and the chairmen of the different committees. The subjects were presented either by outside specialists, whose opinions would be of especial value, by the teacher or teachers of the study under discussion, or by the parents themselves from the parents' point of view.

Such a conference of parents and teachers for free discussion of methods and results was felt to be indispensable to the best working out of an educational system, and such conferences were the meetings of the Parents' Association of the Laboratory School— conferences for the discussion of educational problems in which the parents were individually interested. . . .[2]

In a word, the parents sought to know what the school was doing and why it was doing it. As the meetings of the association were held but once a month, to make the work more effective and intimate, one of the standing committees was an educational one. This committee was to direct the educational interests of the association, particularly in the study of the educational principles of the school and of the ways in which the association could assist in carrying them out. To this committee the parents came with their criticisms and suggestions, and the committee, in quiet consultations with the teachers, was often able to correct a bad habit unconsciously formed in a teacher or, by revealing a teacher's plan to the parent, remove his objections and reconcile him to the particular method in question.

Thus, from such counsels need was felt that the parents must in some way become better acquainted with the real purposes of the school. Through the great kindness of Mr. Dewey, Mrs. Young, and Mr. Tufts, for three consecutive years a class was formed, open to all members of the association, in which the principles of the school were taught. Opportunity was given in the discussions at the close of the class for the asking and answering of questions.

The main value, then, of the educational work of this Parents' Association was to educate the parent in the principles of the school. This brought him necessarily into closer touch and, above all, resulted in a greater sympathy between parents and teachers. It be-

---

[2] The subjects of some of these discussions were "The Question of Reading," "Why Children Should or Should Not Learn to Read at an Early Age," "Some Problems in Modern Education," "The Physical Life of the Child," "The Purpose of Outdoor Excursions," "How to Simplify the Lives of the Children," "The Value of the Study of Literature."

came possible to bring the school life of the child into the home and the home life into the school, so that the two could be welded into a compact and unified whole.

In an article on "The Social Needs of Children," another parent analyzed the social life of the home and school and outlined the suggested program of the Home Committee of the Parents' Association of the School of Education which was to be organized later.[3]

What is meant by a child's social needs? It is his need to learn to coöperate with others, in work and in play, in a manner best fitted for his and his associates' highest development. In these days of social unrest and failure to recognize one's obligation to his neighbor, we all agree that there can be no part of a child's education that is more important. These social needs should be recognized in the school and in the home, and it would be logical and natural to add in the church. But for the purposes of this paper the school and the home centers only will be considered. Social organization takes place naturally when there is something to do. In the words of one of the leading educators, "when occupations are made the articulating centers" of home life and of school life, the social nature of the child grows and expands. Some educators are telling us how this can be accomplished in schools. The school is not a place for the acquisition of knowledge only. It is where the social instinct is recognized, while all of the powers of the body, mind, and soul are unfolding and developing under wise guidance. In order to fully accomplish this, the life of the school and the home must supplement each other. Were the schools social centers, our parents and teachers would meet on common ground for the furtherance of a better social spirit among all sorts and conditions of children. . . .

This group of parents were strenuous in their efforts to infuse into the little community which grew about this school simplicity in thought and action, and knowledge of its methods, and I think we were rewarded by seeing our boys and girls reach the ages of sixteen and seventeen, natural and wholesome. But we did not have our own children only in mind. We hoped that the learning of a university, its rare pedagogical insight, combined with the earnest watchfulness and experience of the teachers and parents, might throw light upon what the social life of children of all communities, and especially of less favored communities, should be. We hoped that all children might be helped to the rich inheritance of what should be theirs, by the perfect growth of all their powers.

---

[3] Hattie Hover Harding, *The Elementary School Teacher*, December 1903.

The parents of the children, as well as others, were in close coöperation with the teachers and administrators in the school, all recognizing that "there cannot be two sets of ethical principles, or two forms of ethical theory, one for life in the school, and the other for life outside the school. As all conduct is one, the principles of conduct are also one." [4]

Holding this common intellectual viewpoint, all were united in a common purpose to make the setting and conditions such as to help the child develop the right "how of conduct," whether at school or at home, by showing him the right "what of conduct." Thus the two-faced quality of ethical theory was made clear to the child, and psychological *and social ethics* entered into the practice of the school life, as much, if not more, than into the home life of the children, and in so doing unified them.

THE CHILDREN OF THE SCHOOL

There is little more that can be said of the third and most important group of coöperating human factors in this enterprise, the pupils of the school. The main purpose of the experiment was to win them to and guide them into joint undertakings. How far this was successful may be judged from the practices of the school already related.

At the close of the school in 1903, most of the oldest class had been under its care from the beginning—seven and one half years. During the last two and a half years (1901 to 1903) biology, physiography, algebra, and geometry, and a year of what might be called preparatory Latin were included in the program. Their school experience with subject-matter throughout had been of a widely varied nature. Their teachers were trained experts in the various sciences, in mathematics, in the languages, and in the industrial and artistic activities. These teachers had been chosen because of a background of life experience which had bred in them attitudes of adaptability, open-mindedness, honesty, fresh enthusiasm, and above all re-

---

[4] John Dewey, "Ethical Principles Underlying Education," *The Third Yearbook of the National Herbart Society*, 1897.

spect for the growing personality of a child and his need of freedom, under guidance, to exercise his developing powers.

In consequence of these attitudes on the part of the teachers, there seems to have been an unusual response in the children, like that of plants to air and sunshine, a response frank, free, and urgent with the driving force of original desire. As expressed in recent letters from one of the teachers,[5] the result was "a home-like atmosphere in which the children worked. Not that the school-room suggested a home, but the spirit of physical and mental freedom between the children and their surroundings (in which the teacher was only distinguishable by her size) made a really living atmosphere."

The children were actors in the scenes of the constantly shifting, on-going, self-planned drama of their daily action. The teachers provided the setting and properties and were the stage directors. A faculty visitor writes of a memory of one of frequent visits to the school: [6]

It was a glimpse of a class in geography—or was it science?—that I most clearly remember. I recall that the little children in the class were engaged in no less a social occupation than that of impersonating the solar system—or at least the sun, earth, moon, and maybe a planet or two for good measure. They took their positions on the floor and revolved about one another in true planetary style, yet with childlike zeal and informality. This is but a snap-shot, a mere random cross-section, but it seemed to me to typify both the simplicity and the audacity of the school's pedagogy. . . .

One of the pupils in the school, now well known in the field of psychological research, also bears witness to the effect of his schooling: [7]

"There is not the least doubt in my mind that the work in research, which has become my profession as a psychological investigator, had its origin in the ideas and methods gained in the Dewey School."

As a result of this guarding and direction of their freedom, the children retained the power of initiative naturally present

---

[5] Katherine Andrews.

[6] Willard C. Gore.

[7] Johnson O'Connor, Director of the Human Engineering Laboratories of Stevens Institute, Hoboken, N. J.

in young children through their inquisitive interests. This spirit of inquiry was given plenty of opportunity and developed with most of the children into the habit of trying a thing out for themselves. Thus they gradually became familiar with, and to varying degrees skilled in, the use of the experimental method to solve problems in all areas of their experience.[8]

A reminiscence of one of the science teachers illustrates how truly the educational process in the school was an experimental one and was actually participated in by the children themselves.[9]

I think the children did get the scientific attitude of mind. They found out things for themselves. They worked out the simplest problems that may have involved a most commonplace and everyday fact in the manner that a really scientific investigator goes to work. Do you remember the disgust of the head of the University ———— Department that the children spent two laboratory periods on a "trifle that they might have found out in a few minutes from a book?"

So habituated were these children to the test and see for yourself attitude, that for the most part they had come quite naturally to look upon the experimental method as their best tool in time of need. The feeling that they had a way by which they could set about the solution of any problem gave them self-confidence. This ability to state their problem, gather the data about it from all possible sources, and after deliberation on these data, decide upon an experimental course of action, established a sense of security in a power within themselves and in their knowledge of the availability of outside resources.[10] They had learned by themselves doing

---

[8] A girl in the oldest class began college work in physics at the University of Wisconsin. She was asked by her instructor where she had had her preparation; he added, "I am interested to know because you are the only one in the class who seems to know what an experiment is."

[9] Katherine Andrews.

[10] A mother who had been most critical as to the effects of the school on two of her children acknowledged many years later that, when comparing the two children who had had the school experience with those who had not, she believed "the markedly greater ability of the first two to meet new situations and to attack problems was due to their early experience in this school."

what man has done and had won through to a philosophy of confidence. In consequence, these children were quite unafraid in new situations, and their later work in college or university was of such outstanding character as to place them immediately in the front rank of their group.

There were few backward or difficult children, mainly because the activities of the school were so varied that many types of personality found freedom for expression. Interest and effort went so often hand in hand that there was no reason to be at odds with one's neighbors or at cross purposes with the teacher. There were some cases of difficult adjustment, particularly where a child came into this school from one of the public schools. Such a child was frequently at a loss to know how to proceed, lacking as he was in power to initiate or direct his own work. The help given such individuals was strictly incidental to the specific block or problem. It can be said with truth that difficulties in the adolescent period were very few, owing probably to the fact that the earlier experiences of these children had been full, free, and satisfying. They had the frank attitude of unthwarted, uninhibited, freely acting persons.

COMMENTS OF PUPILS AFTER THIRTY YEARS

There were also children, who had not had the whole course of the school, who at its close had a hard time readjusting themselves to the system of the public or other schools. One of these pupils when recently asked if he had any remembrance of being a member of the experimental group, especially in regard to his experience in learning to read and spell, answered: [11]

"I never learned to spell—I do not know how to spell now, I have no sense of spelling. Of my group some were spellers and some were not. I had two sisters and a brother in the school. My brother and one sister learned to spell; the other sister and I did not. My brother was of the book type and began to read early. I was of the shop type and was not interested in books. I did not feel the need of reading or writing and hence no desire to learn to spell. There

---

[11] Paul McClintock, 1930.

would have come a time when I would have wanted to write up what I had found out and what I was doing in the shop. Then I would have learned to spell. But the school as an experiment stopped just before we non-book people came to the point where we wanted to write or read. This was bad for the experiment and was very bad for us. . . .

I don't remember any *studying* or *learning* of anything. I don't remember going through the process of learning to read, but I read. However, I never read a book of my own free will until I reached the second year in high school.

I am a firm believer in Dr. Dewey's theory of education, and I believe the university will come to be on much the same basis within the next ten years, though it will approach the problem from the more practical standpoint rather than the theoretical. And this, because our present system of education is a failure.

Handicapped by her lack of hearing, one of the pupils of the school characterizes the influence of the school upon her later experience as follows: [12]

First as to the Sciences, no matter how young we were—too young to understand very much—we were given a chance to use our eyes, to observe facts of nature more closely. Modern customs have been shutting us off too much to satisfy childhood's curiosity. Hence the science not only helped us to understand life better; it also helped us to learn to see, trained our eyes to observe, and thus used and developed our minds.

Secondly—the activities—carpentry, cooking, weaving, sewing, art —all trained our hands and fingers to be useful. Such skills are valuable not only for the sake of economy and usefulness; they are restful to the nerves. People have often asked me where I learned to use my hands, and how it is I so easily learn to do new things with my hands. I tell them it is because I was trained to use my mind and hands and eyes together. I was trained to observe and given a chance to use what I observed in what I did.

Third, the building of the club-house—the real and practical work—helped us to see what architecture really is. We got far more out of that than out of books.

Fourth, I learned responsibility. When I was quite young, I was asked to teach art for two months to a younger class. The experience of learning how to take this responsibility was very good. When I went into the room for the first time I had to realize that I must do something! I learned how to teach that way, and this is responsibility finally realized.

---

[12] Josephine Crane, 1930.

Hence, in the school we got firm foundations for life in every branch of usefulness. We learned to use our hands, our eyes, our heads and to accept responsibility. This is realizing fundamentals. These are very pleasant and precious memories, and I am more than grateful to John Dewey and his ideas.

Some of the alumni of the school, for the most part those who had been pupils in the school from its start, happened to meet recently at a social gathering in Chicago. After comparing notes about themselves and their observations of others of the old school group, they agreed that the outstanding characteristics of all Dewey School pupils, then and since, were adaptability and initiative in meeting life's situations. One of this group enlarged her memories and comments as follows: [13]

When I was a little girl, I had the rarest of educational experiences. I went to the John Dewey School in Chicago, "The University of Chicago Laboratory School." The school occupied a large city lot covered with a sparse and tawny grass, worn bare in spots by the running back and forth of many, busy, happy feet. The lot was cut across diagonally by a gray, dusty path leading to the school-house. That brown house with its good-sized veranda and passageway to the gym and shop held for the children a living world. There were no inhibitory moments of fear or self-consciouess before the teacher, other children, or visitors. We were a large family, anxious to put forth our kindest manners, happy to help the child who was slower to grasp the problem at hand, knowing that when we needed help it would be as gladly given. A most remarkable spirit of normal coöperation existed, the kindliest tolerance, an inspiring pride in work and play. There every child felt as much released, as happy and as unself-consciously contented and at ease as in his own home. Probably more so. This was a victorious educational premise.

It is difficult for me to be restrained about the character building results of the Dewey School. As the years have passed and as I have watched the lives of many Dewey School children, I have always been astonished at the ease which fits them into all sorts and conditions of emergencies. They do not vacillate and flounder under unstable emotions; they go ahead and work out the problem in hand, guided by their positively formed working habits. Discouragement to them is non-existent, almost *ad absurdum*. For that very fact, accomplishment in daily living is inevitable. Whoever has been

---

[13] Helen Greeley.

given the working pattern of tackling problems has a courage born of self-confidence and achieves.

The Dewey School gave us the opportunity to form practical, livable behavior patterns. As I consider in contrast the average students passing out of school into social and economic conditions, we were armed for the battle, they are maimed. . . .

To learn that, through occupation, or more simply, through work, one experienced happiness, to own that point of view as a daily habit is perhaps the greatest gift bestowed. To experience all sorts of things, not just to study them, is Mr. Dewey's plan of education. So our schooling was work in a workshop, and the habits we formed thereby were active habits. The discipline we learned was a practical way of living congenially with our neighbors.

Now that I have children of my own and face the problem of preparing them for life, I find that my greatest aid in helping them is my Dewey School background. As a child I was understood by my teachers. So in bringing up my children I have an initial advantage. I know what it means to a child to be understood and to be guided from that premise. Instead of being forced into an adult imitation, I was definitely allowed to be a child. As a result, my childhood memories are not only vivid but alive. So, even at my age, thanks to my Dewey School experience, I find it possible to enter into my children's childhood life with them and influence them not merely through my point of view born of experience but through theirs too.

Like a voice out of the past, the memories of his Dewey School days come to haunt the consciousness of a grown-up pupil of the school until he voices them in this sketch.[14]

A young American journalist, standing on one of the terraced heights of the ancient city of Genoa, was gazing out upon the wrinkled water of the crescent bay. Between the bay and the spectator rose the serried roofs of the shining city in a wide amphitheatre, broken here and there by terra-cotta domes and striped bell towers of a score of Roman churches lifting their insignia of spiritual dominion high above the sultry squares and tangled, kenneled streets, above even the red and white and green banners of the State, into the blue Italian sky. Far to the left and right stretched the olive-clad Ligurian mountains, in undulating horizons of grey and green, marking the alluring shore of the *Riviera di Levante;* embracing the blue Tyrrhenian Sea, they marched westward towards the tawny, theatrical cliffs of France, beyond San Remo and Ven-

---

[14] Brent Dow Allinson.

tiniglia. Why should Columbus, as boy or man, of imagination all compact ever dream of leaving so delightful a scene?

But was it so delightful to him with its mercenary feuds and political vendettas, continuing to this very day? . . . Suddenly, the young American, who was visiting Italy for the first time in his life became aware of a vague feeling of sympathy for the place, a dim impression that he must have experienced the scene before, that it was not wholly alien to him. But how, or when? He could not solve the mystery of sub-conscious memory— Had he been in Italy and breathed its glamour, as lovers of the beauty that passes understanding are so easily led to believe, in some previous incarnation?

.   .   .   .

Twenty-five years before, in the atttic of a rambling, shingled dwelling house on an indifferent, flat avenue in Philistine Chicago, a brown-eyed child of six or seven years sat cross-legged on the floor, confronting a vast expanse of taut canvas smelling of oil, paint, and the excitement of turpentine. A blue gingham apron was buttoned and pinned under his chin, and in his hand he held a long paint-brush, unmanageable as a chop-stick, dripping with Cobalt-blue paint. *Burnt Orange,* as someone had viciously nicknamed him, because of an auburn glint in his hair, had been authorized to streak waves of blue water, bluer than he had ever believed existed, onto the canvas, by a tall, serene lady who always spoke in the kindest voice. She had shown him somehow the trick of making the water look real, of painting in short rippling strokes the watery shadows in the lee of caravels riding at anchor and the reflections of piles and a pier. Lost in those painted ships upon a painted ocean, the lad was entirely happy, if only the bell would not ring to summon him to some other class. He had to stand upon a chair to paint the masts on the three immortal ships—the *Nina,* the *Pinta,* and the *Santa Maria* (what matters it, if they rode at anchor in Cadiz and not the bay of Genoa?)—and to carry the green wavy line of the hills across the horizon and off the canvas, towards France. . . . The fumes of the turpentine and the glamour of the enterprise combined to stimulate the fresh imagination of the child, under a supervision that was no less tactful than experimental, and to convert the old attic into a halcyon grove. . . . He was learning by doing as the phrase went and perhaps still goes, pedagogically speaking.

Learning what? Learning the feel of artist's paint and canvas, but learning the feel of history also—whether or not it is a legend that has been agreed upon—and the tang of historical adventure. . . . He was painting, not just in order to paint, to cover space with meaningless color and lines, but painting with a purpose. He was helping to paint a back drop, a stage-scene, for a dramatized version of the story of Columbus. The story had been read and written and inwardly learned by the history and English groups of the school; it had been composed as a play by the joint efforts of a dozen or more children of different ages. It would be produced as a major school event, a project they would call it nowadays, after the stage and its footlights had been carpentered, the scenery painted for the different scenes, the costumes designed and fabricated in the manual training, the art, the textiles, and other groups. And the little girl who played Isabella, with her casket of jewels, to the curly-haired, brown-eyed, indigent, ambitious Columbus would be even more than a Queen of the May. . . . There would be coöperations, imaginings, inventions, responsibilities developed, as well as feelings implanted for the primitive constructive crafts and the articulate expressive arts; and who should say what memories would remain, or under what circumstances of after-life they would emerge in the stream of consciousness to make the unfamiliar world more familiar, and action less blind?

SUMMARY

Such memories show a rich background of experience, of daily and hourly meeting situations in which it was necessary for these children to make their own choices and reach their own conclusions as to future plans of action. Both as a group and as individuals, they had been trained to sense situations— to look and to see, to listen and to hear; they had grown able to regard, to compare, and to refer, and such behavior had become more or less habitual. They, therefore, had early come to have their own definite tastes and standards which enabled them to judge, to evaluate, and to interpret with greater ease than is usually the case at the adolescent age.

Their meaningful activities had given exercise to their wits. They had played and dug, hammered and cut, had fashioned things of their own planning, had painted and modeled, and had written, read, and sung much about all they had done. Because of this rich background they seemed more sensitive than most children to the quality and value of many different kinds of experience. Their imaginations were in consequence more alert, and they were able in their reading to seize upon and relate the veiled (to others not so experienced) meaning of the written symbols. The indirect experience of others, therefore, took on a semblance of reality and was integrated more completely into their own experience, thus deepening and enriching it.

It seems a legitimate conclusion that there had come about a gradual widening of the area of the individual vision of these children through the growth in them of the understanding of people in relation to situations. They could size up the latter in relation to the former, and vice versa. There was a noticeable ability to include in this estimate a sympathy with what lay beyond their direct interest. They seemed to have vague inklings of the social as well as intellectual aspects of knowledge, and the latter had a vital value to them, proportionate to its contribution to the solution of their problems and to those of a larger world than their own. When these problems were real and genuine matters for adjustment, problems which interfered with and obstructed real and genuine purpose, the knowledge, the data, the idea, which was most relevant and helpful in the solution of these problems was also the knowledge which was most vital.

In planning the scheme of the school's curriculum, those responsible tried to consider the choice of its activities from the point of view of the needs of its common life. It endeavored, therefore, to place essentials first and refinements second. The things which are socially most fundamental, which had to do with the experience shared by most of those in the school and society in general, were regarded as the most essential; those which represented the needs of specialized groups and technical pursuits were of secondary importance.

It was recognized as of the highest importance that the interest of children naturally attaches itself to the occupations of local surroundings. But it must be fed.[15] "It must not be held down to recapitulating, cataloguing, and refining what is already known. When the familiar fences that mark the limits of the village proprietors are signs that introduce an understanding of the boundaries of great nations, even fences are lighted with meaning. Sunlight, air, running water,

---

15 John Dewey, *Democracy and Education* (New York City, The Macmillan Co., 1916), pp. 248–249.

inequality of earth's surface, varied industries, civil officers and their duties—all these things are found in the local environment. Treated as if their meaning began and ended in those confines, they are curious facts to be laboriously learned. As instruments for extending the limits of experience, bringing within its scope peoples and things otherwise strange and unknown, they are transfigured by the use to which they are put. Sunlight, wind, stream, commerce, political relations come from afar and lead the thoughts afar into fields of romance, of moral and esthetic beauty."

In spite of its mistakes and failures, there seems to have been imbedded in the memories of all who shared in this school experience, students, teachers, parents, children, administrators, a sense of its reality, its relatedness to life, its continuity with the actual processes of life, and its unbroken growth into the larger and finer meanings of living. This has stood the test of time. In those who have written and talked of this experiment, there is the conviction that the facts and skills then learned were not just information and habits soon forgotten, but had been so used to further construction and expression of ideas or in developing social situations, that they had been assimilated and built into the fiber of both individual and group experience.

What has seemed of importance to many was, in effect, a by-product of the things done, an attitude of confidence toward life. This sense of confidence and security seems to have had three main sources. First, it was a consciousness of power within the individual to meet emergent circumstance with planned though experimental action. Second, he was group-conscious; he appreciated the power and satisfaction of group thinking and concerted action. Third, he had a trust in the dynamic power and continuity of life, born out of a study of the history of the race, its inventions, its discoveries, its methods, and the meaning of these for the future. Belief that this meaning would lead on to new discoveries, new fields of creative effort, and hitherto unknown fields of action gave steadiness and purpose to many of this group to follow its gleam along untrodden paths. All felt they had had a share in a new sort of education and in the planting and nourishing of a seed that had dynamic life.

It should be said in conclusion that while the greater burden of development fell upon the teachers, they almost without exception realized that whatever success attended their efforts was due largely to the backing, the inspiration given them, and the faith placed in them by the whole group under the leadership of Mr. Dewey.

CHAPTER XX

EVALUATION OF PRINCIPLES
AND PRACTICES

IN evaluating the significance of this experimental school in the educational situation of thirty years ago, and in its implications for the present, it is necessary to emphasize some of the ideas and principles that were basic to its philosophy of education, masterfully set forth in their entirety in Mr. Dewey's *Democracy and Education.*

PRINCIPLE OF GROWTH

The approach of those guiding the experiment was biological and functional: growth is the main characteristic of life at all levels. The controlling principle of growth, therefore, became the guiding principle of the school's theory. It held that education is growth at all levels and results from intelligent action—from the constant adjustment of an individual to his environment both physical and social as he uses or modifies it to supply his needs or those of his group. Furthermore, normal growth is continuous. It goes on at one or more levels during the whole life span of the individual.

A study of the mental development of early infancy was the key which unlocked the secret of this characteristic and controlling principle of development. Certain questions prompted this study. What is the organism through which mental growth takes place? What are the functioning factors within this organism? How do they work together to produce growth? What unifies and coördinates them? Mr. Dewey describes a simple act, or coördination, as the psychical organism of growth within which three factors function in rhythmical, unified labor. These factors are sensory-stimulus, central connection or idea, and muscular-response. They function in a circuit to maintain, reinforce, and transform the act. Of these three, *idea* links the satisfaction of need with the motor-response to the sense-stimuli. Idea is the *meaning* of the act. It is its controlling factor. Habits are built out of many acts (such as constitute the habit of seeing or hearing) and become parts of larger coördinations, more complex acts. Something heard suggests what can be seen or touched, and the meaning of one act for another enters in. Intelligence thus constituted can control the original impulse, can interpret sense-stimuli, can reinforce or transform, and thus direct the motor-response into a form of intelligent action.[1] The meaning of one act for the next is apparent. In a series of acts which constitutes an activity, there is a continuing transformation of the present in the light of the consequences and meaning of the past action. As a result, recasting of purpose follows; a new plan is set up; and decision to act again is made. This is intelligent action. From such action mental growth results.

The inclusion of intelligence within activity avoids the separation from the total activity (thought, feeling, and action) of the thought-aspect of it as being merely mental. It also avoids the exclusive emphasis on overt activity at the expense of thinking, for the chance of developing even overt activity lies in its increasing mental content, which gives both increased knowledge and skill. Otherwise, an increasing complexity of external movement, acquired without mental counterpart, would amount to nothing more than a rushing around in a squirrel cage, a meaningless activity.

[2] "In contrast a meaningful activity is the definition of an idea which continues to direct that activity in new expressions. Such an activity is a genuine expression and at the same time a development of the self. The whole hypothesis about ideas, as definitely intellectual experiences, is that they arise,

---

[1] The path of an act can be thought of as part of an interlocking spiral, not a closed circle. This concept of Mr. Dewey's came to be known as *the organic circuit concept.*

[2] John Dewey, written for the authors.

are clarified, and defined (developed) in the course of the activity they first guide and later provide the meaning of. Then this development of meaning or idea leads on to new expressions and constructions, and so on. This process constitutes human growth as far as that is something more than merely a physiological development."

Every individual, whether child or adult, acts to reach a desired end. Every act involves choice in every situation where it is possible to choose—a preference for one result of the action rather than another. Choice is made either on the basis of imitation and obedience to tradition, or on the basis of the individual's preference for the consequences which his own thought on end and means has clarified and previsioned. Action based on imitation or obedience is blind. A policy of action based on custom and tradition, rather than thought, is backward not forward looking. It has no insight into the present and hence no foresight for the future. The conception of the act as a unified trinity including sensory-stimulus, idea, and motor-response as factors functioning within it and emphasizing the interpretative function of idea, became the working principle by which the educative worth of any experience might be analyzed and tested, and genuine choices made. It was also the basis of Mr. Dewey's psychological analysis of what constitutes a moral act, moral conduct, and character, for he early pointed out and has steadily maintained the identity of so-called moral education, as well as every other customary division of education, with growth that results from intelligent action. The kernel of his principle is this: *the moral act is the consciously completed act which expresses the unified self.* He pictures the important steps in the psychological process whereby all three factors within the act—feeling, thinking, and muscular-response—come to the coöperative functioning that expresses a unified self. The first phase of the action is impulsive. But when the impulsive act meets resistance, it divides into contrary and competing tendencies. Out of this conflict are born ideas using symbols to represent possible acts. These serve to give meaning to impulses and thus to redirect action. That is, each conflicting line of action is represented by an idea which through communication by symbols expresses an act as a possibility rather than a fact. The interplay of these alternative ideas is deliberation. Thought is thus a substitute for overt conflict in action. Through the balancing of ideas their harmonious coöperation is brought about. This unification is what we know as choice and decision. It marks the forming of a self which is more consciously integrated than was the impulsive self or body of organic tendencies out of which it grew.

The conflict of impulsive tendencies is also a state of emotional disturbance. As the ideas move toward a unified purpose, so the emotions directed by ideas or meaning tend toward a unified desire or affection and finally become a definite interest. The original impulse to act blindly has become an intellectualized desire to act in accord with the new plan. The self of impulse and the self of deliberation coalesce and express themselves as a unity in an act. Intelligent action is thus the expression of the best thought and the deepest desire (or interest) of the whole self. This expression represents a unified person who acts as he both thinks and desires, whose intellectual ideal is backed and reinforced by his undivided interest. The acts of such a person are the result of his full attention and his whole-hearted effort. In other words, such acts represent genuine interests of the self and are, therefore, moral. They are the self in expression.

When such coöperative action is not achieved by thought and will, the deed represents whichever self has proved the stronger and is, therefore, according to Mr. Dewey's theory, not a complete act—one which represents the whole self. It is a partial act representing a divided self, where one self has achieved a victory over the other. Where the objective self (the thinking self) does not carry the subjective, the really interested self, along with it, but insists upon action without such agreement, the act represents only part of the self. The ideal has resulted in deed without the complete backing of the original impulse; full interest in the deed is lacking; and complete satisfaction therefore cannot result. Or, if the subjective, interested self rushes into ill-considered action, the agent is said to have acted against his better judgment. In either case, part of the self is unexpressed and is unsatisfied with what has been done. The deed represents a divided, a disintegrated self. Such a deed is not genuine, and therefore, according to the theory, it is not moral.

[3] "Identification of self in and through an on going process *is* feeling or emotion. Finding himself in an objective (one with meaning) is interest. Engrossment, absorption, wholeness of reaction is interest or emotion. When the thing and the act fit, there is intensity and completeness of response. This intensity of quality may be analytically separated out by the adult and called emotion. To the child it is a direct quality of the experience. It is killed or chilled by being made a separate thing as often in false artistic or aesthetic instruction."

Such expression is a round of dynamic activity, always spiral in form because continually increased in meaning and heightened satisfaction. The motives that are springs to action are the original impulses which have been indentified with purpose through the mediation of thought and communication through symbols and have become ideals. These ideals are not lugged in from without nor put over from above; they are homemade, for they are self-initiated, self-deliberated, self-evaluated, and self-chosen. They are central factors in moral growth.

There is a further point of highest significance in this definition of intelligent moral action. This is that possible social consequences following action must be foreseen and reckoned with. A moral act is thus seen to be a social one.[4] "In a moral act, the will, the idea, and the consequences are all placed inside of the act, and the act itself only within the larger activity of the individual in society." From this corollary to the theory's principle of growth it follows that mental and moral growth results from intelligent action only when action is motivated by social concern and directed to social ends.

---

[3] John Dewey, written for the authors.
[4] George H. Mead, *John Dewey, The Man and His Philosophy*, (Cambridge, Harvard University Press, 1930), p. 100.

CONDITIONS NECESSARY TO GROWTH IN THE
FORMATIVE PERIOD

Among the psychological assumptions underlying the school's theory and guiding its practices were two quite different from those accepted by traditional education. The first of these was that the needs, powers, and interests of the growing child are unlike those of maturity; but that, second, he utilizes the same general conditions as the adult in his intellectual and moral development.

Like the adult, the growing child needs freedom to investigate and experiment. He thus makes the many contacts with persons and things that widen and deepen the range of his knowledge and experience. On the other hand, his abilities to think, to act intelligently, and to control himself are not yet formed as they are in the adult, but are forming, in response to their use in action and in the measure of such use. His interests are primarily in activity, using *activity* to include thinking as well as observing through the use of the senses and muscular effort. His activity is the expression of his ideas in ways that fit and knit together satisfactorily the various phases of his experience and that make him one with it. He is in the process of learning how to act intelligently.

In that process a child, like other growing organisms in coming to maturity, passes through various stages of growth. These are not sharply defined, but shade gradually from one to the other. Clues to the sort of experience that is most educative in these stages are to be found in the child's interests, attitudes and capacities. Recent research on physical growth in bodily development reveals characteristic accelerations and retardations associated with certain age periods. These may indicate possible causal connections with the social and psychological attitudes and interests which it was found in the Dewey School characterize these periods. For example, this research has found that the physical growth in the prepuberty period (about ten to fourteen years) is characterized by a relatively slow gain in height but a very rapid increase in mass or weight. A deduction is that this increase in mass involves cell increase in some organs of the body and cell organization in others including the brain among the latter. This period, then, is the one *par excellence* for development in both physical and psychical skills. As a result, indeed, of the Dewey School's experimentation from the educational point of view it was found that in these years there is great willingness on the part of the child to use drill and repetition because of the growing ability to see facility as a means to desirable ends, a fact now generally recognized and used.

In these relatively rapid stages of the growth process, the child differs from the adult. Youth and adult are alike, however, in that they use the same environmental conditions as the setting for their growth at all levels. For specific purposes these may need to be specialized, but broadly considered both child and adult deal with similar conditions. Both solve their problems and reach their planned ends by: (1) selecting relevant materials and choosing their methods, (2) by adapting these materials and applying these methods, (3) by all the experimenting and testing that accompanies this effort.

[5] "In traditional education, practically every one of these three conditions of increase in power for the adult is denied for the child. For him, problems and aims are determined by another mind. For him the material that is relevant or irrelevant is selected in advance by another mind. And, upon the whole, there is such an attempt to teach him a ready-made method for applying his material to the solution of his problems or the reaching of his ends, that the factor of experimentation is reduced to the minimum. With the adult we unquestioningly assume that an attitude of personal inquiry, based upon the possession of a problem that interests and absorbs, is a necessary precondition of mental growth. With the child we assume that the precondition is rather the willing disposition which makes him ready to submit to any problem and material presented from without. Alertness is our ideal in one case; docility in the other. With one we assume that power of attention develops in dealing with prob-

---

[5] John Dewey, *Psychology and Social Practice* (Chicago, University of Chicago Press), p. 13.

lems which make a personal appeal, and through personal responsibility for determining what is relevant. With the other, we provide next to no opportunities for the evolution of problems out of immediate experience, and allow next to no free mental play for selecting, assorting, and adapting the experiences and ideas that make for their solution."

GROWING CONSCIOUSNESS OF RELATION OF MEANS TO END

As a result of the two years of experimentation in the Dewey School a principle evolved which was used as a basis for differentiation of the psychological levels of the various stages of growth and determined the choice of activities for each stage. Early childhood is impulsive; there is almost no pause between impulse and act and later between idea and action. With increasing maturity, however, as a result of trial and error and experimentation, a child becomes less forthright in action, increasingly willing to stop and think about what it is he is going to do and how he is going to do it. In other words, he is beginning to see the difference between means and ends, the how of action in terms of the what of action, that the one is necessary to the other. This increasing span of interest, which makes a child willing to postpone action for longer and longer periods in order to perfect means to attain desired ends, determined the choice of activities in the school as to kind as well as length of plan. It was the test of maturity. By reference to chapters dealing with the various ages, the details observed and the plans used may be found. These most important issues of the Dewey School experiment are not yet used by the progressive schools as criteria, nor have they been supplemented by further experimentation reported to a consulting central body.[6] Successes are enjoyed; only a few are shared; and even here the psychological as well as the social conditioning is not clearly reported. The result is that schools are too often the theater for specific personality trends

---

[6] *See* John Dewey, "The Sources of a Science of Education," *The Kappa Delta Pi Lecture Series* (Horace Liveright, New York City).

or interests and fail to contribute to a developing science of education.

No experience is truly educative unless interest and effort go hand in hand toward a desired goal. An interest is a form of self-expressive activity which has an objective end (idea or object) in view. This has felt value, and its attainment gives satisfaction. In a young child action is direct and immediate. He is interested in play as play. There is no gap in the mind between means and end. Impulse and idea go immediately into action. The existing experience gives satisfaction. It has no end beyond itself. As the child grows in experience, he is able to see an act, a thing, or an idea, not by itself, but as part of a larger, perhaps coveted whole. This act may be a means of gaining the larger whole, and his interest expands to using this means to attain this end. He meets difficulty in using these means; this stimulates him to think more clearly and intensely of what it is he wants, and what he must do to get it. His end becomes not alone an object of desire; it is something worth working for. Interest, therefore, steadies and enlists effort and stimulates thoughtful action. Increasing willingness to delay action, to perfect means in order to arrive at larger ends, is indicative of increasing maturity.

The school's continued experimentation with the subject-matter of the elementary curriculum proved that classroom results were best when activities were in accord with the child's changing interests, his growing consciousness of the relation of means and ends, and his increasing willingness to perfect means and to postpone satisfactions in order to arrive at better ends. This maturing ability to work for more and more meaningful ends showed itself at different ages in different kinds of activities. Children of eight years, at the end of a long course in experimental cooking, were able to make a general classification of foods, grouping those together which required the same or similar means of preparation by cooking. At eleven years, when their experience had included experiments in solution and osmosis and a physiological study of animals, these same children reclassified foods on the basis of their use to the body.

INDICATIONS AND PRINCIPLES OF GROWTH PROCESS

The important question for those guiding this process of growth, and of promoting the alignment and coöperation of interest and effort, is this. What specific subject-matter or mode of skill has such a vital connection with the child's interest, existing powers, and capabilities as will extend the one and stimulate, exercise, and carry forward the others in a progressive course of action? The emotional accompaniment of such progressive growth of activity, of continual movement, of expansion, and of achievement, is happiness. Persons, whether children or adults, are interested in what they do successfully. They have a sense of confidence and accomplishment. Their absorbed interest means a happiness which is not self-conscious and is a sign of developing power.

Without being conscious of the fact, a young child becomes like the other members of his group as he interacts in doing the same things along with them. He thus reflects in his own personality organization the patterns of the organized behavior and relations of his group. His social self inevitably has those habits, those responses which every one else has; otherwise, he would not be a real member of the group. Each individual, however, has a different make-up and endowment, a unique point of view which places him in a unique relationship to the social process of the group. He, therefore, reflects the social attitudes and relations uniquely. In the process of interaction each child gradually becomes conscious of his active relations with others of the group. He recognizes their interests and attitudes and, at the same time, grows conscious of himself as a self that is a factor in these relations. He thus realizes others and himself in a social situation in which they and he both take part. Growth, therefore, depends upon reciprocal relationships in a suitable environment.

[7] The child is a member of the community, but he is a particular part of the community with a particular heredity and position which

[7] George H. Mead, *Mind, Self and Society*, edited by Charles W. Morris (Chicago, Illinois, University of Chicago Press, 1934), p. 200.

distinguishes him from anybody else. He is what he is in so far as he is a member of this community, and the raw materials out of which this particular individual is born would not be a self but for his relationships to others in the community of which he is a part. . . . Dissociations have centered attention on the self and have shown how absolutely fundamental is this social character of the mind. That which constitutes the personality lies in this sort of give and take between members in a group that engage in a coöperative process. It is this activity that has led to the humanly intelligent animal.

In this progressive process of self-realization, a growing child gradually becomes conscious of his impulses and impelling ideas, his deep desires and purposes. He wakes up to what it is he really wants to do. There are occasional flashes of insight, like those of the laboratory worker, when he intuitively knows how to do what he wants to do or what he should choose, although he cannot explain why. This realization that he has both impulses to action and insights for action make him sensitive to similar processes in others. He also becomes conscious of resources outside of himself in the achievements of other persons, in values that already exist— the values of the stored knowledge of the race, of customs and traditions. It was a fundamental principle of the school to await the dawning of these directive insights, to trust their arrival, and to provide the conditions that foster their awakening.

An important aspect of this conditioning process by means of the school's daily practices was to aid each child in forming a habit of thinking before doing in all of his various enterprises. The daily classroom procedure began with a face-to-face discussion of the work of the day and its relation to that of the previous period. The new problem was then faced, analyzed, and possible plans and resources for its solution suggested by members of the group. The children soon grew to like this method. It gave both individual and group a sense of power to be intelligent, to know what they wanted to do before they did it, and to realize the reasons why one plan was preferred to another. It also enlisted their best effort to prove the validity of their judgment by testing the plan in action.

Each member of the group thus acquired a habit of observing, criticizing, and integrating values in thought, in order that they should guide the action that would integrate them in fact. The value of thus previsioning consequences of action before they became fixed as fact was emphasized in the school's philosophy. The social implication is evident. The conscious direction of his actions toward considered social ends became an unfailing index of the child's progress toward maturity.

SO-CALLED SCIENTIFIC APPROACH TO EDUCATION

The point of view which recognizes these principles as vitally important is in sharp contrast to that which underlies the so-called *scientific* approach to education. This latter view holds that in education there is no need for a consideration of values, that value and choice on the basis of value simply do not enter into this type of scientific education. Three ideas are basic in this view.

First, is the idea that the only way science can be used is to apply it to something already in existence. All that science can do for educational direction and progress is to analyze its present practices in the hope of making them more concrete, more efficient, and more logical in unfolding the pupil's experience. Second is the idea that the various processes and functions of education can be separated from one another, that education has primarily to do with the mental life of individuals and their search for truth, while attitude, motive, conduct, character, and the methods for dealing with them are not the business of education. These are the business of the home and the church, or of the reformatory in case these fail. In the third place, this approach holds it possible to isolate and rate mental ability by certain tests and measurements. In its emphasis upon this phase of education, it has impersonalized personality, for the terms of the highly developed system of tests and statistical measurements can describe only the impersonal. Furthermore, by lifting an individual out of the familiar physical environment in which he lives, his daily associations and social connections are ignored as having any direct bearing on education. This so-called "scientific" approach implies a mechanized, unsocial, individualistic point of view.

SCIENCE IN THE EDUCATIONAL SITUATION

The philosophy of the Dewey School was in sharp contrast at all of these points. Science was not isolated from the significant experience of these children. They acquired technical information along with familiar objects and the operations of daily experience. They discovered that water seeks its own level as they built and equipped the houses in their sand-table villages, or as they constructed their rude balances, they found that weight measures the pull of gravity on an object. Mathematical symbols of measurement, formulae of equality, of ratio and proportion—all took on meaning and became familiar tools in laying out gardens or in calculating amounts of cereals and proportions of water necessary for their proper cooking. By this psychological method of approach a child of this school became increasingly familiar with scientific facts and a scientific method of treating and interpreting the familiar material of ordinary experience through his own observation, thought, and experimentation. Knowledge was the outcome of his activities as they produced changes in the environment. He thus grew by easy stages into the adult, logical point of view and as he grew in maturity was increasingly able to analyze, abstract, generalize, formulate, classify, to form hypotheses and test the same by experiment. At no time, therefore, in its theory or in its practices, was there opposition between science and the school's basic philosophy of value. Scientific method and the assured facts of scientific investigations were used in daily classroom experience; activity based upon the results of both took place; and new consequences of value resulted. Choice operated, and further consequences ensued. Science was the means to the greater attainment of values. In determining relative values, scientifically guarded experimentation had its place in conduct as well as in the manipulation of material things. There was much experimental play in the early stages of growth and many consciously planned illustrative experiments in the later stages. In every classroom the play of deductive and inductive thinking went on as teacher and children burrowed through to the meaning of a new idea or concept, element, animal, or social situation. Science, both as method and as source of needed facts, thus aided choice by clarifying values, and by testing out experience, continued to uncover for both individuals and groups new ways of action and principles of value which became in turn new standards of choice.

The philosophy of the school also denied the second point—that it is possible to isolate the various processes of education from one another and from experience, and the functions of the mind from the formation of character and attitudes of behavior. It held that education, like growth, goes on during the whole life span of an individual. It is a by-product of his activity. True education results in an integrated personality, an individual whose powers of mind, body, and will to action are developed in unison, are aligned and directed by an organizing principle such as a planned activity, a purpose, or a vocation. This basic interest, like an axis, runs through the diverse detail of living and causes different experiences, facts, and items of information to fall into order with one another.

On the third point, the philosophy of the school recognized authentic results of scientific investigation, but built upon the idea that organisms, selves, characters, minds, are so intimately concerned with their environments that they can be studied and understood only in connection with them.

RELATION OF INDIVIDUAL TO SOCIETY

Those who worked out the principles and practices described here consciously sought a new and better type of school as well as a new and better development for the individual. In this double-headed experiment the school was to provide the sort of socially minded environment in which individual children and teachers, playing and working in association, could find and develop their personal interests and powers in creative expression. Here too, they could learn the equally important satisfaction of directing their own efforts toward chosen ends and bringing values that could be shared. On the personal side it was hoped that the principles and practices of the school would become those of the children and teachers individually. Each was to find his interests in the process of his own moving experience, to develop his method of intelligent choice, to learn the uses of knowledge and skills in the expression of his interests in social action.

This double-visioned philosophy saw each individual as a potentially creative personality, but also recognized that he was always an individual in relationships, he was always a member of a society which in turn had powerful influences upon him. It also conceived that a person finds his best expression when his interests and purposes are identical with those of a group as they put through a common project together. Developing practice proved on the whole that such mutuality of effort freed personalities to unusual powers of expression, enriched group life, and fostered the progress of the school as a whole. This, to be sure, did not always work out. Progress varied with the experience and training of the teacher, the choice of subject-matter, the backgrounds of the pupils, and other factors. In many groups, however, individual development flourished in the stimulating give and take of shared activity. An eager but tolerant spirit permeated relationships which seemed to free the abilities and capacities of the boys and girls to organized and integrated thought and action and to a rather unusual appreciation of one another's gifts. It often happened that a child who had contributed to a group enterprise and whose contribution had been appreciated by his mates grew more appreciative of the efforts and contributions of others, in the glow of his own satisfaction. To those who had eyes to see and ears to hear, it became apparent that individuals develop with one another, that normal growth requires a coöperative spirit, but that growth is thwarted, stunted, and perverted by self-interest and competitive processes. The importance of school as a socialized institution is stressed in *The Educational Frontier:* [8]

Social arrangements are to be judged ultimately by their educative effect, by what they do in the way of liberating, organizing, integrating the capacities of men and women, boys and girls. These capacities include esthetic factors, those which lie at the basis of music, literature, painting, architecture in both production and appreciation, intellectual and scientific power and taste, capacities for friendship, and capacities for appropriation and control of natural materials and energies. It is the function of education to see to it that individuals are so trained as to be capable of entering into the heritage of these values which already exist, trained also in sensitiveness to the defects of what already exists and in ability to recreate and improve. But neither of these ends can be adequately accomplished unless people are trained to grasp and be concerned about the effect of social institutions upon individual capacities, and this not just in general but in discriminating detail.

COMPETITION VS. COÖPERATION IN EDUCATION

It grew clear that if the goal of an institution is a social goal, then the means to the achievement of that goal must be social also. The slowness with which educators have awakened to this fact is evidenced by the slow increase in the number of progressive schools which are truly social in aim and method. A gradual breaking down of some of the old rigidities in a number of the newer public schools in progressive communities has been, of course, a great gain. But the distasteful fact must be faced that the vast majority of children still enter at six years of age an educational system which trains them for twelve years to work for grades and individual advancement on a competitive basis. For twelve years, six hours a day and five days a week, each child sits in his place in a fixed row of desks and faces, not his companions as an active, guided, social group, but his teacher as an instructor and disciplinarian. He studies largely by himself and for himself and is, during much of the time, in direct competition with his mates. If a child

---

[8] John Dewey and John L. Childs, "The Underlying Philosophy in Education," *The Educational Frontier*, edited by William H. Kilpatrick (New York, The Century Co., 1933), p. 292.

cannot make the grade, that is largely his own fault. The over-whelmingly prevalent system of American public schools, and of many expensive private schools which might pioneer to the great advantage of all, is still individualistic and their methods basically competitive. The implications for society are increasingly apparent to thoughtful students of education and of the development of democratic society.

The physical set-up of the classrooms of the Laboratory School with their movable chairs helped to make each period a social occasion. In all classes teacher and children started off the day's work with a face-to-face discussion of coöperative plans for individual and group activity. The work of one day was thus linked to that of the day before and suggested the activities of the day to come. These activities being, as they were, relevant to the occupations of life, afforded many opportunities for the observation of nature, for the use and control of natural forces and processes, for the discovery of better ways of living, for the invention of tools and machines, for the observation of conditions and values in the physical environment with reference to living conditions and occupations and the action of natural forces in relation to the evolution of the forms of life and of individual organisms. The interdependence of plant, animal, and human life was constantly under consideration. These merely suggest the possibility of using active occupations as opportunities for experimental scientific study. The opportunities are just as great on the social side in the study of the groupings of humanity and their relationships. A direct road into civics and economics was also found in a study of industrial occupations in social life. The child was thus enabled to repeat and share what the race has learned in the long achievement of the art of living. Activities thus used demonstrated the value of the experimental method. For these children as for the race, it became an excellent tool for "getting on." The spirit of curiosity, the desire to know why and how, develops early in children and a child of six or seven years can be taught to answer his own questions and solve his own difficulties. Little by little he can be guided to think out what to do to find the answer or the reasons for his success or failure. New ideas of something next to do are thus suggested; new plans are made which involve new search for better ways and means; and again new action brings new knowledge.

NECESSITY OF FREEDOM FOR INQUIRY AND EXPERIMENTATION

It is impossible to overemphasize the importance of the spirit of inquiry to the life and growth of a child. If the tip of a growing plant is cut, the growth of the whole plant is checked, and its form altered. So with a child when the inborn spirit of curiosity and adventure begins to peer through and push aside the protective devices which have surrounded it. If these shy beginnings of imaginative thought are nipped in the bud, stunted, or thwarted by repression or inattention, by the lack of a response equivalent to air and sunlight, or by an overabundance of adult attention, the attitude and quality, form and character of the personality is altered. The healthful exercise of imaginative thought, however, gives the pulse of meaning to all growth and results in an increasing ability to find the what and why and how of action.

Science and its methods, processes, and results—as the organ of the social progress of the race—had the same function in the curriculum of the school as in racial history. It secured freedom from deadening routine for both teachers and children by constantly opening new fields for thought and action. Ideas were set free in the process of experimentation for further testing. Results proved or disproved the validity of hypotheses. Natural forces and principles were used to set forward the child's purpose. What worked here might be useful there, and the meaning of one experience was lifted out and used in another situation. The art of abstracting was thus learned little by little and developed naturally into the power to generalize and formulate rules and principles.

The ever-fresh activities of the school demanded a method of seeing and stating problems, of collecting facts, of acquiring materials and necessary skills, of planning the procedure of solution, and of executing the plans. While the problems of each day were new, the method of meeting them became a habit. A very young child has an idea and goes immediately into action. He soon learns by experience to delay action, to think about ways and means. As before indicated, this willingness to postpone action for longer and longer periods, to stop, look, and listen, to devise and to discover better ways, became an unfailing test of increasing maturity.

[9] "The plan of our school attempted to keep scientific principles and social material in vital contact with each other. Emphasis was put upon the inventive and intellectual forces which have caused all significant advance in human culture. Picturesque and personal elements are, of course, always of value in catching the attention of pupils. But they are of permanent worth only when they are used to carry the mind over to a contribution to basic methods of inquiry, discovery, and social progress. The tendency of some progressive schools to devote special attention to periods which lend themselves to romantic and picturesque treatment at the expense of causal factors is to be deplored.

"When chief weight is given to the factors which have made a permanent difference in the conduct of human life, history is kept in its educative perspective. In addition, pupils become habituated to looking for the forces which are efficient in every social situation and are led to appreciate the part played in social life by methods of observation and thoughtful inquiry. They realize that scientific method is not something purely technical, remote, and apart, but is the instrumentality of socially controlled development. As their studies move on from year to year, the subjects labeled scientific and those labeled social and historical are kept in vital unity, so that each side deepens the meaning of the other, instead of, as so often, pulling the mind in two different directions. It may be seriously questioned whether progressive schools will fulfil their purpose until they take the significance of scientific method more seriously than they have done in the past. It is more than probable that the only genuine solution of the

---

[9] John Dewey, written for the authors.

question of social guidance and indoctrination in education will be found in giving central place to scientific method as the key to social betterment."

THE USE OF THE GENETIC METHOD IN TEACHING HISTORY

The use of the genetic method to get insight into a complex process or problem of the present, by tracing the history of each process from its beginning through the successive stages of its growth, meant that past events were not separated from the child's living present, but retained their meaning for the present and became guides or warnings for the future. The study of simple, basic forms of work grew into the history of the industries, that of trade and barter into economic history, while the ways of men in organizing and coöperating for common ends and the good of all, or of competing for private ends and domination became the history of political and social relationships. Each phase of the story came to have meaning and ethical significance for the other aspects of living. This emphasis on the social meaning and aim of all the activities of the school was one of the unique and important contributions of the experiment.

The way general ideas in the field of any subject-matter took form historically proved very helpful to the teacher in planning a course of study. In science, those illustrative experiments were selected which would help the children understand and formulate definite physical and biological theories in the later school years. Man's relation to his physical environment and his increasing control of its forces and resources opened up many fields of scientific interest, which were extended and enlarged in spiral fashion year by year. In mathematics, the children discovered the function of symbols and tools of measurement through their need of them in their activities and formulated for themselves rules and principles, the fundamental concept of an equation as a balance in equilibrium and of proportion as the relation of gears. In their study of the history of a colony, they found that the climate and physiography of its setting determined largely the type of occupations and social organizations that developed.

VALUE OF PURPOSEFUL ACTION

What is really worth knowing are the ways by which anything is entitled to be called knowledge. A child who has learned to think for the purpose of guiding his own action, who has learned to use that which was of repeated value in restricted situations to clarify and direct his action in larger ones, who has seen and mastered the use of the tools of language or other media of expression so that he can make use of the heritage of the past, is well on the way to a mature understanding of the function of intelligence and knowledge. Such knowledge becomes a mode of intelligent practice, an habitual predisposition of mind to guide action. Such understanding is the basis for an appreciation of the interrelation, value, and beauty of all aspects of knowledge and of all the arts whether fine or practical. As in the early days of infancy when something heard means something that can be seen, and something seen means something to reach and handle, so in all later developing mental and social life, there is an organic spiral: activity, which expresses meaning, meaning which reflects back into and changes action, thus continually enlarging and enriching ideas and ideals, guiding action, and generating character.

Beyond the outward act and the visible product of the children of this school, the eye of faith saw a readjustment of mental attitude, an enlarging vision, a sense of growing power, and an ability to identify both insight and capacity with the interests of others. There was a very real directive sense of excellence in their choices and habits, of tastes formed that grew into habitual modes of preference and esteem.

At the start much faith was necessary, first, in the power of living beings to grow, mentally and spiritually, as well as physically, and to find a way out, over, around, under, and through adverse conditions. Faith, also, was necessary in the self-developing power of informed intelligence to make over the self-protecting, self-preserving, self-perpetuating impulses of the immature human animal into the other-concerned, protecting, preserving, perpetuating impulses of the mature human personality. As a plant cannot grow in stony soil nor when choked with weeds, so the human plant needs the gardener's provision, protection, and nurturing care. The setting and conditions of the school garden must be pre-arranged though not rigidly fixed, and its potential program of activities so chosen as to engage interest, enlist effort, link knowledge to action, and inspire each to give of himself to others. Above all, there must be freedom under guidance to test interests and aptitudes and to try out their worth in experimental action. The guidance had to be both wise and intuitive; there had to be enough of both let and hindrance, just the right balance (always adjusted to ability) of the "for-and-against forces," characteristic of human living, so that genuine need be present for the child to exercise his wits, initiative, effort, judgment, and control. Slowly, but inevitably, there would emerge out of such a process a genuinely happy, because satisfied, child —a child who was growing in body and mind and was finding increasingly the enduring values and satisfactions of the spirit in the expression of his deepest and most urgent interests. Such a child, in whom freedom of action goes hand in hand with an increasing capacity for thought, gets an early taste of the wine of creative effort directed to social ends. Such wine is from the very apple of life, and he who tastes it enters an enduring Garden of Eden. Such an educative process is a normal process and covers the whole life span.

RELATION OF THE DEWEY SCHOOL TO PRESENT PROGRESSIVE SCHOOLS

Such were some of the ideals and values, hopes and aspirations, which lay behind this early laboratory school's philosophy of education, which filled those who loved and worked for it with a zeal of crusading ardor. Thirty years have passed, and the present has many "progressive" schools. Some are near

of kin; others bear little if any resemblance to the parent
school. In between lie all varieties, each with some likeness
to the original. Many of them have, as George S. Counts
puts it,[10]

a number of large achievements to their credit. They have focused
attention squarely upon the child; they have recognized the fundamental importance of the interest of the learner; they have de-
fended the thesis that activity lies at the root of all true education,
they have conceived learning in terms of life situations and growth
of character; they have championed the rights of the child as a free
personality. Most of this is excellent, but in my judgment it is not
enough. . . . It constitutes too narrow a conception of the meaning
of education. . . .

If an educational movement, or any other movement, calls itself
progressive, it must have orientation; it must possess direction. The
word itself implies moving forward, and moving forward can have
little meaning in the absence of clearly defined purposes. . . . Here,
I think, we find the fundamental weakness, not only of progressive
education, but also of American education generally; . . . it has
elaborated no theory of social welfare, unless it be that of anarchy
or extreme individualism.

While these comments may be a merited criticism of some
or all progressive schools of today, it cannot be truly made of
this experimental school of thirty years ago. This school conceived of itself as a social institution fostering a new individualism which, in return, would both clarify the idea of
education and establish it as fact in a new society where co-
operation rather than competition should rule. In spite of
the mistakes and failures that inevitably attend original experimentation, the successful coöperative living of all in the
school put enough of this idea into practice plainly to blaze a
new trail.

The school had no definite theory of social welfare; indeed
its philosophy could not permit the formulation of a definite
theory of social welfare for a fast-changing present and an unknown future. However, it had a great faith in the power of
persons to grow spiritually as well as physically, and out of the
wisdom born of experience was content to educate boys and

---

[10] George S. Counts, *Dare the School Build a New Social Order?* (New
York, The John Day Co., 1932), p. 100.

girls for thoughtful action and an attitude of readiness for coöperation in carefully planned social experimentation. It believed in evolution rather than revolution. It evolved a plan and rediscovered scientific method as the tool for the achievement of the plan and the testing of its theory. The cardinal principle of its educational hypothesis was the principle of growth. The essence of its philosophy of social welfare was its development of social individuals who could carry on intelligent social action.

The school held that the original impulse to grow and the initial power for growing are from within, but the renewal of the power to grow is developed largely out of the experience of growing. Through an increasing consciousness of himself as a factor in the midst of an intricate physical and social environment, a person, whether child or adult, gradually becomes aware of impulse and power within himself. He aspires to be and to do. Both impulse and power are augmented from the aspirations and deeds, the needs and sufferings of others with whom he lives in the close fabric of human relationships. He awakes to them, is inspired by them, desires to emulate, to relieve suffering, to answer need, and finds within himself a miraculous increase in the impulse to be and the power to do. The more he thinks, the greater are his thoughts. The more he gives, the more he has to give. The more he concerns himself with suffering, the greater is his concern and more wise his measures of relief. He has discovered sources and resources for impulse and power both within and without himself and has tapped springs so close hidden that only those who seek may find. Hence, in the school, it was assumed that the constant and increasingly intelligent reconstruction and social integration of a person's experience within himself and as it touches others is the business of each individual. The immediate purpose, for which the school assumed responsibility, was the right and adequate conditioning of this process of self-discovery and of the constructive process described here. The school's ultimate social ideal was the transformation of society through a new, socially minded individualism.

As the experiment progressed, the purposes of the large plan held, but the day-to-day, week-to-week detailed program developed, widened, and extended. It was modified by individual and group thinking to fit altering circumstances of availability of materials or equipment, or the changing factors of human relationships. Quite essential, therefore, to theory and plan and to the efficient testing of both as means to the ultimate purpose, was the participation of the individual boy or girl in the common search for a program—the ways, means, and method—of practice which should demonstrate the theory, approve the plan, and insure progress toward the fulfilment of the purpose. The evidences of this participation were shown in the growing skill of boy or girl to note and find in his own moving experience satisfying values in self-realization and contribution and in his own imaginative thinking to lay hold of and test the way these could function increasingly and socially.

Quite as essential, in progressive education as here conceived, is the skilled guidance which aids the individual to taste the larger satisfactions of self-expression for social ends, for here begins the type of development that has no limit. By impregnating self-interest with the dynamic principle of sympathetic understanding and appreciation of others, the desire for personal gain comes little by little into an understanding of the spread and span of catholic interest and the consuming zeal of social concern. To those who taught and those who learned, what was social came to mean that which was ethical or moral. So-called discipline or individual difficulties of children were met by more or different activities which might engage their attention, release creative expression, and thus change their attitudes. There were few difficult children and almost no adolescent problems, perhaps because the earlier years were so releasing and satisfying, so filled with genuine and interested expression and creative, socially motivated activity. This suggests that many problems of the adolescent period and of later life may have their roots in a repressed and thwarted childhood experience. Be that as it may, the school's experience definitely proved the importance of this most formative period of individual growth and that much of later development depends on the experience of these years. It made clear that the teaching of young children requires expert skill, carefully chosen surroundings and equipment and, therefore, an endowment which should approach university standards. The school was a laboratory of the University. Certain features, therefore, need not be duplicated, but its close relationship to the University was of incalculable help and importance in maintaining the stability and reality of the experiment.

Experimental method in the school had two commandments. The first was: "Think in terms of action and in terms of those acts whose consequences will expand, revise, test your ideas and theories." The second was like unto it, so like that it was a corollary: "Concern yourself also with the social consequences of those acts." The school did aim to indoctrinate the child with experimental method and social motive so that he himself might form his attitudes, cultivate his tastes, and initiate the process of inquiry that leads to discovery and invention or creative expression of any sort. It tried not to dictate plans or to formulate rules, but to endeavor to provide in the school the sort of society where the relationship was one of mutual benefit and regard, and where the children trusted the help and appreciated the counsel of their teachers.

The choice by the school of intelligence as the preferred method of action implied, like every choice, a definite moral outlook. As suggested by Mr. Dewey, this moral implication, when followed out, outlines an entire ethical and social philosophy. In the school's philosophy of education, its two main constituents, the relationship of the social and the individual and of knowledge and action, coalesce in this conclusion. It follows that the interests of school and society must also coalesce. Intelligent experimental action and the subject-matter in which it operates cannot be separated. One reason for the measurable success of the experiment lay in the choice of subject matter which was genuine and important—the activities fundamental to the art of living. However, thirty years ago as now, the implications of such a social philosophy meant isolation from and conflict with the larger society for those who went out of its doors. In such a school intelligent choices had come to mean social choices which were also moral choices. Attitudes had been coöperative in spirit; individual ideals and interests had tended largely toward alignment with those of the school society. Now, as then, society brings both shock and conflict to a young person thus trained, even if he be fore-warned. His attempts to use intelligent action for social pur-poses are thwarted and balked by the competitive antisocial spirit and dominant selfishness in society as it is. He finds that the children of darkness have made efficient use of the experimental method, but have turned it in truncated form to private ends. The complete and adequate use of the ex-perimental method is only possible in a certain kind of so-ciety.

[11] Life based on experimental intelligence provides the only pos-sible opportunity for all to develop rich and diversified experience, while also securing continuous coöperative give and take. The method cannot be fully established in life unless the right of every person to realization of his potential capacities is effectively recognized. . . . The experimental method is the only one compatible with the democratic way of life, as we understand it.

It could be added with truth that the experimental method so conceived is the only method compatible with the religious way of life as the way that regards the welfare of all as the concern of each. Just what will help each child develop reli-giously is problematical, but it seems increasingly clear that, in Mr. Dewey's words,[12] "it is a question of bringing the child to appreciate the truly religious aspects of his own growing life, not one of inoculating him externally with beliefs and emo-tions which adults happen to have found serviceable to them-selves. . . .

"To realize that the child reaches adequacy of religious ex-perience only through a succession of expressions which

---

[11] John Dewey and John L. Childs, "The Underlying Philosophy of Edu-cation," *The Educational Frontier*, edited by William H. Kilpatrick (New York, The Century Co., 1933), p. 317.

[12] John Dewey, "Religious Education as Conditioned by Modern Psychol-ogy and Pedagogy," *Proceedings of the Religious Education Association*, 1903, pp. 60–66.

parallel his own growth, is a return to the ideas of the New Testament: 'When I was a child, I spoke as a child; I understood—or looked at things—as a child; I thought—or reasoned about things—as a child.' It is to return to the idea of Jesus, of the successive stages through which the seed passes into the blade and then into the ripening grain. Such differences are distinctions of kind or quality, not simply differences of capacity. Germinating seed, growing leaf, budding flower, are not miniature fruits reduced in bulk and size. The attaining of perfect fruitage depends upon not only allowing, but encouraging the expanding life to pass through stages which are natural and necessary for it."

In every moment of such an expanding experience, the act of acquiring is always secondary and instrumental to the way of inquiring. The latter is a seeking, a quest, for something that is not at hand.[13] "Original research is not a peculiar prerogative of scientists or of advanced students. All thinking is research, and all research is native, original, with him who carries it on, even if everybody else in the world already is sure of what he is still looking for."

This attitude of respect for original research, at all stages of growth from the laboratory of the nursery to that of the adult, gives glimpses of countless avenues for the renewing of human life. It makes endless the possibilities of invention and discovery, of better and more original ways of living, of unveiling still undreamed-of connections, relationships and consequent developments which will lead to enrichment of human experience. In the school it inspired those leading with a reverent respect for personality and a vision of the things to come. With the inner eye one caught glimpses of the "might be" in every child that made the place whereon one stood holy ground. It awakened faith in the power of life and revealed something of the sources of life, and of its power, and revived confidence in the developing ability to use this power.

This way of regarding personality resurrects and revivifies the old vision of a child as a growing, developing person—

---

[13] John Dewey, *Democracy and Education* (New York, The Macmillan Co., 1931), p. 174.

"First the blade, then the corn, after that the full corn in the ear." In its light a child stands revealed—an individual—possessed of an unique combination of bodily and mental equipment, and of spiritual potentiality. He must not be allowed to sell this birthright for a mess of pottage.

The light of this vision has never gone out in the lives of those who caught it. It has burned steadily, a pillar of light illuminating an old way of life and interpreting it anew. In those days it guided and inspired the slow building of the program of the school. It shines through the long years since, an undimmed beacon for a new education and a new society.

Through man's intelligence imponderable waves, caught and timed to sound, are now replacing the heavy under-sea cables as messengers of thought. So, also, must intelligent use of the store of human kindness meet and overwhelm the forces of hate and evil now so subtly aroused by war and directed to individual aggrandizement. Then, and only then, will the great abundance of the new technology be justly shared over all the earth.

APPENDICES

APPENDIX I

THE EVOLUTION OF MR. DEWEY'S PRINCIPLES OF EDUCATION[1]

IN the summer quarter of 1894 there came to the University of Chicago as head of the Departments of Philosophy, Psychology and Education a young philosopher whose thinking and teaching had already begun to shed new light upon the nature of education. John Dewey was graduated from the University of Vermont in 1879 with the degree of A.B. He spent the two subsequent years teaching in the high school of Oil City, Pennsylvania. Part of the following year, 1881–82, saw him getting a first-hand experience in a rural school at Charlotte, Vermont, filling out the remainder of the year reading philosophy with Professor H. A. P. Torrey of the University of Vermont. In the years 1882–4 he was a student at Johns Hopkins where he held a fellowship in his last year, completed his doctorate, and was immediately invited by the University of Michigan to be instructor in its department of philosophy. In 1886 he became assistant professor and continued as such until the Fall of 1888 when the University of Minnesota offered him a full professorship. At the close of one year, however, the University of Michigan again claimed him to fill the chair of Philosophy, left vacant by the death of Professor George H. Morris, whose assistant Mr. Dewey had been in his earlier years at Michigan. Here he remained until the summer of 1894. During these years Mr. Dewey's philosophy in its making exemplified the principles of development upon which it was based. In his *Psychology*, published in '87, his approach

---

[1] Parts of this chapter in slightly different form have been used in pages 377–381 of Chapter XX. At the risk of repetition, it has seemed best to preserve continuity and keep the present chapter intact.

to the nature of thinking was through the field of ethics by by means of a persistent analysis of the moral implications— the meaning and consequences to himself and others—of action.[2]

Like Royce, Dewey was profoundly influenced by James's psychology, though it suggested to him a method of interpretation of knowledge rather than a metaphysical problem to be worked out in Hegelian fashion. . . . It would, however, be an error to ascribe to James's *Psychology*, the starting point of Dewey's independent thought. In his *Outline of Ethics*, 1891, in which are to be found the essential positions of his ethical doctrine, he makes no reference to James among his many acknowledgments to English idealistic and naturalistic writers, and yet here we find him denouncing the "fallacy that moral action means something more than action itself." Here we find the "one moral reality—the full free play of human life," the "analysis of individuality into function including capacity and environment."

The early flowering of Mr. Dewey's philosophy into practice was stimulated by a twofold desire for a laboratory to test his educational philosophy and to provide opportunity for growth and development in his own children. On one occasion when asked how it came about that he had turned his attention to educational philosophy, Mr. Dewey replied, "It was mainly on account of the children." Theories as to the functions of feeling, thought, and activity in promoting growth and development were to him charged with vital meaning, and his own nursery was his laboratory wherein to test these theories. With true scientific spirit he seized upon whatever he could find in the experience of the past that had made for educational progress, particularly as evidenced in the conduct and abilities of his associates.[3] The educational possibilities of the

---

[2] George H. Mead, "The Philosophies of Royce, James, and Dewey in Their American Setting," *The International Journal of Ethics*, January, 1930.

[3] "Eternal vigilance is the price of liberty, and eternal care and nurture are the price of maintaining the precious conquest of the past. . . . If it were not for the work of an aristocracy of the past, there would be but little worth conferring upon the democracy of today." John Dewey, "Current Problems in Secondary Education," *School Review*, January, 1902.

fundamental activities of the home and especially of farm life interested him greatly. The parents of one of his students, many years before, had established conditions for an experiment in education, by moving from a city to a country home where their four children could at one and the same time carry on and learn about the fundamental activities of life. The father of this family treasured in his old age Mr. Dewey's acknowledgment of the value of this experiment in the formulating of his educational theories.[4]

In the summer term of 1894 the University of Chicago invited Mr. Dewey to become the head of a joint department of philosophy, psychology, and pedagogy. This invitation offered him, administratively, a unique opportunity at the right moment, to carry out the making of a philosophy which had as its legitimate outcome a theory of education. His years of study and teaching had centered in the search for a comprehensive answer to the ever-present question of philosophy, *What is the meaning of life?* Nothing was ever presented, therefore, as isolated from or unrelated to life. Along the pathway of logical thinking, Mr. Dewey came to believe that since growth is the characteristic of life, education is all one with growing; it has no end beyond itself. Education goes on, more or less, during the whole life-span of the individual. It is the result of a continuing process of adjustment by the individual to his physical and social environment, which is thus both used and modified to supply his needs and those of his social group.

As a school-child is too far along in the process of development for satisfactory observation of its simplest forms, Mr.

---

[4] An appreciation of the formative influences of early childhood was also held by Professor James. "In speaking of the constructive impulse . . . you fully realize, I am sure, how important for life—for the moral tone of life, quite apart from definite pursuits—is this sense of readiness for emergencies which a man gains through early familiarity and acquaintance with the world of material things. To have grown up on a farm, to have haunted a carpenter's and blacksmith's shop, to have handled horses and cows and boats and guns, and to have ideas and abilities connected with such subjects are an inestimable part of youthful acquisition." William James, *Talks to Teachers.* (Delivered at Cambridge, 1892, published 1899.)

Dewey takes for study the human being in his earliest stages immediately following birth. In this period of development are exemplified those conditions on the mental side which obtain as long as education continues. The new-born infant is a key to the nature of growth which he hopes will unlock the secret of a characteristic and controlling principle of development, both physical and mental. Upon such a principle there could be set up a working hypothesis which should be of the same help in clarifying the world of educational theory and practice as the hypothesis of evolution had been in the world of nature.

Up to this point the principle of sensory-motor action, known as the reflex arc concept, had been the best guiding principle of growth thus far stated by the initiators of the new scientific approach to the study of mind as a growing affair. The reflex arc concept held coördination to be a sensation-followed-by-idea-followed-by-movement process in which the sensory-stimulus was one thing, the central activity standing for the idea another thing, and the motor discharge standing for the act proper a third, these all being separate entities.[5] "As a result the reflex arc is not a comprehensive or organic unity, but a patchwork of disjointed parts, a mechanical conjunction of unallied processes." In Mr. Dewey's view this concept still showed the dominating influence of the older psychology, which also was disjointed in its thinking, whether viewed from the standpoint of development in the individual or in the race, or from that of analysis of mature consciousness.[6] In other words, while the reflex arc represented a great step in psychological thinking, it was only a half-truth.

Mr. Dewey and his associates, approaching the problem with their attention fixed upon continuity of function, find the controlling principle of growth must be essentially unitary.

---

[5] John Dewey, "The Reflex Arc Concept in Psychology," *Psychological Review*, Vol. III, No. 4 (July, 1896).

[6] "The older dualism between sensation and idea is repeated in the current dualism of peripheral and central structures and functions: the older dualism of body and soul finds a distant echo in the current dualism of stimulus and response." John Dewey, "The Reflex Arc Concept in Psychology," *Psychological Review*, Vol. III, No. 4.

Such a principle as would [7] "substitute the idea of gradual differentiation for the notion of separate mental faculties . . . and the conception of organic interdependence and coöperation for the notion of mechanical juxtaposition and external association." In consequence, they held that "sensory-stimulus, central connection, and motor responses shall be viewed, not as separate and complete entities in themselves, but as divisions of labor, functioning factors, within the single concrete whole." This single concrete whole, Mr. Dewey further defined as [8] "that which is not sensation-followed-by-idea-followed-by-movement, but which is primary; which is, as it were, the psychical organism of which sensation, idea, and movement are the chief organs." He termed it "coördination." His interpretation came to be known as the organic circuit concept.

This view of the unity of the act as including intelligence within itself enabled Mr. Dewey and his associates to carry over the statement of the psychology of the act, with its implications, into their *Studies in Logical Theory* then being carried on and later published by the University. [9]

Under the stimulating effect of the new interest in the child-mind as a growing affair, much observation of child-life had gone on, and a large amount of valuable data had been collected. These data were being interpreted, however, according to the rubrics of the old psychology and were being classified and stowed away under such headings as *sensations, movements, ideas, emotions*. These, when studied and reviewed, presented only a disconnected series of facts and not "the living unity which is a child." They showed little more than that

---

[7] John Dewey, "Principles of Mental Development as Illustrated in Early Infancy," *Transactions of the Illinois Society for Child Study*, Vol. I, No. 3.

[8] John Dewey, "The Reflex Arc Concept in Psychology," *Psychological Review*, Vol. III, No. 4 (July 1896). (A study made in the psychological laboratory of the University of Chicago by Mr. James R. Angell and Mr. A. C. Moore, and published in *University of Chicago Contributions to Philosophy* also confirms this interpretation.)

[9] John Dewey, "Studies in Logical Theory," with the coöperation of Members and Fellows of the Department of Philosophy (Chicago; The University of Chicago Press, 1903), XIII (University of Chicago; The Decennial Publications, Second Series, Vol. XI.)

certain things happened earlier and other things later. What connected those earlier and later actions into a living unity was not apparent. The cord of continuity was lacking. To quote Mr. Dewey [10] ". . . through forcing the observed facts under the captions of the old faulty psychology, we miss precisely the peculiar scientific value of the genetic method. The fact of growth, of continuity, is completely obscured in detail, even though there may be much talk about it at large. There is no insight into continuity of function, no way of connecting earlier and later facts into a living unity. In any biological study, or study using the genetic method, while the persistent and minute study of details is absolutely indispensable, the minutiae of structure and the exact succession of changes are of importance simply as they throw light upon the growth of the life process itself. It is the life principle which is the real object of study, and to sort the observed facts into pigeon-holes, irrespective of their relation to life history, is to have the name but not the reality of the genetic method. . . . Many intelligent parents, especially mothers, are repelled from the work of infant observations simply because there appears to be only a jumble of disconnected facts, all on the same level, with no lead-points of survey or standards or reference. Moreover the individuality of the child is completely concealed in the uncontrolled accumulations of facts with resulting disjointed arrangements."

In this same article after defining the confused psychological thinking of the period, Mr. Dewey states his problem as "the question whether any continuous function of a typical character can be detected and traced, in its growing differentiations and ramifications, amid all the diversity of phenomena which the infant life exhibits." He finds that such a function can be found and his working hypothesis is finally formulated thus: "the principle of coördination or of sensory-motor action supplies us with just such a centralizing principle—a principle which can be employed equally on the physiological and the psychological side. In popular language this unit is an act,

---

[10] John Dewey, "Principles of Mental Development in Early Infancy," *Transactions of the Illinois Society for Child Study*, Vol. IV, No. 3.

whether of greater or less complexity." He points out in this connection that seeing, hearing, are just as much acts as are reaching, grasping, and locomotion. *Sensation* is simply one element in the act. Starting from the act, coördination, or sensory motor adjustment as a fundamental fact, Mr. Dewey traces the growth of the act through its typical stages in the first year or so of infant life and, with this principle in mind, proposes to organize in outline the chief facts brought out by observers of infant psychology. These facts he groups under three heads, corresponding to three typical periods. Each of these shades into the other, but is nevertheless marked off from the others by a certain type of coördination which is in the process of development.

The characteristic of the *first period* is the simultaneous and relatively independent maturing of the functions corresponding to such organs as eye, ear, and hand—independence in both a psychical and physiological sense. When each of these functions reaches adequate operation, it becomes a habit and gradually ceases to act in an isolated way. This gradual process ushers in a *second period,* and [11] "the stress of activity is now transferred to the elaboration of larger or more comprehensive coördinations into which two or more of the established habits enter as subordinate and contributing factors. That which has been an end in itself now becomes a means, in coöperation with others, to reaching a larger end. . . . The interaction of the various functions with one another means that the organism as a whole is coming into play. . . . When the eye reacts to light as light, the ear adjusts to sound, and the hand to contact simply as contact, there is no further significance involved. But when there is translation from the terms of one activity into another, when what is heard means something for what can be seen, and what is seen means something for reaching and handling, there is significance; one experience points to, is a sign of another. *This cross reference constitutes the essence of intelligence.*"

The characteristic of the *third period* is the use of motor con-

---

[11] John Dewey, "Principles of Mental Development in Early Infancy," *Transactions of the Illinois Society for Child Study,* Vol. IV, No. 3.

trol—habits now acquired—so as to gain new experiences from other senses.

The principles typical of these periods are: [12] "(1) Each coördination is at first worked out more or less blindly, simply by some reaction to some excitation. (2) Periods of such development alternate rhythmically with periods of use, of application in which the given coördination becomes a part of a larger coördination by actively coöperating with others of its own general order. (3) Development is not even and equable in all directions simultaneously. There are shifting dominant centers of coördination. While one coördination is building up, all other activities are secondary and contributory. The forming coördination locates the center of interest and decides the stress of effort in any particular time."

These laws governing the earliest developing coördinations of the infant are also seen to be the same laws that operate in the building of the more and more complex coördinations of later development. Observation guided by these laws reveals a thread of continuity in growth. Such a method of observation can be used at any stage of growth, and by its intelligent use new and better ways to assist growth are discovered.

It was natural, therefore, that those guided by such a method conceived of education as a continuous process covering the whole life-span in which the individual constantly obtains a wider command of body and environment as tools of thought. Ideas become richer and more effective. As one experience acts in reference to another there is an increase in the complexity of the activity and the definiteness of adjustment. This is the fundamental way of mental growth, of all growth, whatever the stage. It is characteristic of all the adjustments of the developing individual to his physical and social environment.[13]

---

12 Dewey, *loc. cit.*

13 "There is a most important element in this conception of growth that deserves special attention. The non-recognition of it is the greatest weakness of the present-day educational theory. It is the return of the circular activity into the impulse in which it originated, and the four effects resulting from this return: (1) an interpretation of the impulse as to its meaning and worth, (2) an increasing definiteness in the aim of the impulse, (3) a greater certainty in its expression, (4) a development of the activity into a

This view of the act as a unified trinity including sensory-stimulus, idea, and motor-response, all as factors functioning within it, and emphasizing the interpretative function of idea, became the working principle by which the educative worth of any experience can be analyzed and tested. The three factors function to maintain, reinforce, and transform the act or co-ordination. The state of experience before the motor phase is altered in value, reconstituted by movement; hence the state of experience which follows movement is the preceding state reconstituted and it is, therefore, quite different and in itself a unique event. In a series of acts there is a continuing reconstitution whose meaning is interpreted as a revaluation of the present act in the light of the meaning of the past, out of which, and as a result of which there follows a recasting of the purpose of the act on the basis of which the decision to act again is made.[14]

This view, known at that time as *behaviorism*, included intelligence, or meaning within the act and can thereby be differentiated from its later offshoot, also known as "behaviorism." In this later version, however, sensory-stimulus and motor-response are regarded as distinct psychical entities. Behavior is treated as a simple chain of reflex acts, in which stimulus and response have a merely external relation to each other. In such a conception there is no room for conscious behavior, action with a deliberate purpose as distinct from automatic and unreflective action, no room for a conflict of ideas, and hence none for emotion as a form of conscious life. According to the earlier version of *behaviorism*, reflex acts in human beings are for the most part, the product of high specialization of activities which originally involved the entire organism. The absence of emo-

---

habit whose flexibility partakes of the nature of intelligence." Mrs. Ella Flagg Young, *Some Types of Modern Educational Theory*, University of Chicago Press.

[14] "In the animals, so far as can be judged, the stimulus and the response seem to assume purely serial order, one impulse calling forth its appropriate act, this its proper sequence, and so on. The later acts or experiences do not return into the earlier; they are not referred or reflected back. The animal life is one of association, not of thought or reflection." John Dewey, *Study of Ethics*, 1894, pp. 14–15.

tional quality is due to an acquired mechanization of behavior, since emotion involves the organism as a whole.[15]

The inclusion of intelligence within activity avoids the separation of some activity, as merely mental, from other forms of activity. This inclusion also avoids the exclusive emphasis on overt activity at the expense of thinking, for the chance of developing even overt activity lies in its increasing mental content, which gives both increased knowledge and skill. Otherwise, as increasing complexity of external movement acquired without the mental counterpart would amount to nothing more than a rushing about a squirrel cage, a *meaningless* activity. In contrast, a *meaningful* activity is the definition of an idea which continues to direct that activity in new expression. Such an activity is a genuine expression and at the same time development of the self. The whole hypothesis about ideas, as definitely intellectual experiences is that they arise, are clarified and defined—developed—in the course of the activity which they first guide and later provide the meaning of. Then this development of meaning or idea leads on to new expressions and constructions in action, which in turn normally produce new developments in ideas, and so on. *This process constitutes human growth* as far as that is something more than merely a physiological development.

This formulation of the principle of growth was also the basis of Mr. Dewey's psychological analysis of what constitutes a

---

[15] A recent writer points out the historical connection between the two behavioristic views. "Whatever we may think of behaviorism [referring to the later view], and it has lately indulged in excesses which merit drastic criticism, no one will deny its being distinctly modern. It savors pungently of science and presents what I would even call an industrialized conception of human personality. With whom did its basic idea originate? On the occasion of the republication of his *Essays in Experimental Logic*, Mr. Dewey himself wrote that these essays had been composed in the spirit of 'what has since come to be known as *Behaviorism*.' These essays were first issued in 1903, the year in which Mr. John Broadus Watson received the degree of Doctor of Philosophy for researches in animal training, from the department of which Mr. Dewey was the head. At that time Mr. Dewey's *School and Society*, probably the most influential educational pamphlet ever issued in America, had already been three years in circulation. Its title is sufficiently indicative." C. E. Ayres, Book reviews, "Philosophy and Genius," *International Journal of Ethics*, January, 1930.

moral act, moral conduct, and character. This analysis is, there-fore, an essential part of his basic concept of all education which results in growth, for he early pointed out and has steadily maintained the identity of so-called moral education and of all kinds of education and growth. The kernel of his principle is this—*the moral act is the consciously completed act which expresses the unified self.* Moral acts as described by Mr. Dewey are the structural units of moral character. He pictures the important steps in the psychological process whereby all three factors within the act—thinking, feeling, and muscular-response—come to coöperative functioning. The first phase of action is impulsive. But when the impulsive act meets resistance, it divides into contrary and competing tendencies. Ideas are born out of this conflict and then serve to give meaning to impulses and thus to redirect action. That is, each conflicting line of action is represented by an idea—the formulation of a possible act not yet a fact. The interplay of these alternative ideas is deliberation. Thought is thus a substitute for overt conflict in action. Through the balancing of ideas, their harmonious co-ordination is brought about. This unification is what is known as choice and decision. It marks the forming of a self which is more consciously integrated than was the impulsive self or body of organic tendencies out of which it grew. The conflict of impulsive tendencies is also a state of emotional disturbance. As the ideas move toward a unified purpose, so the emotions directed by ideas or meaning tend toward a unified desire, or affection, and finally become a definite interest. The original impulse to act blindly has become an intellectualized desire to act in accord with the new plan. The self of impulse and of deliberation coalesce and express themselves in an act as a unity. Action is then the expression of the best thought and the deepest desire (or interest) of the whole self.[16] This expression

---

16 When action is not achieved by the coöperation of thought and will, the deed represents whichever self has proved the stronger and is, therefore, according to Mr. Dewey's theory, not a complete act—one which represents the whole self, but is a partial act representing a divided self, where one self has achieved a victory over the other. Where the objective self (the thinking self) does not carry the subjective, the really interested self along with it, but insists upon action without such agreement, the act represents

represents a unified person who acts as he both thinks and desires, whose intellectual ideal is backed and reinforced by his undivided interest. The acts of such a person are the result of his full attention and his whole-hearted effort. In other words, such acts represent genuine interests of the self and are therefore moral. They *are* the self in expression. In such a person there is a continual round of dynamic activity, always spiral in its form because of its continually increased meaning and its heightened satisfaction. In such a person the motives that are springs to action are the original impulses which have been identified with purpose through the mediation of thought. These impulses have been made over into ideals. These ideals are not lugged in from without. They are homemade, for they are self-initiated, self-deliberated, self-evaluated. They are self-improved and finally result in a truly moral self-expressive act.

This sort of ideal enlists the agent's full attention, his whole-hearted effort, and, therefore, his undivided interest. "The resultant act becomes a definition of the self. It is a complete co-ordination." It is the self, moving the way it would go and doing the things it would do with the full and complete sanction of the mind. "There is no factor in the complete act that is foreign or alien to the agent's self; it is himself through and through. No action is moral (that is, falling in the moral sphere) save as voluntary, and every voluntary act is the self operating and hence is free. Impulse is self; the developing ideal is self; the reaction of the ideal as measuring and controlling impulse is self. The entire voluntary process is one of self-expression, of coming to consciousness of self. This intimate and thoroughgoing *selfness* of the deed constitutes freedom."

---

only part of the self. The ideal has resulted in deed without the complete backing of the original impulse, *full* interest in the deed is lacking, and complete satisfaction therefore cannot result. The agent convinced against his will is of the same opinion still. Or, if the subjective interested self rushes into unconsidered action, the agent is said to have acted against his better judgment. In either case, part of the self is unexpressed and is unsatisfied with what is done. This partial self has been suppressed, and the deed represents a divided, a disintegrated self. Such a deed is not genuine and therefore is not, according to the theory, moral.

Such an ideal, in so far as it modifies conduct, is directive and effective. It is a "very present help in time of trouble." It has a self-executing, a moving power. It is dynamic. It is itself progressive in development and makes for progress in social action. As it moves, it instructs and informs regarding the particular thing that needs to be done next; "it translates itself into terms of the next concrete individual act." In other words it is a working principle for the achievement of what has to be done.

What are the ethical meanings that lie hidden in this concept of the way of mental growth? What does it mean for the development of the child's power to initiate, to think, to plan, to weigh, to decide, to evaluate, and finally to make a choice and act on the basis of his own evaluation? What does it mean for the young child that one moral act should follow another with no breaks in the formation of the moral habit of acting in this way? The answer is plain. A living sequence of moral acts each including within itself the factors of impulse, intelligence, and choice based on reflection eventuates in moral conduct and constitutes moral character.

To those holding this theory and planning this experiment in education, therefore, *the child* as a growing person was the first concern. How could *he* find the best expression for that which in *him* lay, that which *he* wanted to do, to say, and to be? How could *he* develop *his own* working ideals by which *he* could go into action, moment by moment, hour by hour, and day by day, and thus build within *himself* habits of moral behavior and advancing ideals and goals? How could *he* be given the manna that would be of use to *him* in the fashioning of such ideals? And what was the environment in which this could best be done?

Two working principles stand out among the many educational implications of this theory, one of which is a corollary of the other: first, to foster the development of the child's own inner self, and second, to foster its development in social relationships. The first of these must be in order that the second may be, but neither can be considered apart from the other, for both must grow together. From this previous analysis, he who runs may read at the heart of this theory the belief in responsibility for consequences, for constant recognition by every person that he is not alone in a physical world, but that he lives in a world of men. Responsibility, therefore, lies in the process of deliberation and choice, of estimating and constituting value (to others as well as to himself), of proving and approving the worth of the deed. As ability to estimate value increases, so increases the demand for revision or "mediation" of the plan of action. Hence, as the plan develops, responsibilities increase. The self must be true in thought and will in order that the deed may also be true.

[17] "In a moral act, the will, the idea, and the consequences are all placed inside of the act, and the act itself only within the larger activity of the individual in society." This was a twofold commandment for those who held this theory: to guide the child in the making of his deeds so that they become better and better deeds and, at the same time, more helpful deeds. A moral act is thus seen to be a social act. The school must be a place where individual activity can be social also in character, where the child by working on and in his physical environment can develop his individual powers and at the same time use them in furthering the larger activities of his group. The supplying of every available aid to this process constitutes the function of any system of moral education, for Mr. Dewey's conception of education is identical with moral education thus conceived. Certain assumptions are always implied. The growth of an individual implies and depends upon a developing society which in turn is constantly changed by the contributions of the individuals who constitute it.[18] Growth of an integrated personality, however, necessitates freedom from undue social pressures during the maturing process. Rhythmic periods of solitude are essential that the individual may develop his own

[17] George H. Mead, "The Philosophies of Royce, James, and Dewey in Their American Setting," *The International Journal of Ethics*, January, 1930.

[18] "Society is a society of individuals, and the individual is always a social individual. He has no existence by himself. He lives in, for, and by society, just as society has no existence excepting through and in the individuals who constitute it." John Dewey, "Ethical Principles Underlying Education," *Third Year Book*, National Herbart Society, 1897.

ideas and ways of bettering and adjusting his actions to the activities of his group. *This rhythm the school must provide.*

Although many of these ideas have now become so acceptable to educators as to be taken as a matter of course, at least as far as formulae are concerned, it must be remembered that, at the time they were advanced, prevalent educational theory was, for the most part, in close accord with the tenets of the older psychology. It viewed the mind of the child as something that became more of a mind by direct and naked contact with isolated facts and materials. This process could go on apart from a social environment in which facts and materials took their natural places as contributory factors. It held, with respect to the child's mind, that it possessed a number of faculties, such as "perception," "memory," "reasoning," and that these powers develop by training like that required for the fixing of a muscular habit.[19]

The educational practice of the time closely applied, for the most part, the rubrics of this psychology. The public schools, both higher and lower, were (and still predominantly are) places where accumulated knowledge about the world of nature and its processes was retailed by the middle-man, the teacher, to the learner, who received, memorized, and, without assimilation, regurgitated such facts. These facts were (and are) selected with little reference to their actual incorporation in the child's world of experience. Such a selection completely divorced the

---

[19] This is akin to the reasoning of a later hybrid view of "behaviorism." Backed by the brilliant physiological experiments of Pavlov in conditioning the reflexes of animals, this view bases the training of children, even beyond the infant stage, on similarly conditioned reflexes which are frequently devoid of any organically related meaning for the child. It attempts to build up habits and skills by repetition of isolated acts, depending, for retention by the child, upon the application in teaching of the so-called "laws of learning"—forced association with unrelated factors, or former successes attending the act. In contrast, *the original behavioristic view* seeks to establish a *course* of action which, leading through a series of varied acts, results in the perception by the child of the meaning continuous in those acts. This course of action, thus intelligently motivated, becomes, if serviceable, a useful habit. Further, training for emotion, even esthetic emotion, cannot be a direct aim in education. Emotion is never normally separated out by the child. How this applies in the current fad of "Education for art—for artistic appreciation" is clearly apparent.

intellectual content of knowledge from the active experience
of the child, robbed it of value to him, and made a bore of
learning.

This was stony ground for the radically different conception
which held the mind of a child to be a growing, changing thing,
with developing and varying modes of self-expression. However, other educational experimenters were also searching for
a unifying idea. Here and there, the seed of new thinking was
finding good soil. Experiments in progressive education, fostered by the advance guard of the newer psychological thinkers,
were springing up. Self-initiated activity was of primary importance to all of these educators. The interaction between
mind and body was assumed, not discussed, as inseparable from
this fundamental activity. In short, harmony in the great principles of these thinkers show they are at one in their general
aim. Their widely varying applications in educational practice, however, have resulted in very different systems of education. In Mrs. Young's estimate,[20] It would be difficult to give
adequate praise to the endeavor of these early pioneers, and in
particular to that of Colonel Francis W. Parker, one of the
foremost of these progressive prophets. To break away from a
strongly intrenched theory of education which restricted the
child to a process of listening and memorizing, to make self-
development primary in importance and life the central study
of education—these were accomplishments the value of which
cannot be overestimated. The way of teaching, however, was
not clear to these pioneers. They, too, like the initiators of the
child-study programs, were in danger of losing sight of the
forest because of the trees.

With the growth of civilization had come a great increase in
knowledge, in the number of facts to be learned. The gap between the capacities of the young and the information of the
adult had widened. Education alone could span this gap. There
was need of conscious teaching. As a result of the gap, however,
there had come a split between experience gained in direct asso-

---

20 Mrs. Ella F. Young, *Some Types of Modern Educational Theory.* This
study includes the theories of Arnold Tompkins, Mrs. R. Alling-Abor,
W. W. Speer, Francis W. Parker, John Dewey.

ciation and that acquired in school. Learning was being more and more divorced from doing.

These early educators, viewing the child as the first concern in their program and realizing that a training in the techniques of the three "R's" alone could not educate a child, were confronted with a staggering mass of knowledge that must somehow be taught to the child. To curricula, already overburdened, were being added many content-furnishing subjects under the titles of *nature study, domestic science, manual training, geography,* and many of the arts. While many of these activities under certain teachers were successfully made a part of the child's experience, the large unsolved problem was the unselected, ununified and therefore overburdened nature of a curriculum, so unrelated to the school community that it was in danger of swamping the very child who was the chief concern.

Just at this moment, Mr. Dewey appeared with his new vision of the school as a selected social environment that was to set the children free by giving continuity and direction to their activities. With the ideal of education as *a freeing of individual capacity in a progressive growth directed to social aims,* those guiding this experiment saw clearly that the break between the school and the life of the child before coming to school and throughout school life must be mended in order to preserve continuity of development. The school must be made intermediary between the home and the community. It must reproduce, in miniature, the activities fundamental to life as a whole and thus enable the child, on the one side, to become acquainted gradually with the structure, materials, and modes of operation of the larger community, upon the other side, it must enable him to express himself individually through these lines of conduct and thus gain control of his own powers.

In this plan, the activities of the home—the fundamental activities of living—become logically the activities of the school and continue with ever-widening horizons. The child, interested in these activities, does things to and with others for a purpose he understands and assents to willingly. He does them for the attainment of an immediate end which he desires and which leads him on into further attempts. His experience thus becomes a continuous and unified living. Under wise direction he forms habits of doing which necessitate thinking, thus maturing his own power of expression. The most important result of such an educative process is a byproduct of it—*the development by the child of his own method of learning*. Each day his mind, stimulated by genuine interests and desired ends, directs his activity as initiated by himself. He uses what was profitable in his own past to further the next steps of his on-going occupation. With such a method of his own he has the key for solving problems at any stage of his development.

Just as the organic circuit concept with its emphasis upon the reactive function of the act had organized psychological thinking, so, Mr. Dewey conceived, constructive coöperative activity was the organizing principle that would bring unity, order, and social concern into the chaos of educational practice. In his own words,[21] "We need a pedagogy which shall lay more emphasis upon securing in the school the conditions of self-expression and the gradual evolution of ideas in and through the constructive activities, for it is the extent in which any idea is a projecture of self-activity that measures its weight—its motor-power—its interest."

---

[21] John Dewey, *Interest as Related to Will.* Second Supplement to the Herbart National Year Book for 1895, National Herbart Society.

APPENDIX II

THE THEORY OF THE CHICAGO EXPERIMENT

THE gap between educational theory and its execution in practice is always so wide that there naturally arises a doubt as to the value of any separate presentation of purely theoretical principles. Moreover, after the lapse of some thirty years, there is danger that memory will have done its work of idealization, so that any statement that is made will contain a considerable ingredient of the conclusions of subsequent experience instead of being faithful to the original conception. In the present instance, the latter danger is avoided because the exposition of the underlying hypothesis of the educational experiment is drawn from documents written during the earlier years of its existence.[1] Irrespective of the success or failure of the school in approximating a realization of the theory which inspired its work and which in some directions unexpectedly exceeded anticipations, there is some value in setting forth the theory on its own account. It will assist the reader in interpreting the report of the actual work of the school, lending it a continuity, not wholly specious, for that continuity did obtain; it will aid in evaluating the failures and successes of its practices, whatever their causes; and whatever there is of lasting value in the theory itself may suggest to others new and even more satisfactory undertakings in education.[2]

---

[1] "Pedagogy as a University Discipline," *University (of Chicago) Record*, 18 and 25 (September, 1896), Vol. I, pp. 353-355, 361-363. Brochure privately printed in fall 1895.

[2] This experiment had the backing of an exceptional group of University experts, a fact which accounts largely for its daring invasion with suggestive results into so many fields new in elementary subject-matter. See adaptations of experiments made by pupils of A. W. Michelson for Group X, also of John M. Coulter's material later published by him in *Plant Relations*.

There is a specific reason for setting forth the philosophy of the school's existence. In the University of Chicago, at the outset, the Departments of Philosophy, Psychology, and Education were united under a single head. As that head was trained in philosophy and in psychology, the work of the school had a definite relation in its original conception to a certain body of philosophical and psychological conceptions. Since these conceptions had more to do, for better or worse, with the founding of the school than educational experience or precedent, an account of the actual work of the school would be misleading without a frank exposition of the underlying theory. The feeling that the philosophy of knowledge and conduct which the writer entertained should find a test through practical application in experience was a strong influence in starting the work of the school. Moreover, it was a consequence of the very philosophy which was held. It was intellectually necessary as well as practically fitting that the lecture and class instruction in the department of pedagogy (as the department of education was at first called) should be supplemented and tested in a school which should bear the same relation, in a broad sense, to theory that laboratories of physics, chemistry, physiology, etc., bear to university instruction in those subjects. The combination of the various departments in one afforded the opportunity.

Reference to the article printed under the title of "Pedagogy as a University Discipline" (in September, 1896) will show that the school by intention was an experimental school, not a practice school, nor (in its purpose) what is now called a "progressive" school. Its aim was to test certain ideas which were used as working hypotheses. These ideas were derived from philosophy and psychology, some perhaps would prefer to say a philosophical interpretation of psychology. The underlying theory of knowledge emphasized the part of problems, which originated in active situations, in the development of thought and also the necessity of testing thought by action if thought was to pass over into knowledge. The only place in which a comprehensive theory of knowledge can receive an active test is in the processes of education. It was also thought that the diffused, scattering, and isolated state of school studies provided an unusual situation in which to work out in the concrete, instead of merely in the head or on paper, a theory of the unity of knowledge.

Under the title of the *Plan of Organization* (a document privately printed in the autumn of 1895) there is a schematic outline of the main bearings of the philosophic theory upon education. The account, contained in the preceding chapter of this appendix, may be extended further by a summary of the leading points of this document. First in importance is the conception of the *problem* of education. In substance this problem is the harmonizing of individual traits with social ends and values. Education is a difficult process, one demanding all the moral and intellectual resources that are available at any time, precisely because it is so extremely difficult to achieve an effective coördination of the factors which proceed from the make-up, the psychological constitution, of human beings with the demands and opportunities of the social environment. The problem is especially difficult at the present time because of the conflicts in the traditions, beliefs, customs, and institutions which influence social life to-day. In any case, it is an ever-renewed problem, one which each generation has to solve over again for itself; and, since the psychological make-up varies from individual to individual, to some extent it is one which every teacher has to take up afresh with every pupil.

The formula of a coördination or balance of individual and social factors is perhaps more current today than it was a generation ago. The formula which then had the widest currency was probably that of the harmonious development of all the powers—emotional, intellectual, moral—of the individual. It was not consciously asserted that this development could be accomplished apart from social conditions and aims. But neither was the importance of social values consciously stated. And, especially in progressive schools, the emphasis today is often so largely upon the instincts and aptitudes of individuals as they may be discovered by purely psychological analysis, that coördination with social purposes is largely ignored. Moreover, a doctrine of individual economic success is often pursued in schools as if that were the only significant side of social life. On the other hand, the doctrine of "social adjustment" is preached as if "social" signified only a fitting of the individual with some preordained niche of the particular social arrangements that happen to exist at the time.

In the theory of the school, the first factor in bringing about the desired coördination was the establishment of the school as a form of community life. It was thought that education could prepare the young for future social life only when the school was itself a coöperative society on a small scale. The integration of the individual and society is impossible except when the individual lives in close association with others in the constant and free give and take of experiences and finds his happiness and growth in processes of sharing with them.

The idea involved a radical departure from the notion that the school is just a place in which to learn lessons and acquire certain forms of skill. It assimilated study and learning within the school to the education which takes place when out-of-school living goes on in a rich and significant social medium. It influenced not only the methods of learning and study, but also the organization of children in groups, an arrangement which took the place occupied by "grading." It was subject-matter, not pupils, that was thought to need grading; the important consideration for pupils was that they should associate on the terms most conducive to effective communication and mutual sharing. Naturally, it also influenced the selection of subject-matter for study; the younger children on entering school engaged, for example, in activities that continued the social life with which they were familiar in their homes. As the children matured, the ties that linked family life to the neighborhood and larger community were followed out. These ties lead backward in time as well as outward in the present, into history as well as the more complex forms of existing social activities.

Thus the aim was not to "adjust" individuals to social institutions, if by adjustment is meant preparation to fit into present social arrangements and conditions. The latter are neither stable enough nor good enough to justify such a procedure. The aim was to deepen and broaden the range of social contact and intercourse, of coöperative living, so that the members of the school would be prepared to make their future social relations worthy and fruitful.

It will be noted that the social phase of education was put first. This fact is contrary to an impression about the school which has prevailed since it was founded and which many visitors carried away with them at the time. It is the idea which has played a large part in progressive schools: namely, that they exist in order to give complete liberty to individuals, and that they are and must be "child-centered" in a way which ignores, or at least makes little of, social relationships and responsibilities. In intent, whatever the failures in accomplishment, the school was "community-centered." It was held that the *process* of mental development is essentially a social process, a process of participation; traditional psychology was criticized on the ground that it treated the growth of mind as one which occurs in individuals in contact with a merely physical environment of things. And, as has just been stated, the *aim* was ability of individuals to live in coöperative integration with others.

There are, of course, definite reasons which account for the notion that the school was devoted to personal liberty and that it advocated rampant individualism. The more superficial cause was the fact that most visitors brought with them an image of the conventional school in which passivity and quietude were dominant, while they found a school in which activity and mobility were the rule. Unconsciously, such visitors identified the "social" element in education with subordination to the personality of the teacher and to the ideas of a textbook to be memorized. They found some things quite different and, accordingly, thought there was a riot of uncontrolled liberty. A more basic reason was the fact that there was little prior experience or knowledge to go upon in undertaking the experiment. We were working in comparatively unbroken ground. We had to discover by actual experimentation what were the individual tendencies, powers, and needs that needed to be exercised, and would by exercise lead to desirable social results, to social values in which there was a personal and voluntary interest. Doubtless, the school was overweighted, especially in

468   THE DEWEY SCHOOL

its earlier years, on the "individualistic" side in consequence of the fact that in order to get data upon which we could act, it was necessary to give too much liberty of action rather than to impose too much restriction.

In leaving behind the traditional method of imposition from above, it was not easy for teachers to hit at once upon proper methods of leadership in coöperative activities. At the present time there is much known which was then unknown about the normal acts and interests of the young. Methods of insight and understanding have reached a point where the margin of un-controlled action which was demanded by the experiment at that time is no longer required. It is still true, however, that while some schools have gone to an extreme in the direction of undirected individual action, there are more schools in which artificial conditions prevent acquaintance with the actual chil-dren, where fictitious beings are treated on a fictitious basis, and where genuine growth is made difficult. Our schools have still much to learn about the difference between inspiring a social outlook and enthusiasm, and imposing certain outward social conformities.

The reader of the early documents will find that next after the idea of the school as a form of community life came that of working out a definite body of subject-matter, the material of a "course of study." As a unit of the university, it had both the opportunity and the responsibility to contribute in this direc-tion. Custom and convention conceal from most of us the ex-treme intellectual poverty of the traditional course of study, as well as its lack of intellectual organization. It still consists, in large measure, of a number of disconnected subjects made up of more or less independent items. An experienced adult may supply connections and see the different studies and lessons in perspective and in logical relationship to one another and to the world. To the pupil, they are likely to be curiously mys-terious things which exist in school for some unknown purpose, and only in school.

The pressing problem with respect to "subject-matter" was accordingly to find those things in the direct present experience of the young which were the roots out of which would grow more elaborate, technical, and organized knowledge in later years. The solution of the problem is extremely difficult; we did not reach it; it has not yet been reached and in its fullness will never be reached. But at all events we tried to see the problem and the difficulties which it presented. There are two courses which are easy. One is to follow the traditional arrangement of studies and lessons. The other is to permit a free flow of experiences and acts which are immediately and sensationally appealing, but which lead to nothing in particular. They leave out of account the consideration that since human life goes on in time, it should be a growth and that, otherwise, it is not educative. They ignore continuity and treat pupils as a mere succession of cross-sections. It is forgotten that there is as much adult imposition in a "hands off" policy as in any other course, since by adoption of that course the elders decide to leave the young at the mercy of accidental contacts and stimuli, abdicating their responsibility for guidance. The alternative to the two courses mentioned is the discovery of those things which are genuinely personal experiences, but which lead out into the future and into a wider and more controlled range of interests and purposes. This was the problem of subject-matter to which the school was devoted.

This work also involved the searching out of facts and principles which were authentic and intellectually worth while in contrast with wooden and sawdust stuff which has played a large part in the traditional curriculum. It is possible to have knowledge which is remote from the experience of the young and which, nevertheless, lacks the substance and grip of genuine adult knowledge. A great deal of school material is irrelevant to the experience of those taught and also manifests disrespect for trained judgment and accurate and comprehensive knowledge. In the earlier days of our country these defects of school material were largely made good by the life of the young out of school. But the increase of urban conditions and mass production has cut many persons off from these supplementary resources; at the same time an enormous increase of knowledge in science and history has occurred. Since no corresponding change has taken place in the elementary school, there was the need for working out material which was related to the vital experience of the young and which was also in touch with what is important and dependable in the best modern information and understanding.

The thirty and more years which have passed since the school in Chicago undertook the development of a new type of subject-matter have seen great improvements in the content of studies. The latter are not so dead nor so remote as they once were. They still show, however, the effect of modern increase in knowledge by way of sheer quantitative multiplication, resulting in congestion and superficiality. The "enrichment" of the curriculum has often consisted in the further introduction of unrelated and independent subjects or in pushing down into the "grades" topics once reserved for high-school study. Or, in the opposite direction, there are introduced under the name of projects disconnected jobs of short time-span in which there is emotional stimulation rather than development into new fields and principles, and into matured organization.

It was an essential part of the conception of proper subject-matter that studies must be assimilated not as mere items of information, but as organic parts of present needs and aims, which in turn are *social*. Translated into concrete material, this principle meant in effect that from the standpoint of the adult the axis of the course of the study was the development of civilization; while from the standpoint of those taught, it was a movement of life and thought dramatically and imaginatively reënacted by themselves. The phrase "development of civilization" suggests something both too ambitious and too unified to denote just the materials actually used. Since some forms of social life have made permanent contributions to an enduring culture, such typical modes were selected, beginning with the simple and going to the complex, with especial attention to the obstacles which had to be met and the agencies which were effective, including in the latter new inventions and physical resources and also new institutional adaptations.

The details corresponding to the central principle are found in the story of the experiment. But some interpretative comments are here included, based particularly upon objections most frequently raised and misconceptions entertained. Perhaps the most fundamental one of these was the notion that the material was merely "historical" in a sense in which history signifies the past and gone and the remote, that the material used was too far away from the present environment of children. I shall not stop here to engage in a justification of the educational value of history. What is to the point is that the material was historical from the standpoint of the adult rather than of the children, and that psychological and physical remoteness have little to do with one another, until a considerable degree of maturity has been reached. That is, the fact that certain things exist and processes occur in physical proximity to children is no guarantee that they are close to their needs, interests, or experience, while things topographically and chronologically remote may be emotionally and intellectually intimate parts of a child's concern and outlook. This fact is recognized in words at least whenever the importance of play for the young child is emphasized—to say nothing of glorification of fairy tales and other more dubious matters.

Such terms as primitive life, Hebrew life, early American settlements, etc., are, therefore, mere tags. In themselves they have no meaning. They may signify material of antiquity quite outside the range of present experience and foreign to any present interest and need. But they may also signify perception of elements active in present experience, elements that are seeking expansion and outlet and that demand clarification, and which some phase of social life—having for the adult a historical title—brings to the focus of a selective, coherently arranged, and growing experience.

The word *imagination* has obtained in the minds of many persons an almost exclusively literary flavor. As it is used in connection with the psychology of the learner and there treated as fundamental, it signifies an expansion of *existing* experience by means of appropriation of meanings and values not physically or sensibly present. Until the impulses of inquiry and exploration are dulled by the pressure of unsuitable conditions, the mind is always pressing beyond the limits of bodily senses. *Imagination* is a name for the processes by which this extension and thickening of experience take place. Such imagination naturally finds outward and active manifestation; instead of being purely literary, it uses physical materials and tools as well as words in its own expanding development. Subject-matter that to the adult is remote and historical may supply the intellectual instrumentalities for this constant pushing out of horizons and internal deepening within the child's present experience.

Superficially, there was a similarity to the "recapitulation" theory in this method of enlarging the intrinsic experience of the children by means of subject-matter drawn from the development of the culture of mankind. In reality, there was no adoption of the notion that the experience of the growing human being reproduces the stages of the evolution of humanity. On the contrary, the beginning was made with observation of the existing experience of a child, his needs, interests, etc., and then some selected phase of cultural life in a generalized and idealized form was looked to for material which would feed and nurture the needs and do so in a way that would give the child a greater understanding and increased power over his own present life and environment. Moreover, there was always an attempt to secure a rhythm of movement, beginning with conditions already familiar to the child, passing through something more remote in time and space, and then returning to a more complex form of existing social surroundings.[3]

Moreover, the entire process of the school was subject to the condition which has already been emphasized:—the need for a *present* community life in which the pupils, along with the teachers, should be sharing, emotionally, practically—or in overt action—and intellectually. Physical materials and constructions, implements, tools, dramatization, story-telling, etc., were used as resources in the creation and development of this immediate social life, and with the younger children—or until the social sense was linked to a sense for history as temporal sequence— "historical" material was subordinated to the maintenance of

---

[3] Thus, present family life was studied before "primitive" life; the setting of Chicago before the earlier Colonial settlement of Virginia and Massachusetts, etc.

community or coöperative group in which each child was to participate.[4]

The misunderstanding which is most likely to arise in connection with the idea of the "ways of civilization" concerns a seeming exclusion of science and scientific method from the picture. Schools are habituated to a sharp separation of social subject-matter and that which is labeled scientific. The latter thus becomes technical and lacking in humane quality and appeal. But at the same time the social and historical subject-matter becomes far-away and literary and of value as a means of escape from the troubles and roughnesses of the present.

It is more than probable that the only genuine solution of the question of the place of social guidance and indoctrination in education will be found in giving a central place to scientific method as the key to social betterment.

The importance which is attached—both in the statement of theory and in the actual work of the school—to preparation of food, to clothing, rugs, etc., and to means of shelter, is to be understood, accordingly, by being placed in the context just mentioned. Socially, these give a fairly constant framework of fundamental activities of humanity and a concrete, definite center from which the enlargement and deepening of culture could be approached. Psychologically, they give opportunity for the exercise and satisfaction of all the impulses of construction, manipulation, active doing and making. Through the divisions of labor and the coöperations involved, they fit naturally and almost inevitably into the life of the group as a directly present, appealing, and controlling social form.

It follows that the importance that was attached to the practical and motor activities, spinning, weaving, cooking, woodworking, etc., was not because of so-called utilitarian reasons, whether the importance of mastery of the processes involved in the future life of the pupils or that of tangible material products and results.[5]

---

[4] From the first, the name *group* was deliberately substituted for the traditional word *class*.

[5] Coming as the children did mainly from professional families, there was little prospect of any utility of this sort.

The reason for the activities, on the contrary, was the fact that on one side they conformed to the psychological hypothesis that action (involving emotional and imaginative as well as motor elements) is the unifying *fact in personal development,* while on the social side they furnished natural avenues to the study of the dynamic development of human culture and afforded the children opportunities for the joy of creation in connection with their equals. In the working hypothesis of the school the idea of "occupations" was central in the survey of human development; and occupations as engaged in by the pupils themselves were means of securing the transformation of crude and sporadic impulses into activities having a sufficiently long time-span as to demand foresight, planning, retrospective reviews, the need for further information and insight into principles of connection. On the moral side, this same continuity demanded patience, perseverance, and thoroughness—all the elements that make for genuine as distinct from artificially imposed discipline.

In 1895, the Illinois Society for Child Study sent out a questionnaire in which it was asked, "What principles, methods, or devices for teaching, not now in common use, should in your opinion be taken as fundamental and authoritative, and be applied in school work?" A reply, from the pen of the present writer adds nothing new to what has been said, but because of its early date, and because it was definitely written from the standpoint of application of theory to a new school practice, it is here inserted.[6]

In stating the following principles, it is taken for granted that there are no results that are "foregone" in the sense of being beyond further investigation, criticism, or revision; but that what is wanted is a statement of results sufficiently assured to have a claim upon the parent and teacher for a consideration as working hypotheses.

(1) The radical error which child study would inhibit is, in my judgment, the habit of treating the child from the standpoint of the teacher or parent: i. e., considering the child as something to be

---

[6] John Dewey, *Transactions of the Illinois Society for Child Study,* Vol. I (1895), No. 4, p. 18.

educated, developed, instructed, or amused. Application of this particular principle will be found in connection with the positive statement following:

(2) The fundamental principle is that the child is always a being, with activities of his own, which are present and urgent, and do not require to be "induced," "drawn-out," "developed," etc.; that the work of the educator, whether parent or teacher, consists solely in ascertaining, and in connecting with, these activities, furnishing them appropriate opportunities and conditions. More specifically: (a) sensory and motory activities always are connected; (b) ideational activity is perverted and cramped unless it has a motor object in view and finds a motor outlet; (c) the sensory-motor and idea-motor coördinations tend to ripen in a certain order; (d) the larger, coarser, and freer coördinations always mature before the finer and more detailed ones; (e) all normal activities have a strong emotional coloring—personal, characteristic, dramatic deeds and situations, moral, and esthetic; (f) curiosity, interest, and attention are always natural and inevitable concomitants of the ripening of a given coördination; (g) finally and fundamentally, a child is a social being, hence educationally

THE FOLLOWING METHODS

(1) Reading, writing, drawing, and music should be treated as ways in which a given idea under the influence of its own emotional coloring find its own expression. The work of the teacher is to see that the mental image is formed in the child, and opportunity afforded for the image to express itself freely along lines of least resistance in motor discharge. Reading is psychologically dependent upon writing and drawing, needs observation for stimulus, and the stirring of the social instinct—the demand for communication—for object.

(2) Number arises in connection with the measuring of things in constructive activities; hence arithmetic should be so taught and not in connection with figures or the observation of objects.

(3) Nature study, geography, and history are to be treated as extensions of the child's own activity, e. g., there is no sense psychologically in studying any geographical fact except as the child sees that fact entering into and modifying his own acts and relationships.

(4) Minute work is to be avoided, whether it is (a) mainly physical as in some of the kindergarten exercises, in many of the methods used in drawing and writing, or (b) mainly intellectual, as starting with too much analysis, with parts rather than wholes, presenting objects and ideas apart from their purpose and function.

(5) The intellectual and moral discipline, the total atmosphere, is to be permeated with the idea that the school is to the child and to the teacher the social institution in which they *live*, and that it is not a means to some outside end.

This summary of the philosophy upon which the work of the school was to be based may be concluded with an extract from a writing of a later date, but one which was based upon the earlier theory as that was developed by the experiences gained in the School itself. "All learning is from experience." This formula is an old one. Its special significance in this particular connection is derived from the conception of the act as the unit of experience, and the act in its full development as a connection between doing and undergoing, which when the connection is perceived, supplies meaning to the act.

[7] Every experience involves a connection of doing or trying with something which is undergone in consequence. A separation of the active doing phase from the passive undergoing phase destroys the vital meaning of an experience. Thinking is the accurate and deliberate instituting of connections between what is done and its consequences. It notes not only that they are connected, but the details of the connection. It makes connecting links explicit in the form of relationships. The stimulus to thinking is found when we wish to determine the significance of some act, performed or to be performed. Then we anticipate consequences. This implies that the situation as it stands is, either in fact or to us, incomplete and hence indeterminate. The projection of consequences means a proposed or tentative solution. To perfect this hypothesis, existing conditions have to be carefully scrutinized, and the implications of the hypothesis developed—an operation called reasoning. Then the suggested solution—the idea or theory—has to be tested by acting upon it. If it brings about certain consequences, certain determinate changes, in the world, it is accepted as valid. Otherwise it is modified, and another trial made. Thinking includes all of these steps—the sense of the problem, the observation of conditions, the formation and rational elaboration of a suggested conclusion, and the active experimental testing. While all thinking results in knowledge, ultimately the value of knowledge is subordinate to its use in thinking. For we live not in a settled and finished world, but in one which is going on, and where our main task is prospective, and where retrospect—and all knowledge as distinct from thought is retrospect—is of value in the solidity, security, and fertility it affords our deal-

---

[7] John Dewey, *Democracy and Education*, pp. 164 and 177.

ings with the future. . . . To learn from experience is to make a backward and forward connection between what we do to things and what we enjoy or suffer from things in consequence. Under such conditions, doing becomes a trying, an experiment with the world to find out what it is like, the undergoing becomes instruction —discovery of the connection of things.

Two conclusions important for education follow. (1) Experience is primarily an active-passing affair; it is not primarily cognitive. But (2) the *measure of the value* of an experience lies in the perception of the relationships or continuities to which it leads.

A child or an adult—for the same principle holds in the laboratory as in the nursery—learns not alone by doing but by perceiving the consequences of what he has done in their relationship to what he may or may not do in the future; he experiments, he "takes the consequences," he considers them. If they are good, and if they further or open other ways of continuing the activity, the act is likely to be repeated; if not, such a way of acting is apt to be modified or discontinued. Whichever it may be, there has been a change in the person because of the meaning which has accrued to his experience. He has learned something which should—and which will if the experience be had under educative conditions—open up new connections for the future and thereby institute new ends or purposes as well as enable him to employ more efficient means. Through the consequences of his acts are revealed both the significance, the character, of his purposes, previously blind and impulsive, and the related facts and objects of the world in which he lives. In this experience knowledge extends both to the self and the world; it becomes serviceable and an object of desire. In seeing how his acts change the world about him, he learns the meaning of his own powers and the ways in which his purposes must take account of things. Without such learning purposes remain impulses or become mere dreams. With experience of this kind, there is that growth within experience which is all one with education.

APPENDIX III

A LIST OF TEACHERS AND ASSISTANTS IN THE LABORATORY SCHOOL [1]

Anderson, Miss K. S.
Andrews, Katharine (Mrs. John Healy)
Armentage, Mr. H. F.
Armitage, Miss Anne W.
Ashleman, Mlle. Lorelei [2]
Atwood, Mr. Wallace
Averitt, Miss Mary Judson

Bacon, Miss Georgia F.
Baird, Miss Grace
Ball, Mr. Frank H.
Barnet, Miss Bertha
Baxter, Mrs. Ellen C.
Bickell, Miss E.
Bolli, Miss Ellen
Bradshaw, Mrs.
Brown, Mrs. Fannie
Bruere, Miss E. Cornelia
Bulkley, Miss Julia E.
Butlin, Mrs. Minerva [2]

Camp, Anna R. (Mrs. R. H. Edwards)
Camp, Katherine B. (Mrs. D. P. Mayhew)
Case, Mr.
Churchill, Miss
Clark, Mr.
Comstock, Miss Clara
Cowles, Mr. Henry S.
Crawford, Mrs.

Cushman, Lillian S. (Mrs. Charles Brown)

Delpit, Mlle. Louise
Dewey, Mrs. Alice C. [2]
Dey, Miss Helena
Dolling, Miss Grace
Dunlap, Miss Elizabeth E.

Entemann, Miss
Erickson, Miss Helen

Feuling, Mrs. Mary Dynes
Foster, Miss May
Fowler, Mrs. S. W.
French, Sarah (Mrs. Sumner Miller)
Fulmer, Miss Grace
Furniss, Miss Ida

Garrey, Mr. George
Gillett, Mr. Harry O.

Harmer, Althea (Mrs. Charles Bardeen)
Hart, Walter S.
Hill, Mary (Mrs. Gerard Swope)
Hoblitt, Miss Margaret
Hornbrook, Mrs.
House, Miss Gertrude

Ingres, M. Maxime
Irons, Mr. Foster H.

---

[1] This list is as complete as the authors have been able to compile through the searching of records. Many of these records at the University of Chicago were destroyed just before this book was written.
[2] Deceased.

479

Jones, Arthur Tabor
Jones, Miss Elizabeth

Kern, Mrs. May Root

Lachmond, Miss Alice E.
Lackersteen, Miss Wynne
Landry, Mlle.
Lane, Miss Winifred [2]
Laver, Mrs. M.
La Victoire, Miss Florence
Loeb, Dr. Leo

MacClintock, Mrs. Lander Porter
McClellan, Mr.
McMannis, John F.
McMillan, Mr. D. P.
Manney, Frank
Marferding, Mrs. Janet S.
Marks, Mr. Charles E.
Miller, Helen Topping
Mitchell, Miss Clara Isabel
Moore, Miss Anne
Moore, Dr. Dorothea
Moore, Mr. Ernest C.

Neal, Miss Kate

Osborn, Mr. Clinton S.[2]

Pattee, Miss Martha
Perlett, Mlle.
Peterson, Mr. Clark
Port, Miss Elsie [2]
Post, Mr.

Radford, Miss Alice
Radford, Maude B.

Rodgers, Mr. R. R.
Row, Robert Keable
Ruger, Miss Sylvia
Runyon, Miss Laura L.[2]

Sanveur, Mlle.
Scates, Miss Georgia
Schertz, Fraulein Anna
Schibsby, Miss Marian
Sexton, Miss Edith
Sinclair, Mr. S. B.
Small, Dr.
Smedley, Mr. F. W.[2]
Stewart, Mr. A. T.
Stewart, Dell

Taylor, Mr.
Taylor, Miss Jennie
Taylor, Miss May [2]
Teller, Miss Charlotte
Thompson, Helen (Mrs. H. T. Woolley)
Thurber, Mr. Charles
Tough, Miss Mary
Tuttle, Marcia Wallace

Vincent, Mrs. George

Weatherbee, Miss
Wells, Mr. Guy F.
Welsh, Cora
Wheeler, B. N.
Whiting, Miss
Willis, Gwendolin B.
Wood, A. W.

Young, Mrs. Ella Flagg [2]

Zuckerman, Miss

INDEX

Aber, Mrs. Alling, 286
Abstraction, acquiring power of, 97; conscious use of, 204; growth in power of, 222-223
Abstractions, 272-273
Action, purposeful, value of, 433-434
Activities, as basis for development, 474; as source of knowledge, 425; by Group III, 80 ff.; by Group V, 138 ff.; by Group VII, 169 ff.; by Group IX, 205; club-house as source of, 228 ff.; correlated, on Group-VI level, 151; on Group VIII level, 196 ff.; dramatization by Group III, 85 ff.; drawing and painting, 359-361; experimental, developing origins and background of social life, Ch. XVI, 310 ff.; developing scientific concepts, Ch. XV, 271 ff.; developing skills in communication and expression, Ch. XVII, 336 ff.; fundamental, in sub-primary curriculum, 60; in accord with child's interests, 421; making clay vessels, 105; making woolen cloth, 109; musical, 356-359; organizing curriculum through, 42 ff.; primitive-life study, 100 ff.; processes of textile industries, 290; selected psychologically, 420; selection and development of, for sub-primary groups, 63-69; selection of, guided by growth principles, Ch. XIV, 250 ff.; specialized, experiments in, Ch. XI, 200 ff.; experiments in, Ch. XII, 220 ff.; experiments in, Ch. XIII, 237 ff.; study of occupations, 282 ff.; study of plant life, 284; study of processes, 283; study of

shepherd life, 107; the lumber camp, 92 ff.; typical of social situations, 254
Activity, constructive coöperative, 462; form and function of, 23 ff.; meaningful, 414, 454; originating with child, 61; purposeful, as basis of learning, 154; self-directed, 71; study of cotton, 88 ff.
Adjustment, of program, to child's level, 382-391
Administration, of the Laboratory School, 373-374
Algebra, work in, by Group X, 236; by Group XI, 238 ff.
Allinson, Brent Dow, on Dewey School, 407
America, early study of, 133 ff.
American Revolution. See Revolution, American
Andrews, Katherine, 49, 74, 285, 402, 403
Angell, James R., 4, 10
Animals, domestication of, study by Group III, 106
Architecture, 230
Arithmetic, articulation of algebra with, 343; work in, by Group X, 236
Art, as a subject, Dewey on, 25; first steps in technique, 95; methods in, 359-361; study of, by Group VI, 163; work, by Group V, 139; by Group VI, 154; by Group IX, 219; by Group XI, 247
Artistic expression, methods in teaching, 347-349
Assembly, 392; developing expression through, 245 ff.
Astronomy, work in, by Group IX, 213
Atwood, Wallace, 10, 243, 295

**Other Current
Atheling Books**